A NEW CHRISTIAN IDENTITY

A NEW CHRISTIAN IDENTITY

Christian Science
Origins and Experience
in American Culture

Amy B. Voorhees

THE UNIVERSITY OF NORTH CAROLINA PRESS
CHAPEL HILL

Published with the assistance of the Authors Fund of
the University of North Carolina Press.

© 2021 Amy B. Voorhees
All rights reserved

Set in Whitman by Copperline Book Services, Inc.
Manufactured in the United States of America

The University of North Carolina Press has been a member
of the Green Press Initiative since 2003.

Handwritten notes, letters, and unpublished works by Mary Baker Eddy and some letters and reminiscences not authored by Eddy from The Mary Baker Eddy Collection are © The Mary Baker Eddy Collection. Used by permission.

"The Heart's Unrest," by Mary Baker Eddy, © The Mary Baker Eddy Collection.
Used by permission.

All other sources not authored by Eddy from The Mary Baker Eddy Library
and The First Church of Christ, Scientist, Boston, are used courtesy of
The Mary Baker Eddy Collection.

Cover background © shutterstock/Nik Merkulov

Library of Congress Cataloging-in-Publication Data
Names: Voorhees, Amy B., author.
Title: A new Christian identity : Christian Science origins and
experience in American culture / Amy B. Voorhees.
Other titles: Christian Science origins and experience in American culture
Description: Chapel Hill : The University of North Carolina Press, 2021. |
Includes bibliographical references and index.
Identifiers: LCCN 2020035432 | ISBN 9781469662343 (cloth ; alk. paper) |
ISBN 9781469662350 (paperback ; alk. paper) | ISBN 9781469662367 (ebook)
Subjects: LCSH: Eddy, Mary Baker, 1821–1910. | Eddy, Mary Baker,
1821–1910. Science and health. | Christian Science—History.
Classification: LCC BX6941 .S 2021 | DDC 289.5/73—dc23
LC record available at https://lccn.loc.gov/2020035432

Galatians 6:3–4, 7

To MHB and JTB

CONTENTS

List of Illustrations ix

Preface xi

Acknowledgments xiii

A Restoration Story and a New History 1

PART I. ORIGINS
15

Chapter One. Youth 17

Chapter Two. Loss and Exploration 28

Chapter Three. Unrest 41

Chapter Four. Portland 44

Chapter Five. Accident and Recovery 57

Findings: Part I 59

PART II. TEXT
63

Chapter Six. Genesis Manuscript 65

Chapter Seven. Claiming Her Experience 71

Chapter Eight. *Science and Health* 78

Chapter Nine. Readership, Rhetoric, and Transmillennial Religion 93

Findings: Part II 108

PART III. REVISION
111

Chapter Ten. Reform and Salvation 113

Chapter Eleven. Naming Her Experience 131

Chapter Twelve. Holy and Unholy Challenges:
Divine Healing and Theosophy 139

Findings: Part III 161

PART IV. PASTOR
165

Chapter Thirteen. Church Body 167

Chapter Fourteen. Public Perceptions, Private Experiences 187

Chapter Fifteen. Final Words 207

Chapter Sixteen. Into the Twentieth Century 216

Findings: Part IV 227

Christian Science Identity 231

Appendix: Major Copyrighted Editions and Content
Revisions of *Science and Health with Key to
the Scriptures* by Mary Baker Eddy 237

Notes 243

Bibliography 279

Index 297

ILLUSTRATIONS

Congregational church in Sanbornton Bridge, N.H. 82

Popular American engraving of Jesus by John Sartain 84

Diagram in the typical style of Protestant prophetic tradition 103

Notes by Mary Baker Eddy in her first edition of *Science and Health* 104

Calendar and bookmarking tools used by Christian Scientists 173

Early Christian Scientists with their religious books 176

Stylized devotional art of the Bible and Christian Science literature 177

Cartoon in *Puck* depicting women reformers 188

Notes by William McKenzie in his copy of *Science and Health* 202

Notes by Mary Baker Eddy in some of her Bibles 203

William P. McKenzie 221

Marietta T. Webb 222

PREFACE

MARY BAKER EDDY and her early church organization left a massive amount of archival material, and to employ it in a scholarly manner requires placing each source within simultaneously broad and detailed historical context and a complex, extensive historiography. Further, her private papers make sense only in context with her published writings, as many are drafts or discussions of published pieces. A close understanding of her theology is obviously requisite. I have done my best with each of these tasks.

I have favored sources produced at or near the event described, referred in general to scholarly and peer-reviewed biographies that also do this, and treated contextually materials produced primarily for either polemical or devotional purposes. I have given special weight to primary sources the author did not write for an audience or publication, while understanding these must be deeply contextualized and used sparingly, as they cannot tell a story on their own.

This work does not seek to provide an exhaustive catalog of textual changes in Mary Baker Eddy's book *Science and Health*, nor does it interpret or religiously explain her book's content. It rather provides historical context for aspects of her book's development as her religion coalesced around it and the Bible in North America. As a historical work in the field of religious studies, my work does not venture into the fields of textual studies or comparative literature. It is not primarily biographical, but it attends to the inseparable link between author and text. For readers unfamiliar with the main editions or revisions of Eddy's book, which can be tracked from a few different angles, the appendix provides an overview.

I hope any Christian Scientists who encounter this book find it interesting and recognize something authentic to their tradition within it. I also hope they bear in mind a few things. First, although historical questions in the study of religion necessarily touch on theological matters, this work is historical and not religious in nature. It does not explain their textbook or religion to them. Any questions it might raise should be resolved with reference to religious texts and not my own. No archival silver bullet exists to suddenly explain a religious leader to adherents. Understanding Mrs. Eddy's religious place is by definition a devotional activity, which is not the purpose of this book.

Second, religious titles denote respect and affection, and they are naturally meaningful to adherents. With the exception of early chapters, where I refer to Mary Baker Eddy by her first name to distinguish her from other Bakers in her family, I call her by the surname she gained when she married Asa Gilbert Eddy in 1877. Also, I do not capitalize Discoverer, Founder, or Leader. I hope adherents neither reject this book out of hand because of these academic conventions nor feel compelled to adopt them for religious use. They have no meaning in a religious sense. I call her "Mrs. Eddy" among Christian Scientists and in her own church. Finally, over the past few decades, I have noted that some religious readers (and some self-identified detractors) tend to make too much or too little of particular historical points. I hope this can be tempered by an understanding of my book's scholarly method and purpose.

In answer to a reader's 1894 query, "How much do I study the Bible, and how?," the Baptist minister and Christian Science booster O. P. Gifford quoted the famed Presbyterian preacher Lyman Beecher, who said he had been writing a particular Sunday sermon all his life. "All his thinking life went into it," commented Gifford, and this must be the case with "every work that is well done." All of my thinking, feeling, and acting life has gone into this book, and I can only hope that it is well done.

Amy B. Voorhees

ACKNOWLEDGMENTS

IT TOOK ME THE BETTER PART of two decades to write this book. Naming all the excellent archivists and researchers who provided outstanding support at more than two dozen archives during this time would take more space than I have. My sincere thanks for on-site support goes to staff at the Boston Athenaeum; the Congregational Library and Archives, Boston; Longyear Museum, Chestnut Hill, Massachusetts; the Maine Historical Society, Portland; the Mary Baker Eddy Library, Boston; the New Hampshire Historical Society, Concord; and the Sophia Smith Collection at Smith College, Northampton, Massachusetts. My thanks go also to those who helped at the American Antiquarian Society, Worcester; the Boston Street Railway Association; Jenks Library at Gordon College, Wenham, Massachusetts; Huntington Library, San Marino, California; the Library of Congress; Newberry Library, Chicago; Manassas National Battlefield Park Archives, Virginia; the Salisbury Confederate Prison Archives, North Carolina; the Supreme Court of Ohio Law Library, Columbus; the Theosophical Society in America Archives, Pasadena; and the W. E. B. Du Bois Library at the University of Massachusetts, Amherst.

Several reviewers provided meaningful input on portions of my manuscript at various stages. Catherine Albanese, Patrician Cline Cohen, and especially Ann Taves offered exceptionally insightful comments and support on early iterations and, in Ann's case, portions of later drafts. Thomas C. Johnsen provided key insights early on and later arranged needed support in a timely and generous manner. For their helpful input at various points, I thank Margaret Bendroth, Ann Braude, the late Thomas E. Buckley, SJ, Rosemary (Hicks) Corbett, Heather D. Curtis, Heather V. Frederick, the late Stephen Gottschalk, David F. Holland, Margaret McManus, Keith McNeil, Eva Payne, Randi J. Walker, and the anonymous reviewers at various scholarly journals.

As my work developed, colleagues thoughtfully commented on drafts at several colloquiums and conferences, including the American Academy of Religion, the American Society of Church History, the Berkshire Conference of Women Historians, the North American Religions Colloquium at Harvard Divinity School, the Reception Study Society, the Society for the Scientific Study of Religion, and the Western Commission for the Study of Religion. I am grateful for over a dozen anonymous reviewers at the National Endowment for the Humanities, who provided encouraging critiques that reinforced the strengths of my project at a critical time and helped me sharpen my thesis. Margaret Washington's work stood as a beacon for how not to push *against* persons but *toward* new evidence in presenting revisionary historical work. I thank every thoughtful, observant historian of Christian Science who preceded me and paved the way for my own work. Though few in number, quality over quantity is always preferable. I also build on the interesting work of many historians of American religions and of religious healing. Whether agreeing with or suggesting modifications to the points these esteemed scholars make, my own work is richer for the conversation.

Three discerning and rigorous anonymous readers at the University of North Carolina Press encouraged me to feel that my manuscript could make an original contribution while also providing challenging critiques and practical advice. All pushed me to highlight crucial observations and evidence at the start rather than the conclusion of my manuscript, where I had buried them almost out of shyness. I greatly appreciate their confidence in my manuscript and their willingness to take Mary Baker Eddy, her work, and Christian Science adherents seriously. My editor at UNC Press, Elaine Maisner, secured outstanding readers, offered helpful and sound advice, and patiently guided my manuscript through to completion. Her advocacy and superb professionalism made all the difference, and I thank her for her careful work. The entire UNCP staff has been sincerely a pleasure to work with.

My gratitude goes to Simeon D. Youngmann, whose professional services as an artist produced on short notice the sensitively rendered portrait in this book of Mrs. Marietta T. Webb, when I was unable to secure archival permissions. David Brooks Andrews took expert photographs. Amron Gravett was a model of patience and produced an excellent index.

I am grateful for well-timed fellowships and awards, especially the few affording me freedom to focus exclusively on this work during critical phases. My thanks go to the Albert Baker Fund, the American Congregational Association–Boston Athenaeum Fellowship, the Brython Davis Endowment, the Marlène F. Johnson Fund for Scholarly Research on Christian Science, the Mary Baker Eddy Library Fellowship, the Mensa Education and Research Foundation, and the New England Regional Fellowship Colloquium.

Material from two chapters was published previously in "Mary Baker Eddy, the 'Woman Question,' and Christian Salvation: Finding a Consistent Connection by Broadening the Boundaries of Feminist Scholarship," *Journal of Feminist Studies in Religion* 28, no. 2 (2012): 5–25, and "Understanding the Religious Gulf between Mary Baker Eddy, Ursula N. Gestefeld, and Their Churches," *Church History* 80, no. 4 (December 2011): 798–831. I thank the *JFSR* for granting permission to republish this material here. I am grateful to Ralph Byron

Copper for allowing me access and publishing rights to items in his private collection. Longyear Museum generously granted me permission to publish material in its fine collections. The kind staff at the Mary Baker Eddy Collection graciously helped me navigate a large-scale permissions process to publish copyrighted works. I thank them for their professionalism and diligence.

My research, claims, and conclusions are, of course, independently produced and entirely my own. The epigraph at the start of this book points to this fact. The verses came to me when I first began writing. They assured me that my job was simply to do my work as conscientiously and as well as I could; if anything good is in it, that will stand. If not, it will be as if never written. Finally, I dedicate this book to my parents.

As I complete this book, public health concerns are playing out on a massive scale those of us in the United States have not seen in a century. My thoughts turn to the Christian Scientists in this book who recorded their own questions and struggles alongside many academically unexplainable accounts of healing during earlier times of pandemic and uncertainty. Whatever we might think or make of Christian Science identity and experience, the unusual and interesting historical records around its development stand as an intervention into many of our basic assumptions about modern life. I thank everyone who helped me investigate and make sense of these records to some degree for present and future readers.

A NEW CHRISTIAN IDENTITY

A Restoration Story
and a New History

I OPEN WITH the story of Marietta T. Webb, whose life as a Christian Science adherent was both distinctive and representative of her church's experience writ large during the infancy of its history. As such, it is both exceptional and typical of American religious experience as it moved more fully into modernity.

Webb entered the world in Virginia in 1864, just after emancipation, the third child of an African-descended couple named Georgina and Randall Jones. The growing family relocated to Massachusetts between 1869 and 1872. From Acton Street on the outskirts of Boston, the three Jones boys fanned out to work at a hotel, lumberyard, and depot. The two Jones daughters stayed in school. Georgina kept house. Randall worked as an "engineer," census records report, and could read though not write.[1]

Husband and wife ensured that all their children achieved the full literacy they were denied. Webb received a substantial secondary education. She later recalled her childhood as "unlike those of the majority of children, for I grasped every opportunity to read the Bible" and to attend church with her parents. Naturally inquisitive, she "went on in this way for years, pondering certain serious questions of religion, and consulting many of the theologians."[2]

In early 1892, Marietta wed the older Washington, D.C., native Hiram Webb, an engineer like her father.[3] In 1893, she delivered the couple's only child, Hiram Orlando, and called him by his middle name.[4] Orlando's birth record is the only African American entry in an 1893 Massachusetts birth index table showing the children of bookbinders, sawyers, guilders, and laborers, mostly immigrants from the Canadian maritime provinces, the United Kingdom, and Europe.

By the time he was three, Webb later wrote, Orlando "was hovering between life and death. Some of the best physicians in Boston had pronounced his case incurable, saying that if he lived he would always be an invalid and a cripple." These may have been elite African American physicians, who had recently convened in Boston to form the National Medical Association after the American Medical Association excluded them. "He suffered to the extent that he would lie in spasms for half a day," Webb later wrote. "He also had rickets; physicians saying that there was not a natural bone in his body."[5]

The Webbs lived close to Massachusetts and Huntington Avenues, where adherents of Mary Baker Eddy's new Christian Science religion had just completed a Romanesque worship space in 1894. The church called itself (and its building) The First Church of Christ, Scientist, or The Mother Church. Several decades before, Eddy had engaged in a wide-ranging search for the gospel law many Americans assumed must or should govern the cure of the sick.

She claimed to identify this law by the end of 1866, linking it to a healing experience earlier that year. Grappling with how to explain it within the overall arc of her lengthy search, she produced an unrefined, provisional, and highly distinctive biblical exegesis that spoke of revelation, inspiration, discovery, and divine science. Gradually she found the footing to understand and articulate her scriptural interpretations with increased clarity.

In 1875, Eddy published *Science and Health with Key to the Scriptures* (though it took a few years for the entire title to appear in print). When existing churches declined to formally embrace her novel explanation of a "Christian science" that made Bible healings relevant and repeatable in modernity, she resigned her thirty-seven-year membership in the Congregational church. She founded her own church in 1879.

Accounts of Christian Science healing spread across the United States through the 1880s, as did distribution of Eddy's book alongside the Bible. These were met with a wide range of public responses, personal temperaments, and agendas that produced dozens of conflicting descriptions of the religion within the broader culture. The church entered a new phase of organizational expansion and development in the 1890s.

After a friend invited her to a testimony meeting at The Mother Church in 1897, Marietta Webb reported that she had found "the religion for which I had been searching for years."[6] Narratives of healing prompted her to seek help for her son, but the Christian Science healer or "practitioner" her friend recommended was swamped with requests. Some testifiers had recounted experiencing healing while reading Eddy's *Science and Health*, so Webb borrowed her friend's copy.

She "read it silently and audibly, day and night, in my home, and although I could not seem to understand it, yet the healing commenced to take place at once. The little mouth which had been twisted by spasms grew natural and the child was soon able to be up, playing and romping about the house as any child should. . . . I constantly read the Bible [and] Science and Health. . . . The child's limbs grew perfectly straight," he fully recovered, "and for years he has been a natural, healthy child in every way."[7] Webb also chronicled several illnesses from which she found herself freed.

Yet the physical cures were "nothing," she concluded, compared to "the spiritual uplifting" she felt. She ended, as testifiers usually did, by gratefully crediting Eddy with explaining the New Testament gospel of Christian healing to modern people. In the reader-supplied columns of the church's weekly *Christian Science Sentinel*, Webb later declared the Bible and Eddy's interpretation "my daily guides, the heavenly manna on which I feast and live." She added that she found Christian Science "to be the only salvation of my race" in the United States because through it, "man is not only learning what the true love of God is . . . but he is getting out of his old prejudiced self, into the spiritual sense of man's union with God."[8] In 1907, Eddy approved placing Webb's testimony of Orlando's healing as one of several in the final chapter of her book, where it remains today.

Scholars treating claims to spiritual healing usually consider the question of efficacy a values-based rather than historical topic, and following a well-trod path in religious studies, my goal is to neither endorse nor debunk them.[9] The historical point of departure here is that Webb's testimony is like thousands of Christian Science testimonies printed throughout the 1890s, tens of thousands from 1883 onward, a major and almost entirely unstudied body of primary sources. She spoke anecdotally, as testifiers typically do, but presumably not fictionally, in the sense that she recounted her understanding of lived personal and bodily experiences.

Testimonials are but one of many types of sources I draw on for this study, as my bibliography shows. I highlight Webb's testimonial here, however, for its simultaneously subjective and representative qualities: it is distinctive to herself yet echoes thousands of her era. Contextualized among scholarly sources and major threads of American cultural life, it orients our view of Christian Science experience as part of the story of American religious history, opening onto the topics in this book.

This study is an *origins* project in that it focuses on four aspects of *Science and Health*: who wrote it and why, who read it and why, what some of its main topics are, and how a wide variety of people responded to it in the long nineteenth century. And it is an *identity* project in that through this exploration, the takeaway for the field of religious studies is a more accurate understanding of Christian Science identity, or the essence of how we can define and differentiate this religion from others in America.

With this as my starting point, I argue four interconnected theses. First, as early Christian Science adherents engaged the Bible as interpreted by Mary Baker Eddy's *Science and Health with Key to the Scriptures*, they forged a new Christian identity. This new religious identity mediated modernity in distinctive ways, not least through experiences deemed *healing*, understood not as ends in themselves but as waymarks pointing to something Christians by definition consider more important: salvation, or the redemption of human life based on a new view of God and Jesus Christ.

Like Webb's, accounts of these experiences tended to value what they identified as spiritual benefits over whatever physical changes they might report. Whether sudden or gradual, triumphal or modest, in process or complete, in conversation with medical views or wholly apart from them, Christian Science healing experiences were and are thought to link the human and the Divine. As scientific materialism gradually replaced the cultural authority of religion, these healing accounts described a novel path to experiencing the presence and relevance of God in the modern era.

Second, this new religious identity was not simply an invention of Christian Scientists but embodied the central features of Eddy's book as it developed over time. This is especially evident if we pay attention to the origins and reception of *Science and Health*. Christian Scientists received Eddy's text most fundamentally as a God-revealed message concerning the principle, law, or science that had once activated biblical healing, a discovery they now claimed should renew and extend apostolic life in the modern era.

Critics, observers, and adherents described Christian Science as an intervention, welcome or not, into the surrounding network of theological, scientific, and curative options. Its textbook stood as a singular intervention into the hotly debated viability of Christianity in modernity. Exploring how its claims emerged, expanded, and continued to operate in relation to a variety of cultural materials and historical domains helps us to capture the identity of Eddy's religion in a more precise manner than previously.

Third, this dual intervention was at the heart of the outsize influence historians agree Eddy's denomination has had on American culture. Scholars have argued that the outsider, dissenting status of American-born minority religions—Shakers, Mormons, Jehovah's Witnesses, Pentecostals, Christian Scientists—is the very characteristic that makes them paradoxically and quintessentially American.[10] Emergent Christian Science constituted a form of dissent against conventional views of life, religion, and healing that simultaneously claimed to develop and confirm the true meaning of this triad in modernity. This combination of dissent and affirmation has both reflected and rippled out across American culture in formative ways.

Observers called this both paradoxical and axiomatic, idealistic and practical, and they supported or railed against what it implied, sometimes both at once. An astonishing variety of people received Eddy's book across established and emerging religious groups (or occasionally no group). They variously argued for or against, cribbed and criticized, adopted or rejected it, again sometimes simultaneously. Many developed or refined their own religious texts and practices in conversation with hers to varying degrees, as she did with them.

Conversations with or about Eddy's book and its actual or presumed contents factored into the formation of many aspects of modern American religion and culture. Eddy's book, the religion it inspired, and the academically inscrutable healing events they involved conversed and interacted with these networked aspects while also constituting a singular intervention into that network. Its intervention was less a *via media* compromise than a reworking of the issues altogether.

As these points suggest, Christian Science landed all over the plot lines commonly employed to narrate religion in modernity. We cannot capture its identity by aligning it with either side of the conservative-liberal dichotomies generally used to describe the religious features of modern America, including its later postmodern condition: science versus religion, therapy versus theology, secular versus sacred, mind versus heart, revelation versus reason, subjective versus objective, enchantment versus disenchantment, the presence versus the absence of God. We cannot accurately describe it using predominantly liberal or conservative tropes, though it aligns with some elements of both. Our present views of modernity cannot be employed retroactively to accurately describe Eddy's experience, as I will also argue regarding our current definitions of feminism.

This makes emergent Christian Science one of many forms of nineteenth-century religion we cannot profitably use bifurcated, dichotomous, twentieth-century descriptions to retroactively define. The long nineteenth century saw the emergence of such polarized forms but not their full development or calcification. A certain fluidity held sway. For similar reasons, historians such as B. M. Pietsch, R. G. Robins, and Grant Wacker have cautioned against interpreting early Fundamentalism through the lens of a thoroughgoing anti-modernism ascendant only in later decades.[11]

In broad perspective, religion in nineteenth-century America appeared less a series of fixed dichotomies (on or off their spectrums), less a triad or quad or other neat geometric arrangement, than a vast overlapping network having nodes handling greater or lesser amounts of traffic. As the century wore on, some nodes receded and others stood in greater relief. Some changed meanings; some slipped between primarily religious and other cultural meanings. Like some other new religious expressions of its era, Christian Science was both multi-nodal and distinctive—that is, it tracked across multiple existing nodes while constituting a new one. Rather than combining existing nodes to create a subset of them, it dialogued with these as it developed its own.

Following Stephen Gottschalk's landmark 1973 study, scholars have agreed that Christian Science emerged as an organizationally distinct movement.[12] Yet scholars have not clearly arrived at the singularity of its religious message. My fourth and final contribution is to demonstrate how it was and is theologically distinct. I show that in Christian Science, Eddy introduced a postwar restorationism with a revelatory rationale that constituted a multi-nodal intervention into modernity via a singular system of applied Christian metaphysics expressed in healing. *In short, Christian Science is a singular expression of Christianity with a restorationist, revelatory, healing rationale.*

By *postwar*, I mean emerging with the suite of religious and other cultural developments that followed the American Civil War. By *restorationist*, I mean claiming to restore apostolic Christianity in the modern era. By *revelatory*, I mean claiming to result from divine Self-disclosure. By *multi-nodal*, I mean that it traversed and conversed with traditions and movements on many nodes across the network making up the wide cultural landscape of the long nineteenth century. By *modernity*, I mean the era of emerging authority for scientific materialism, its offshoots, and its implications. By *healing*, I mean claiming and reporting healing experiences. By *singular*, I mean it variously bridged or bypassed, invoked or ignored existing religious and cultural options while forming its own distinctive intervention into modern American life. This is the crux of what made Eddy's religion multi-nodal and distinctive in an academically descriptive sense, though Christian Scientists do not use those terms to describe themselves.

The chapters in this book unfold in four parts, which build on each other to elucidate my thesis regarding how Eddy, adherents, and Americans generally (in a manner part-serial, part-overlapping) came to view Christian Science. Together, they show the role Eddy's book played in cohering a movement around a new biblical understanding; the controversies, praise, accusations, befuddlement, and acclaim it attracted; and its impact over time and space. Each part delves into a major period in the development, reception, and use of Eddy's book *Science and Health*.

A brief summary of findings at the end of each part orients readers to major evidence and arguments as the book progresses. Later chapters loosely correspond to major editions of *Science and Health*. (For a chart of these editions, see the appendix.) This arrangement is not simply a chronological convenience but best conveys the multilayered history of *Science and Health* in all its tremendous religious and cultural importance. It anchors my discussions and serves as a springboard or point of entrée into larger historical and cultural issues.

Part 1, Origins, begins with Mary Baker Eddy's cultural and personal milieu in New England after her 1821 birth and ends prior to her authorship, with the 1866 accident and recovery that her earliest texts indicate as the gateway to something religiously and experientially new. A fuller slate of biographical details can be found elsewhere, but this part of my book provides needed background for the people, terms, and events inhabiting Christian Science history.

It also introduces the extent to which author, book, and religion are inseparable in this story. In his work on religious copyright, Andrew Ventimiglia sees Eddy employing copyright activism to emphasize "the fundamental unity of author and the Truth that author has worked diligently to express," and I add that even without conscious effort, her life and text speak to this link.[13] In a basic way, her book grew out of her life.

My treatment of Eddy's formative years expanded well beyond my initial research interests as I became immersed in primary sources having little to do directly with her and realized the extent to which leading cultural conversations of the 1840s through 1860s served as an incubator for her later work. This discussion picks up in the middle of chapter 2. These middle years are often portrayed as a wasteland for Eddy, and personally, they rather were. Yet the philosophical and curative dimensions of the conversations surrounding her, permeated with debates in Christian theology, were substantial. The intellectual and cultural richness of the period provided a cushion on which her developing views rested, informed the way she began to articulate them, and served as an elastic buffer zone for her intellectual and spiritual wrestlings.

Through new consideration of primary sources, I position Eddy as an early advocate of antislavery through "moral suasion" rather than "agitation" (that is, intellectual and moral persuasion rather than radical activism) and eventual adopter of abolitionism. I contextualize her early illness within her era's medical history on spinal neuralgia, a frequent and "fearful malady" with an elusive pathology. Physicians distinguished this malady from hypochondria and hysteria as they studied to classify it.

I further contextualize Eddy's quest for health within the popular expectation that new, cutting-edge cures may well be vessels for Christian healing that acted on the mind—the seat of the sentiments, reason, conscience, and piety of the individual—in some definite and likely scientific yet unexplained way. Eddy's eventual explanation is singular in its revelatory assurance and definitive detail. Finally, I find the Civil War more formative for Eddy than is usually acknowledged, and though she was still appreciably sick, dependent, and tentative, her independence during these years bears greater emphasis. Throughout this part of the book, I call Eddy and her family members by their first names in order to distinguish them from one another.

Wacker has said of Adventist leader Ellen Harmon White that while her historical significance needs to be assessed with reference to the "basic ingredients" of her cultural age, "she cannot be reduced to her age," as she "cut against the grain of the age" as well.[14] The same might be said for Eddy. In treating her life, I seek to thoroughly contextualize and understand the historical record she left, especially in relation to the development of her book and religion. Throughout, a major goal is to take her seriously as a theologian.

The literary critic Ashley Squires has recently noted that Christian Science, like its history, "remains poorly understood" by scholars and public alike, aided by "frustratingly enduring" reliance on century-old polemical sources.[15] In addition to scholarly studies, I rely on hundreds of primary sources woven together to engage Eddy's story. I consider her story as it unfolded in real time apart from later historiographic tropes, with herself as the central agent of her life. If this sounds obvious, it has not been consistently the case.

Part 2, Text, picks up with Eddy's new ability to write in a sustained way after her landmark accident and recovery experience in 1866. It covers her immediately subsequent exegesis of the first Bible book, Genesis, and other early texts. I show that Eddy's jumbled Genesis manuscript both embodied and submerged her own experiences while providing our first look into her mode of biblical interpretation, which was highly distinctive. I then discuss the development of her book *Science and Health with Key to the Scriptures* in the American cultural scene of the 1870s. Overall, her texts cannot be described using the bifurcated categories readily available to scholars of American religions. They represent the emergence of a new Christian identity that mediated modernity in singular ways.

Only a few other American women have founded a well-known church on their claims to biblical interpretation and religious authority, notably Ann Lee, Ellen Harmon White, and in some respects Aimee Semple McPherson. Most significantly for this study, Eddy's interpretive method was singular. She identified her book as a God-revealed biblical explanation that required conscious, careful, divinely guided individual human agency to articulate over time.

Stephen Gottschalk comments that unlike Joseph Smith, who claimed to find and translate golden plates containing a fixed divine message, Eddy "maintained that the revelation that came to her . . . had the character of a gradual process of unfolding."[16] Robert Peel notes that she once wrote "S.&H. as first written" next to the Scottish philosopher Thomas Carlyle's "description of the Koran" as a work composed with "headlong haste." To Peel, a similar "'headlong haste' is apparent in almost everything Eddy drafted" immediately after 1866, but this soon gave way to a settled approach in which "she revised, rerevised," and sought "literary advice," sifting through it to better bring out the message she described as divinely revealed to her.[17] A main point my book introduces is that this unfolding, sifting, gradual process is interesting not only as a biographical and stylistic element but as a major intervention into the production of religious texts considered revelatory and constitutes a major new contribution to world religions.

These are historical observations about religious claims. As Ann Taves contends in *Revelatory Events*, it is not only academically possible but productive to study "a particular type of experience that has played a central role in the formation of many spiritual paths—experiences of presence that some consider 'revelatory.'" Rather than shying away from the term, she invokes its "loaded" meanings to create a roadmap for investigating religious formation.[18] In Jamesian fashion, she sees claims to revelatory events as evidence of neither pathology nor divine intervention, which cannot be proved historically, but as useful tools for scholarly explanation. I agree with such observations here.

I further demonstrate that while the Bible is the only scripture to students of Christian Science, Eddy's book can be considered a new sacred text. The historian Stephen Stein has observed that *Science and Health* "does not replace the Bible for Christian Scientists" but is instead "a 'textbook' that seeks to clarify and explain the Bible." He notes that Eddy's book is "regarded as an inspired text," written according to divine inspiration and according to the author's "spiritual sense."[19] This is in accord with Paul Gutjahr's definition of sacred texts: "momentous, spiritual texts that lay claim to special insights, and thus call for special levels of allegiance, on account of some form of divine authorship."[20]

Others propose that *Science and Health* is a scripture because, for example, scriptural status lies in the interactive relationship between text and community.[21] Christian Scientists themselves do not subscribe to this view. Neither do they claim that *Science and Health* reopened the biblical canon, as members of the Church of Jesus Christ of Latter-Day Saints do regarding the Book of Mormon. Early Christian Scientists, I find, spoke of Eddy's book as an interpretative work that reinstated apostolic activities and fulfilled prophecies within the existing, sealed biblical canon. In this way, they cohered a new, largely uncharted Christian identity around the teachings in her book.

Eddy claimed to have discovered the "Science of the Scriptures," or the law of God that animated the works of Jesus and the prophets, and in so doing to restore and fully explain them in modern terms for people to practice today. She described her book as the Bible's "best interpreter."[22] I show how in *Science and Health*, Eddy engaged essential Christian concerns to present her religion in practical, restorationist, democratic terms as a new branch of experiential or provable Christian metaphysics and a revelation from God to carry on Christ's church in the modern era.

Finally, Eddy wrote at a time when confidence in the new reach of a massively expanding print culture leapfrogged the last stages of manual typesetting with its many errors. I show that Protestant culture simultaneously replaced its resignation to the linguistic imprecision dictated by God at Babel with confidence in the scientifically precise possibilities of the written word. *Science and Health* and its author participated in both these developments. They also engaged a handful of clerical critics who found her text an unacceptable expression of Christian heterodoxy—though as was usually the case, they did not dispute her healing claims.

Eddy's outsize confidence in her book rested on her distinctive view that it played a central role in aiding the present and coming kingdom of Christ. I coin the term "transmillennial" to describe the stance of those like her who were neither premillennial nor postmillennial but bridged these two widely known options. It has been difficult for us as scholars to grasp and map viewpoints such as this, as they fall outside our established categorical descriptions. Such views had a major impact on American religiosity, however, and in this case became a key part of the newly distinctive religious identity Christian Scientists forged in modernity.

Part 3, Revision, charts both revised public views of Christian Science and revised versions of *Science and Health* throughout the 1880s. The book's author and readers engaged an ever-widening array of conversations and controversies around social reform movements, established churches, and emergent religions. It first addresses a perennial question within feminist scholarship, as within Eddy's milieu: Was she a supporter of social reforms and social justice causes? Further, to what extent can we call her work "feminist"? I argue that Eddy's support for women's rights was emphatic and radical yet qualified and ultimately subsumed by her soteriology.

As with all social justice causes, her sympathy for women's rights corresponded to how closely the methods used to achieve them conformed to her understanding of Christian salvation. I also show that race, religion, reform, gender, liberty, and millennial designs mingled to shape the egalitarian basis on which Eddy expressed her entire vision for human liberty. Her distinctive theological statements on these fronts both influenced and reflected American culture, though they lie outside our usual scholarly descriptions of this period.

Next, I delve into a public controversy that spurred Eddy to clarify her religion's discovery narrative. I show that although her successive texts had always included unmistakable elements of both phenomenal discovery and religious revelation, these were not seamlessly joined in her main narrative of religious origins until 1883. This blending process occurred under the magnifying lens of media coverage, and somewhat ironically, it resulted in a more accurate statement of the distinctive religious identity she introduced. Various groups continued to single out one thread over the other, however, in evolving their own public and private characterizations of Christian Science.

Just as Eddy felt her book became more clear, and as public perceptions of Christian Science identity began to solidify around what the *Boston Sunday Globe* called its "cures astonishingly like those quoted from the New Testament," public views and characterizations of the religion underwent major changes. The 1880s were a forum in which Christian Scientists, Protestant divine healers and ministers, mind curists, and Theosophists parsed their beliefs over against one another and clarified assumptions regarding compatibility. The actual or perceived contents of Eddy's *Science and Health* were at the center of this animated discussion.

Divine healing and Christian Science held some resonance and some dissonance, both often obscured by cultural confusions. Esoterically inclined inquirers initially interested in Eddy's unorthodox teachings found public impressions that these were eclectic belied by a totally Christian self-identity, especially an exclusive focus on the Bible and teaching of special revelation. Eventually, esotericists decided this constituted a gulf too wide to cross. As New Thought emerged, it accommodated the eclectic, theosophically inflected, esoteric healing views neither Christian Science nor divine healing found amenable. Interested Christian inquirers, on the other hand, accepted and in some cases championed Eddy's message, using her book while remaining within their own denominations. Perceptions of what constituted Christian Science shifted radically from one group and individual to another.

The cultural confusion that arose around this diversity of conflicting views about Christian Science was not simplistic or minor. It obscured basic theological points, permeating American society with disagreements about what Christian Science was, who founded it, which tradition and texts it involved, and who practiced it. This section conveys the cultural magnitude of such conversations, the difficulties of capturing them using established scholarly rubrics, and why societal perceptions of Christian Science as an eclectic religion have so often differed from parallel perceptions (and its primary source record) as a novel Christian one.

The historian of American women and religion Eva Payne has noted that while Christian Science historiography has often dwelt on the experiences of those who left the faith to innovate their own religious teachings, we cannot gain an accurate understanding of the religion's identity without a clear profile of those who stayed.[23] This is an axiomatic yet largely unfulfilled premise of Christian Science history. Accordingly, part 4, Pastor, steps toward a vernacular history of Christian Science.

These chapters highlight not only core experiences of Eddy as church founder but the experiences of those who read the Bible and *Science and Health* as they sought to put Christian Science into practice. We see pictures of them, read their first-person narratives, and investigate artifacts they left behind. Adherents represented a lived element of Christian Science as they sought to embody Eddy's distinctive teachings about the Bible in their new religious identity, and she chose to literally complete her book with their experiences.

Just as Christian Science historiography has tended to focus on former adherents, it has tended to focus on controversy. This is an important aspect, which I discuss in this book. Yet it does not give us a sense of why people became Christian Scientists, as tens of thousands did. It also sidelines important primary sources referring to Christian Science experience. A main goal of this section is to provide what Heather Curtis, in her work on divine healers, calls a "'retrospective ethnography'—a finely grained, richly textured account—of the spiritual practices" adherents employed and recounted.[24]

Testimonials and artifacts, such as books thick with reader annotations, serve as main sources. I include them unfiltered and apart from my scholarly voice to illustrate rarely seen private views of Christian Scientists. They show how the worship lives of adherents revolved around the Bible as Eddy interpreted it, thus consciously establishing a new Christian identity that cannot be described using dominant scholarly categories.

Adherent experiences raise matters of social position, race, worship, and efficacy. I also briefly cover legal and authorship controversies and the production of Eddy's final book editions. A sketch of organizational polity will satisfy readers wanting to know how her church was and is structured. As she took the unusual step of ordaining the Bible together with her book as her church's dual "pastor" in 1894, she placed this pastor at the center of newly cohering activity unifying the Christian Science movement as it headed into the twentieth century. Most of that later story is beyond the scope of this book, but I sketch out a few main points and close the book as it begins, with Marietta Webb's experience.

The tone and texture of this book shifts throughout, according to which sources predominate. Part 1 converses almost entirely with primary sources to reconstruct key parts of Eddy's early New England era and how she lived within it. Parts 2 and 3 are richly academic and comparative. They put primary texts in steady conversation with scholarly sources on American history and culture. Part 4 takes an ethnographic approach as it seeks to establish a view from within adherent experiences, in all their sameness and diversity. The more "interior" tone of part 4 also reflects Eddy's biography after she retired to New Hampshire in her last two decades, concurrently with a huge increase in adherents and media attention.

As we more precisely map the multivalent contours of this distinctive religion, we begin to see Christian Science operating historically from its own singular node on a network within a field of networks, its distinctive characteristics in conversation with many other cultural elements. Mapping Christian Science in this manner opens new ways of conceiving the boundaries and patterns of American religions generally. This is true to form for outlier and minority religions.

As we trace the themes in this book, we find a singular story of the arrival and development of an unorthodox religion, accounts of religious healing practices and modes of worship, textuality and embodiment, social position and religious experience, the origin and reception of a major new biblical interpretation, the new landscape of Christian variety this invokes, and conversation and contestation about modernity and religiosity within American culture. And through all this, the creation of a new Christian identity.

Throughout the early history of Christian Science, adherents practiced what they experienced as an unorthodox and restorationist religion meant to, as Eddy put it, "commemorate the words and works of our Master," Christ Jesus, "which should reinstate primitive Christianity and its lost element of healing."[25] This restorationism had a revelatory rationale that mediated modernity with a new system of applied Christian metaphysics expressed in healing. Public perceptions sometimes matched this identity and sometimes did not, for reasons I detail in the following pages. Yet by tracing the production, reception, and use of Eddy's *Science and Health with Key to the Scriptures* in and on American culture, we can clearly identify Christian Science as a singular expression of modern Christianity with a restorationist, revelatory, healing rationale.

PART I

Origins
(1821–1866)

CHAPTER ONE

Youth
(1821–1844)

In which Eddy is a Congregationalist of decisive antislavery persuasion and a neuralgic having a regionally normative upbringing and a decent if irregular education

IT MAKES SENSE THAT Mark Baker would buy a stereotyped edition of the Bible. Introduced to America in 1812, stereotyping reduced costs and errors in printing, sure to appeal to his Yankee frugality, Calvinist bent toward scriptural exactitude, and yeoman's affinity for pragmatic invention.[1] The 1828 tome now sits at a museum in dust-free, airless repose, but scuffs and page wear recall how Mark put it to work at the saltbox farmhouse in Bow, New Hampshire, he shared with Abigail Ambrose Baker and their six children. He used it in lengthy, sometimes interminable family worship and animated, stubborn debates with local divines.

Abigail and her husband's mother, Mary Ann, used it for personal guidance and family education. Like most of their neighbors, the household's children learned recitation and reading from this and earlier family Bibles. The youngest of them, Mary Morse Baker, would later become the religious leader known as Mary Baker Eddy.

The outlook of most antebellum New England farming families was straightforward yet complex, folksy yet literate, both provincial and global, with dry and subtly sarcastic humor. An 1837 issue of the popular *Yankee Farmer* (later *New England Farmer*) illustrates their culture. News about beet sugar preceded items from Niger, Liverpool, Ohio, Boston, Mexico, and Georgetown. A story set in Glasgow needed no introduction; readers knew Scotland's geography and culture. Poetic verse was requisite and ample. Morality sketches meant to illustrate the ideal farmer and his wife (smart and attentive, respectively) coexisted with congressional voting reports, political analysis, and ads for feathers, spoons, mulberry bushes, and cast iron plows.

The clever humor came with a straight face and a wink: "A dog in Boston having been taught some lessons on the harp, was found alone one morning practicing by himself"—a rural dig at city folk and their presumed superiority. An especially popular joke ran, "A boy having been praised for his quickness of reply, a gentleman observed, 'When children are so keen in their youth, they are generally stupid when they advance in years.' 'What a very sensible boy you must have been, sir,' replied the child." This type of politely irreverent humor would pop up in Mary Baker Eddy's letters and memoirs for the rest of her life, speaking to the value system that shaped her.[2]

Like most families around them, the Bakers were intellectual but not erudite, comfortable but not wealthy, civically engaged as a matter of course. Mark filled a series of elected and appointed civic positions in addition to farming (such as selectman, school board member, town meeting moderator, town counsel, road surveyor, militia chaplain, almshouse agent, Sunday school superintendent, and church clerk—literally part of citizenry until 1819, when New Hampshire voted to end taxation funding Congregational churches).

Abigail kept the family's preindustrial domestic life running. Artifacts from their home give a window into daily activities: Abigail's spinning wheel, Mark's ledger detailing over 500 business transactions (some savvy, some charitable, some neither), hair curlers Mary and her two sisters used, a shaving mirror for their father and three brothers, a candle mold, an oil lamp. Mary's needlepoint sampler looked like hundreds of others from her era.[3] The *New Hampshire Patriot and State Gazette*, of Jacksonian Democrat persuasion, often lay on the table. Most in their region read it avidly.

Notwithstanding the occasional "village atheists," religious questions were the overriding concern in the Bakers' community.[4] Mark was a Calvinist of the most stalwart and inflexible variety then possible. He railed against universal salvation and loved his children with a fierce loyalty that included rigid correction for the good of their souls. In contrast, Abigail's Calvinism brimmed with affection, sobered by requisite thoughts of creation's fallen state.[5]

Her letters show her especially endeared to her youngest, Mary, whose religious tendencies aligned with her mother's and sometimes clashed with her father's. The Bakers moved to nearby Sanbornton Bridge (later Tilton) in 1836, and in 1838 Mary's parents transferred their church membership to the Sanbornton Congregational Church (Trinitarian).

Records at the back of a church manual show that Mary joined by profession at the same time, meaning the minister and church examined her claim to salvation before admitting her.[6] She would remain a member for thirty-seven years, until 1875, when she was approaching her midfifties. This was a lifetime in the nineteenth century. Understanding Mary's long-term Congregational church experience, locally and denominationally, is key to understanding her developing religious sensibilities.

Mary's first and most influential pastor, Enoch Corser, was known as a "Boanerges of the New Hampshire pulpit" and successful revivalist.[7] He was considered blunt, sincere, and "firm in the Calvinistic view of doctrines of the Gospel," though his strict successor deemed him not quite enough of a disciplinarian. Corser preached in the traditional New England manner from summary headings in an outline, beginning "to extemporize, rising, by degrees" to a state of "eloquence and deep pathos," his audience listening "in breathless silence."[8]

The room itself was rarely silent, though, as Corser possessed not only a thunderous voice but "tremendous muscle, which he often used on the desk and Bible in moments of intense fervor."[9] Orderly sermonizing delivered with deep feeling, considered neither too restrained nor extra emotional, was the standard. It captured hours of Mary's attention. She later wrote that Corser and the church welcomed her along with her objection to the doctrine of predestination that would have doomed her siblings, none of whom had professed salvation.[10] So many Protestants of her generation registered similar objections that this stance would become a defining marker of Protestant belief by midcentury.

Like many rural churches, the Sanbornton church was evangelical with a tradition of interdenominational exchange, mostly out of necessity. Baptists and Methodists shared the meeting space before the Congregationalists built a church of their own. So did the pacifist, dress-reforming, faith-healing Osgoodite sect from nearby Warner, a few years before the Bakers joined. The Reverend Liba Conant, who led meetings while the Bakers were making their membership decision, presided over revivals characterized by "prayer, earnest, ardent and agonizing" in their sincerity. His Sunday school pupils memorized "hundreds" of scripture verses, a common regional and denominational practice. Ministers were chronically undercompensated, and the families they served had constant pastoral needs. Conant found his duties "sufficient to crush an angel," were it not for the sustaining prayers of the congregation.[11]

Notably for Eddy's later career, Conant's ministry oversaw an important national shift toward the temperance movement. At his ordination ceremony, copious consumption of liquors had preceded marching "to the music of the fife and drum, to the place of examination, and back in the same order" to get "liquored up again, before supper." Ministerial examining committees were considered remiss without this practice, which was repeated a few days in a row.[12]

In 1828, however, the year Mary turned seven, the temperance movement created a divisive stir in the region. Revelers taunted teetotalers with rum, declaring they would "sprinkle" it on them in baptismal fashion, and lit gunpowder at their feet. Increasing numbers nevertheless pledged to forgo "spirituous liquors," and in 1833, the Sanbornton church's officer of discipline published a resolution to exclude or censure any member who "traffics in, or manufactures ardent spirits."[13] The same year, a few states to the west, Joseph Smith codified temperance for Mormons in his Doctrine and Covenants. Mary Baker Eddy would later become the only other American religious founder to invoke this standard for adherents, though she would describe it in her church's textbook rather than its rulebook.

Temperance was a messy, contested, hard-won moral stance as Mary Baker began to seriously weigh the state of her soul. When she joined the Sanbornton church, choosing the influence of the Holy Spirit over liquid spirits was not a formality but a raggedly new and vital act. Individual conviction, rather than rote rule-following, was key. A speech on temperance from the 1830s by Mary's brother Albert can be taken as representative of the general regional and family position.

Albert argued that it would cheapen the cause to "strip it of its moral aspects wholly and make of it a mere political question by carrying [it] to the Ballot Box and to the Halls of Legislation, and identifying it with every possible enterprise and transaction." Though a lawyer himself, he found law intrinsically powerless to give people "an abiding interest for a moral cause."[14] Legislating aspects of human behavior was sometimes an unavoidable practicality, he argued, but it ran serious risks: rote compliance, reversal, backlash. Better to first work with reason, religion, and conscience to win people over. This democratic stance, especially characteristic of New Hampshire, equated caution in legal regulation with the gradual and sure establishment of democracy through moral conscience.

Congregational churches in New Hampshire extended this logic to antislavery as well in the 1830s, when gradualist antislavery views trumped the immediacy of abolition. Increased radicalization took over from the 1840s onward. Congregationalist antislavery was not without robust conflict, which should not be minimized. It is not a neat or tidy story. Yet while reading through hundreds of issues of *The Congregationalist* from 1830 to 1860, as well as several issues of the dozens of lesser-known Congregationalist periodicals and archival letters among lay adherents, I found myself surprised at how thoroughly these sources expressed antislavery sentiment.

Biographers have debated the extent of Mary's early antislavery views, often assuming her family's democratic orientation precluded clear commitments in this direction. This debate is apropos of her postwar authorship, which engaged abolitionist tropes in treatises of spiritual freedom. The spiritual politics of her early church, however, provide essential context for understanding how

Jacksonianism consistently and increasingly yielded to Congregationalism on this matter throughout the region, including within her own congregation.

It was "the imperative duty of Christians to make slavery a subject of prayer, inquiry and discussion," New Hampshire Congregationalists voted in 1834, "with a view to its cessation at the earliest possible period."[15] Churches celebrated antislavery leaders, but the ideal at first was to end enslavement as prayerfully and quickly as possible without undermining progress through intemperate radicalism that (this view held) risked deepening national divisions.

Among the few early "radical agitators" in New Hampshire, one was reportedly thrown out of a church and at least one arrested. Jacksonians considered abolitionism a threat to the Union; Congregationalists simultaneously thought it divisive enough to weaken or delay the desired goal of antislavery legislation and, by extension, the sinless state of the coming millennium.[16]

From the 1830s to the 1850s, this latter line of reasoning predominated almost exclusively and without variation in Congregationalist periodicals circulating in Mary's home state. Several carried items by her family's pastors and acquaintances. These published fervently and increasingly persuasive antislavery features and lecture reports. A typical newspaper acknowledged in 1836 that dissolution of the Union was the most awful thing to contemplate for some, yet "the hosts of heaven are not indifferent" to slavery, and neither should be the church.[17]

A minister of Jesus in New Hampshire should not attempt to "throw the garments of an angel over and around such a monster as slavery."[18] Even those who struggled with the intellectual questions involved in the politics of freeing the enslaved, and who might note that at one time enslavement may have had a place in the Bible, must have a feeling that "slavery is a dreadful wrong—a withering and tormenting *curse* to the human family," and the moral heart must condemn it.[19]

When a congregation in Keene, southwest of Concord, hosted an antislavery talk in 1837 featuring a formerly enslaved man named Girly (possibly a feminized name created by enslavers, a name he chose, or a surname akin to Gurlie or Gurley), a European American attendant filled a letter to his sister with Girly's biblical rhetoric, finding it critically brilliant. The talk's high drama was justified, he concluded, as "the evils of slavery could not be told" otherwise.[20] In 1841, New Hampshire Congregationalists renounced the Southern Presbyterian Church over its endorsement of slavery. An 1843 church gathering in Manchester declared the practice a "heinous sin," while a minister declared it "intolerable" for slaveholders to "hold the image of God as a *chattel*."[21]

During the 1850s, antislavery was no longer enough, and abolitionism became the norm as New Hampshire Congregationalists radicalized even more, leaving behind their earlier "moral suasion" stance. In 1854, a cadre of ministers exercised their heritage as "protest-ants" (as they put it) by signing an abolitionist petition. One explained that as a "Democrat 'dyed in the wool,'" he had not been an abolitionist previously, but now he hoped God could forgive him for voting for Franklin Pierce. By the time the Civil War arrived, Congregationalists welcomed "ardently patriotic sermons and supported Lincoln and the union," tied these to absolution for the sin of enslaving people, and even recognized in some cases "that the North was not without responsibility for the crime of slavery."[22]

This arc from antislavery to abolitionism trumped democratic views and held practically exclusive sway in Congregational churches across New Hampshire, including Mary Baker's own. As her Sanbornton congregation worked to secure a lot for its church building right after the Bakers joined, it "had the offer of a good site for nothing on condition that we would never have the emancipation of the slaves named in the church," a minister later recalled. Declining the offer, the church paid for a site instead, and "has been free for a pure gospel to this day, and we have lived to see the ultimate and glorious triumph of Freedom in our beloved America."[23]

Though written after the Civil War, this narrative matches the record unfolding in real time in the years around 1840. For Mary to step outside this record and hold contravening views would have been practically unthinkable and is, in any event, unsustained by documents about her early life. The arc from antislavery to abolitionism was certainly hers as well. As she would write in 1865, long before fame or public image entered in, the "tears of the bleeding slave poured" on the "breast" of the newly reunified nation to be "wiped away" by God, who knew "best."[24] Such sentiments built on her earliest sympathies and experiences.

IF SALVATION AND FREEDOM of the soul was the predominant concern among early New Englanders, education was a close second, deemed "the handmaid of religion" by New Hampshire state historians.[25] By 1850, the rationale for educating girls and women had shifted from a primarily religious to a human rights basis. When Mary Baker Eddy was a girl, however, Congregational Protestants still assumed young people must learn to read, write, and reason in order to gain a proper sense of their own depravity and need for salvation in Jesus Christ.[26]

Reading the Bible allowed them to examine the natural wonders of God's creation and their state of thought comprehensively, intensely, and regularly in writing, an expectation applied equally to both sexes. Mary's parents assumed she would be educated for the same reason as other girls: to meditate on religious topics and properly attend to her soul as the nation waited for the coming Lord.

Religious convictions about the necessity of educating girls pushed up against cultural and medical views in the opposite direction. Echoing popular views, a New England newspaper announced in 1830 that women could not understand men's passions, vices, business, or characters or the affairs of the world, mainly because of the "disabling delicacy that pervades [female] conceptions and feelings."[27] Prevailing medical conceptions held that girls would not properly develop into womanhood if overstimulated; too much education could have only debilitating effects on their brains and nervous systems.

Physicians applied this theory almost exclusively to Anglo girls from socially elite or "established" backgrounds, as they usually considered girls of color and working-class white girls either to be physiologically different or to have no need of becoming "ladies."[28] Prevailing rhetoric about white girls in the 1830s persisted through and well beyond the end of the century.

The president of the New Hampshire Medical Association opined in 1891 that mothers were often alarmed over daughters who "were never quite strong, but were the brightest and most ambitious scholars in their classes." A female physician agreed that "school-life is responsible for much of the ill health of young girls."[29] As ample secondary and primary literature shows, throughout the long nineteenth century, girls exercised their brains at the expense of their bodies, and vice versa.[30]

Within this simultaneously expansive and restrictive educational environment, Mary Baker gained a decent if irregular education. She heavily marked passages in *Young's Night Thoughts* and Milton's *Paradise Lost*, pieces with orthodox religious themes echoing those in her family and church environment. Her main schoolbook, Lindley Murray's popular reader, contained mostly eighteenth-century works. In her girlhood notebooks, she wrote down passages from Byron, Wordsworth, Shakespeare, and the popular romantic poet Felicia Hemans.[31] When she was ill, tutors replaced school attendance whenever possible.

Mary's main tutors were Corser (her pastor and a Middlebury graduate) and her brother Albert, a Dartmouth graduate who left farming to read law with future U.S. president Franklin Pierce, returning home regularly. Another Corser student, Lucian Hunt, recalled the minister as a regional educational draw and standout Latin teacher. Dyer Sanborn, author of a widely used grammar book, was deemed "of no deep scholarship" but an excellent pedagogue and popular teacher.[32]

Sanborn almost certainly taught Mary; so did Sarah Bodwell, relative of local minister Abraham Bodwell, who sat on the Woodman Sanbornton

Academy's executive board.[33] Through these avenues, the bulk of Mary's education focused on the standard subjects of the day: natural philosophy or what was then called "moral science," logic, some language, basic mathematics. She learned enough of ancient and European languages to be considered respectable in her social circles but probably not enough to make a splash at a Boston finishing school.

Mary's girlhood poems were typical of her time, gender, and place, mingling imagery of patriotism, natural beauty, some social commentary, and Christian salvation. Her meditation on the beauties of nature inspiring her to "form resolutions, with strength from on high," and to "kneel at the altar of mercy and pray" for "pardon and grace, through His Son," meshes thematically with the poems of New England Baptist Persis Sibley Black, who produced a twenty-page meditation in 1836 on the coming apocalypse, a common theme.

The Boston Unitarian Ann Greene Chapman began journaling her thoughts on sermons at age eleven, agreeing with a preacher that "religious anxiety" was essential to faith, as "the passions of hope and fear" would be meaningless unless they held religious purposes. She brought them to God in her "secret struggle" to discern worthiness for church membership. She also found joy in bucolic scenery, chafed against the compulsory silence of women in mixed company, and, like Mary, thrilled at a commemoration of the Battle of Bunker Hill. Congregationalists and Baptists tended to consider Unitarians heretical, and Chapman was of a more elite social class than both Mary Baker and Persis Black, but all three produced fairly typical antebellum female writings.[34]

In addition to poetry, Mary, like Chapman, practiced the traditional habit of self-examination and religious reflection through writing. She held onto it her entire life, the practice much later picked up by a sometime–Christian Science convert who circulated among several Christian groups. William Strachan eventually chose the Paulists but carried with him the Protestant practice of spiritual journaling, which he credited to Mary Baker Eddy.[35]

Medical concerns about the deleterious effects of education on female physiology, however, were compounded by the fact of Mary's actual illness. Nineteenth-century American letters are often full of gritty reports of sickness and its symptoms and effluvia, usually combined with religious hopes for recovery or at least endurance. The Baker family letters singled out Mary as their main source of worry on this front, registering serious concern about a degree of suffering that sometimes overwhelmed her.[36]

DESCRIPTIONS OF SICKNESS from the era are difficult to translate to twenty-first-century ailments, but Mary's nervous inflammation and digestive problems or "neuralgia of the spine and stomach" fit somewhere on the continuum mapped out by nineteenth-century research on the spinal column as the locus of bodily health.[37] Neuralgia today is considered a nervous disease characterized by sharp, shocking pain, but medical historian Andrew Hodgkiss notes that "its meaning expanded between 1840 and 1880" before contracting to its present sense.[38]

A prizewinning 1852 essay by Charles M. Parsons in the *American Journal of the Medical Sciences* judged spinal neuralgia, inflammation, or irritation (the terms were synonymous) common but difficult to diagnose. Parsons leveraged years of study and treatment in his landmark essay. Neuralgia, he decided, resided either in nervous dysfunction or "disorder in some internal organ . . . the spinal cord serving as the medium" rather than the cause of illness. As a secondary symptom, patients experienced relief that was "sometimes surprisingly prompt as to show that some other condition than inflammation has existed."[39] This matches accounts of Mary's chronic symptoms sometimes advancing and receding quickly.

Letters from regular folk around New Hampshire also describe symptoms like hers. A gentleman hoped to be rid soon of "weakness of the spine"; a minister's invalid teenage daughter "will probably die before a great while, yet she may live years," as she had the awful and mysterious "spinal disease"; a doctor's wife could not go to prayer meetings and tired easily, and her husband "says it is spinal irritation the cause of all my troubles he thinks my lameness originated in the spine and having sprained my hand it located there that being the weakest spot. [I]t looks quite reasonable he says of the weakness that caused me to fall down so much was of the Spine."[40] Fatigue, unpredictability, falling down—all characterized this ubiquitous yet unmanageable condition.

Researchers contrasted neuralgia to "the pains of hypochondriasis," which were "boring or burning" instead of "acute" and could recede when the patient was "suitably distracted," which "was not seen in neuralgia."[41] They also decided neuralgia was categorically unlike hysteria, a nervous affliction thought to be induced by disorders of the womb (*hyster*) and attended by different leading symptoms, which were said to affect mostly dissipated denizens of high society who read novels and danced too much.[42] By 1871, a phenomenally popular assessment by George H. Napheys would contrast hysteria ("always curable" and perhaps psychologically rooted) with neuralgia ("a more fearful malady is hardly known to medicine"). Napheys's book went through seven editions in five years and came recommended by dozens of ministers, physicians, and their respective professional periodicals.[43]

As definitions of neuralgia narrowed after 1880, definitions of hysteria simultaneously expanded to take on a set of distinctive physiologically rooted, heavily psychologized, and contentious meanings. By 1910, these retroactively affected descriptions of Mary Baker Eddy's illness as they appeared in early biographies.[44] According to medical literature at the time of her illness, however, her affliction was squarely neuralgia.

However frustratingly evasive its pathology may have been for physicians, it was a widespread ailment. One doctor who advertised his services to Congregationalist readers claimed to have treated 42,000 patients between 1826 and 1854 at his "spinal institution" for symptoms exactly like Mary's.[45] "Whatever the nature of spinal irritation," Parsons concluded in his medical journal study, "there is reason to believe it means something, and that this something" produced symptoms that need treatment.[46]

THE 1840S SAW a downward slide for Mary and her family. Albert's health had been tenuous and began to fail. He died in 1841 after a brief illness. He had become a radical populist in the New Hampshire legislature and a representative of the Democratic State Committee; ardent eulogies appeared around the state. Further, Enoch Corser abruptly left the Sanbornton pulpit in 1843. The brief tenure of an interim minister was not a happy one, dogged in part by controversy over Corser's departure. When Corbin Curtice finally took his place as the formally installed pastor, some congregants still felt Corser might have stayed with "proper treatment."[47]

Curtice asked his parishioners to talk less and pray more about such matters, and they complied, mostly out of courtesy. He eventually built up the Sunday school and brought together the congregation. Personal tragedy caused him to be "plain, faithful and sympathizing with the sick" and mourning, helpful traits for the Bakers at the time.[48] He would remain Mary's pastor from the time she was twenty-two until she was almost fifty, though later mostly at a distance as she moved around New England.

Mary's situation brightened considerably when she wed George Washington Glover in December 1843. "Wash" was a friend of her brother George, who was unlike the studious and refined Albert. Wash and George traded energetic letters about the kinds of "men's passions, vices, business," and exploits from which Mary's alleged "disabling delicacy" excluded her, and about the "solled comfut" Wash found so welcoming in the Baker home.[49] Wash focused solely on such homey and delicate matters with Mary, who did an end run around her father's objections to the older suitor by corresponding with him while on a trip with her brother to the mountains. While there, she also penned a poetic tribute to the famous natural granite formation the Old Man of the Mountain. It was the kind of meditation on natural and national themes magazines loved to publish, as in this case one did.[50]

Mary and Wash married in her parents' home and set sail for Charleston, South Carolina, blissfully unaware of their limited time together. Wash died of yellow fever six months after the wedding. He had met with entrepreneurial success but was not well established and left his widow without resources.⁵¹ Six months pregnant, she returned to New Hampshire to deliver their baby.

In 1844, Darwin published the arguments he would later refine in his 1859 *On the Origin of Species*. The pressures of scientific inquiry were inexorably changing the shape of faith, but on the surface at least, nature still appeared firmly in the control of God's hand. Religious utopia, perfectionism, and rapture abounded. The Disciples of Christ founder Barton Stone and Mormon founder Joseph Smith both died that year, signaling new eras for different types of American restorationism. The leader of the small faith-healing sect that had once shared worship space with Mary's home church, Jacob Osgood, also died, but divine healers were on the cusp of establishing significant ministries in America patterned after Europeans such as Dorothea Trudel.

Whatever their sect or tradition, nearly everyone seemed to be talking about the end of the world. Congregationalists circulated end-time publications increasingly linked to the sin of slavery.⁵² Harriet Livermore, too radical for her New Hampshire Congregational roots, found purchase with those inclined to take the Bible's millennialist calculations literally.⁵³ The most popular millennialist come-outer, William Miller, delivered an imminent end-time message to huge interdenominational crowds. The apocalypse, Millerites knew, was upon them.

CHAPTER TWO

Loss and Exploration
(1844–1865)

In which medical advice for neuralgics to avoid stress, lest their symptoms inflame, meets with bad prospects for Mary, who spends midlife searching for the gospel and science behind various cures, like many Americans

IN THE FALL OF 1844, when the world was supposed to come to an end, Mary was at her parents' home in Sanbornton Bridge slowly recovering from the difficult delivery of her son, George Washington Glover II. Georgy arrived on 12 October. Ten days later, thousands of Millerites gathered in public places to welcome the end-time and the advent of the millennium. This non-event of national proportions immediately became known as the Great Disappointment. For Mary, it must have felt like the end of the world for different reasons, riddled with her own private great disappointments. More were to come, along with a new spirit of exploration, perhaps born of necessity, that was both highly personal and meshed with the times.

Quick on the heels of the Millerite flameout, Ellen Harmon White found visions in its embers and began shaping her Adventist teachings in Maine. In 1846, John Humphrey Noyes introduced complex marriage at his Oneida Community. Multiple religious innovations emanated from the same "burned over district" of upstate New York, a region named for its unusual concentration of spirited visions and fiery revivals. The evangelical stirrings of Charles Grandison Finney and the Second Great Awakening were long gone, but the Fox sisters heard table rappings in Rochester in 1847, kicking off the nation's widespread engagement with Spiritualism.

The American Bible Tract Society, aided by the burgeoning print industry, was busy distributing unprecedented quantities of tracts, preparing Americans for salvation through the written word.[1] Radical evangelicals mounted increasing challenges to enslavement, clerics, and religious authority. A questioning spirit was in the air. "Conventionality is not morality. Self-righteousness is not religion," wrote Charlotte Brontë in *Jane Eyre*. "To attack the first is not to assail the last."[2]

Most of these developments were distant news at best to Mary, surrounded as she was by domestic trials. Her mother died in 1849. Abigail Baker had been instrumental in helping her ill daughter raise a child in the restrictive atmosphere of Mark Baker's home. Family letters continued to refer to the poor health that prevented Mary from consistent work. Just before Abigail died, Mary relocated to a nearby town for two months to take medical treatment from her regular doctor, Parsons Whidden, with middling results.[3]

She briefly ran an experimental kindergarten, one of the first in New England, and wrote mostly inconsequential pieces for local magazines. Publishers appear to have paid her for these, if modestly, a new development for women authors at the time. Her bid for independence was constantly thwarted, however, not only by illness but by her father's proscriptions. "O, how I wish that I had a *Father* that had been *ever* willing to let me know something," she wrote. That not being the case, she resigned her latest idea of moving away and learning piano in order to teach it.[4]

Marriage offered the only practical way out of such circumstances. Abigail died probably comforted by her daughter's engagement to a childhood friend, John Bartlett, whom Mary had accompanied to his graduation from Harvard Law School in 1848. Bartlett sought his fortune with thousands of others in the gold rush, however, and just a few weeks after Abigail's passing, Mary received word that he had died in Sacramento.

Mark Baker soon remarried and made clear that Mary and her son were no longer welcome in his home. Out of a combination of misguided concern for his daughter's continually compromised health, an aging realization of the amount of work caregiving would require of himself and his new wife, and possibly personal frustration or antipathy for George or his father, Wash, Mark sent George to live with aunts, uncles, and eventually a neighbor, Mahala Sanborn, who was an occasional hired family helper and a warm friend to Mary.

Mary sent letters suggesting her sister might provide a new home for herself and George, but she had no leverage. By 1851, Mahala had married Russell Cheney, and Mark supported their move with Georgy to the remote village of North Groton by the White Mountains. As recent work on family law by Tracy A. Thomas so fully illustrates, women lacked the financial independence and legal standing to be involved in custody negotiations, much less object to them. Elizabeth Cady Stanton had just forcefully illustrated to the New York legislature in the 1840s how pathetically and dangerously unable women were to make legal decisions about the welfare and placement of their children.[5] This right was reserved for their nearest male relatives. In his unrelenting way, Mark probably thought he was making the best choices for those under his patriarchal care.

Biographers have suggested that this experience stayed with Mary far into her life. It was doubtless a factor that led her to later support women's rights. She responded to these losses with grieving poems of the type that appeared in her church's periodicals and combined resignation, despair, anxiety of soul, loss of hope, and religious expectations for a brighter future.[6]

Seeking to rebuild her family, in 1853 Mary wed the family dentist, Daniel Patterson, a relative of her stepmother, Elizabeth Patterson Duncan. Elizabeth gifted her a book about New Hampshire families, and Mary proudly marked the Patterson name.[7] The two developed a warm relationship over time, but neither had a say in Mark's decisions. The newlyweds followed Mary's son and the Cheneys north, but the menfolk were stubborn. Russell and Mark dug in their heels for the status quo, and Daniel became unwilling to make a home for the boy. Mary's hopes for reunification appear pathetic in retrospect as, unknown to her, a legal contract prevented it. The Pattersons would have had to pay a $400 bond to redeem young George from this arrangement, though Mary's "disabling delicacy," exacerbated by the dreaded spinal disease, excluded her from such discussions.[8]

Under murky circumstances, in 1856 the Cheneys relocated to Minnesota, when George was twelve. Mark likely financed their move in part. George was given to believe his mother was dead. Mary's family told her that her son had wandered into the wilderness, apparently again out of their collective inability to contravene Mark. To some degree, they were also motivated by continuing misguided concerns to preserve Mary's health.

PREDICTABLY, THIS TACTIC had the opposite effect. Standard medical advice that neuralgics should avoid stress and worry, lest their symptoms inflame, met with bad prospects for Mary.[9] She continued taking extreme care with her diet and hoping in the Lord, but her neuralgia deepened considerably.

The next six years were among the most difficult in Mary's life. She was often bedridden. An engraving of the Pattersons' home in North Groton shows a small cabin set hard against the relentlessly churning stream that powered a sawmill.[10] Outside their front door, the mill ground away the landscape all summer. In the winter, snow blocked the way out. Debt also piled up. The stresses of their beleaguered lives probably led to sharp arguments. Decades later, Mary Baker Eddy would write "horror" next to Tolstoy's description of domestic friction in *The Kreutzer Sonata*: "I did not know that in all households they, like myself, imagined that it was a misfortune exclusively reserved for them."[11] It is hard not to feel her backward gaze to Groton.

It was not all bad, though. When Daniel traveled, affectionate letters continued between him and Mary, replete with imagined embraces, family news, anticipated visits, and thoughts of warm kisses. More dramatically, in 1856 a newspaper in nearby Nashua reported that Mary had flung herself between Daniel and two attackers, saving his life. The issue was probably bad debt, though Daniel did not escape the womanizing reputation of most itinerant dentists, and his infidelity was the leading factor in their later divorce. In any case, "almost helpless by long disease," the account ran, Mary "rushed from her bed to the rescue of her husband, and, throwing herself before their intended victim, seized, with unwonted strength, the son who held the axe and prevented him from dealing the intended blow. Help soon came, the assailants fled, and the feeble but brave wife was carried back to her bed."[12]

To those around her, Mary was either a living example of "female courage and virtue"—the type chronicled in a popular 1850 book noting that although not her "natural province," a woman's "integrity, fortitude, courage, and presence of mind, may frequently be called forth by adventitious circumstances"— or a pretender at illness. The medical observation that neuralgia symptoms could be relieved "sometimes surprisingly prompt[ly]" was new among physicians in the 1850s and little understood by observers.[13]

Whatever factor was at work, Mary's "unwonted strength" doubtless surprised her.[14] Her biographer Robert Peel surmises that in addition to her practice of homeopathy at the time, this experience may have caused her to reflect increasingly on how thought and body might interrelate under God's providential supremacy.[15] As we will soon see, many Americans were considering similar matters.

Daniel was unable to make a living in the remote northern area where they had moved, and his business failures resulted in the loss of their home a few years later. Mary's sister owned it but was unable to pay the mortgage without Daniel supplying rent, and she had to foreclose.

The Panic of 1857 was partly to blame. As a New Hampshire farmer wrote to his sister that year, "The hard times are cramping almost every kind of business. . . . People now can have time to reflect what they are and what they have been doing and what is the end of all these things—All earthly things are vanity & vexation of Spirit saith the preacher—We can all learn wisdom."[16] It is difficult to say how reflective Daniel was. At the time of foreclosure he was away on a dalliance, desperately working to secure dentistry income, or both. Mary's sister resettled her at nearby Rumney in 1860.

Throughout this time, Mary found meaning in her surroundings by reading her Bible at home, in church when she was well enough, through visits from nearby children and in tutoring a young neighbor, and by scrapbooking, a major mode of information retrieval "supported by a large commercial apparatus throughout the 19th century." In recent years, scholars have begun to construct a narrative of this practice that counters "powerful critical accounts . . . [that] tended to devalue scrapbooks as the 'trifling' hobby of women and children."[17] Principally, as Mary sorted and systematized, she explored treatments to improve her health.

FOR ABOUT TWENTY YEARS, and like many Americans at the time, Mary experimented with various popular curative approaches in addition to regular medicine: food reforms, homeopathy, and hydropathy or water cure. Most Americans were familiar with the spectrum of food reforms that gained cultural traction when William Beaumont, the "father of gastric physiology," published his digestive experiments on Alexis St. Martin in 1836. Mary practiced variations on the popular Graham system, named after the inventor of the graham cracker, Sylvester Graham, whose Christian convictions led him to link moral purity to dietary practices somewhat akin to veganism.

The diluted drugging regime of homeopathy had food rules of its own imported and modified from the broader culture. An 1850 pamphlet of alimentary instructions for sick people under homeopathic treatment, penned by a New Hampshire physician, outlines the type of medical advice Mary followed in the 1850s. This included "only the lightest and most simple kinds of nutrients," water, broth, and fruit. Patients could add starches and proteins in moderation, including light breads and biscuits as long as they were "not too fresh." Two columns of "forbidden" and "strictly forbidden" foods follow.[18]

In the antebellum era such "irregular" cures were often more popular than "regular" allopathy, which was considered common and traditional but not necessarily the most progressive or proven system. Christians then did not describe them as "alternative therapies," an anachronistic label, though Christians today tend to use alongside the general public. Rather, they most often experienced such cures as practical, forward-thinking treatments built on the latest scientific facts, explainable through Christian theology, and endorsed by respectable reform-minded figures. Judges, ministers, famous authors, and regular folks pursued them.

Physicians frequently prescribed allopathic and homeopathic remedies together because, as Candy Gunther Brown notes, "patients wanted the best of both medical systems."[19] This was not difficult, according to David Nartonis, since homeopathic practitioners "came largely from the conventionally trained medical profession."[20] Homeopathy had enough influence that by 1875 the president of the New Hampshire Medical Society noted that regular doctors "do not object to small doses" of medication, "nor even to no doses at all," as long as the methods of homeopathic practitioners were transparent to the sick.[21] As this suggests, the majority of "irregular" patients and practitioners were regular people looking for any effective medical cure.

Practitioners debated to what extent their method rested on divine activity. "The New Hampshire pioneers" of homeopathy, writes Nartonis, "were unsure about what side to take in the battle between spiritual and material explanations."[22] Founder of homeopathy Samuel Hahnemann advocated a rather vitalist theory; others felt that the shaking mechanism involved in dosage preparation loosened medicinal particles. The latter explanation increasingly gained traction as the field developed.

The mechanistic explanation, however, was not necessarily at odds with the tendency to credit God with healing experiences and explain them in Christian terms. In midcentury New Hampshire, patients and practitioners alike often found it important to do this. In 1851, for example, O. A. Woodbury, MD, quoted the book of Genesis in the *Homeopathic Advocate and Guide to Health* to note that when "God created man in his own image" and then "breathed into the material body" a spiritual soul, he enacted a law of divinity in the material realm that explained homeopathic success.[23]

Most or all of the advertisers at the back of the *Advocate* saw homeopathy in light of their Christian views: John Le Bosquet authored the standard manual for Congregational churches in 1841, J. F. Whittle was a Unitarian Universalist, and Alpheus Morrill of Concord was a Trinitarian Congregationalist.[24] We are "now well—thanks to our Heavenly Father, and his faithful devout Homeopathia," a mother who was one of Morrill's patients and pupils wrote in an 1853 letter.[25]

Morrill was also Mary Baker Eddy's cousin by marriage. At a time when women leveraged their family caregiving roles to pioneer key aspects of homeopathic practice, he encouraged and mentored them in this as well as in standard medical practice. He advised and encouraged Mary in homeopathy just prior to her marriage to Daniel Patterson.[26] Morrill and his wife were in the circle of Armenia White, a notable Concord reformer who had ties to the most well-known political agitators of the time, from Alice Stone and Henry Blackwell to William Lloyd Garrison and Frances Willard.

One of White's correspondents was "glad to see so many good people interested" in homeopathy, meaning socially respectable and established folks like "our good friends, Dr. & Mrs. Morrill," and hoped the more staid crowd living near the town center on School Street would endorse both antislavery and homeopathy, progressive causes considered compatible by their advocates. Tongue in cheek, he added, "If salvation dont flow out of School Street to the whole town, I am afraid we are *done for*."[27]

Mild irony aside, the common popular view was that such methods and causes were vessels for Christian cure and progress, and this extended to hydropathy, or water cure, which Mary's sister encouraged and paid for her to take. Their church newspaper advertised a "hydropathic cook book" in a section of devotional titles alongside such offerings as *The Priest and the Huguenot* and *The Prairie Missionary*.[28] More notably, Harriet Beecher Stowe's religious conversion led her to turn to water cure as a means of regaining health.[29] Rather than a secular mimic of perfectionist piety, water cure was generally seen as an extension or expression of religious convictions.

The human mind was thought to play an especially distinct role in such curative activities. A dedicatory sermon at the Clifton Springs, New York, Water-Cure elaborated, emphasizing the curative action of God on the human mind. Supported by four regular physicians and other pillars of the community, the minister homed in on "the great *new* idea of the age in the science of medicine . . . the value of the mind as a recuperative agent, always to be addressed, in every attempt at a restoration of the body from disease."[30]

This "spiritual health for the mind of every inhabitant of earth" operated because "God is not an idle being[;] . . . He is the only living Being," and fallen man could access his perfection only through the restorative powers of Christianity. "The christian religion must begin to be received, in its practical, regenerating, and restorative operation, as the first agency to be employed in the theory and practice of the healing art," and the Clifton Springs water cure "was established for the purpose of making practical piety a leading agent in raising the diseased and disabled to a state of recovery and health." As an added benefit, regular medicine is expensive, but "the christian system of salvation, even as a medical agent, is free to all."

TO MIDCENTURY PEOPLE educated in antebellum texts laden with late Enlightenment precepts, the mind was not a strictly psychological or biological construct, as we conceive of these today. It was the sum of individual sentiments and feelings, reason and rationality, the arbiter of moral and spiritual experience. It was the seat of character, conscience, and conduct, devotion, the duty of piety, revelatory insight and reception; reciprocity and benevolence, all as defined by widely influential works on "moral science" or the "science of the soul."[31]

Thus the mind harbored diseased conviction that could be cast out only through Christianity, posited Frederic Henry Hedge. A Unitarian minister and early moderate Transcendentalist, Hedge preached that Jesus's healing of a sick woman shows that in some chronic cases, disease "becomes a fixed idea, a stubborn mood, a prevailing consciousness . . . causing the patient to live in his disease, to be mentally as well as bodily possessed with it." In such cases, "no drugs will avail. . . . The body in such cases can be reached only through the mind[,] . . . some great revelation, some new love, some inspired and inspiring purpose, giving thought and will a new direction," and only by "divine authority" and "agency can the demons of disease be cast out." How exactly this might happen, Hedge could not say. The lesson, he concludes, is "the healing and restorative power of faith . . . in this episode of evangelical history."[32]

Hedge's type of evangelical healing was not the "healing in the atonement" of Jesus espoused by the "faith cure" or the divine healing movement practiced by people such as Charles Cullis or Dorothea Dix, nor was it the homeopathist Woodbury's divine law of healing in the breath of biblical creation or the Clifton Springs hydropathist's "christian system of salvation, even as a medical agent." It was not one of the "miraculous signs" that followed laying on of hands or "rubbing upon" the body with sacred objects (such as a walking stick) by Mormon elders in 1849, nor was it the supernatural miracle at Lourdes that captivated the attention of American Catholics after 1858.[33]

Neither was it quite what the *Congregational Journal* meant when it matter-of-factly stated in 1843 that redeeming faith in God was needed, as "it is well known that there is an active sympathy between the mind and body, and what more natural than a depressed and embarrassed spirit should derange an organ" (though quite in sympathy with such views).[34] Yet even while the most orthodox Protestants persisted in relegating healing works to the apostolic era, each of these models urged Christ's healing presence in the modern era.

The element so many sought to identify and explain was the "law of divinity," Christian truth, or spiritual principle behind this healing. How exactly did God act on human sentiment and reason, thus redeeming human bodies? By what mechanism had he wrought these healing experiences in the natural world?

No one knew for sure. The Clifton Springs orator wondered "where this healing agency of the true religion stops" and it becomes only a "*sedative* virtue," making the mind passive to receive physical medicine, as opposed to "a positively *curative* power, in the indwelling, of God within the mind."[35] The Christian ideal here was specifically *not* for God to render the brain a transmitter of material medicine. Rather, it was for God to render the body alive to his power through physical treatments that ensured his immanence in and on the mind—the character, conscience, and conduct of the human self.

Woodbury took things further, positing that "the *mind* is the power which produces, in the human body, not only the *intellectual* and *moral* but also the vital phenomena. The mind produces all the varied phenomena of the body." He theorized that God operated on the human mind to curative effect through "the medium of the most refined of all material agents, the natural element of the universe, the medium which fills all space.... It matters not by what name we call it, whether it be the nervous fluid, electricity, or the vital principle. All recognize it, under one name or another."[36]

The last point overreaches, in keeping with the totalizing aspect of vitalist theory. Educated people were generally familiar with popular debates about the proposed "vital fluid," but its definition and viability were as yet indistinct. Most Christian healers interpreted the invisible principle at work in their cures in terms provided by the doctrines of creation and immanence, sometimes creatively defined. Whether or not this immanence operated in or on a theoretical vitalism to cure the human system (through its gateway, the mind) was a finer point on which few agreed.

NEITHER DID SURETY EXIST about whether physical electricity and magnetism shared properties with a proposed vital or animal magnetic fluid, perhaps as different phenomena of the same underlying scientific principle or force. Instead, perhaps these were strictly aspects of the scientific law of electromagnetism that James Clerk Maxwell was on the cusp of explaining. Regardless, an era was beginning in which these would-be explainers would need to parse how electricity, magnetism, and their proposed or actual phenomena did and did not fit into their healing theologies.

This question was not a fringe matter but rather at the contested heart of scientific, medical, and spiritual discussions at the time. Before Darwinism fully emerged, Sara Paretsky shows, developments in geology and philology were already breaking down the Scottish commonsense mode of learning predominant in northern seminaries, and the scientific inquiry taking its place posed a challenge to traditional theology.[37] Magnetic theory centrally took part in this trend, expanding and deepening the fertile ground of questioning that set the stage for later debates over science, biblical authority, and God's activity in creation.

On 27 December 1843, the same day Mary and Wash Glover sailed for Charleston, the Congregational church in Shelburne, Massachusetts, crystallized the nature of this debate. Did a congregant have standing to object to his minister's study and employment of animal magnetism as a curative agent? The church body sought to settle if such an objection were a permissible expression of conscience or rather an unlearned insult tantamount to libel.

The star witness, Edward Hitchcock, was a geologist, collector of dinosaur footprints, interplanetary theorist, resisting dyspeptic, venerable Congregational author, and third president of Amherst College. The church is "the spot where God's Spirit descends," he noted; thus the controversy grieved him.[38]

Yet his views were clear. If the Shelburne church were more educated, congregants would "know what progress has been made with respect of Mesmerism" and that "men of distinction . . . consider it a science established." If Christians do not investigate this new science, "shall infidels, materialists[?] They have had the field long enough. No: Christians & Christian ministers are the men."

Hitchcock argued that Christians might realistically find mesmerism scientifically explainable like the "phenomena of light & heat & electricity." It might be a medium for divine communication and a potential means for convincing materialistic unbelievers of God's curative and saving power. It was a topic of urgent cultural importance: "Thousands will know of this case and its decision." Would Shelburne be found wanting?

The trial ended with a whimper. By the time the question was called, the quorum had disappeared. Procedural issues eventually scuttled the affair. Yet the Shelburne case signified a new era in which Christian intellectuals, scientists, traditionalists, physicians, and innovators (many of whom wore many hats at once) debated passionately over what science and scripture meant in the modern world.

What did new phenomena like animal magnetism mean? Was it godly, curative, and helpful, or a devilish distraction? Was it an invisible natural phenomenon like the wind and waves that God caused to exist and act, just as he stirred all creation into being? If so, how did God conduct and use this natural force to his glory, as he did other elements of the created world?

Was it part of the raft of new scientific discoveries, like the telegraph and steam engine, that so many people assumed contributed to the millennial rumblings of God's coming kingdom? Was it the medium through which Christians could perceive God's voice, even perhaps a manifestation of his voice itself, or was it a rank counterfeit? Was it seemly or unseemly? Was it law? If so, natural or divine?

Magnetism and electricity were scientific forces, yet their invisible, uncharted powers and properties acted on the human mind and self in unprecedented ways. To the extent they did, they continued to be a legitimate if mysterious factor in the holy work of ministers.[39] In 1852, the unorthodox Congregationalist Horace Bushnell (then in the midst of his heresy trial relating to the divinity of Christ) preached at length on a law of "unconscious influences" that operated invisibly like many of the laws of nature, working through the sentiments and feelings of the mind rather than as a "verbal proposition."[40] He was hardly a vitalist and also not a participant in the divine healing movement. Spiritualism and occultism frankly disgusted him. He was rather an innovative minister grappling with the unexplained scientific forces of his time.

Unlike Bushnell, some ministers sought to merge Spiritualism and Christianity into a new construct. A few left to build new esoteric religious identities in which the proposed animal magnetic ether corresponded to the Holy Spirit, with the Bible playing a supporting or minor role (rarely did it play no role).

In a world grappling with how to classify a multiverse of rapidly separating scientific and theological threads, Spiritualism (which Krister Dylan Knapp calls a "logical extension" of traditional Christian teachings on the eternality of the soul outside the body) evolved a "scientific wing" that "hoped to use science to prove the objective reality of spirits." This attempt to align itself with a Geertzian "aura of factuality" signally failed by 1900, but the legacy of psychical research continued to have enduring implications for the study of religion.[41]

For its part, as Emily Ogden shows in her recent history of mesmeric phenomena, mesmerism had long moved in and out of respectability.[42] It now experienced a gradual historical split. Most ministers, including those in Mary's Congregationalist circles, stayed in the traditional pulpit and increasingly grouped mesmerism, spirit rappings, and the clairvoyance of Andrew Jackson Davis together as diabolical manifestations or "evil agencies." Yet aspects of mesmerism that appeared to corroborate scientific research on suggestion, brain, nerves, and mind became absorbed into the evolving basis of mainstream psychology by the turn of the new century (which in turn began to blend with many denominations that had ironically eschewed the mesmeric tradition fifty years prior).[43]

Thus throughout the nineteenth century, overlapping religious, medical, and scientific communities diligently worked to pin down newly emergent phenomena and to parse their actual or theoretical causes and effects.[44] These forces were culturally neutral in that they lent themselves to dozens of interpretations, from the biblical to the mechanical, chemical, psychological, or esoteric. The meanings people assigned to them varied profoundly and were often at odds. The weight of cultural authority, however, increasingly shifted toward the natural sciences.

In his widely known 1858 work *Nature and the Supernatural*, Bushnell pushed against a world in which the laws of the Spirit were becoming effete compared to scientific laws and methods. He looked for "the living God, immediately revealed," so that "religion is not more a tradition, a secondhand light, but a grace of God unto salvation, operative now." The next year, Darwin published his *On the Origin of Species*. From then on, the concerns Bushnell pointed out and lamented would increasingly become a defining feature of American Christianity.[45]

IN THE LATE 1850s, this suite of debates had considerable purchase in popular imagination. Mary was familiar with some through her circle of Protestants pursuing popular cures and social reform movements for reasons they described as biblical, even if these sometimes flummoxed the more staid elements in town. As a homegrown practitioner, she did not yet participate in broad public discussions. She had no way of knowing that would change in the coming decade.

For the time being, she was still a member of the Congregational church in Sanbornton Bridge, and that covenant relationship radiated out to her series of remote dwellings to warm the core of her worldview. Whatever her worship life was like in the White Mountains, her home church was not only her most enduring early religious connection but possibly her longest early relationship.

Her husband occasionally sent sermon news about the Sanbornton church from his dentistry trips. She may have heard about the meeting in winter 1858, an unusually cold Sabbath evening when only a few attended, "those who *really desired to be there*." Many experienced a tearful revival of Jesus's love in their hearts. "A Methodist brother being asked how he had enjoyed the meeting, with tears replied, 'I never so felt the mighty power of God as here tonight.'"[46] Methodists were well known for their heart-based,ardent religiosity, and it was clearly a badge of pride in Mary's congregation that this brother *felt* God's power with tears in the meeting.

Most of the social reform set in her church tradition modified their Trinitarian beliefs by the 1850s. She may well have, too; we know she certainly did by the 1860s. Like many Americans by midcentury, she also held onto her conviction in universal salvation. As a Congregational farmer outside Concord wrote to his cousin in 1858, "I cannot believe there is a person on earth so revengeful and vindictive that he would if he had the power sentence even his mortal enemy to *eternal* torture. . . . I fear I could not love God if I believed he had invented this scheme of punishment." Rather typically for his cohort of agrarian New Englanders, he backed up his view with evidence from "the best Greek scholars."[47] Carried on a sea of such popular sentiment, reformers including Bushnell, Ellen Harmon White, Elizabeth Cady Stanton, the Beecher siblings, and Sojourner Truth would reshape (or, in the case of Stanton, reject) evangelical religion to arrive at widely varied teachings they considered both tender and fair.

For most Americans, the significance of apocalyptic dates also came into unprecedented focus with the drumbeats of the Civil War. Apocalyptic rhetoric swirled as they saw the fulfillment of end-time prophecies unfolding in the nation's blood atonement.

Mary would eventually come to know Hitchcock, of the Shelburne trial, through his contributions to an 1856 book on the Bible's "chief prophetic periods," which she marked up in pencil. She doodled on the endpapers, jotted numbers in the margins, and drew a line next to the statement that "most prophetic interpreters" dated the first resurrection of the saints between 1864 and 1885. This would be known by "the peal of the resurrection trumpet, and the living saints that are on earth shall leap for joy."[48]

In the antebellum era and through the Civil War, she was thinking alongside many Americans about the urgent relationship between scripture, science, health, mind, identity, apocalypse, and salvation, while looking for the Second Coming.

CHAPTER THREE

Unrest

(1860–1862)

*In which evangelical poetry is forthcoming and mourning
and national strife mean everything is unsettled*

IN 1860, when she had few friends and no audience, Mary Baker Eddy wrote "The Heart's Unrest," a poem in which she "long[ed] to inhabit a world more bright" and lamented the "mournful memories" surrounding her. Depressed by life's turns, she felt the flowers strewn on the "bright path . . . never will blossom on mine." However, the last stanza takes a different tack, showing the core of her religious inclinations at the time:

> Yet through the rough billows and pitiless storm
> The Pilot acquires his art
> And thus our dear Savior by conflict forms
> The meek and enduring heart
> These these are the teachings of wisdom & love
> To lean on thy Father's breast
> Tis the fold for the lambkin the cote of the dove
> Where the love of thy heart *can* rest[1]

Such conclusions aligned with popular Protestant devotional sensibilities. In a typical letter, a New Englander consoled his sister in the midst of pressing difficulties by assuring her that "peace is not now. But soon, in a brighter world, it will come." Our "nobler solace" comes from Saint Paul, who wrote that "'All things work together for good.' You are in the midst of a storm. A calm comes next."[2] Without family members close at hand to assure her of this, Mary sought to reassure herself.

A calm did not come next in her case, however. "You will be amazed to learn that I am in prison," she heard from her husband, Daniel, in 1862.[3] "My anxiety for you is intense but be of as good cheer as possible and trust in God."

Entrusted with funds for northern sympathizers, Patterson had been captured on the site of the first Battle of Bull Run (First Manassas). Battlefield sightseeing and souvenir gathering was common during the Civil War, and historians at today's Manassas National Battlefield Park judge Daniel's capture a fluke, noting that he was on the field with several others well after the conclusion of the fight. The party stumbled onto a group of Confederates whose presence these historians cannot easily explain.[4]

Like many other Northerners, Mary and Daniel lost their "romantic innocence" about the war overnight.[5] Mary had published a poem about Major Robert Anderson and written to Union generals John C. Frémont and Benjamin Butler—"Give us in the field or forum a brave Ben Butler and our Country is safe," she wrote in August 1861, when Butler was still behaving like a gentleman—but now she spent her time and energy trying to secure her husband's release.[6]

"I am so sad," she wrote to her brother-in-law in May 1862, grieving over Daniel's capture and signing off, "Your desolate sister."[7] Months later, she relived the uncertainty and worry when her enlisted son, George, was found with a serious neck wound. He somehow had learned his mother was alive and engaged a fellow soldier with literacy skills to write to her. Afterward they kept in touch, though they would not meet again in person for several years. George recovered, but not before Mary's thrill at receiving his letter, and her pride in his enlistment, gave way to panic.

Drew Gilpin Faust describes a war in which news of death or capture was not standardized or assured, causing great anxiety for an unprecedented number of families. In one sense, Faust comments, "information as much as individuals" was "missing" in the Civil War.[8] Mary could count herself among the fortunate to receive notice of her husband's whereabouts, but soon she was lamenting the "last intelligence from my poor husband[.] O! How dark are the mysteries of His hand when it is laid so heavily upon us! Still my soul utters—'be still and know that I am God.' I have just written again to our member to Congress to see that my husband is exchanged. . . . I learn from the newspapers there have been some recent exchanges of Officers."[9]

Daniel was not among them.[10] One soldier characterized Salisbury prison, where they both had landed, as "more endurable than any other part of Rebeldom," perhaps explaining why Robert Peel could characterize Daniel's earliest letters from the site as "not . . . uncheerful," though they also clearly sought to convey an even tone in an effort to minimize Mary's distress.[11] Still, Daniel had the obvious benefit of his race, and conditions at Salisbury in early 1862 were not close to what they would become by 1864 or to those at the infamous Andersonville prison.

By summer, though, they were bad enough. Reports of favorable conditions began to seriously decline, especially for civilians.[12] The constant stress caused Mary's neuralgia to flare up again. "I was getting well this spring," she wrote the Maine curist Phineas P. Quimby, whose circular Patterson had collected before his capture, "but my dear husband was taken prisoner of war by the Southrons," and the "shock" of it brought on a "relapse."[13]

Homeopathy, allopathy, and dietary changes had not produced stable improvements for Mary, and she now sought Quimby's help. Her familiarity with him was limited to his circular, which stated that he cured without drugs and rendered his cures through "the Truth." To an evangelical Congregationalist who had spent years looking alongside others for the Christian law behind every cure, only to be disappointed at every turn, and whose homeopathic practice had taught her to regard drugs as placebos, this must have sounded promising. Did not Jesus say, "Ye shall know the truth, and the truth shall make you free"?[14]

Eddy's sister was footing the bill, though, and she first arranged for Eddy to take in a water cure retreat. Eddy stayed about three months at Dr. W. T. Vail's Hydropathic Institute in Hill, New Hampshire, but her health declined further. She was ready for Portland, Maine.

CHAPTER FOUR

Portland

(1862–1865)

In which Eddy's health comes and goes, she hopes she
has found the truth that will make her free, and 1864
is a landmark year for her wobbly independence,
though nothing much comes of it

COSMOPOLITAN, individualistic, and influential, Portland, Maine, in the fall of 1862 was in the running with Rochester, New York, as an intellectual center for social reform. Its dozens of newspapers circulated international headlines across multiple states and overflowed with intellectual news and lecture announcements.[1]

Portland colleges produced authors of nationally known texts, high-profile statesmen, and President Franklin Pierce. African American stevedores worked the waterfront, unloading barrels of molasses with new Irish arrivals. On Sundays, European American families detoured to the docks after church to hear them sing.[2] The city would be sustained by its large shipping industry through the war. Maine's economic and cultural influence receded after the 1860s, but both were booming when Mary Baker Eddy arrived in the company of her brother Samuel and his wife, Mary Ann.

Portland's religious scene was a microcosm of the nation's cultural diversity in its early wartime years. African American families attended any of the fifteen churches in Portland willing to bring them "down from the balcony," notably the Congregational church at the Abyssinian Meeting House, a newly forming AME church, or the State Street Congregational Church, cofounded by William Foye, a former Millerite of African heritage whose preaching had inspired Ellen Harmon White as a teenager.[3] Wealthy Portlanders, like the Longfellows at First Parish, Unitarian, debated changing worship service times to accommodate people working as servants. Broadsides detailed a steady flow of church dustups, regular proceedings, and sermon transcripts, as ubiquitous as they were earnest. The Free Will Baptist minister's adultery trial was hot news.[4]

The deaf ex-Quaker Jeremiah Hacker strode through town with an ear trumpet under one arm and copies of his newspaper, the *Pleasure Boat*, under the other. The *Boat* took thousands of readers in several states on a tour through Captain Hacker's radical antislavery, anti-presidential pacifism (targeting both Abe Lincoln and Jeff Davis with equally strident pacifist rhetoric).[5] He felt he spoke prophetically and could not care less if people disagreed. Plenty in Portland did, including a small but vocal "white men's rule" group backed by a southern lawyer and favoring scriptural interpretations of its own. Portlanders were not wholly contrarian, but neither were they inclined to walk in lockstep.

In this yeasty Portland scene, Eddy found the reform-minded elements of her experimental years magnified around her. Radical evangelicals attacked clergy and pulpit, convinced that any sincere reader could interpret the Bible well.[6] Adventists filled the region. The abolitionist Frances Ellen Watkins Harper had just completed a tour. A man who freed himself from a ten-pound ball and caged collar left the remnants of his enslavement with a Portlander who had served under General Butler.[7]

Temperance sashes and medals occupied closets and cupboards.[8] Advertisements for new and experimental medical treatments filled the pages of local papers. Women embroidered stacks of bookmarks with achingly sweet, guileless floral designs intertwined with matter-of-fact morals and scriptural mottos to remind them of their greater obligations as they turned pages.[9] The sincerity of their finish work and handmade goods echoed their social views, which their menfolk elaborated daily in print. Just as Longfellow joined head and heart in his poetry, these people joined practicality and sentiment in their everyday lives.

On 11 October 1862, Eddy woke up fresh from her appointment with Phineas Quimby at the newly built International House the day before. Hoping to find local amenities and news of her husband in Confederate prison, she would have scanned the *Daily Press*, which on that day described how African Americans were employed in the war effort, the rebel steamer *Alabama* was "creating havoc among the American whalemen," and General Franz Sigel was ill with "fever, exhaustion, and professional annoyance."[10]

Items recounted murder and debt (which they were wont to treat with similar degrees of outrage). Legislative news appeared next to accounts of pain and poison. Ocean steamships would sail at the appointed hours; the Maine Fifth had interesting experiences. "Considerable fun" occurred on Middle Street, when "a crowd of urchins" scrambled for apples spilled from a farmer's cart. Eddy's family probably had mackerel for dinner, as winds had driven "innumerable quantities" to shore, where restaurant cooks snapped them up at a low price.

Frank, fine-grained reports of illness and promises of cure filled the pages of daily public discourse. "I vomited for three days," read a typical testimonial, "and the third day I threw up something that resembled a lizard."[11] Ample details followed. Sexual dysfunction was a popular topic. Farmers could hardly afford to be squeamish about sexuality and reproduction, and medical ads assumed that "impediments" to sex should be removed in both men and women. In line with Protestant theology, sex between husband and wife was considered a natural function to be neither repressed nor overindulged (perhaps one reason Eddy later marked a book on friendship and marriage approving pure love of the soul yet against "prudery").[12] "Self-abuse and solitary habits, their effects and consequences," were another matter, yet these could now be treated professionally, without mercury (once thought a cure-all but now known to kill all). Papers announced such cures alongside ads for Christmas wreaths and goods shipped from Liverpool. These were ailments everyone had or knew about, like pulmonary catarrh and ailing backs.[13]

Eddy would have taken this all in stride while catching up on war news and anticipating her next appointment with Quimby, whose advertisement ran amid those of dozens of other curists'. He was an "irregular" doctor but more popular, if less established and respectable, than many regulars (a name that belied a situation in which little regulation took place).

According to estimates from his correspondence, he saw about 12,000 patients over twenty years, equivalent to about 5 percent of the Portland population per year (though like Eddy, many patients were not local). His treatment lacked drugs but, she had found on arrival, not physical administrations. He believed an etherealized, charged substance could be conducted by water on his hands to his patients by massaging their heads. He had fixed Eddy in his piercing gaze, strongly suggesting she was well—and so she was, for the time being.

Today we tend to link his treatment to a form of suggestion or hypnosis, but at the time, those labels were not used and did not clearly apply. Quimby could have sought to combine mesmerism with any number of Christian or scientific inclinations of his day to explain his work, as the Shelburne trial and other sources indicate. Yet as a former stage mesmerist, he denounced his former art as unhelpful, even opportunistic, and now embraced a life of curative aid he described as unrelated to mesmerism. Patients wanting a practitioner who identified as mesmeric could instead visit the likes of "Dr. Stackpole, the celebrated clairvoyant & electropathic physician," down the street.[14]

What, then, explained Quimby's method at the time? Was he practicing a cutting-edge medical treatment based on actual scientific phenomena tied to the invisible physical force of electromagnetism? Did his treatment leverage the "great *new* idea of the age in the science of medicine," the "value of the mind" in healing disease, as people did at Clifton Springs—through water and the Holy Spirit?

Like them, had he possibly struck on a new Christian claim to medical cure? Did he seek to reach the body "through the mind," as the Unitarian Frederic Henry Hedge declared Jesus did? Or was his work similar to that of Mrs. S. Brown, also of Portland, who "can tell what a person's diseases are by looking at them," or of Mrs. Manchester, who wrought "astonishing cures" by telling patients their "feelings exactly" after physicians "laughed" and dismissed them as "nervous"—and if so, by what means?[15]

No one knew. Quimby took notes on his practice in the form of phrases or concise notations, perhaps written in his brief free time between sessions, and he allowed patients and copyists (notably the sisters Emma and Sarah Ware) to change punctuation, add words, complete sentences, alter capitalization, and make other redactions.[16] These offer interesting glimpses into his work and suggest he sometimes presented it, to at least some extent, in the manner so many exploratory curists then did, as a science of some type relating somehow to the cures of Jesus.[17]

Yet his notes also suggested leveraging a patient's belief in the Divine in the curative process. They do not consistently revolve around any one cohesive rubric. This would wait for later advocates to retroactively piece together and theorize. He was apparently focused on being of curative help and was content with making no clearly overarching explanatory bid.

He fit well into his surrounding world in this way. Exactly how a proposed etherealized substance transmitted through wet hands may have operated like electromagnetic phenomena in the scientific and medical realms remained indistinct in public thought. Many, however, claimed that it did operate in this manner. Dozens of applications and devices were springing up, claiming to channel electricity for health, such as an 1860 electromagnetic machine "for nervous diseases" employing wet sponges that was owned and operated by a regular graduate physician of Dartmouth College. "As lightning purifies the air, so must electricity purify the blood," read an advertisement for another. "Throw Away Drugs! Try Nature's Remedy!"[18]

Regarding his method, Quimby's terse advertisements gave nothing away. They stand out as brief and businesslike among the bevy of medical notices dominating the columns of daily newspapers. From 1862 to 1865 he announced only that "he will attend to all wishing to consult him" at No. 13 International House, followed by a list of prices.[19]

The circular that had drawn Eddy to Maine stated only that he gave "no medicines or outward applications," though she later learned of the water application and "rubbing," or massage. He told patients "their feelings and what they think is their disease," and in "correcting their error, he changes the fluids of the system and establishes the truth, or health. *The Truth is the Cure.*"[20] This echoed many other curative explanations at the time and in cultural context could have had a diversity of meanings.

Eddy was steeped in a milieu that assumed the omnipotence of God, saw his hand in everything, and sought a divine law of gospel healing behind every cure. Quimby's notes presented multiple conceptual frameworks without one consistent explanatory thread, but Eddy would have thrilled to see the few linking his work to spiritual truth, science, and Jesus.[21] As she sought to reconcile this common cultural sentiment with the phenomena she saw in his practice, she pieced together her own explanations under long-considered rubrics, but the pieces would never quite fit. Her own ideas always came out differently than his. Though friendly, he never quite recognized nor endorsed them.

Onto the relatively blank slate that was Quimby's presentation of his treatment, she wrote her own explanation, and it involved the fulfillment of the long-held hope for the renewal of Christian healing she shared with many in society. Her deepest, most meditative hope in 1861 had been for "the teachings of wisdom & love / To lean on thy Father's breast," and after meeting Quimby in 1862, she clearly felt his "wisdom" was the means to this God-dependence. She may have even felt she had stumbled upon the dawn of the new millennium.

DESPITE A PROMISING START, Eddy's health under Quimby's care fluctuated greatly. Between 1862 and 1865, it was punctuated with more pronounced and closely clustered ups and downs than previously. When she was better, she at times seemed much better, and when she was worse, she was just as badly off as before. Unfortunately, increasingly over the next two years it would be the latter.

On the first day of 1863 she triumphantly wrote from Sanbornton Bridge that she was "to all who once knew me a living wonder, and a living monument" of Quimby's power. She had already assumed the role of interpreting his cures, though her explanation "surprises people," apparently including Quimby himself. Regardless, "I eat, drink and am merry; have no laws to fetter my spirit now,—though am quite as much of an escaped prisoner as my dear husband was." Some "stomach pain" persisted, she noted, but overall her health and high spirits were vastly improved.[22]

By the end of the month, however, Eddy was writing that her old pains had been troubling her for "several days."[23] This relapse did not affect her belief in Quimby; she continued sending friends and relatives to him for treatment, including a nephew with the "easily besetting sins" of smoking and drinking (though he could not travel to Maine until after the "period of excitement in N. Hampshire," the political season when "the ballot box controls"). In early

1863, Eddy herself was "suffering somewhat from my old habits [that is, pains], pain in the back and stomach, a cold just now, and billious."[24]

Daniel had rejoined her by then in the most dramatic way possible. After escaping prison in September, he struggled northward on foot and eventually found his wife in Maine. Of the 15,000 Union soldiers to serve time at Salisbury prison over the course of the war, only 300 escaped. By contrast, about 2,000 defected to the Confederacy.[25] The harrowing trip left Daniel's health and resolve compromised, but he was able to join the circuit of war lectures to get somewhat back on his feet, charging $0.15 for admission (equivalent to about $3.75 in 2020). He proved an ineffective public speaker, however, and undertook to rebuild his itinerant dentistry practice. This took him away from home again.

Several months later, about a year after she first went to Portland, Mary wrote to Daniel's brother in Saco, Maine, that she was unable to visit as planned due to extreme illness. "I have had so much pain," she wrote, and need "a room with a fire and bed as my side is so bad I cannot be dressed all the time." She was a complete invalid again, she apologetically explained. She hoped to be well enough to travel soon, and though she was "sorry to afflict you with the afflicted," she was too ill to remain in her current boardinghouse. In a postscript she added, "O! I want to see my Daniel so much I cry half the time." Yet she still hoped her relapsed health problems would improve: "The Dr's patients tell me all difficult cases are worse after a time[;] same with divers maladies. I have lost no faith even if I am worse."[26]

Her letters to Quimby stopped until 1864, when she wrote from Warren, Maine, that she felt even "less physical strength this spring than I did last" and that she "had a jaw of trouble" and "can't eat enough."[27] She again reported the same physical ailments that had initially plagued her in 1862. Finally in spring came significant relief, which, she wrote to Quimby, demonstrated "the truth you practice." She was "up and about to-day," she wrote, "by the help of the Lord! (Quimby)."[28]

Her faith had begun to sink, but it was now restored with (mostly) her health. "I did feel once Why hast thou forsaken me? Ie, your wisdom; am all right now," but she asked him to please treat her "occasionally" to keep her well. His view of treatment from a distance is unclear but probably included ideas about the circulation of an unseen electromagnetic ether. This went untheorized and undiscussed, and Eddy clearly referred to him as a latter-day New Testament figure, which he seemed to neither confirm nor deny. Her focus, however, always tracked from him personally to the "truth" or "wisdom" she assumed must operate in his work.

Yet by the end of the month she was "very ill again," she wrote flatly, with the old neuralgic "spinal pain and heat," and felt so poorly that she resolved to make a last-resort visit to Portland.[29] Almost a year later, in March 1865, she wrote to Quimby's son George for a list of boardinghouses near his father, and we can surmise this indicated a visit for treatment. Her letters, however, had by then become brief and reserved. She reported no healing successes under Quimby's care after 1864, as she had so effusively done before.

The year 1864 is largely unremarked in Eddy's biography, linked to few specifics, but looking closely at these letters shows it was a landmark year. After becoming "very ill again," no reports of improvement or hopeful comments followed. Her letters to Quimby began to taper off. She began to question him, gently challenging him. Her identity as an independent agent, which she had begun to forge through her own curative experiments under difficult life circumstances throughout adulthood, came even more to the fore. She also began to express a longing to work out in writing the "model" of her own career.[30]

In the spring of that year, Eddy met Ann Mary Jarvis from Warren, Maine, whose large family had been decimated by consumption, or tuberculosis.[31] Like most of Quimby's patients, Jarvis had come to his Portland office after hearing reports of miraculous cures. When she returned home still feeling ill with consumption, Eddy accompanied her and, in what she called her own "poor way," took the case herself.[32]

In a letter to Quimby about her experience, Eddy reported her patient had suffered from breathing problems brought on by "'easterly winds.' I sat down by her, took her hands and explained in my poor way what it was, instead of what it *was not* as she understood it. In a little, her breath became natural and to my surprise even, she raised phlegm easily and has scarcely coughed any since."[33] In her next letter she confirmed, "Miss Jarvis has got well."[34]

When Mary Baker Eddy published the first edition of her book eleven years later, in 1875, it included a matching account of Jarvis's healing, adding only that she sat "silently by her side a few moments" before "her breath came gently" and naturally. The weather vane still pointed "due east," but "her difficult breathing had gone; therefore it was not the wind that produced it, and our explanations broke this mental hallucination, and she never suffered again from east winds" (1875:337–38).[35] The account remains essentially the same in the final edition of *Science and Health*.

Eddy's letter about Jarvis's healing experience is interesting for what it shows us of her emerging practice in 1864. Rather than fixing her eyes on Jarvis, channeling the force of inner will to command her into wellness, or dipping her hands in water and rubbing Jarvis's afflicted body—all earmarks of Quimby's practice—she held Jarvis's hands apparently in affection rather than as a healing technique, then somewhat tentatively and unexcitedly explained "what it was, instead of what it *was not*."[36] Registering surprise at Jarvis's recovery, she indicated that she had little idea how it was done, a theme recurring in her letters of the period. Some divine law, wisdom, or gospel truth informed this healing, she indicated, and at the time she felt it must also inform Quimby's cures, no matter how different their approaches. Exactly what that meant remained elusive.

This letter is also interesting because of the mixture of dependence and independence it shows on Eddy's part. She "laughed" while telling Jarvis about Quimby's powers. Yet beneath the high spirits and humor that peppered her letter—"I like people of common sense, and common justice, or else I like to laugh where the joke comes in"—she was serious and searching.

She represented herself as studying to practice the "wisdom" or truth that lay, she was convinced, behind the phenomenon of healing and was the same "wisdom & love" that in 1861, a year before meeting Quimby, her poem saw the Savior forging from life's tragedies in order that all might "lean on thy Father's breast," the great heart of God.[37] In the same manner, if healing Jarvis was possible through the "Spirit," she was still trying to identify the "letter" or explanation.

Perhaps in part as a result of this healing, Eddy's confidence and independence grew in traceable amounts. In her letter from Warren a month after leaving Jarvis's home, she reported a lecture she was about to give. Her first foray into public speaking was itself a marker of increased confidence, at a time when audiences were just starting to consider women at the lectern acceptable. The content of her talk would distinguish, she said, Quimby's "spiritual science" from Deism and Spiritualism. The topic built on an emerging cultural and scientific preoccupation with identifying, separating, and classifying the threads of new phenomena. She commented to him with a sense of ownership, independence, and emerging confidence, "I have changed my lecture to suit the need of the occasion[.] This seems to me a spiritual need of the people."[38]

Eddy questioned and pushed on Quimby's work, again implying she was far from understanding it and must know more. "What is your truth if it applies only to the evil diseases that show themselves," she asked both rhetorically and searchingly, when it is our unseen "spiritual foes" that pose the greatest need? She felt the need "to be *perfect* after the command of science," a need he could not fulfill for her.

Then she posed a question to Quimby: "Would *you* have the *courage* to attend if here? *Sometimes* wisdom is known by her followers." Casting "wisdom" in the female (in contrast to his equation of it with a "Father" God), she may have hoped at least for his ever-elusive approval of her independent efforts on his behalf, though it never came. At most, she signaled a truth she was following, whether he would or not. Either way, her question carries a challenge.

Eddy's letter simultaneously reflected the homage and deference more typically found in her earlier notes to Quimby. "Who then is wise, but you," she remarked, implying his work followed the healings of Jesus. Her short letter contains five Bible quotes or references, which she uses to frame and explain her understanding of his work. She seems to have thought of Quimby as modeling the biblical "truth" to which she was still in "pupilage."[39]

Like others who spoke with him and sought his services, she could not find a single explanatory rubric within the writings he generously shared. Unlike those in his closest orbit, however, she at first assumed she could grasp and describe a biblical "truth" behind his work in her own way. Yet her experience with Jarvis only raised more questions. Her questioning reflected not only independence but uncertainty, and she remained somewhat hesitant, declining to expand her practice.

Reflecting this same hesitance, her first lecture on Quimby's work also proved to be her last. That fall she entered the lecture circuit again at Waterville College (later Colby College)—Baptist, like her husband—speaking on "The South and the North."[40] Her talk undoubtedly sought to interest war-weary Northerners in her experiences and observations as a young wife in Charleston prior to becoming widowed.

According to the newspaper writeup, she was a well-received speaker. Yet Eddy would not lecture again until 1875, a world away in both experience and explanation (her topic then in Lynn, Massachusetts, would be "Christ Healing the Sick"). In 1864, however, she remained fundamentally uncertain how to explain Quimby's work and unsure about the parameters of her own.

This hesitance coexisted with her challenges to her doctor, the tapering off of her letters to him, and the development of her independent practice and speaking engagements. Other factors underscore her autonomy. Wartime uncertainties and her family's needs were a major preoccupation during this period, and they constituted a significant realm of independent action outside Portland. While in Maine, also, Eddy and Quimby operated in a larger cultural milieu that encompassed them both. Her reform-minded leanings bubbled up and coalesced in that yeasty scene outside Quimby's office, and her few lectures show that to some degree, she followed and participated in this scene independently of her doctor.

Perhaps most significantly, when she arrived on Quimby's doorstep in 1862, Eddy was forty-one years old and had already spent years probing the Bible and experimenting with various cures in a quest for health. She was accustomed to questioning data about illness and cure, health and purpose, God's will and creation's status, on her own. Her first letter to Quimby shows that she had arrived in Maine with an agenda: not simply to be healed, but if that worked, to codify and explain how in biblical terms. Building on her previous experiences, she immediately assumed the role of his interpreter. Her jumbled explanation, she told him, "surprises people."[41]

HER EXPLANATION apparently surprised Quimby, too. She wrote to him as one would a confidant, and although he rarely replied, contemporaneous accounts characterize him as warm and humane. Whether actively or passively, he supplied space for her intellectual and spiritual wrestlings when formal collegiate circles, seminaries, and everyplace else did not. Antoinette Brown (later Blackwell) may have managed to graduate Oberlin with a theological degree in 1850, but an 1866 report found her analysis of Greek texts all the more fetching when it yielded to male authority and her own "maidenly" demeanor, as well as to mores regarding women speaking in church.[42] Eddy's circumstances would have ruled out a theological degree even had she wanted one (and there is no evidence she did). Both women, however, like others of their era, carved out a path where they could.

Yet Quimby stopped short of endorsement. He did not embrace or champion the way Eddy represented his work or perhaps fully comprehend how she pursued her own practice (neither did she). If nothing else, this demonstrates something of her independence. To Quimby, it seems, Eddy was conspicuously doing her own thing.

Quimby's papers are notoriously difficult to work with, as I have noted, but given this caveat, it is clear he looked and hoped for an heir to his practice while consciously bypassing Eddy as a candidate. In an undated letter to an anonymous patient, who was probably male and might have been his son George, he wrote, "My patients feel my influence in you and like the children of Israel they want a leader which they will find in you."[43] The letter's intimate tone and the circumstances it describes rule out Eddy as the recipient.

Part of this might have been gendered; although Quimby was socially liberal and left several notations decrying slavery, few exist on the position of women. An 1860 piece suggests their "true position" was teaching children and ministering to the sick (valuable roles, he noted, that men did not consider filling, perhaps out of pride).[44] Quimby's patients later agreed he hoped his practice would carry on under George, who demurred, and that he left no chosen heir. Eddy represented herself as explaining his work and offered to champion him, but he apparently had different plans and declined multiple opportunities to agree.

Several years after Quimby's January 1866 death, his widow, Susannah, emphasized this in a negative light. Prompted by a letter that was critical of Eddy, Susannah offered that Eddy "evidently thought when she so strongly endorsed the Dr['s] theory at her first visit to him that he would put her forward to explain *for him his doctrine*, and she never fully abandoned the idea while he lived."[45]

Susannah Quimby recalled Eddy arriving in Portland ready to explain Phineas Quimby's practice, confirming the background and agenda she brought with her. During one of her last visits, Susannah wrote, Eddy "hung around" hoping to give a lecture on his behalf, "but the Dr did not encourage it, and did not invite her to *preach* for him at all, so she did not stay long."

Gillian Gill suggests that Susannah's "nose was out of joint" because her husband had "a little too much" affection for Eddy and spent too much time with her, and that this influenced her recollections.[46] However, Keith McNeil points out that Susannah spent most of her time at home in Bangor, coming to her husband's Portland offices only rarely, and knew little of Eddy's visits there.[47] She may have formed opinions about Eddy later, for a host of reasons having little to do with events in 1864. Whatever the case, Susannah's recollections have an unusually disparaging edge.

Yet Susannah's memory that "Park" (as her late husband was known) did not see Eddy as a viable candidate to represent or speak for him was basically accurate.[48] He did not prevent her from doing these things on her own time, but neither did he mentor her in them. Former Quimby associates later recalled his attentiveness and concern for all his patients, and those who championed him in the 1880s and beyond recalled no personal strife between him and Eddy. Yet they invariably claimed a disjunction between her method and his. George Quimby underscored the point by writing of his father, "Don't confuse his method of healing with Mrs. Eddy's Christian Science, so far as her religious teachings go. . . . The religion which she teaches certainly is hers."[49]

When it comes to assessing the extent of Eddy's independence in 1864, these sources are helpful. In 1864 Eddy began to represent herself in a manner that mixed dependence on Quimby as a patient with an independent questioning, exploring, challenging quest to explain the gospel she was sure was at work behind his practice.

She seems to have seen herself in "pupilage" to a biblical truth he might or might not be following and either did not or could not fully explain. He did not disagree. This is not to say he necessarily disliked her message, as his wife later did, but he never claimed it represented his own. He did not select Eddy to represent him and did not publicly endorse her ideas. Neither did he criticize or prevent whatever it was she was doing. Neither of them seems to have fully comprehended it.

In a paraphrase of John Keats's *Endymion*, Eddy identified one thing she knew without doubt in 1864: she wanted to be writing. In high-minded tones she had reserved early in the war for battlefield descriptions of heroes and patriotic ideals, she referred to the "good, honorable, and brave career" she hoped might await her and then added, "If I could use my pen as I long to do and not sink under it," meaning not chronically tire and fall ill, "I would work after this model till it should appear a 'thing of beauty which is a joy forever.'"[50]

Keats's next lines are oddly apropos to Mary Jarvis's experience, ending with an ideal of "health, and quiet breathing." His "uncertain path" through "flowers and weed" uncannily echoed Eddy's at the time.[51]

EDDY WAS UNABLE to fulfill her desire to write after her own "model" in 1864. Continued poor health was her most major and basic concern. She had written to Quimby in April, the same month she healed Jarvis: "I long, *long*, to be strong! and then would I not be happy saying just what I wish to, and letting people read it?"[52] The complicated, multilayered process of daily dressing followed by toiling at a writing desk was out of reach.

As in so many wartime families, an unstable and intensely demanding family situation also required much of her attention. Biographers have only minimally explored Eddy's war experience, yet in many ways, it dominated her life in the early 1860s, leaving a deep imprint that appeared in her later work. As in revised considerations of Emily Dickinson and her poetry, the trope of an isolated female figure with the war as a distant backdrop recedes to show formative intimacy with wartime realities.[53]

The wartime experiences of Eddy's husband Daniel and son George were her own experiences. Her family situation seemed to fracture and reconfigure in newly broken ways at each turn, as if viewed through a sad kaleidoscope. Her collapsed domestic ideals mirrored those across the nation, as the national family experience began to pattern what it had inflicted on the enslaved, some said in wrenching accord with divine penance and justice.

Daniel and Mary did their best to set up a stable home when he returned, but their attempts were unfortunate. After Daniel's prison ordeal, Robert Peel notes, "the serious privations he had suffered seemed to have damaged his health, weakened his will, and increased his restlessness."[54] In 1864 Mary sent a brief note to Quimby mentioning help for her sick husband, who was apparently resisting her own ministrations. Continued worries over her son's location and condition added to her stress.

She sent her last letter to the doctor from Lynn, Massachusetts, in July 1865, a few months after the war's official end on 9 April. Her son had served two tours in the army and was now ill while traveling, which had deeply affected her and "well nigh separated soul and body." She had few confidantes at the time and seemed desperate to share the news, hoping in this last short letter that Quimby could "save him."[55] Glover survived, but without seeing Quimby or his mother. Nothing else about the episode is clear.

With the failure of her marriage to Daniel Patterson and the gradual unraveling of her once tightly knit family circle, Eddy entered a phase of poverty largely disconnected from the more refined country culture of her youth. She kept her manners, which read as affectations to some and dignity to others. They can be understood basically as a safety mechanism. As an 1860 etiquette book noted, "There is no situation in which a lady is more exposed than when she travels, and there is no position where a dignified, ladylike deportment is more indispensable."[56] Constantly uprooted and moving from house to house, Eddy did her best to deflect unwelcome attention through careful deportment.

The slew of poor health, wartime family demands, and the distinct problems of female poverty: even as Eddy emerged into a new experience of independence, this trifecta made sustained authorship an impossible ideal for her in 1864. They also provided a context in which she was able, even required, to embrace new experiences.

CHAPTER FIVE

Accident and Recovery

(1866)

In which Eddy has an accident, recovers, falters, regroups, and moves on, finding that earlier barriers to independent action are no longer in play

ON SATURDAY, 3 February 1866, the *Weekly Reporter* out of Lynn, Massachusetts, ran an item announcing that Eddy

> fell upon the ice near the corner of Market and Oxford streets, on Thursday evening, and was severely injured. She was taken up in an insensible condition and carried into the residence of S. M. Bubier, Esq., near by, where she was kindly cared for during the night. Dr. Cushing, who was called for, found her injuries to be internal, and of a severe nature, inducing spasms and internal suffering. She was removed to her home in Swampscott yesterday afternoon, though in a very critical condition.[1]

Little other documentation exists detailing the incident as it unfolded in real time, but what does shows that the two women who cared for her in Swampscott considered her back broken, noted paralysis, and thought she was likely close to death, with the result that a minister was called in. Dr. Cushing left homeopathic medicines along with his grim prognosis and withdrew. No visitors later recalled what became of the vials, but she continued to decline. Those present later concurred it was considered miraculous when, on Sunday afternoon three days after the accident, Eddy asked to be alone with her Bible and then got out of bed and walked across the room unassisted.[2]

At first Eddy's recovery was little understood, not least by herself. For most of 1866 she sought to come to terms with it, and that was a messy and far from clear-cut process. Phineas Quimby had died a few weeks before, and she now haltingly began to sort through the mixture of independence and dependence she brought to his legacy. A few weeks after her accident, she wrote an overwhelmed letter to his former patient Julius Dresser (who with his wife, Annetta, had been in the doctor's inner circle) seeking help to maintain her forward progress, but Dresser politely declined.[3]

She seems to have questioned what had happened, felt a victim of circumstance, and struggled with feeling a return of either recent or prior symptoms as she sorted through the mental and physical aspects of her experience. She filed a lawsuit with the city of Lynn seeking damages for the fall, which biographer Gillian Gill posits came at the urging of her husband or friends out of financial desperation, then reconsidered and withdrew the suit. Daniel was an intermittent presence in her life by then. Her father, Mark, had died in late 1865, underscoring how alone she was.

By the end of 1866, however, something radically shifted. Eddy's letters after that date abandon the theme of chronic illness, registering an unprecedented degree of health. Gill notes that religious explanations aside, photographs of Eddy after this date show her looking well-fed and contented, even confident, a qualitative difference from prior portraits. Whatever happened in 1866, her papers document an experience that essentially flipped from one of chronic illness with brief and occasional periods of wellness to the opposite, regular health with brief and occasional periods of illness.

At the same time, the war had ended, leaving the nation bedraggled, shocked, and closer to its ideals of freedom. Americans "lost their own lives as they had understood them before the war," writes Drew Gilpin Faust, changing materially, emotionally, and spiritually in ways they could not have foreseen.[4]

The war shook open new spaces for activity and leveraged an unprecedented capacity for growth; this is how Tera Hunter describes African American women after the Civil War and how Eric Foner describes Abraham Lincoln during it and is a main quality of George Frederickson's "inner Civil War."[5] Equally important for Eddy, the turmoil of her home life finally resolved in a sobering way when Daniel permanently abandoned her after his latest episode of infidelity. They would remain married well into the next decade but never again formed a close family. Poverty persisted for her, though Daniel sent a small sum for a few years.[6]

Overall, the impediments to independent action that Mary Baker Eddy had experienced were gone or greatly minimized by late 1866. Most significantly, she was well. The war was over, she had a meager sum to get by on, and her home was empty but quiet. This finally enabled her to write.

FINDINGS: PART I

FOLLOWING HER rather typical rural New Hampshire upbringing, the commonly intractable neuralgia affliction combined with Mary Baker Eddy's increasingly experimental Congregationalism as she explored cures alongside many antebellum and wartime Americans. Her middle years were occupied, fittingly for her cultural moment, with the urgent interrelationship between scripture, science, health, salvation, and the anticipated Second Coming of Jesus Christ. The mind—the seat of character, conscience, piety—was considered central to such inquiries and the linchpin of scientific, devotional, and curative activity in some definite yet not fully explained way. As the sermonizer at the Clifton Springs Water-Cure noted, "the great *new* idea of the age in the science of medicine [is] the value of the mind as a recuperative agent, always to be addressed, in every attempt at a restoration of the body from disease."[1] The Unitarian Hedge preached that Jesus was able to heal a sick woman because in some cases disease "becomes a fixed idea, a stubborn mood, a prevailing consciousness," and in such cases, "no drugs will avail." Instead, "the body . . . can be reached only through the mind," through "some great revelation, some new love, some inspired and inspiring purpose, giving thought and will a new direction," and only by "divine authority" and "agency can the demons of disease be cast out."[2] Such models urged Christ's healing presence in the modern era, advancing different interpretations of how to "present your bodies" to God and "be transformed by the renewing of your mind," as Saint Paul put it (Romans 12:1–2).

Yet none of these models could identify *how* God acted on the mind and thus the body. What "law of divinity" might be at work? How could it be explained, its phenomena repeated? What speculative or actual scientific processes or substances were involved? No one could say. Within this environment, Eddy sought not only to be cured but to find and explain the gospel truth operating on human individuality to effect the cure. She brought this agenda with her to Portland in 1862, immediately undertaking to explain her experiences under the care of the irregular curist Phineas Quimby from within the fold of her progressive, exploratory, sometimes radical Congregational world, which was then morphing, spinning, reinventing itself. In recent years, scholars have suggested that a perceived need to establish a male authority figure for Eddy and her work has resulted in overly dependent portrayals of her in the 1860s.[3] This is valid; I emphasize the substance of her independence.

Under Quimby's treatment, Eddy's health fluctuated greatly, first improving and then declining. Yet experiencing and observing his treatment provided fully convincing evidence of what earlier curative experiments had shown: that unseen factors and beliefs could affect the human mind and thus body for better or for worse. This evidence so far was phenomenal and not religious or teleological in nature.

Quimby's generous nature, however, supported Eddy's independent questioning about these phenomena, which helped her thoughts on healing to emerge in a different direction from his own, though neither of them at first could identify how or what this meant. To an extent, he presented his cures in culturally resonant terms, in which science and cure and possibly Jesus mingled in some unexplained way. She was culturally predisposed to see his work engaging controversial yet cutting-edge scientific principles, rooted in modern views of God and what it meant to follow Jesus.

Eddy championed her own views of Quimby's work for a time, deciding his practice must offer answers about the gospel truth of healing she and so many other Americans sought, and that she would explain how. He was never on board with either assumption, but neither did he object. He simply steered away. He was by all accounts kind and too busy with his daily practice to develop a comprehensive view of it.

As she began to tentatively articulate a novel expression of her own healing work in 1864, using her own distinctive methods, Eddy quietly challenged Quimby, tapered off their interactions, and began to speak more authoritatively about her views of both his work and her own. She called healing possible through the "Spirit" but still could not identify the "letter" or explanation. These new steps mingled with a significant degree of continued dependence on and deference to the doctor.

Eddy's time in Maine could be considered a capstone to her years of medical experimentation and discovery from roughly 1845 to 1865. It involved key experiences and central observations alongside key disappointments and central disagreements. Without these years, she could not have taken her next steps toward Christian Science.

No one took those for her, though. At the end of 1865, no next steps were particularly on the horizon. The war had interfered; her family was fragmented. She did not have the content to parlay into a new religion of any significance, and even if she had, she did not have the stamina such an undertaking required. She still seemed vaguely hopeful yet was overwhelmed again by sickness and other problems.

Something radically shifted by late 1866, when after a dramatic accident and recovery experience Eddy found impediments to independent action gone or greatly minimized. Her letters, photographs, and papers began to register an unprecedented degree of health. Whatever academics might attribute this to, she found herself with a newfound ability to write and with something radically new to say.

In part 2, we now turn to the production of Eddy's religious texts, which progressively embodied and made sense of her curative search and 1866 experiences through novel Bible interpretation.

PART II

Text
(1866–1880)

CHAPTER SIX

Genesis Manuscript
(1866–1869)

In which Eddy seeks to provide the Bible's revealed meaning "in science," yet her own discovery and revelation experience is rather submerged in her jumbled text, and a stark dissonance exists between how she introduced this early manuscript and what she wrote in it

BY THE END OF 1866, Eddy seemed to settle into some understanding of her recovery experience. It proved to be a galvanizing impetus to her writing. The exegesis of Genesis she produced in the three ensuing years does not discuss this event; raw and new, it sits submerged, the work's unacknowledged experiential basis. It is present, however, in the very fact of the manuscript, which represents a major uptick in health and stamina and the consequent ability to work in a sustained way. Her manuscript also thickly embodies her experience in its rationale, themes, and explanations.[1]

Originally titled "The Bible in Its Spiritual Meaning," this is our earliest evidence of Eddy's intent to write a book to explain the scriptures.[2] It is qualitatively and quantitatively different from anything she had written before. In this initial effort—rudimentary, rough, and equal parts opaque and lively—a tumble of words jostles for position to capture something new. There is a certainty and even urgency in her writing. "Despite her muddled exposition," writes Robert David Thomas, "there were some things that [she] was absolutely clear about, even in this early stage as she sought to redefine the meaning of illness in the nineteenth century and to reconstruct the meaning of the sacred in an increasingly secular, scientific world."[3]

Though her book *Science and Health* came out much differently a decade later, with most language revised or discarded and her Genesis notes eventually filling a single chapter, her central goal was essentially unchanged from this early manuscript. By 1866, her tentative, experimental days were behind her. She now sought to provide not a second or supplementary Bible but the "true meaning" of the scriptures "in science," whatever that might prove to mean.[4] To this end, both texts show a dual focus on principle and practice, discovery and experience. In both texts, she also worked to explain her experiences, though initially that effort was quite provisional.

Following the traditional manner of reading scripture, her Genesis manuscript gives a sense of deep personal engagement and identification with the biblical figures, as though her life were an extension or a mirroring of their narratives. It reads as if Eddy were seeing events in her own life echoing Jacob's or mapping the children of Israel's successive and progressive experiences onto her own.

Her vocabulary often trends exploratory and novel. Yet when she writes of a "science" being revealed to Jacob and Joseph in their moments of spiritual inspiration, we catch a glimpse of how she might have begun to understand all of the experiences leading up to events in 1866. Before that year, she had heard of and tried many cures claiming to mingle science and gospel, yet like her experience of the cures themselves, her explanatory efforts had fallen short. Now she expressed something different, with a new sense of authority.

As she wrote, she dynamically, imperfectly, and incompletely began to work out the relationship between divine source, human agency, and textual development that singularly marked her text. Words such as "explanation," "discovery," "inspiration," "revelation," and a host of other terms appear as she began defining their relationship to each other. In one passage, she tentatively switched between "revelation" and "explanation," then later went on to describe revelation and its resulting explanation of the Bible's true spiritual sense with "the ladder . . . of [Christian] Science" bridging earth and heaven. Her explanation of biblical truth, she noted, was like Jacob's ladder at Bethel, with angels "ascending and descending" between the wide open divine realm and the stony, uncomprehending ground.[5]

A few chapters later, she replaced "vision" with "revelation," only to cross that out (perhaps because it duplicates the word "reveal" used earlier in the sentence).[6] Whatever "revelation" may have meant to Eddy religiously, it did not involve blank passivity, mediumship, or trance. It required and allowed divinely sourced, humanly individualized inspiration, vision, and agency to perceive and explain God's disclosure.

Later in the text, "false" explanation or revelation is that which originates in human opinions rather than in divine inspiration. Human reason could be imbued with divine grace to grasp and explicate the inspiration God bestowed, or it could concoct its own erroneous falsehoods.

Through vigorous editing Eddy shifted back and forth between the terms "interpretation" and "explanation" several times, exploring the nuances between them. In the end, her many uses of the terms in this context were quite similar in meaning: the human discernment and statement of truth established by God through spiritual inspiration and revelation. Scriptural interpretation and explanation without these signified the human invention of falsehood (the "interpretations of belief").[7] In these passages, her biblical explanation described revelation. Without this, exegesis was "false" and obscured God's Word rather than elucidated it.

Eddy's Genesis manuscript is filled with references to revelation that reappear, deeply revised yet recognizable, in her later book in all its editions. In understanding revelation, she emphasized the importance of the "new birth," or spiritual rebirth in Christ where childlike innocence has the advantage over "errudition and pride."[8] Science is then the "gospel" explained, the "only revelation of truth and God."[9]

All spiritual inspiration involved a degree of revelation, in biblical times and now, but this new statement of Christian science embodied God's complete Self-disclosure, the likes of which had not been seen since the time of Jesus.[10] The early patriarchs perceived some "revelations of Science," but neither they nor the apostles could explain its letter comprehensively, which was now her momentous task.[11] "Inspiration is a revelation of science," Eddy wrote.[12] On whatever scale, it happened in human life according to a divinely rooted principle, plan, or pattern, rather than being randomly or materially generated. Belief in "isms," doctrines, or creeds stood in contrast to these.[13]

In her discussion of the imprisonment of Joseph with Pharaoh's butler and baker, Eddy made clear that her exegesis united "literal" and moral readings. Literalism, however, had not yet become equated with textual inerrancy, as it would in twentieth-century Fundamentalism and earlier foes of textual and higher criticism.[14]

In the 1828 Webster's dictionary, "literal" meant "according to the letter; primitive; real; not figurative or metaphorical." This "primitive" and "real" sense of scripture is key in both her early and later biblical interpretation. Together with inspiration and revelation, it marked what she would later call the "inspired Word" of the Bible. She would later call Christian Science itself the higher criticism, not academically but practically.[15] Such views do not fall neatly into the opposing inerrant and higher critical camps scholars generally use to categorize nineteenth-century Christian expressions.

In another passage, she compared Christian Science to the discovery of other scientific principles operating to better the human realm, such as the science of the steam engine discovered by Robert Fulton.[16] This analogy, though she acknowledged its limitations, would also become a constant in her later work.

The continuities between Eddy's Genesis manuscript and her later *Science and Health* are unmistakable in rationale, essence, tone, and some expressive choices. Yet like all her early documents, she eventually either discarded or fundamentally reworked much of the Genesis manuscript. In 1866 Eddy still tended to write with a relatively traditional theodicy, which would change as she worked out the implications of God's allness and sovereignty, as Robert Peel has pointed out.[17] As he and David Weddle have further noted, the immediate, unedited, urgently composed style of her early notes is singular in her oeuvre and makes them almost impenetrably difficult to work with, at least on the surface.

The unclear, submerged place of her own experience in this manuscript contributes to this. Eddy had spent years combing her Bible and trying new cures, like so many Americans, to find the gospel rationale of modern healing. Finally, she wrote, she had discovered it. She would now convey "the spiritual meaning of the Bible," her brief introduction announced. This, in turn, would describe the science of healing the sick that "controls man"—or was it the science that controlled her former doctor Phineas Quimby's work?[18]

She considered both, then decided on the latter. By any measure, her manuscript begins to advance a highly original explanation. Textually, its wording is her own. Experientially, it represents something fledgling and new. Yet in her introduction, she framed it as kindled and illustrated by Quimby's cures, a "phenomenon at first trifling" as he described them, though this could, would, or might have been the foundation of his later work. These phenomenal observations stirred her to give "the world a new version of the Scriptures," the true spiritual meaning of the Bible, the principle behind all gospel cures, which she could explain though he could not.[19]

This setup creates a stark dissonance between her brief introductory remarks and what she wrote in the jumbled body of her text. Quimby's name does not reappear, though he hovers in the background in some words from her time in Portland, alongside others garnered from her full range of experiences and their larger shared cultural context. He is also inferred in the special, interesting, as yet indistinct place he had held in her development. She seemed caught between principle and personality. Her introduction still looked backward to him as healer, doctor, physician to herself and others, provisional illustrator of her scriptural expositions, but this meant overlooking her earlier letters to him describing recurring symptoms as well as her own influential experiences since his demise. Meanwhile her own experiences, wording, interpretations, biblical exegesis, and authorial vision flood the following pages.

As with her letters to him before, with their tapering pauses, challenging assertions, and reports of recurring symptoms of illness mixed with lingering dependence and gratitude, there is a disconnect. She continued to offer the biblically based explanations of health and cure that made most sense to her, whether or not the good doctor would have agreed, while working through how to understand his experience in relationship to her own. The whole text is clearly a work in progress.

Eddy's other writings during this period show an outward-facing variety and a new emphasis on teaching. A brief exegesis of three chapters in the gospel of Matthew served as an 1867 classroom text for her first student, a Lynn shoe factory worker named Hiram Crafts.

For a while Eddy also tinkered with a short document of unclear provenance dating to her days with Quimby titled "Questions and Answers," which she provisionally retitled "Science of Man" (and was once probably called "Science of Soul"). She may or may not have penned parts of it herself while in Portland but definitely added a preface and revised some passages later. She did not teach from it, however, and wrestled basically with its Quimby-like contents during this time.

"To make matters more confusing," Keith McNeil writes, by 1870 she had "completely changed the text of the manuscript," dropped everything that had appeared in Quimby's writings, "and promulgated to her pupils a completely new text, but with the same title." She copyrighted and later revised this latter original work for publication in an 1876 pamphlet, also titled *Science of Man*, which she later parlayed into her teaching chapter "Recapitulation," starting with the third edition of *Science and Health* in 1881. Thus the *Science of Man* on which Eddy based part of her book's text was her own creation and a wholesale different document from the earliest, unpublished piece in her possession of the same name. (Understandably, early biographers in particular mixed up these manuscripts.[20]) This rapid rethinking and jettisoning of content related to Quimby, while still grappling with what his memory meant to her, was typical of the late 1860s for Eddy.

In 1870, the year she opened a joint healing practice with a student in Lynn, Eddy used yet another document, titled "The Soul's Inquiries of Man," to teach her first two classes of five and six students, respectively. A student who took a class in late 1870, Samuel Putnam Bancroft, much later recalled the sessions revolving around Eddy's exegesis of Genesis.[21]

In the early 1870s, attending to students and her growing healing partnership took significant time. She taught one class each in 1871 and 1872, charging $300 per session, though subsidizing several working-class students. In comparison, the well-to-do Isaac H. Sears family of Boston spent $49 on a "Full Set Teeth with Spring" and $54 on other medical bills during the first half of 1871, $109 in 1872 on home goods, and $40.50 on pew number ten at the Episcopal Church of Our Saviour.[22] Her students, even those later disaffected, said they found her price fair, citing teaching that continued outside the classroom, reduction in medical bills, and their ability to make a living long after.[23]

Eddy attended First Congregational Church in Lynn at least occasionally at this time and may have rented a pew with a student.[24] Her views, like others', had shifted from Trinitarian to Unitarian Congregationalism by then as New England religion trended liberal.

She continued to clarify her message and position it within broader religious culture, as in an 1872 manuscript contrasting her position with John Tyndall's materialism.[25] Tyndall, a British professor of physics and chemistry, issued his scientific challenge to the efficacy of Christian prayer in 1872 and toured Boston that year.[26] After his sensational American debut, notes Rick Ostrander, "it became almost obligatory for Americans writing on prayer in the nineteenth century" to refute Tyndall and his cohort of skeptics.[27]

A small flurry of Bibles exchanged hands as gifts among Christian Scientists in the 1870s, many including jottings that may seem inconsequential but show the unselfconscious self-concept of the earliest Christian Scientists, recorded in small notes and gestures they never expected to be publicly noted. Eddy wrote a ditty in one on Christmas 1871 to George Allen:

> Take this, 'tis a gift of love
> That seeks thy good alone,
> Keep it for the giver's sake,
> But read it for thine own.[28]

In return, in 1872 her students gifted her with an embossed King James Bible along with Cruden's Bible concordance. Calling themselves her "Students in Moral and Physical Science," they judged the book "a token of their appreciation of her valuable services to them, and as a fitting emblem of her moral worth and goodness." She wrote one notation in it: "II Cor. 12th chap.," a Bible passage that begins, "I will come to visions and revelations of the Lord."[29] By the end of her life, Eddy would keep forty-one Bibles in her library, many heavily marked.

By the late 1860s, Mary Baker Eddy represented herself as discovering, with absolute certainty, something new in the religious and scientific realms. Her Genesis manuscript confidently explored but tentatively framed it. How to acknowledge, write about, understand, compare, and contextualize her own experiences, past and present, remained major questions. Eddy's timorous womanhood at the time also still reflected a lifetime of conflicting messages regarding her presumably weak yet worthy nature and special yet secondary status. The fact that she would grow out of this was as much a miracle as anything.

The way this all changed is clear enough in the historical record. In 1872, largely unnoticed by the world outside Lynn, Massachusetts, a set of events laden with cultural resonance caused Eddy to fully claim her own experience.

CHAPTER SEVEN

Claiming Her Experience
(1872)

In which Eddy finally surfaces, claims, and explains her own religious experience, resolving many previous contradictions and uncertainties, and then begins her book manuscript

BACK IN 1869, Eddy's stepmother had gifted her with a volume titled *Scenes and Incidents in the Life of the Apostle Paul*. Eddy marked a series of passages that show her contemplating the world's reception of religious innovation. "The manner in which new views and opinions in philosophy and religion have been received in our world is one of the most remarkable things in history," wrote the author, the renowned Presbyterian theologian, abolitionist, and temperance advocate Albert Barnes. Eddy also marked subsequent passages noting that Aspasia, Socrates, Plato, and Galileo were persecuted for new ideas, while of course the incomparable "Saviour of the world was put to death on a cross." As Christianity expanded, "the pure religion of Christ has somehow encountered the opposition of men. . . . In every case of persecution, whether in science or religion, the CAUSES are to be sought in something peculiar in the views advanced, as bearing on received opinions and on the state of the world."[1]

What her religious experiences meant, how to articulate them, and how to handle the inevitable blowback all Christians knew came with delivering a message from God to the world: these were among the main questions Eddy sought to answer in 1872. Rather unexpectedly, she found an opportunity to answer all three at once that year.

First, the massive cultural conversation around mesmerism came into play regarding her work, as it did with every other new religious, medical, or scientific claim at the time. An item in the *Lynn Transcript* asked whether Eddy's work was of God or mesmeric. In a manner echoing hundreds of broadsides and articles seeking to classify new phenomena, the author argued the latter.

Like many Americans, he did not necessarily feel mesmerism to be a bad thing; his objection was that Eddy refused to identify her discovery with it. He would be thrilled to see "this science in the hands of some one better fitted to represent and develop it," notably himself, "and if *perfection* is in it, to bring this out to the public."[2] This early case of mansplaining mixed with noblesse oblige, a combination that would persist throughout Eddy's career, echoed broader public discourse.

Had she been so inclined, Eddy could have followed the suggested tack on a presumably Christian basis. Although mesmerism as stage performance had a bawdy, "promiscuous" reputation, as a provisional science it had a fluctuating reputation depending on context and audience. Among others, Rev. Edward Hitchcock of Amherst College had claimed in 1843 that Christians were duty-bound to investigate this new phenomenon in order to leverage its possibly holy benefits, and to some degree the jury was still out on this concept.

Many Christians questioned whether universal biblical laws (regularly assumed to be both) informed scientific activity and whether this included mesmerism. Yet others, including most Congregationalists, consistently lumped mesmerism with Spiritualism as erroneous works of the devil having no biblical or scientific principle behind them. The situation was, to say the least, in flux.

Eddy sealed for her then-tiny readership a basic component of Christian Science identity when she replied to the *Lynn Transcript* "that Christianity and mesmerism 'are separated by barriers' that are complete and impassable."[3] Mesmerism was not controlled by the spiritual, scientific law of God, she noted, but true Christian healing was. She also noted that she was "preparing a work" to explain this and the rest of her teachings "to the public," though her heavy workload created a "delay in publishing."[4]

In 1872, a student began using focused mental suggestion as an instrument to harm. Details are not entirely clear, but the primary sources register a fair amount of shock around the problem. Eddy described the student, Richard Kennedy, "as an *experimenter*" in harmful practice. Robert Peel calls him moved by a "fascination with evil, a 'motiveless malignity'" having an uncanny resonance with Dostoevsky's 1872 *The Possessed*. Gillian Gill focuses more on Kennedy's alleged seamy prurience, typical of broadsides against male mesmerists.[5] Perhaps the two combined in some manner. Whatever the case, in one of many dramatic episodes in her religion's early period, Eddy and Kennedy disaffiliated by year's end.

These events pushed to the surface key questions. If healing could occur through prayer entirely as a mental process, could harm as well? What distinguished this from the avidly discussed realms of mesmerism and animal magnetism? Was mesmeric practice harmful or helpful? If harmful, what constituted a safeguard against it? What implications did this have for teachings about God's allness, or theodicy?

MANY OF THESE QUESTIONS would also soon be engaged by divine healers, Protestants who rejected earthly medicines and physicians in favor of spiritual healing alone.[6] According to Heather Curtis, this involved "training the mental faculties to dismiss sensory evidence" and behaving accordingly through faith in the atoning power of Jesus on earth, as in heaven.[7]

Public divine healing practices included shouting, stomping, and falling down, thought to be inspired by the Holy Spirit. Such phenomena are notably absent from accounts of Christian Science practice. More basically, though both groups agreed that healing came through faith in the atonement, they defined this faith differently, with Christian Scientists emphasizing faith they equated with "spiritual understanding."

Yet a distinct resonance exists between these two groups. Other religious groups selectively rejected what they called "means" (that is, physical means of healing), but only Christian Scientists and divine healers did so completely on the basis of their radical theodicies. Both were criticized and dismissed as mesmerists, like other new groups. In the 1880s, critics would attribute divine healer Maria Woodworth-Etter's apparent successes to magnetism and charge the healer Charles Parham with hypnotizing his followers, just as the critics of Christian Science did from 1872 onward.[8] Both groups foundationally rejected traditional theodicy, arguing that sickness was never God's will.

However, some divine healers also selectively embraced traditional theodicy, apparently out of deference to the preexisting beliefs of many adherents. "Like Woodworth-Etter and [John Alexander] Dowie," writes Jonathan Baer, "Parham identified Satan as the ultimate source of all sickness, but he recognized a minor role for God's permissive will in allowing sickness to come to the disobedient."[9] Woodworth-Etter and Dowie both invoked what they described as a righteous curse on those who disagreed with their religious beliefs, extending the theme of human ability to spiritually invoke and direct harm toward those who "mocked" God's will.

When the possibility of exercising a religious harming tradition first arose among Christian Scientists in 1872, Eddy essentially defined it as prayer gone awry. The themes of mesmerism, harming, and theodicy were linked for her. She classed religious cursing, prayer gone awry, or intent to harm as mesmeric and entirely evil. She eventually would call this impulse "mental malpractice." She brought out that mesmerism and mental malpractice were disconnected from God's will and sharpened her theodicy to make clear it excluded the possibility of divinely willed harm. This theology then took clear shape in her book *Science and Health*.

In her Genesis manuscript a few years earlier, Eddy had focused heavily on God's goodness, sovereignty, and absolute will for healing, but she had not spelled out the implications for the ontological existence of Satan. By the time she published her book, this had changed. God's will was still purely and only good, sovereign, and omnipresent. Anything that claimed to say otherwise was a hypnotic and mesmeric suggestion using the medium of personal or corporeal sense to entice the innocent away from obeying the first commandment, as the snake had enticed Eve. In this manner, she defined "satan" (lowercase to deprive the word of ontological personality, as opposed to the one Person, God) or evil as mesmerism and illustrated it by means of the snake-talker in the first chapter of Genesis.[10]

The first edition of *Science and Health*, in 1875, would use the term "mesmerism" in a negative sense, and the third edition, in 1881, would adopt the term "animal magnetism" to describe the base, hypnotic nature of evil. Both usages stood in contrast to the mesmeric tradition, which defined animal magnetism as a vital healing fluid. "In rejecting animal magnetism" as a healing influence, writes Ann Taves, Christian Science showed "a theological attitude and strategy toward other religions similar to that of other evangelical Protestants and Seventh-Day Adventists."[11] This is unsurprising, given Eddy's religious background; she was still a Congregational church member in 1872.

In formalizing within her new theology this long-standing rejection of mesmerism, she found that the pauses, hesitancies, and lingering questions she had long held regarding Quimby came into focus. Before 1872, she had no explanation for the cycle of relapse her letters to him described, why he was personally gracious yet never fully welcomed her into his inner circle, why he declined to connect his partial writings to an overarching explanatory rubric, what his occasional references to Jesus meant.

Now she understood his healing method as mesmeric, based on the temporal human will rather than divine and enduring, and thus inherently unstable and cyclical.[12] Now it was clear to her that he had welcomed her personally but declined to endorse her work because he recognized they were not following the same approach, and he was too honest to suggest differently. Eddy represented Quimby as well-intentioned, unlike some others, occasionally including her own students. Yet his personal goodness could not cancel a basic theological difference.

Eddy had previously offered an uneven framework for Quimby's cures by magnifying his references to divine things and overlaying them with her own Protestant spirituality. His imprecisely defined beliefs in a higher power were apparently sincere, and he had been fairly open in an untheorized way about leveraging the patient's belief in the Divine to effect a cure. Now she classed this as a type of hypnotism, the newer term for mesmeric practice, or "blind faith."

He did not put forward a consistent theory, according to this view, because his practice rested on a conglomerate of insights originating in the human mind. It thus lacked an eternal Christian principle emanating from spiritual reality. She could not call his practice a response to God's will in the Christian tradition, because it sought a response entirely to and from a personal mind and will (however benign).

Though she could not now accommodate Quimby's work within her particular Christian rubrics, Eddy retained an endorsement of her own work while she knew him, as in her healing of Mary Jarvis (which would later appear in *Science and Health*). This asserts the ways in which her practice had long developed independently of his, however tentatively at first, though only now could she identify how and why that was important.

Further, the issue of physical manipulation had been something of a mystery to her before 1872. She never practiced this herself but allowed it as an apparently harmless gesture, perhaps in line with apostolic "laying on of hands." After 1872, her teaching was decisively and totally different. She now wrote with confidence that physical manipulation broke the first commandment by making the physical and electrical sense of touch a god that could heal. The fact that Quimby used physical touch routinely (apparently to leverage the patient's faith in it, not solely as a means in itself) seems only to have confirmed this conclusion for Eddy. Among multiple manuscript versions of her *Science of Man* belonging to her or her students, three out of eight pre-1872 versions make an allowance for the manipulation of patients (notably head rubbing). Each of these references is crossed out after 1872, reflecting her classroom teaching specifically disallowing the practice.[13]

Following this logic, Eddy now reasoned, Quimby's practice could not be truly classified "mental healing," because it relied on physical processes. When practiced at a distance, a theoretical ether was apparently thought to conduct his healing energies, themselves invisibly physical. As she put it three years later in the first edition of *Science and Health*, "The doctor that depends on manipulation (and he cannot employ it honestly without such dependence), works from a matter basis," whereas Christian "science is the spiritual predominating over the material; Truth [God] mastering error; the very opposite of mesmerism and the mal-practice aforesaid" (1875:378).

Taves notes that Quimby saw Jesus as a "clairvoyant," while, conversely, Eddy saw Jesus as a "demonstrator" of God's law, and that Quimby rejected special revelation "in keeping with both Spiritualism and the later New Thought tradition, while Eddy's insistence on revelation aligned Christian Science strategically" with Jonathan Edwards, John Wesley, and Seventh-Day Adventists. When the Portland doctor framed his magnetic passes as a benign manipulation of the patient's belief in magnetism or his own power to heal with it, this can be classed an early and foundational instance of psychologizing the mesmeric tradition. Thus Quimby's "healing practices were derived from the mesmeric tradition," while to Eddy, Christian Science and mesmerism were "incompatible."[14]

IT IS OBVIOUS THAT 1872 was a watershed year for Eddy and her later book on these counts. Her audience was small, and arguably few cared, but she clarified for herself and anyone listening that Christianity and mesmerism were mutually exclusive and that her Christian Science healing had always, if initially without full awareness, developed apart from mesmerism and could not be reconciled to it. Thus the significant conversation she had maintained with Quimby's work came to a close.

Perhaps in this process she felt "forced into accepting her own status as an independent thinker, along with the weight of responsibility that went with it," as Stephen Gottschalk puts it.[15] Perhaps she found this liberating. Presumably a mixture of both. She may have felt the same way when she finally came to terms with Daniel Patterson's final desertion of their marriage vows and divorced him in 1873, after twenty years of union.[16]

In 1875 she would write that Quimby "never studied [the] science" she discovered, but "he was a good man" and, though in retrospect she now understood him as a mesmerist, she felt he had been "growing out of" it (1875:373).[17] Years before, he had viewed her developing interpretations of his work with benign distance, making space for her without endorsing them.

The tables now turned, with Eddy viewing Quimby's practice in a benign way she could not now endorse. The matter was not personal but theological, and in a basic sense not essentially about her former doctor. Rather, it was about resolving how her own theology would answer pressing questions regarding laws of nature, science, Christianity, special revelation, and healing, including her recovery and discovery experience.

Christians who later developed a "sacralization of the self" through psychological modes and methods claimed a positive identity in the mesmeric tradition that, at least in this one respect, paralleled the psychological approach to cure found in New Thought. The fact that New Thought itself would grow out of a rejection of the Christian Science skepticism of the mesmeric tradition and its concomitant embrace of special revelation is a historical plot twist that often has been read as a conundrum but in fact only underscores the point.

While Eddy was sorting through all of this in 1872, her Congregational church held its fiftieth anniversary celebration in Tilton, New Hampshire.[18] She had been a member most of that time and would stay three more years. Like many, she was not an orthodox member. The works of Horace Bushnell, Darwinism, German criticism, and other major cultural shifts had opened new options for those in the pews.

Yet neither was Eddy a come-outer, meaning one who found established denominations inherently so unsatisfying they withdrew to seek a new religious path, as did Ellen Harmon White and Joseph Smith. She had gravitated away from Trinitarianism but in the early 1870s still attended Second Congregational Church (Unitarian), Lynn. She was in the process of completing her book, which she hoped her church would accept.

A printer would have to accept it first, which did not happen until late 1874. At Christmas that year, Eddy gifted a Bible to her student Miranda Rice, inscribing it to her "much esteemed friend . . . from the author of the 'Science of Life.'"[19] When she found another book with the same title, she changed hers to "Science and Health" and in September 1874 delivered her manuscript to the printer.

As before, she would still claim to give "the spiritual meaning of the Bible." Her explanation of the gospel rationale of Christian healing remained highly distinctive. Yet now her 1866 recovery experience surfaced. No longer submerged, she began the work of shifting it into place within a developing discovery narrative that would introduce and frame her distinctive take on "moral science," the "science of Soul," or Christian Science.

CHAPTER EIGHT

Science and Health
(1875)

In which Eddy presents her religion in practical,
restorationist, democratic terms as an unusual discovery
of experiential or provable Christian metaphysics
and a revelation from God to carry on Christ's
church in the modern era

AN 1875 CORRESPONDENT to *The Congregationalist*, Eddy's denominational periodical, wanted to know if matter was actual and eternal. Since the chemist Edward L. Youmans, founder of *Popular Science Monthly*, had decided material forces were the only persistent universal constant, what defensible reasons existed for a Christian to doubt "the eternity of matter" and to believe "that God is its Creator?"[1]

This is a long-standing question of "pure metaphysics," the columnist replied. The scalpel and microscope assume they see and touch matter, but they cannot prove it exists. They "reveal certain qualities" but "they do not touch the substance, if substance there be. The existence of matter cannot be demonstrated by logical reasoning. It is assumed and must be accepted by faith."

The columnist cited John Stuart Mill, Thomas Henry Huxley, John Locke, Paul Janet, Herbert Spencer, and John Fiske on these points but centrally employed scriptural reasoning. We see around us the "things that do appear," as Saint Paul put it, not the actual and eternal substance of God's creation. "The evidence of the existence of an Infinite Spirit disproves the self-existence of matter. The one truth excludes the other." Only a pantheist such as J. Allanson Picton would disagree. "We will not—because we need not—go into the proof of the existence of an Omnipotent God," concludes the author. "It is the complete and sufficient refutation of the notion that matter is eternal."

Mary Baker Eddy's completed book was then at the printer, and when it came back a few months later, some of its core metaphysics grappled with similar themes. God is "the first and only cause of all that really is," and matter could not share God's characteristics of immortality, omnipotence, and so on (1875:11–12). To believe otherwise is pantheism and breaks the first commandment by worshipping matter as an idol. Although idealistic, she immediately set herself apart from G. W. F. Hegel's synthesis (by all accounts unintentionally, and definitely without reference to the philosopher's work). "Spirit never requires matter to aid it, or through which to act" (1875:9), she wrote, in contrast to Hegel's vision of Spirit acting on and through matter.

Then there was the core radicalism in Eddy's book: the claim that she and others had proved her Christian metaphysics by healing not only sin but disease, and her readers could, too.

Observers including scholars have puzzled over how claiming Spirit's reality, to the exclusion of matter, could result in healing or even in valuing the world around us. Someone would ask Eddy a similar question in 1899. "If all matter is unreal, why do we deny the existence of disease in the material body and not the body itself?" She replied, "We deny *first* the existence of disease, because we can meet this negation more readily than we can negative [*sic*] all that the material senses affirm." Jesus, after all,

> does not require the last step to be taken first. He came to the world not to destroy the law of being, but to fulfil it in righteousness. He restored the diseased body to normal action, functions, and organization, and in explanation of his deeds he said, "Suffer it to be so now: for thus it becometh us to fulfil all righteousness." Job said, "In my flesh shall I see God." Neither the Old nor the New Testament furnishes reasons or examples for the destruction of the human body, but for its restoration to life and health as the scientific proof of "God with us." . . . The *spiritual* body, the incorporeal idea, came with the *ascension*.
>
> Jesus demonstrated the divine Principle of Christian Science when he presented his *material* body absolved from death and the grave. The introduction of pure abstractions into Christian Science, without their correlatives, leaves the divine Principle of Christian Science unexplained, tends to confuse the mind of the reader, and ultimates in what Jesus denounced, namely, straining at gnats and swallowing camels.[2]

It is also true, however, that back in 1875 Eddy referred to her theology and metaphysics as truly understandable only through experience. Healing with the "unction of primitive Christianity" allowed readers to "have part in the atonement, and to understand wherefore Jesus suffered and triumphed." Yet "those not having touched its garments and felt in their body it has healed them, will persecute it" (1875:306).

Eddy was unapologetic about the radicalism of such positions. "Some of our present readers may wish to tone down the radical points in this work, others to cast them overboard," she wrote (1875:455), yet the gospel demanded demonstration in a way the modern world would recognize, not vice versa.[3]

The eight chapters of her 1875 volume elucidate these points and more. The book opens with a discussion of natural science as it relates to metaphysics in Christendom generally compared with her "practical Christianity that casts out devils and heals the sick" (17). The next chapter discusses phenomena of "tricks or belief" (64), such as mediumship and mesmerism, that would impose on and impede the human demonstration of Christian healing. Chapter 3 covers the relationship between Spirit and matter, while chapter 4 discusses creation, including the "person of God" (221), the Trinity, the basis of individual existence, and an exegesis of Genesis.

Chapter 5, "Prayer and Atonement," covers purposes and methods of prayer and the atoning mission of Jesus. Chapter 6, "Marriage," rests on Eddy's complementary view of manhood and womanhood. She endorses legal physical union for the purpose of parenthood and opposes "free love," which declares its "sin as Sodom, and hide[s] it not" (315). Next she discusses physiology as it does and does not relate to essential identity. The final chapter, "Healing the Sick," includes several testimonies emphasizing phenomenal recovery from disease using her system of "taking up the cross and following Christ" (349). It stresses the need for morality in healers and ends with an allegory illustrating Christian Science healing.

Throughout, Eddy used innovative terms and constantly explicated scriptural passages that grounded her discussions. The subtitle "Key to the Scriptures" would not pop up in print until 1883, but she jotted it by hand on the title page of her first edition. She also copied on the inside front cover the scripture "The keys of the kingdom of heaven," connecting her book to the founding of the early Christian church.[4] This speaks to the restorationist sense in her book.

Several churches already claimed to restore early Christianity, notably the Churches of Christ, the Church of Jesus Christ of Latter-Day Saints, and some Methodists and Baptists (and, later, Pentecostals). Nathan Hatch characterizes the Churches of Christ and to some extent Mormons as part of the "democratization" of American Christianity that rejected creeds and traditions in favor of placing the Bible and therefore, as Richard T. Hughes has it, the "power in the hands of the people." Hughes notes the strong sectarianism present in the Churches of Christ, but he agrees with Hatch about the anticlerical emphasis.[5] Eddy never issued wholesale or sustained anticlerical statements in the manner of Barton Stone, Alexander Campbell, or Joseph Smith, but she eventually formed her own church and would later substitute scripture and its written interpretation for clergy.

Thus Eddy fit this overall restorationist model, but quite unlike the cessationist Churches of Christ, she claimed that healing should replace creeds and traditions. "Anciently the followers of Christ, Truth, measured their Christianity by the control it gave them over sickness, sin and death," she wrote, "whereas the more modern forms of religion leave out the first proof." Her system of religion restored it, as we "require the primitive tests of Christianity" (1875:167). Further, "man-made theories have taken the place of primitive Christianity," and this tendency needed to be reversed (330).

Further, whereas Campbell found apostolic Christianity pairing *with* "science, technology, education, and republican institutions" to bring in the millennium, Eddy found primitive or apostolic Christianity now expressed *as* a divine science, "more important morally and physically than the discovery of the powers of steam, the electric telegraph, or any other advanced idea that science has revealed," and in fact capable of guiding the development of these human sciences.[6]

Science and Health presented anew core aspects of traditional Christian theology as well. In Eddy's unorthodox Trinity, God comprised three offices in one incorporeal Person, rather than three Persons in one office, which she described as pantheistic. (Decades later, in 1901, she would lay out in detail her distinctive understanding of God as Person.)[7] She asserted Christ's divinity wholly in Sonship and overturned the doctrine of natural depravity.

Radical Christians had moved in such directions in Europe prior to the New England experiment, building on events such as the Christological debates of the fourth century C.E., and Unitarians initially carried on the tradition in America.[8] Bushnell, the Trinitarian Congregationalist, had recently picked up the Unitarian William Ellery Channing's mantle in this regard. The church of Eddy's youth saw Unitarians as grossly heterodox, but this was changing by 1875. Unorthodox Christians of all stripes were offering views on the nature of God and his Christ that had not aired recently, if at all. Eddy's were also singular and innovative.

Back in 1872, she had procured a booklet on baptism by the Quaker Joseph Phipps from a neighbor, a merchant of "table luxuries" in Lynn. She had some social connections with Quakers; one who later became a Christian Scientist would recall that Eddy asked her friends the married Quaker couple Charles and Abigail Winslow to review her newly completed book manuscript (one recommended publishing it, the other not).[9]

In the Phipps booklet she marked a passage beginning, "Those who are obedient to [Jesus's] call are his followers, whether they are water-baptized or not." The formality may make a "nominal" Christian, but "baptism of the Spirit only can make a real one."[10] In her book, she developed this radical tradition anew. Rather than the ritual of water baptism, she wrote, healing the sick was the primary means of following Christ Jesus, "keeping his precious

CONGREGATIONAL HOUSE OF WORSHIP, TILTON.

Mary Baker Eddy belonged to this Congregational church in Sanbornton Bridge, New Hampshire, for thirty-seven years and while she was a member wrote her book *Science and Health*, engaging key concerns for the survival of Christianity in modernity. She initially expected established churches to embrace her new interpretation of the Bible. Moses Thurston Runnels, *History of Sanbornton, Vol. 1* (Sanbornton, N.H.: A. Mudge and Sons, 1882), illustration inset between pages 96 and 97.

precepts" in order to "be baptized with his purity" (1875:309). She continued contemplating this topic, marking similar passages about baptism in the 1901 book *The Messages of Paul*.[11]

She took a similar approach to sacrament. In his discussion of Communion, John Calvin had been deeply concerned with the "danger of venerating matter, on the one hand," writes Ernst van den Hemel, "while avoiding a purely metaphorical interpretation of the presence of Christ, on the other."[12] This tension was familiar to Eddy as a serious concern, and she named her answer to it by locating sacramental grace in healing the sick, as well as in adherents experiencing direct "communion with Spirit," God, in prayer (1875:94).

The year Eddy published *Science and Health*, the Methodist author Edward Eggleston published *Christ in Art*, which included Alexandre Bida's engraving of Jesus sitting on a rocky outcropping, gazing at the sea. *Jesus by the Sea* became one of the most popular images of Jesus, as Bida's "plain style" tapped into interest in the historical Jesus among Bible students and scholars on both sides of the Atlantic.[13] Eddy owned several pictures of Jesus, and one of her favorites reflects her own stance on emerging debates regarding higher criticism and the historical Jesus.

Her student Julia A. Bartlett commissioned the painting as a gift to Eddy, who received it in 1885.[14] It is based on an engraving by John Sartain of Philadelphia from around 1860–70, which he in turn based on the purported sole historically authentic portrait (*imago veritas*) of Jesus, a Roman likeness and cut in emerald on the orders of Tiberius Caesar. Sartain did not produce evidence of the original emerald likeness, but the picture he created gained wide popularity nonetheless. Ellen Harmon White reportedly favored Sartain's engraving, claiming that it matched her visions of Jesus.

In regard to higher criticism, it is fitting that what Eddy called "the just picture of Jesus" carried the most advanced claims to accuracy yet was itself ultimately unverifiable. In the final consideration, she would later write, the "spiritual noumenon and phenomenon" of Jesus "silenced portraiture."[15]

Similarly, she followed biblical scholarship with interest, but if the Bible's events could not be historically proven, what of it? They could be accepted on faith but only truly explained by inspired understanding, revelation, and Christian demonstration. As she later told a Unitarian clergyman fixated on historical proof-checking, if scholarly corroboration of Christ's life were not forthcoming, that made little difference to her; revelation trumped it anyway.[16] Scholarship had a respected and sometimes quite useful place. Yet academics could not verify spiritual experience.

This approach subscribed to neither extreme in the higher critical debates, though it responded to elements within both. Eddy registered concern over literalism that eschewed spiritual inspiration, but she found real facts as well as moral worth in the Bible. Referring to her well-used *Smith's Bible Dictionary*, she found spiritual meaning to be partly "literal" (real, primitive, not metaphorical) and partly "moral" while also abounding with "metaphor" (1875:45).

Her work embraces scriptural metaphor and typology but remains grounded in what she considered to be the lived fact of Christ Jesus's virgin birth, fleshly incarnation, death, and resurrection. Her interpretation of these events was decidedly unorthodox, but her acceptance of them was not. The flesh may amount to the "things that do appear," not the actual and eternal substance

The creator of this popular engraving of Jesus claimed it was historically accurate, but that proved unverifiable. Mary Baker Eddy favored this picture and owned a copy of it, like many Americans of her time, but wrote that the spirituality of Jesus was verified by revelation, not scholarship or portraiture. This perspective mirrored her approach to higher criticism. John Sartain, *Our Saviour from the Only Authentic Likeness of Our Saviour Cut on an Emerald by Command of Tiberius Caesar*, Library of Congress Prints and Photographs Division, LC-DIG-pga-08227, http://loc.gov/pictures/resource/pga.08227/.

of God's creation. Yet mortals depended on Jesus for salvation from all that was temporally apparent.

Overall, *Science and Health* tends to describe the scriptures as a record of spiritual ideals, actual events, real facts, revelation, and moral teachings (sometimes all at once). For example, it counts the Bible's first chapter on creation as a record of revelation, the story of Adam and Eve as an allegory with a moral, and Jesus's virgin birth and resurrection as historical facts pointing to eternal spiritual truths. From the three Hebrew boys surviving the fiery furnace of a tyrant king to the healings of Jesus, she treated biblical miracles as divinely natural and real events.

Nineteenth-century secularization was accompanied by a contrasting and vigorously renewed interest in "miracles"—so vigorous that, according to Robert Bruce Mullin, by the twentieth century the question of the miraculous would vie with or even replace the Catholic-Protestant axis on which Protestant identity and theology turned.[17] This gradual breakdown of the Reformers' cessationist argument provided broad space for new views and practices of the miraculous to interact. John Tyndall's prayer-gauge test, Charles Darwin's challenge, and the influx of Catholic immigrants and their views of intercessory prayer all caused efficacy and miracles to be much on Protestants' minds.

Thus regular columns in *The Congregationalist* discussed the "Efficacy of Prayer," where in 1870 a Sunday school teacher detailed his crisis of faith over miracles. As a schoolteacher, he taught students "scientific principles" and "the immutability of the laws of the universe," only to be asked on Sunday "to teach these same young men . . . that these laws are not immutable, but that God is constantly working miracles." The tension led him to the verge of resigning.[18]

Reverend Jones of Natick, however, saw no conflict. God creates immutable laws *and* works miracles, he responded, and "in fact, all miracles are wrought according to those laws; and if they occurred in sufficient numbers, there might be constructed a science of miracles, just as well as a science of botany, or of engineering." God is both the creator and maintainer of the universe, and who is to say that he cannot enact and fulfill the laws he has created in new ways at new times? The author's ultimate rationale ended on a different track than Eddy's, but his speculative "science of miracles" mirrors what Eddy claimed to have proved real.

Such views sought to reconcile science and the Divine, or more precisely to rearticulate their recently challenged unity. Theories in the natural sciences, especially organic evolution, implicitly separated threads of science, medicine, and religion that long had been presumed merged.

One main response among American Protestant intellectuals, writes Jon Roberts, was to articulate a new basis for reconciling these threads. The other was to declare reconciliation impossible, a stance that led to deeply literal readings of scripture and, later, Fundamentalism. A tapestry of less publicized viewpoints not represented in highbrow intellectual circles also existed, such as those that were "more immanentist" and revelatory in nature.[19]

Eddy's views might be considered in this latter category. Her views, says Kimberly A. Hamlin, add a different voice to the tableaux of women who rethought biblical teachings in light of evolutionary theory.[20] "Mr. Darwin is right with regard to mortal man or matter," Eddy wrote, "but should have made a distinction between these and the immortal, whose basis is Spirit" (1875:265). She did not describe two creations, one mortal and the other immortal, but two *views* of the one real, spiritual, immortal creation. The temporal, material view represented by Darwin was one of the "varied hypotheses of man," by which "we think as a child," Eddy wrote in an echo of the Pauline phrase. However, "putting away childish things and asking more earnestly after God," we find the spiritual view, which Darwin's theories could not grasp (1875:272).

Darwin's evolutionary theory, Louis Agassiz and his theory of embryology, geologists and philosophers, and the second chapter in Genesis all might make perfect sense to those seeking a material explanation of a mortal universe. Yet the mortal record described only the "things that do appear" to material sense, not eternal reality. It could not flow from the same source as the immortal view, as this would be "contrary to revelation" (1875:384).

On the whole, nineteenth-century religionists did not simply take the mantle of natural science with its emergent dominance as a way of legitimizing their views. This would be a simplistic analysis, as their goal was more to preserve the dominance of theology through science, a dominance that in midcentury had not yet faded much. In Eddy's case, it was far more than that still, as she sought to describe an immortal view of reality that could be experienced by human beings through her Christian Science.

SCIENCE AND HEALTH EMERGED into an era in which people sought to tell what was scientific phenomena, what was religious, and what held the deepest authority in the world where they now lived. As methods of scientific inquiry made inroads into institutions of learning after 1820 and the intellectual underpinnings of Scottish Realism and its faith-imbued reasoning had begun to crack, this hastened the shift of authority from theology and ethics to biology and the natural sciences.[21] Spurred on by Darwinism, the year 1875 marked a turning point in this "transfer of cultural authority and prestige from theology to science."[22] The pervasiveness of this shift registers in Victorian book titles, which in 1874 carried the word "science" more often than any other year of the century.[23]

At the same time, in America as in Britain, the term "science" underwent a shift in meaning. At the start of the century, it meant "systematized knowledge" in a general sense; by 1900, it applied predominantly to the natural sciences. When not using the word "science" in a new way coined by herself, Eddy often used the word in its earlier, more general sense.

This made for some unexpected connections. As the historian Kathi Kern asks, "Who would expect to find Charles Hodge, the orthodox Presbyterian theologian from Princeton, in theoretical agreement with Mary Baker Eddy in the belief that 'science' should not be limited to the 'external world'?"[24] From another angle, this assertion could be considered a hallmark of the more general view.

HUNDREDS OF USES of the term "Christian Science" prior to 1875 illustrate this sea change in the meaning, relative authority, and interrelationship of these two words and provide historical context for Eddy's eventual use of the phrase. By midcentury and just after, the words were loosely connected not to denote a specific movement or teaching but as a culturally common synonym for the ubiquitous "moral science." Sometimes "mental science" was tossed into the mix as well.

Representative titles circulated, such as *The Elements of Christian Science* (1851), "Three Graces of Christian Science" (1854), and "An Oration Delivered on the Public Square at New Haven" on the topic of "Christian Science" (1851).[25] In the transatlantic realm, after 1875 the Dutch Reformed theologian (and later prime minister of the Netherlands) Abraham Kuyper postulated a "Christian science" in contrast to a "non-Christian science." In 1872 the Oxford divine John Richard Turner Eaton offered an eight-lecture apologia on the endurance of revealed Christianity that included speculation on "the realm of Christian thought perhaps yet unexplored, and, certainly, not yet taken into possession," whereby "side by side with physical studies and philosophical deductions, Christian Science may still climb the starry heights of Thought and Being, and draw ever nearer the eternal springs of Intuitive Truth."[26]

A common thread in such pieces is how to ascertain, judge, and reconcile phenomenal versus revelatory truth. This was one topic taught in schools across the United States between 1850 and 1870 by the likes of Rev. J. D. McCullough, rector and instructor in Christian Science and belles lettres in South Carolina, or Rev. George Benton, rector and instructor in mental and Christian Science, modern languages, and history in that state, or the proprietors of a young ladies' institute in West Virginia who offered "Mathematics, History, Belles-Lettres, Natural History, Physical Science, Christian Science, Ancient and Modern Languages, and Fine Arts."[27]

Moral science treated questions related to character, conscience, and conduct; revelation, devotion, the duty of piety; reciprocity and benevolence; and, in the antebellum North, the "violation of personal liberty" wrought by enslavement.[28] Authors sometimes distinguished between *moral science* as an ethical inquiry and *mental science* as a cognitive inquiry, though just as often the two were interchangeable.

These studies inevitably treated such questions as the relation between mind and matter, sensation and perception. "The connexion between Matter and Mind is unknown" and "external objects are known only relatively," wrote a typical early author, suggesting that our assumption of material causation "takes for granted the existence of an external world" containing objects to act on organs of sense.[29]

Moral science thus sometimes leaned metaphysical and cognitive, sometimes ethical and theological. The latter was the case when the Christian Moral Science Association convened in June 1871 with the goal of "creating and applying a science of Christian morals" and other gospel-based ends through a unified Church of Christ.[30] Rev. Dr. Cather of London toured the United States in 1870 and 1871 to promote the association. With the exception of a few spicy speculations based on personal intrigue, dozens of newspapers reported on the tour with illustrious approval from St. Louis to Baltimore, Little Rock to Philadelphia.[31]

"Christian," "moral," and "mental science" underwent major changes in meaning throughout the nineteenth century, like "science" itself. By 1900, studies of ethics and cognition merged into the field of psychology as one of the new social sciences, with metaphysics as either a separate philosophical discipline or a subset of the newly isolated field of theology, while earlier natural philosophy evolved into biology and chemistry.[32]

Midcentury, however, saw considerable flux and a loose equivalence or overlap among these terms, as well as the related "Science of Soul." From the 1840s through the 1860s, when Mary Baker Eddy was clipping articles from newspapers and searching for the divine law behind physical cures, the term "Christian Science" or "Christian science" was an occasional and loosely employed synonym of the ubiquitous "moral science." This usage gradually declined as Christianity lost its footing as cultural arbiter of societal mores and morals. It appeared just over 100 times in one representative sample of American newspapers between 1841 and 1870 and slipped from a peak of 79 in 1851 to 22 in 1870. Only 2 instances were found in 1875. During the same time, the term "moral science" was everywhere, appearing over 10,000 times between 1830 and 1875, not to mention showing up constantly in school syllabuses and textbooks.

This provides context for why in her first public statement about her developing book, in 1872, Eddy defined it as a work of "moral science," the phrase her earliest students also used in describing her teachings.[33] Yet her 1875 book uses the phrase only once, and she dropped it entirely by 1890. The term "mental science" follows a similar trajectory, appearing increasingly after 1875 until she dropped it from her book by 1890 (though she continued to use the term "mental healing"). "Metaphysical science" appears ten times in the 1875 edition, but only once by 1910. The considerable evolution of that term, too, must have played a part. She referred to the "Science of Soul" multiple times in her first edition, two in her last.

These latter terms were well known and had already been claimed for specific projects with which they remained thoroughly associated. None of them quite fit Eddy's work. Though she emphasized the ethics and morality of healers, her work did not describe a "moral science" in the popular sense of the term nor its "mental science" subset. It involved some of the same questions about self, identity, mind, matter, sensation, perception, conduct, morality, and Christianity but unusually invoked and radically resolved, not only as a system of ethics but in terms of an eternal law of God she had discovered through his Self-disclosure.

In the end, the term "Christian Science" fit best. This loose synonym for "moral science" had declined in popularity from its notable but never fulsome heyday in the 1850s, and by 1875 it was not attached to any single movement. Eddy decisively fixed the two words together for the first time as a proper noun with a specific definition, essentially introducing a new term with a narrowly specific meaning. Her 1875 edition uses it five times, and in 1878 she designated students of her religion "Christian Scientists." Her book would include dozens of instances of the phrase "Christian Science" in 1886, hundreds by 1910.

Similarly, in 1882, usage of the phrase was rare enough in popular culture that when the *Boston Globe* reported on the "miracles" of Christian Scientists, it deemed their religion's name "new and strange" for most readers.[34] Following the arc of the new sect's popularity, mentions of the term exploded into the thousands between 1887 and 1888 and reached 14,500 by 1900. Additionally, phrases such as "Science of Life" and "Science of Health" had some circulation prior to 1875, but "Science and Health" was a unique title Eddy copyrighted, and specific mentions of it grew exponentially in media outlets by 1910.[35]

Thus the year 1875 marked another cultural shift in which the meaning of the term "Christian Science" changed. Prior to that year, it was a general phrase used as a declining and loosely connected synonym for moral science. After 1875, it became a specific and fixed proper noun referring to Eddy's system of applied Christian metaphysics producing testimonial records of healing the sick. It would remain that way in the long run, though its specificity would undergo new challenges in the 1880s.

BY THE TIME EDDY was done revising her book, it would contain some 680 Bible quotes and references. Including testimonials, it would top out at 700 pages. The book's chapter order, titles, and syntax would change in coming years, but later readers would easily recognize its content. The first edition contained a few terms she would eventually drop, too.

The term "Wisdom" for God was a traditional divine descriptor Eddy had invoked, uncapitalized, in her 1860 evangelical poem "The Heart's Unrest." The Portland ex-Quaker Jeremiah Hacker capitalized "Wisdom and Love" for the Divine in 1863, just as Phineas Quimby used the term "Wisdom." Churchmen well before all three had done the same, both capitalized and not.

It is the favorite term for God in an 1828 Bible history, appearing at least fifty times, capitalized to distinguish between the divine synonym and the human attribute stemming from it (the "wisdom" of Moses was effective only when supported "by the Wisdom which sees all things").[36] After her time in Portland, Eddy described God as "Wisdom" more before gradually dropping the word altogether by 1903, in a minor edition. She kept the term, uncapitalized, as one of God's biblical attributes (the "wisdom and knowledge of God" is deep, wrote Paul to the Romans).[37]

The same 1828 Bible history amply uses the term "error" as the opposite of said Wisdom, based on biblical usages ("Who can understand his errors? cleanse thou me from secret faults," wrote the psalmist).[38] Congregational sermons of the era are thick with this use of "error." Eddy used this amply as well. Some groupings of "error, sin, and disease" appear in newspapers between 1850 and 1875, peaking around 1860.[39] Quimby had used "error" in a similar manner at the time, which must have resonated with his largely Christian New England clientele, including Eddy. Congregational periodicals in the 1870s roughly echoed Saint John by occasionally using the phrase "Divine Love" for God, a term Eddy later popularized anew.[40]

In employing such terminology, Eddy gave culturally resonant phrases new meaning, capitalization, and endurance in her singular theological context. Some phrases circulated in places she could not have seen during her experimental and early writing years.[41] All reflect a shared religious sensibility or verbal culture. After 1875, Eddy's book began the reverse process of gradually introducing new or newly employed religious terms into the larger culture, where her book would have significant impact by the 1880s.

Around 1875, however, her work was still little known. While proofreading and copyrighting *Science and Health*, Eddy taught a few students, lectured on Christ healing the sick, and, though they would not form their own church until 1879, agreed when a small group asked her to lead Sunday services. To this end, she obtained a letter of dismissal from the Tilton Congregational Church after thirty-seven years of membership. It was a mutually warm parting. Yet people might struggle over her interpretations of the Bible and accept them "later than the others," in her confident if less than popular 1875 estimation, because those interpretations "are more spiritual" (1875:266).

She still hoped to meet a positive reception, if not immediate acceptance, among some churches. In some ways, based on the evidence in this chapter, it is easy to see why. Eddy observed and engaged a broad cultural rethinking of theological questions about the nature of healing miracles, natural science, and metaphysics and, if the inquirer after Youmans is any gauge, how the fact of an omnipotent God impacts the appearances of matter.

Oxford University, she noted in her book, had asked for essays "'on Natural Science, to refute the materialism of the present age, or the tendency to attribute physical effects to physical causes, rather than to a final spiritual cause,'" and "this demand for metaphysics coming from the very fount of erudition meets the wants of the age, and is the one question towering above all others" (1875:9).

As an added bonus, it was easier than ever before to get her ideas out to the public. The rapidly expanding book trade was in the midst of its "industrial" era, which saw it grow and cohere on an unprecedented national level, as was the case in everything from travel to currency to institutions.[42] This new coherence in book production and distribution was so pronounced that one historian, Trish Loughran, has argued that in its nascent antebellum stages, it was a causative prelude to secession and the Civil War.[43] Bookmakers and readers alike saw technological progress in the book industry as a means for virtue to flourish through dissemination of information.

Major shifts resulted in glut and competition for the American Book Trade Association in 1876, however, and Eddy had her own contractual, printing, and financial difficulties.[44] Further, her new terms for God, unusual capitalizations, run-on style, and unpolished grammar were perhaps fit for the revelation she claimed and its modest initial audience, but not for the erudite class producing book reviews. Not a few readers felt these stylistic elements betrayed the female weaknesses that must have occasioned them.

Some were more sanguine. Bronson Alcott noted in his journal in early 1876 that he had written to Eddy "thanking her for her remarkable volume entitled *Science and Health*, which I have read with profound interest. She purposes curing bodily disease by metaphysical methods, and teaches the soul's power over the body, its spirituality and immortality. Her book is an earnest and thoughtful appeal to the faith and reason of Christians, and will serve the ends of human culture by its appeals." As Robert Peel carefully details, Alcott later met Eddy to compare "views on the transcendent themes" in her work, which yielded sympathetic yet limited results tempered by their lack of alignment on key matters.[45]

Reading her book convinced Alcott, however, that she "appears to have attained her revelations through deep physical experiences, and writes as a seeress of divine things. The popular Spiritualism finds no favor from her divining spirit. I cannot vouch for the details of her teachings, but am sure of her having truths to impart deserving the attention of every well-wisher of his race."[46]

Eddy also inscribed a copy of her book to John Greenleaf Whittier, a lifelong Quaker she had met in 1868, when they both lived in Amesbury, Massachusetts. In 1872, she wrote to a friend that he had commented favorably on a manuscript she sent him, though no other documentation has survived.[47] Apart from the world of letters, Asa Gilbert Eddy (known as Gilbert) became her husband in a ceremony conducted by a Unitarian minister on January 1, 1877. This midlife marriage was finally a happy one.

In an early advertisement for *Science and Health*, Eddy's publishing agent used a tone paralleling other popular ads of the time ("The Wonder of the Age!"). The ad highlighted the testimony of one Clara E. Ladd, a Congregational church member. Her fellow members and pastor, John C. Paine, signed as witnesses. After six years of illness, she had become unable to talk, walk, or lie down. After about six weeks and ten visits from a student of the author of *Science and Health*, she found herself able to "walk, ride, talk as well as I ever could, lie down and sleep well at night," and so on. As Ann Taves has noted, the communities of religious founders cooperated with authors to receive and produce texts they considered revealed.

Centrally, the ad highlighted core claims Eddy made for her book: that it was not theoretical but provable; that she had written it in obedience to scripture ("Go, write it before them in a table, and note it in a book"); that it explained the Bible "with reason and revelation"; that it allowed practitioners financial autonomy; that doctors of physics needed it to teach metaphysics, Christians to explain how their religion heals disease, and sinners to find hope and salvation; and that it "restores primitive privilege for theology to embrace pathology, and gives the power into the hands of the people."

Practicality, Christianity, restorationism, democracy, and self-sufficiency were all selling points.[48] Few read Eddy's book in the late 1870s, and fewer still accepted its premises, but this mirrors how readers, casual observers, and critics alike tended to describe it. At the same time, critics showcased the fact that Eddy's hope for universal acceptance of her new Christian Science book would not be forthcoming.

Looking beyond her book's unconventional style and major printing problems, some critics also proved able sparring partners whose complaints factored into how Eddy shaped subsequent editions of her book, highlighting further dimensions of Christian Science identity. That part of the story comes next.

CHAPTER NINE

Readership, Rhetoric, and Transmillennial Religion

(1878)

In which the reach of a massively expanding print culture
abounds, and Protestant culture replaces its resignation
to linguistic imprecision thought to be dictated by God at
Babel with confidence in scientifically precise language; Eddy
participates in both while responding to clerical critics, even
while her confidence in her work rests most basically
on the transmillennial view that her book aided
the present and coming kingdom of Christ

FOR THE AMUSEMENT of readers, a news piece titled "Printer's Mistakes" announced in 1864 that an English general "and thirty-seven of his men had been lost in a bottle (battle)." On the crime beat, a man had "stolen a small ox (box) from a lady's work-bag," which he put "in his waistcoat pocket."[1] And so on. Many pieces commented on the problem of typos for years before and just after the appearance of Eddy's book.

In 1876, an in-house periodical to the printing trade sought to interrupt the hilarity by asking who was responsible for such mistakes—"Reporters or Printers?"[2] Editorial errors abounded, it noted (Princess Louise went to Wimbledon "to witness the shooting of her husband"; the Prince of Wales had a son who was "an amiable boy like his mother"). Printers defended their demanding and important work and took pride in the status it gave them as arbiters and conveyors of information. A widely circulated 1876 poem, "Song of the Printer," asks rhetorically, with swagger, who "can rival the printer's power? . . . God only knows / When his might shall cease to tower."[3]

The introduction of linotype or automated printing in 1884 led to increased accuracy in print and punctured the debate between typesetters and reporters, but the era before it was one of rapid expansion in publishing without the benefit of advances in typesetting technology. Readers in this midcentury transatlantic book culture were sympathetic to the difficulties of typesetting by hand, and they responded with a combination of amusement and frustration.

Yet as an 1857 snippet from the *New Hampshire Journal of Education* noted, few readers understood that limitations in printing technology meant the greatest care in proofing could not prevent "errors and blunders." A publisher in Glasgow, it reported, hired six proofreaders and offered a cash incentive to university students who could spot errors on the publicly posted galleys of a book the publisher hoped would be "a perfect specimen of typographical accuracy." Despite this effort, "several errors were discovered, one of which was in the *first line of the first page!*"[4]

Eddy initially had related problems with her book. "All that could be understood of our first and second editions was barely rescued from the abuses of their printers," she wrote in her third edition (1881:196).[5] In 1875, W. F. Brown printed the first edition with a mistake every four pages, on average.[6] For the second in 1878 she switched to Rand, Avery & Co., a larger and more established Boston printer, but the number of mistakes increased exponentially.

Some chapters had to be scrapped; in those that remained, the misprint count quadrupled.[7] "*Correct this*," she emphasized next to a misprint reading "the world" instead of "the word" of God, hardly a small nuance in a religious text (1878:165).[8] About half the page headings carried an incorrect book title; the first chapter title was wrong.[9] Eddy crossed out some with energetic strokes and made several edits, but they look like a drop in the nearby Atlantic, and she eventually quit. Ironically, typos appear even on the woefully incomplete errata sheet included with the book, bringing new meaning to the term "error" in her writing.

Brown was a relatively low-volume printer but not usually sloppy. He printed a book of poems nearly error-free in 1876, and Eddy's book contained more than seven times the number of errors that appeared in a catalog he produced in 1883.[10] Similarly, Rand, Avery was well-respected and its output usually far better. In both cases, the proofreading process for *Science and Health* appears to have broken down so that the author either had limited access to copy or made changes that never appeared in the final text. For her third edition in 1881, Eddy finally moved operations to John Wilson and Sons of University Press, Cambridge, who corrected her book's typesetting and became her long-term printer.

Eddy's verdict, however, was in before then. "Badly as it was printed and bound," she wrote of her first edition, her "book has so far proved a complete success."[11] She was not unusual among midcentury American readers in separating form from content in evaluating her book's effectiveness.

Rather than typesetting perfection, she based her assessment on testimonials from readers professing inspiration, cure, and Christian regeneration. What could be salvaged from the printer for her second edition came out with a stamp of Noah's ark on the cover. From a printing perspective, it barely stayed afloat. Religiously, though, she remained convinced it would "go forth like Noah's dove over the troubled waves" of the world "to find, if possible, a foothold on earth."[12]

THERE WERE ALSO, HOWEVER, her book's developing religious statements to consider. "Pardon its defects," she had written to Bronson Alcott; "'tis a work difficult to write to this age."[13] A week later she elaborated in an article, "When writing this book we found the utter vastness of Metaphysical science overwhelmed thought and discouraged expression."[14] The temporal and worldly nature of language, she asserted, tended to operate as a barrier to articulating spiritual and eternal considerations. She continually sought to close the gap between idea and expression.

Until 1875, Americans mostly found that gap to be natural, insurmountable, and God-created. The revivalist *Christian Palladium* expressed a combination of frustration and submissive wonder in the article "Incapacity of Language for the Expression of Feeling," asking in the antebellum piece, "Why! oh why! was the eloquence of the soul given without an equal gift of speech!"[15]

An 1862 literary magazine declared of words, "How inadequate are they to express what is worthiest of expression. The best things in us can never be spoken or written."[16] "Words Are Inadequate," agreed an 1871 poem in another circular. It spoke for every "rapt beholder" overcome by the "splendor" of a sunrise, the genius of "noble" friendship, and other inexpressively meaningful earthly displays of the right and true.[17]

An 1875 meditation on language and its expression in a periodical devoted to phonographic writing, an early type of shorthand, noted that after the diversification and dispersion of language at Babel, "language has been artificial." As a result, it now needed constant improvement to reach its *"highest art,"* an elusive goal.[18]

The reference to the Tower of Babel had precedent. This was a major theme in Sabbath school sheets, children's magazines, and periodicals of arts and literature in the 1840s and 1850s, around the time the ruins of the tower were thought to have been discovered.[19] Readers usually took literally the Babel story that God confounded the prideful nations by disrupting unified and seamless language. To the degree this view predominated in American culture, the use of language as a tool for perfect expression was suspect as arrogant and unbiblical.

By 1875, however, this trend had begun to reverse, as the phonographic writing reference above shows. Faith in scientific efficiency was extending to the field of linguistics just as the expanding print industry changed views about the possibilities and power of printed language. Peter Mark Roget's *Thesaurus of English Words and Phrases*, first published in 1852, was both cause and indicator of this trend. Its novelty may be hard to grasp today, but it marked a profoundly new focus on precision in language use.

A flood of advertisements and reviews emphasized the book's unprecedented usefulness throughout the second half of the century. When "we wish to convey a certain thought, and our treacherous brain refuses the right word," one announced in 1872, "a book like this will then be invaluable."[20] The thesaurus quickly became a staple for writers, including Eddy.

Eddy portrayed her early book as defective in expression yet true in concept, a work of great import still in progress. As Horace Bushnell argued, mediating understanding of one's self and of God by pressing it through the discursive sieve of language could never be as authentic as "immediate" experience. Yet his theory of divine communication held that "in language itself we have a revelation of God," and thus "at the root of language there are types or forms which God implanted in nature to represent and express thought."[21] This was not quite Eddy's view, but to both theologians, the inherent limitations of language could be mitigated by divine inspiration.

BRONSON ALCOTT thought so, too. After receiving *Science and Health* in 1876, "defects" and all (as she had written to him), he wrote to Eddy that her "work has the seal of inspiration" and added, "And joy is heightened the more when I find the blessed words are of woman's divinings."[22] The same year, George McLaren of Boston wrote to "my dear sister Mary of Lynn, Author of a *Wonderful Book*," with its "strange statements . . . down comes the metaphysical sword, cutting & slashing[.] Who is to be your Armour bearer in this battle of Life?"[23]

The two men were definitely in the minority. Others saw no redeeming qualities in her "strange" prose. Clerics would later both lambaste and champion her work, but in 1876, the few who publicly paused to take note of it fell into the former category. Eddy's critics did not doubt she healed people. Instead they mixed concerns about gender, "learning" or class, salvation and heresy. Often, they expressed these concerns by dismissing her work as female blab.

One critic, H. S. C., contested Eddy's right to authorship by classing her work a type that "babbles philosophy," like "men with the merest smattering of picked up learning." Today, he lamented, "even spinsters and young girls" venture into realms "where Spinoza would not have dared to set his foot," and if Eddy knew what was best, she would not either. He counseled the "gentle authoress" to quit attempting explanations that "have sent many a philosopher to bed with the head ache." Her unorthodoxy may have been an initial draw, but he found it wholly unlike his favored author, Emanuel Swedenborg, to whom he recommended readers instead.[24]

H. S. C. would rather she continue "healing the sick," he added, "and leave the writing of books upon philosophy and religion to others." He did not doubt her prayers were efficacious, but he felt she had no natural right or ability to explain how and why in a book, the province of learned men. "We had a good deal rather have her cures than her reasons for them," he wrote. Her metaphysics were lacking, he felt, and skewed faith like all manner of "modern" trends. He finally admitted he had not given Eddy's book "that careful reading necessary" to fully understand it but still felt it was heretical "rubbish." At base, his gendered snipes covered a central concern about the preservation of tradition.

The Reverend Mr. Silver was more gentlemanly and civil than others and not outwardly concerned with Eddy's gender. He had "feelings of delicacy" on offering his critique; he was aware of "the apparent sincerity and earnestness, and decisiveness of character of the authoress" and hoped his friends knew "enough of my heart to believe that I have none but kind feelings towards [her], and would do anything in my power for her good."[25]

Yet he felt Eddy's "entire 'Science of Soul' of God of human nature and of man's destiny is the most egregious fallacy I have ever seen offered for human acceptance." He feared for gospel believers throughout his long critique. "Nothing but the love I bear for you and to your salvation," he told his readers, "could have induced me to waste so much time over a book fraught with falsities painful to behold." Her book contained some "true remarks," he noted, especially "in the chapter on Marriage," which espouses increased egalitarianism, mutuality, and affection between husband and wife within legal wedlock. Overall, though, he felt the book gravely misled the faithful.

Eddy's second edition addressed concerns like this through her readers. She published in it the letter of a Colonel Letts, who wrote that *Science and Health* had saved him from becoming a "confirmed infidel," allowed him to "understand the beauties of the Gospel of our Master,'" and "restored my health'" (1878:155).[26] Whether this would have convinced Silver is another question. He gave no response to the second edition (tragically he did not live to see the third, drowning in the Charles River early in 1881 at age eighty-four).

Eddy rarely responded to her critics in gendered terms, preferring instead to focus on the substance of their theological concerns. On the few occasions that she did invoke gender, it is incidental to her overall reply. Responding in the *New York Sun* to an unnamed critic of her first edition, she suggested both he and his editors "wait until your beards are grown before you growl, and bark only where you can bite." Her barb casts their remarks as adolescent, unmanly, and effete compared with her womanly strength and maturity. Yet she centered her reply on a challenge to accept her work based on a growing body of healing evidence produced by practitioners of her new and disruptive Christian metaphysics: "The future alone can justify so daring an attempt and explain its merit by proof."[27]

George McLaren, Eddy's proposed "Armour bearer," also invoked the relationship between prayer and proof that was such a major issue for Americans in the 1870s. "You have thrown down the gauntlet to Prof. Tyndall," he wrote, "and you have called the world to battle on this issue."[28] Though Eddy did not engage John Tyndall by name in her writings after her 1872 draft opposing his ideas, her book engaged the issues of prayer, proof, and what constituted "science" in a manner readers could understand as a challenge to his work.

These issues were central to the new chapter "Reply to a Clergyman" in her second edition. Traces of her replies to H. S. C. and the anonymous *Sun* critic can be found in the chapter, but she focused mainly on the concerns of Silver (perhaps a nod to his relative civility). By comparing Eddy's chapter with Silver's manuscript, it is possible to trace her responses back to his particular critiques.

Their exchange revolved largely around the "knowledge of Metaphysics that deal[s] with cause and effects, and the essence and attributes of Deity."[29] Did God heal in the manner Eddy proposed? Who had adequate proof for their position? Which of them was pantheistic? Who had the proper understanding of atonement, theodicy, and creation? Here and elsewhere, Eddy showed profound confidence in her arguments and, unlike her responses in later years, replied to pointed critiques in kind.

Silver, like others, readily accepted that Eddy healed the sick and so did her book. He claimed, however, that this resulted from "making [patients] believe that she has a wonderful power from the Holy Spirit to remove disease." Physicians attained the same results through administering placebos, he wrote, and "this healing a person may do, when his views of God and human nature are the very opposite of Truth."[30] Eddy replied in *Science and Health* that faith in herself or her system was often absent among those cured. "We have healed many an infidel," she wrote, "whose only objection to our method was, that we had faith in the efficacy of Truth, or the 'Holy Spirit,' whereas they had none" (1878:169). At least her cures offered proof of "the efficacy of Christ, Truth," she argued, rather than dogma or tradition alone (164).

Eddy did not respond to her critics by trotting out cases she had healed and even seemed to find their acceptance of her cures a bit annoying, as if they completely missed the point by classing it a personal ability rather than the "scientific" system of biblical healing that anyone could practice. In the *Sun* she complained about her anonymous critic's "tedious narration of cases cured by her," while he "never even gave the title of our book!" The omission was important for reasons of truth and salvation: although *Science and Health* "bears the burden of many typographical errors," it also "bears . . . to the sick the foundations of Health, and to the sinner the way of salvation, and to the saint refreshment and encouragement." She quoted Jesus to underscore the point.[31]

She was as concerned as the clergy about winning souls. Her responses sought to convince them and other readers that what she taught and practiced was Bible truth. By 1886, Eddy was convinced the clergy "have got to be talked with lovingly," was at least guardedly glad that her revised book appeared to be "reaching them," and was willing to continue accepting some clerics into her classes (six applied in March that year).[32] In the 1870s, however, at least in public, she basically contended that if they would not listen, it was their own loss. H. S. C. may have sternly recommended Eddy quit her books and leave the writing to those more learned and masculine, but as Robert Peel dryly notes, she "disregarded the advice."[33]

When H. S. C. criticized Eddy's work as female "gush," he presaged Mark Twain's dismissive use of the term "Eddygush" years later.[34] As Peel comments, "Let good ladies who wrote metaphysical disquisitions remember that older and wiser masculine heads had long ago settled" the difficult and important questions of theology. "It was one thing for Thomas Aquinas to divide theology into two disciplines—Divine Science and the Science of God—and to write of God as Principle. It was quite a different matter for Mrs. Glover of Lynn to set forth a Science of Soul" that characterized the relationship between God and creation, among other ways, "as that of Principle to idea."[35]

H. S. C.'s criticisms floated on an undercurrent of serious religious and existential concern. Among these was a common preoccupation with millennial questions. "We do not know that the Prophets have foretold this time, nor are we certain that *we* have a proper understanding of it," H. S. C. wrote with searching honesty, but this new era of "philosophical gush" was just "possibly the [fraught] period before a new dispensation." According to Eddy, though, that new dispensation was both fully present and now arriving.[36]

EDDY'S OUTSIZE CONFIDENCE in her book rested to a large degree on her faith in its millennial significance. The historian David Weddle observes that she frankly described her work revealing "a new age in Christian history" and fulfilling "the biblical drama of salvation," likening early Christian Scientists to "the first Christians."[37]

For nineteenth-century American Christians, the drama of global salvation often played out as *premillennialism* (in which Christ was expected to return before the establishment of God's kingdom on earth) or *postmillennialism* (in which Christ was expected to return after the establishment of God's kingdom on earth). Eddy fit neatly into neither dichotomous option. She instead described a kingdom that was both fully present (to the spiritually inspired view) and also on its way (to the materially imbued view). We might call her stance *transmillennial*. Actually, this term describes well the traditional millennial view in the New England religion in which Eddy had been raised, though like everything else, her way of approaching it was distinctive.

As Adventists toured New England shopping around William Miller's endtime chronology in the 1830s, seeking to start something akin to an interchurch Bible study movement, Eddy and her family took a definite pass.[38] Congregationalists calculated the urgencies of the millennium differently and tended to consider the Millerite craze a "raving madness" that, in its very lunacy, itself signaled the imminent Second Coming.[39] Eddy never became a millennialist in the popular sense or an Adventist. Years later she elaborated in a note reading "Luke 17–20 Millerism," pointing to the gospel passage in which Jesus tells a group of Pharisees, "The kingdom of God cometh not with observation."[40]

Millennial calculations are usually associated with the visual culture of American Adventism and with Millerites and other groups more commonly acknowledged as restorationist (and might include a cultural propensity toward quantifying that has led one historian to call early Americans "a calculating people").[41] Specifically, they recall the detailed Adventist charts refined between 1843 and 1873 (with "keys" added after 1863 supplied by the likes of Merritt Gardner Kellogg, part of the cornflakes dynasty).[42] In eschewing Millerism, Eddy bypassed such complex charts and their illustrated explanations.

However, Congregationalism had engaged in a sober and distinctive prophetic tradition well before Millerism or restorationism became American trends. In 1812 Abraham Bodwell, the Sanbornton Bridge minister whose daughter taught the Baker girls and who sat on the local academy board, dated the millennium to "about the year 1866."[43] This date, James Moorhead shows, became quite common by the Civil War.[44] Bodwell built on the calculations of Jonathan Edwards, who, as John F. Wilson notes, used "traditional arguments" based on texts from Daniel and Revelation to locate "the beginning of the millennium either in the middle of the nineteenth century . . . or very early in the twenty-first century."[45]

Wilson adds that C. C. Goen sees Edwards characterizing "manifestations of the Awakening in his own lifetime" as possible millennial "harbingers" or even "the beginning of the event itself."[46] George Marsden also finds Edwards operating within a larger Protestant tradition of apocalyptic calculation, which he contextualizes as a response to the realm of widespread war and religious conflict lived by eighteenth-century New Englanders.[47] Bodwell's sermon stands as an interesting inheritance of Edwards's.

"Nineteenth-century postmillennial traditions adapted Jonathan Edwards's ideas even as they adopted them," writes Wilson, most notably by reworking them within "a broadly Enlightenment-derived frame of reference." He notes that Edwards clearly presented what might be called postmillennial views, but with a major caveat: within the Puritan milieu, "claims about Christ's presence in his churches were not propositions to be proved or disproved, but truths axiomatic to church communities that evoked understandings of the self and of history based on biblical precedents and promises."[48]

To Wilson, this says that "the basic distinction upon which so much turned in the nineteenth century among the literal-minded—whether Christ would return before the millennium (yielding premillennialism), or after it (constituting postmillennialism)—was foreign to the seventeenth and eighteenth centuries. For the earlier period, Christ was both present now and to be more thoroughly present later."[49]

That this viewpoint extended well into the nineteenth century is shown in an 1854 essay by Nathan Lord, president of Dartmouth, the Congregationalist college in New Hampshire (and alma mater of Eddy's brother Albert). The doctrine of millenarianism has waxed and waned in popularity throughout the history of Christianity, Lord noted. The European reformers paid it good attention yet saw that it "would belong more intimately to a future, and, as some affirmed, our present period."[50]

Unfortunately, lately it has fallen "into the hands of the speculative and curious" and become an "exercise of a romantic ingenuity" and "popular delusions." Lord hoped for "scientific inquiry into those laws of prophetic interpretation, by which alone the meaning of Scripture, and the orthodoxy of the primitive age, in this respect, could be re-established." Invoking the church fathers, then John Calvin and Huldrych Zwingli, Lord felt a "millenarian believes . . . in a kingdom of Jesus Christ now, and from everlasting to everlasting." He represented the millennial teachings of D. S. Burnet, William Whiston, Daniel Whitby, William Miller, Emanuel Swedenborg, Ann Lee, and Joseph Smith as "heretical philosophies," too speculative to be primitive and traditional. In response, a reader penciled lightly by the binding strings, "There seems to be too much egotism & prejudice in this Essay for me." Lord probably would have classified Eddy a heretic, too, given the opportunity.

Yet Eddy was intimately joined to this long-standing prophetic Protestant tradition in a way we can observe was neither premillennialist nor postmillennialist. The view Lord describes of a "kingdom of Jesus Christ now, and from everlasting to everlasting" resonated with her outlook. Sometimes she used the phrase "second appearing" (as opposed to "Second Coming"), indicating her "present now and also appearing" approach.

God's kingdom may not come "with observation," such as scanning the future horizon with mortal eyes, but it did appear in human consciousness to transform earthly experience now, and now, and now, and now—and according to God's plan, more fully at distinct and prophesied times throughout history.

Her work, she noted, was part of this plan. An enduring passage from her first edition recounts a Methodist hoping *Science and Health* would "dwell much on the atonement," with Eddy responding that her volume would impart the "unction of primitive Christianity" enabling healing—and in this way, readers could participate in the "regeneration" of atonement, "to understand wherefore Jesus suffered and triumphed," which would "revolutionize the world" and "bring in the millennium" (1875:306–7; also see 1911:34). Each regeneration experience involved a glimpse of millennial glory.

Importantly, Eddy never wrote, published, or endorsed literal end-time dates. "Heaven only knows," she wrote, "what searching methods, what agonies, what ages of crime, what revolutions, may be required" for the "coincidence of the human and the divine" to "struggle up to freedom" in our lives.[51] Instead, she sketched out a few notations linking the arrival of her book to traditional Protestant prophetic teachings.

In a copy of her first edition, she worked with traditional biblical figures, the span she considered to occur between the first and second appearing (the life of Jesus and 1876, the year her book began widely circulating), and the span from her book's appearing to the conclusion of a millennial grace period. Quoting *Smith's Bible Dictionary* and various scriptures (Genesis, 2 Peter, and Revelation), she explained that "error will continue prevail seven thousand years, from the time of Adam, its origin," when "at the expiration of this period Truth will be generally comprehended."[52] The numeral seven, she often noted, was a biblical symbol for completeness. Never a literalist, her notes convey to me not so much historical time frames as the certainty that her book participated in the advent of Christ's kingdom, by which all sin and error were to be completely redeemed.

This is likely around the time Eddy annotated the 1856 book *Time of the End* by "a Congregationalist," Frank M. Messenger (and containing an entry by Rev. Edward Hitchcock of the 1843 Shelburne trial). Was this a pseudonym for a "frank messenger" relaying news to the faithful? Or was it Frank Mortimer Messenger, industrialist and promoter of the gospel?

Either way, Eddy marked it in several places: a "diagram showing . . . the chief prophetic periods" converging in 1875; a comment finding it "remarkable that most prophetic interpreters" date "the first resurrection" between 1864 and 1885 ("bounding periods" between which "the living saints that are on

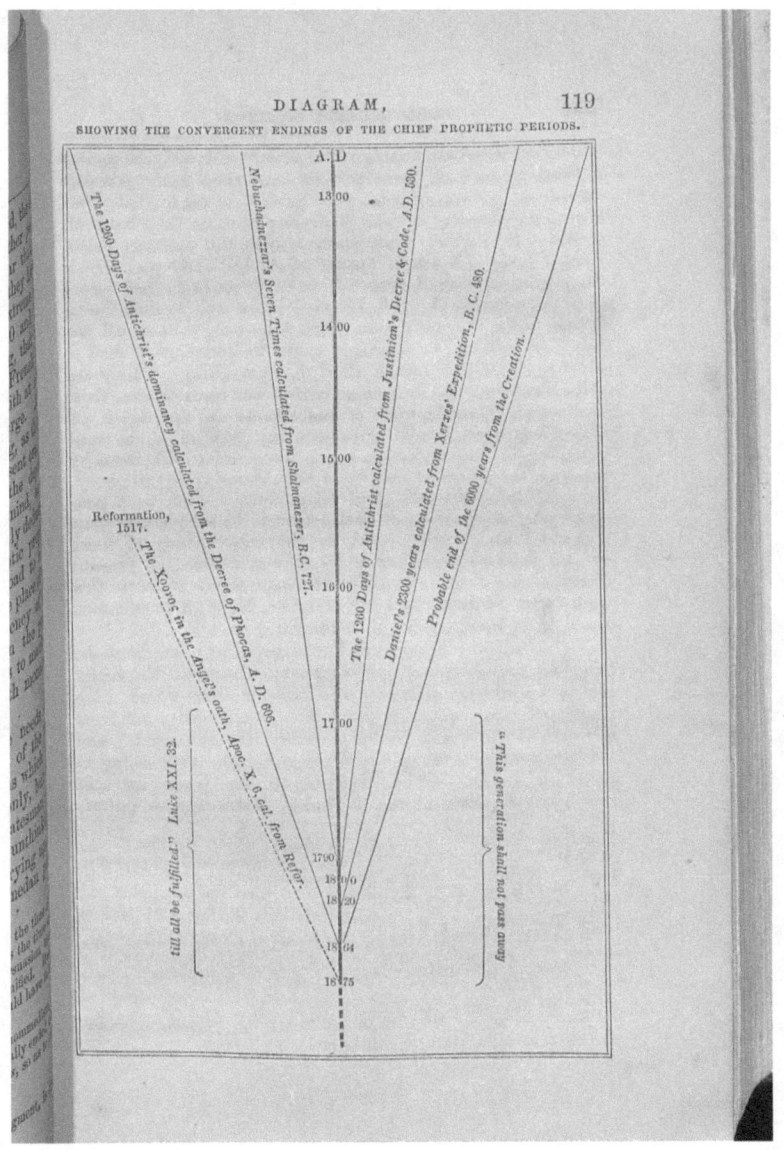

Congregationalism engaged a biblical prophetic tradition dating the Second Coming of Christ to about 1875. Sermons and charts on this topic circulated widely in early and, especially, antebellum America. Mary Baker Eddy owned and marked this book. Image from the Mary Baker Eddy Collection, B00236, Diagram Showing the Convergent Endings of the Chief Prophetic Periods in Messenger, *Time of the End*, 119.
© The Mary Baker Eddy Collection. Used by permission.

> *[margin top:]* no night will be there but the beauty of holiness will shine as the *[prevail]*
>
> *[margin left:]* will have done *[?]*

282   SCIENCE AND HEALTH.

thought embraced the science of being, man's longevity would increase ten-fold, and immortality be brought to light; the years of man will be extended as the belief of intelligent matter is destroyed, until at length a full recognition of Truth shall destroy all sin, sickness, and death. Error will ~~continue~~ seven thousand years, from the time of Adam, its origin. At the expiration of this period Truth will be generally comprehended, ~~and~~ science ~~roll back~~ the darkness that ~~now~~ hides the eternal sunshine and ~~lift the curtain on Paradise, where earth produces at the command of Intelligence,~~ and Soul, instead of sense, govern man.

> And as it was in the days of Noah, so shall it be also in the days of the Son of man. Luke XVII – 26. viz 120 years warning
>
> And I saw an angel come down from heaven, having the key of the bottomless pit and a great chain in his hand. And he laid hold on the dragon, that old serpent, which is the Devil, and Satan, and bound him ——
> Revelations XX – 1 – 2.
>
> 4004
> 1876
> "120"
> 6000 = 6 day
>
> 1000 years.
> 7000 = 1 week
>
> But, beloved, be not ignorant of this one thing, that one day is with the Lord as a thousand years, and a thousand years as one day. II Peter III – 8.

Mary Baker Eddy eschewed Millerism and the adventism of related end-time groups. Instead, she linked the arrival of her book *Science and Health* to older Protestant prophetic traditions and to an acceleration toward their complete fulfillment, now and ongoing, as represented by biblical typology. She wrote these notes around 1876. Image from the Mary Baker Eddy Library, B00424, © The Mary Baker Eddy Library. Used by permission.

earth shall leap for joy"); the sentence "I look for no *sensuous* Millennium—no Pagan Elysium."[53] She seemed to be contemplating traditional dates and times while simultaneously looking beyond them.

In her third edition in 1881, Eddy emphasized scriptural justification for looking beyond computations to the spiritual eternality they represented. Understanding God's creation becomes possible, she wrote, "as we lay aside finite calculations and accept the computation of Scripture, that 'one day with the Lord is as a thousand years'" (1881:120). She later defined the millennium as "a state and stage of mental advancement, going on since ever time was," with an "impetus . . . accelerated by the advent of Christian Science."[54]

That acceleration, she reminded her church in 1900, took place when her book arrived, even if the end result was not presently discernible in totality. Her book was published in 1875, she noted, which "some modern exegesis on the prophetic Scriptures" identified as "the year of the second coming of Christ."[55] In 1906 she received a letter from a Christian Scientist, Maria Louise Baum, who reported from nearby Duxbury that after a period of spiritual study and "awakening" she was "led to look into" Jonathan Edwards's *A History of the Work of Redemption* (1739). There, wrote Baum, she found unsuspected confirmation of her faith in Edwards's apocalyptic dating.

After citing Edwards's figures relating to the restoration of the apostolic church, Baum noted his 1866 date and commented, "He wrote better than he knew." Eddy's affection for Edwards made that a high compliment, and she wrote on the envelope, "Jonathan Edwards prophecy of the coming of *Science and Health*."[56] In 1910 she reiterated a similar sentiment, this time with calculations and scriptural passages, in a dictation to her student Laura Sargent.[57]

These figures vary from her calculations in 1876, underscoring her relative unconcern for the details of millennial math. Both engage roughly the same traditional dates, however, showing her concern for historically appreciable prophecy in relation to her book's arrival. In her book's final edition, she held that "the opening of the sixth seal [of St. John's revelation], typical of six thousand years since Adam," was intimately connected to "the present era" (1911:55). She had told a student as much in nearly identical language back in 1877.[58]

Again, she declined to pin down literal apocalyptic timelines. It is certain that the red dragon in Saint John's revelation "is at last stung to death by his own malice," she noted, but as in her first edition, "how many periods of torture it may take to remove all sin, must depend upon sin's obduracy" (1911:569). This was so just as the scriptural days of creation "can never be reckoned according to the calendar of time" but appreciated only as "thought accepts the divine infinite calculus" (520).

Eddy was decidedly not a millenarian in the usual sense nor a numerologist, biblical or otherwise. She leaves no record of crunching future end-time numbers in a literal fashion or of finding hidden mystical meaning in sums. Rather, she marked the historical advent of her book with prophetic significance and with confidence it would aid millennial glory to its completion according to biblical plan, however that plan might unfold in history. As she did this, she drew on and reworked the eighteenth-century prophetic tradition of her early church culture.

She never endorsed a particular set of apocalyptic figures, filling her text instead with more suggestive passages and typology on such topics. Her ultimate focus remained on what she called the "divine infinite calculus." Whatever that term might have meant to Eddy and to religionists, and however we might describe such views, the premillennial versus postmillennial dichotomy clearly does not apply.

THIS DICHOTOMY is inapplicable to others in the nineteenth century, too, suggesting a need for historians to revisit the range of views on such topics and how we describe them. There is often a limited likeness among such groups, so grouping or classifying them together is not necessarily appropriate. Their highly individualized differences from mainstream options, however, bear better scholarly description. In many ways there was little overlap between Christian Scientists and the Shakers, or United Society of Believers in Christ's Second Appearing (the Believers, as they styled themselves). They had different millennial beliefs, but these are usually more or less uncharted on our overall map of American religions.

An 1879 edition of the *Shaker Manifesto*, for example, declared that "millions, who are clamoring for a *second coming* of the Lord," are unaware it will arrive immediately after they have fully accepted the "*first* appearance." They will simultaneously find they have "united themselves with the Shakers." This "inward rather than outward" nature of the second appearing, notes Stephen J. Stein, emphasized a select few paving the way for future beneficiaries. Through them, "the order destroyed in the fall" of creation will be "restored to a higher degree, and the lost union recovered and made eternal."[59]

This possibility seems to have emerged for Shakers during the lifetime of Ann Lee (1736–84), or "Mother Ann," and at least in the nineteenth century they looked for confirmation through apocalyptic dating. The reformer and Lincoln appointee Elihu Burritt and other "notables," the *Manifesto* indicated, had recognized the probability of the second advent, which may produce research "affixing the date . . . to 1770! Let us all keep our eyes and ears open."[60] In some cases, according to Shaker belief, Lee was thought not to be Christ but rather the first to live wholly within the era of the second appearing, full of his millennial glory.

In such cases, this glorified state was not restricted to Lee, although for Believers she held a special place as the first to experience it and bestow its legacy on others through her church. In other cases, Shakers personified this advent. The Ohio Believers "declared that the Savior appeared as a woman, to the bedevilment of natural comprehension" and the consternation of most Christians who expected the second appearing to be masculine.[61] Lee was sometimes seen as the bridegroom in the book of Revelation, made ready for the bride.

In contrast to such views, Eddy noted that Christian Science, not herself personally, embodied the second appearing. "The second appearing of Jesus," she wrote, "is, unquestionably, the spiritual advent of the advancing idea of God, as in Christian Science."[62] Thus to adherents, Eddy delivered the message of the second appearing but did not herself constitute it. She had restored the primitive church and held a special and unparalleled place as its continual leader. In this configuration, there is always a definite and total difference between Eddy's identity and that of the Christ. This is not the case regarding Lee and the Shaker Christ.[63]

The Canterbury Shakers once gifted Eddy with a hymnal, and Stein recounts a historical openness to some aspects of Christian Science within Shaker communities (notwithstanding Eddy's practical acceptance of sexuality for procreation). Like Lee, Eddy's early students called her "Mother," in her case a term of Christian affection similar to "Sister" and "Brother" (book inscriptions to Eddy using this term surged around 1900, and she asked Christian Scientists to drop it when it raised misunderstandings among critics, the press, and sometimes Christian Scientists themselves).[64]

Similarly, we might call both Eddy's and Lee's eschatologies transmillennial, but the similarities end there. As David Holland shows in his work on Eddy and Ellen Harmon White, mapping the likenesses and differences of such religious innovators helps historians expand our map of the nodes and networks that have operated within American religious history.[65]

I cannot define Eddy's full teachings on the millennium, which are outside the scope and interest of my book. Yet it is relevant to the character and content of Christian Science identity that as it cohered around her interpretations of the Bible, she engaged and refigured an earlier Protestant tradition describing the kingdom of God as both fully present and now arriving. Printing blunders, language limitations, and critics aside, this distinctive transmillennial view saturated Eddy's understanding of *Science and Health*, making her confidence in it inevitable. As it turns out, the millennium also played a central role in her engagement with women's rights and the entire enterprise of social reform in the 1880s. This is where the first chapter in the next part of the book heads.

FINDINGS: PART II

BY THE LATE 1860S, Mary Baker Eddy represented herself as discovering, with absolute certainty, something new in the religious and scientific realms. She described this in terms of vision, revelation, inspiration, discovery, science, and biblical interpretation, jumbled together yet clearly moving in some distinct direction.

"The Bible in Its Spiritual Meaning," or the Genesis manuscript, her first extended interpretation of biblical texts, embodied the impetus and rationale of her 1866 experiences. Yet those experiences remained submerged within her jumbled text. Her work was both highly original and provisional. In her brief introduction, she tentatively framed her newly emergent, singular views as illustrated by prior associations and observations, creating unresolved tensions. She grappled with how to reconcile her past curative search with her new vision.

This shifted decisively in 1872, when a series of events caused her to finally understand her former doctor, Phineas Quimby, as working in the mesmeric and not the Christian tradition. Heretofore she had seen him through the lens of her experimental, unorthodox Congregationalism, as if his practice were (or could be made) part of that world. Now she saw him as a thoughtful and kind hypnotist, but a hypnotist nonetheless. Many Americans were undecided about the character and potentially scientific components of mesmerism or animal magnetism, but to Eddy and others more orthodox, those phenomena and Christianity were "separated by barriers" that could not be bridged.[1]

This apparently explained to her why she had long been unable to discern and describe a systematic Christian description of Quimby's practice. It also answered a set of other unresolved questions and concerns she had retained about his practice since 1864. Thus the close conversation she had maintained with his work became theologically unviable and drew to an end. Though she had hardly any audience to take note, she retained the value of her own independent work when she knew him and began to claim and definitively narrate her own experiences at the center of her always singular biblical interpretations. Beginning in 1872, she recorded these in a new book manuscript.

When Eddy published *Science and Health* in 1875, she presented it as her practical, restorationist, democratic, anti-mesmeric explanation of experiential or provable Christian metaphysics and a revelation from God to carry on Christ's church in the modern era. Her book presented new understandings of restorationism, higher criticism, and the natural sciences. It explained the sacraments and other elements of traditional Christian theology (the Trinity, the Christ, baptism) without ritual.

In conversation with established metaphysical questioning, but quite radically and in new terms, she most centrally offered a system of applied Christian metaphysics illustrated by testimonials of healing. Rather than taking the mantle of natural science to legitimize her religious views, she presented herself as preserving and extending the legitimacy of the Bible through her moral, mental, or Christian science, culturally circulating terms to which she applied new meaning.

Eddy wrote her book as a Congregational church member and expected the established churches to embrace it. The evidence here shows why, and also why this did not happen. Her teachings struck readers as variously heterodox, practical, inerudite, revelatory, outrageous, compelling. Their varied responses to her book illustrate how readers and reception are a core part of the Christian Science story.

Eddy's early critics accepted that her religion healed and was some iteration of Christianity, but they found most of it unappealingly unorthodox. She responded to the substance of their critiques in her text. Her confidence in her book rested to a large degree on the view that it centrally aided the present and coming kingdom of Christ. She left no calculations or timeline for its culmination but rather articulated a new expression of traditional Protestant teachings we can call transmillennial, in which Christ is both arriving now and ever-present.

Christian Science adherents, meanwhile, began to forge a new religious identity around the teachings in her book and the experiences they attributed to these. In America prior to 1875, the term "Christian Science" was a general phrase used as an increasingly rare and loosely connected synonym for the ubiquitous "moral science," its occasional subset "mental science," or the "Science of Soul." After 1875, it became a specific and fixed proper noun referring to Eddy's system of applied Christian metaphysics producing testimonial records of healing the sick. In 1879, Christian Scientists formed their own church based on Eddy's distinctive biblical teachings.

Eddy presented a new model among world religious founders by describing an experience of complete and final divine Self-disclosure that resulted in her progressive understanding and explanation of it over time, guided gradually by humanly individualized divine agency. This approach and the text and claims it produced are singular, unduplicated in other denominations or traditions.

As *Science and Health* entered the 1880s, critics, observers, and adherents disagreed on its value and interest. Yet all agreed that it was a highly distinctive and unusual entry in the Christian world. This agreement would soon change.

PART III

Revision
(1881–1890)

CHAPTER TEN

Reform and Salvation
(1881)

In which Eddy's gendered commitments are seen to be neither Victorian nor "feminist" but in service to her larger religious project—that is, her emphatic support for women's rights is qualified and subsumed by her soteriology—and in which race, reform, gender, and millennium mingle to shape how Eddy expresses her religious vision for human liberty

IN THE THIRD EDITION of *Science and Health*, in 1881, Mary Baker Eddy revised her exegesis of Genesis in several places to use the feminine pronoun for God.[1] "Spirit blessed the multiplication of Her own ideas," she writes, and "She names them all, from an atom to a world" (1881:115). She further implied that God's nature should be more fully acknowledged in feminine terms.

Yet in her working copy of this two-volume edition, Eddy's penciled comments show her thinking more about Jesus than gender. An indexed list of notations at the back of the second volume includes only one overtly gendered reference, while half of the fourteen discuss Jesus: his crucifixion, "The reason of [his] sufferings," "Gethsemane & Calvary," his ascension, the "Spiritual significance" of his life. Turning the page, she wrote the longest notation in either volume: "Peter said 'in the name of Jesus Christ of Nazareth, rise up & walk:' recognising him as the *Way* the *Truth* and the Life. As the rule is the product of the principle, and conformed to brings out the correct result, so the man Jesus, was the perfect model, the *Way* for us. There is no other name given under heaven, among men whereby we may be saved."[2]

Numerous feminist studies about Eddy seek to explain what scholars have dubbed her "ambiguous feminism."[3] Here I problematize both terms in relation to Eddy's gendered theology and practice, instead focusing on the larger religious project within which her gendered work finds its seamless, unambiguous significance.

Following the women's historian Nancy Cott, who positions "feminism" as a twentieth-century term and cautions against employing it anachronistically, I assume that placing Eddy on a feminist spectrum and moving her back and forth on it cannot properly contextualize or represent her within her historical setting. Feminist historiography is better served by a comprehensive view that places gendered elements holistically and therefore more precisely, even (and perhaps especially) if the feminist label does not historically apply to the religion or person under consideration. Asking how we might codify or classify "Eddy's feminism" can be seen as a presentist and perpetually elusive preoccupation. Not a new answer but a new question is needed.

Here I ask, What is the larger religious project within which Eddy's gendered work finds its unambiguous significance? I find that Eddy's early, temporary use of the female pronoun for God, placed in context with her emphasis on Christian salvation, mirrors her relationship to the Woman Question as a whole: it is emphatic and radical, yet qualified and ultimately subsumed by her soteriology, not lost but included within it.

IN 1882, Eddy marked up a book on women's friendships that included a passage about voting. Women have many "outward trials and disabilities," it notes, but their "grand want is freer, deeper, richer, holier, inward life." They may "reach out for the ballot—enter on a larger range of work and possibility," but let them not forget that their "foremost, weightiest need is a more thorough intellectual possession and moral fulfillment ... leading to a closer union with friends and an *absolute* surrender to God."[4] Eddy supplied the underline and put her trademark sympathetic check in the margin.

In a basic sense, she still carried the formative family and regional understanding of moral and political reform, explored in the first chapter of this book, holding that while legislating aspects of human behavior sometimes proved necessary, reactions might occur such as rote compliance or backlash. Reason, religion, and conscience were therefore the best tools to win lasting and constructive social change. Immoral things can easily be made legal. What is moral cannot be legislated until the majority is persuaded it is right. This viewpoint persisted through Eddy's career and made up a key part of her stance not only on temperance and abolition but also on women's rights.

Even given this framework, however, the scope and diversity of Eddy's writings on women's rights over time have constituted a puzzle for historians. In handwriting that archivists place at or near 1895, she wrote what is clearly a response to Elizabeth Cady Stanton's *Woman's Bible*. Titled "Womans Bible," the unpublished draft reads in part,

The Bible is the learned man's masterpiece[.] It is wisdom to comprehend it and to challange or berate it before understanding it is to be ignorant of its worth and incompetent to comment upon it.

It is a book of Truth a book of Life a book of Love[.] Its ideals are high above human conception and . . . are Divine.

The man's Bible is the woman's bible[.] We cannot have two if the sexes are equal[.] Man is the generic term for both men and women and if the most radical suffragist cannot ask or would receive a greater emolument than to be made in the image and likeness of God[,] I must dissent from their ideal and accept gratefully as humbly woman's rights and birthright to be an heir with Christ and joint heir with Jesus[.][5]

This "dissent" from Stanton's views illustrates why in 1910 Edward Bok, the conservative publisher of the *Ladies' Home Journal*, hopefully awaited a public statement from Eddy opposing votes for women.[6] Her several statements in support of women's rights show why Bok waited in vain. From 1875 to 1910 she summarized her qualified support for suffrage in largely unchanged terms: "If the elective franchise for women will remedy the evil without encouraging difficulties of greater magnitude, let us hope it will be granted" (1911:63). Apparently she considered the antibiblical "ideal" of a suffragist like Stanton to pose just such a difficulty.

In 1904, Eddy modified a bylaw in her church manual that had initially prohibited Christian Scientists from joining "organizations which exclude either sex." Equal access for women, however, was apparently not her first concern. She eventually struck the bylaw's gendered language after learning it would extend to all-male groups such as "Press Clubs that give the toil-worn aged Journalists a Home."[7]

The final 1910 version of the bylaw asks members to refrain from joining "organizations which impede their progress in Christian Science," leaving them to weigh the requirement and decide the matter individually.[8] Similarly, a decade earlier when Eddy specified that a man and a woman should read from the Bible and her book *Science and Health* at Sunday services, the primary concern she named was not promoting women's leadership or gender parity. It was rather stemming a worrisome trend toward what she considered theologically inaccurate sermons in the pulpit.[9]

Such instances are in accord with the well-established observation that Eddy, who was focused on the daily demands of building her church, was not a political activist for women's rights. Susan B. Anthony noted this as well. In 1887, Harriet H. Robinson, a suffragist from Massachusetts, offered to send Eddy the latest volume of Stanton and Anthony's *History of Woman Suffrage*, noting that the first volume was already in Eddy's library. Eddy hastily wrote at the bottom of the letter, in a nod to Anthony's tireless fundraising efforts, "Gave Miss Anthony $5.00 for bequest to Soc[iety]. . . . [D]o not think best to sub[scribe] have *no* time to read it & can give help in some other way."[10]

Reflecting the high profile Christian Science held in American culture at the time, later that year Anthony took a course in the faith from an influential Christian Scientist in New York, Laura Lathrop. She was never active in the church, however, and ultimately declared herself unsuited to any religion.[11]

In 1899 Anthony asked, "What of Mrs. Eddy? No man has ever obtained so large a following in so short a time." Then she added, "When woman does write her creed, it will be one of right actions, not of theological theories."[12] The *Christian Science Sentinel* amicably highlighted the comment, but Eddy continued on her parallel course as well and did not respond to a solicitation for funds from Anthony in 1903.[13]

Eddy's mixed record on the "Woman Question" also raises the question of the degree to which her church represented an increasingly imperative commitment to the rights of women qua women, or even to sexual egalitarianism. Citing an important passage about the conjoined purpose of husband and wife in marriage, in which Eddy changed the phrase "separate spheres" (1875) to "united spheres" (1886) "to reflect her developing notion of gender equality," Rosemary Hicks argues that Eddy's move away from narrow Victorian notions about gender roles created a more level environment for women within her church (and promoted one in broader society) on presciently progressive and "counterhegemonic" grounds.[14]

Hicks's challenge to classifying Eddy as Victorian is convincing, and Eddy's writings do show a developing sense of sexual complementarity by moving from a "separate but equal" to a "united and equal" view of the relationship between a man and a woman in marriage. Her gendered terms for God also became increasingly complementary over time. Her book first refers to God as Father but not Mother (1875), then to God as "Father and Mother" (1881), and finally to God as "Father-Mother" (1900).

Other changes are interesting but appear less portentous. Eddy changed the sentence, "The rights of woman are discussed on grounds that seem to us not the most important" (1875:321) to "grounds that seem to us the most important" (1881:159), inverting her conclusion. Yet barring the possibility of a misprint in the first edition (a serious problem, as we have seen), the passage still shows no discernible change in her view of women's rights, only the platform or "grounds" on which they are pursued.[15]

She later simplified the sentence to "The rights of woman are discussed on important grounds" (1886:161) and then dropped it altogether (1891:273). The remainder of the paragraph is substantively unchanged throughout the book's ten major editions. In 1875 as in 1881, and through 1910, it expresses Eddy's convictions about temporal women's rights in almost identical wording.

In 1891 Eddy removed one set of separately gendered qualities from her book but added another that would remain nearly unchanged: "The ideal man corresponds to creation, to Intelligence, and Truth. The ideal woman corresponds to Life and Love" (1891:498). Elsewhere she referred to "the intelligent individual idea" of God, "be it male or female" (1911:508).

Thus the neuter gender existed in languages and parts of creation such as flora and limited fauna, but it apparently did not apply to the male and female whom God created, who were meant to express all the qualities of God equally but also seem to express special and distinct natures that complemented one another. In the poem "Woman's Rights," Eddy identifies how woman earned the right

> To nurse the Bethlehem babe so sweet
> The right to sit at Jesus' feet . . .
> In short, the right to work and pray
> "To point to heaven and lead the way."[16]

She first published this in 1876 and reprinted it unchanged in 1896 in a collection of her work meant to instruct her students.

This is in line with her exegesis of the account of Adam, Eve, and the fruit from the tree of knowledge of good and evil (Genesis 3), which many theologians, women in particular, reinterpreted in the nineteenth century.[17] Eddy's view is singular. She casts Eve as transgressive in a new sense: rather than following Adam in seeking to hide her guilt and blame it on another, she forthrightly and "meekly" owned her error and was first to admit she had been wrong.

This honesty, independence, and strength of character reflected spiritual insight and prescience, Eddy implied, showing that woman had been first to drop "the belief in the material origin of man and to discern spiritual creation," which later allowed her to conceive and mother Jesus, be first to see him at the tomb after his resurrection, and, in an apparent reference to Eddy's own work, "be first to interpret the Scriptures in their true sense, which reveals the spiritual origin of man" (1911:532).

Further, in 1907 Eddy wrote to a woman student that "our sex seems to be needed at this period to lift the darkness and cheer the faithful sentinels at their posts of love and duty." Men, on the other hand, she wrote in 1910, bring "the male element," which is "a strong supporting arm to religion," and Christian Science was in great need of "the strong, the faithful, the untiring spiritual armament" they contributed.[18] Consistently throughout her writings spiritual individuality is genderless, but until this is fully realized on earth, women and men would fulfill distinct and separate yet increasingly harmonizing functions in the institution of the church as in marriage.

Eddy's much-discussed appointment of male administrators was practical in the sense that men would encounter fewer roadblocks in the worlds of publishing, finance, law, and construction, thus ensuring more efficiency, and men were certainly more accustomed than most women to serve in such roles (and probably more available or willing in many cases, as women tended to have inflexible domestic responsibilities and also found that public work begat specially gendered public exposure and criticism, as Eddy well knew).

In 1900 Eddy explained the gendered dynamics of her appointments in an unpublished rough draft, writing that she chose to give most of the public functions of her church to the "masculine element," implying that the qualities men brought to this work better suited them for it (whether naturally or socially is difficult to discern), even while emphasizing that the overall basis of Christian Science was strictly one of sexual equality.

She also wrote that Christian Science "involves no usurpation of power on the part of women," either spiritually or institutionally. This article initially seems to have been meant for publication and was probably intended to address criticisms about her gendered appointments, but it matches up with her private writings on the matter.[19]

Self-sufficiency was a quality Eddy appeared to value in her male appointees, as with women. As she wrote in 1892 to Edward Kimball, then a prominent student in Chicago and later one of her most trusted church officers, she wished he would not speak to others about some matters as if "I in any way decide for you, and do not let me do this. Act as you have done wisely in the light from the oil that is in your own lamp."[20]

Turning to her writings was one thing, but looking for her personal influence was another. A few days earlier she had responded to his request for advice by dictating to her secretary, "It is not necessary for her [Eddy] to ans[wer], God will ans[wer] . . . if you are faithful."[21] In her last years she continued to supply directions, guidance, and bylaws that she described as God-revealed rather than personally mandated, while increasingly leaving both church business and her finances, no matter how quotidian or important, to her mostly male appointees.

Parity between men and women was clearly important to Eddy, yet taken as a whole, her views were varied and situational. Her focus on the rights of women simultaneously increased, diminished, and shifted over time. Her views developed in ways that reflected a basic sympathy with sexual egalitarianism, but they also remained static, developed laterally, and even declined in importance.

Rather than pointing to "ambiguity" in Eddy's work, however, these multivalent changes suggest an even larger context, one that has to do with the shared "birthright to be an heir with Christ and joint heir with Jesus." Enter religious reform, and the millennium.

THE RIGHT TO BE an "heir with Jesus" was one women already had and shared with men, but, Eddy protested, conventional religious theories routinely and systematically denied this fact, just as society denied women their most basic temporal rights. The elimination of African American enslavement was evidence of God's hand in human affairs, foreshadowing the need for all people to realize their spiritual freedom; in like manner, the elimination of discrimination against women was a worthy goal awakening both sexes to realize their already existent spiritual equality.

This offers an explanation for the continued need in Christian Science to sustain some focus on the rights of women qua women, though always as a subset of this greater religious purpose.[22] It contextualizes Eddy's opposition to the securing of women's rights when done via methods that conflicted with her primary spiritual commitments, while leaving open a space that shows why she was so ardent in her qualified support of them.

This ardency is, as others have shown, not difficult to find. It is "the right of woman to fill the highest measure of enlightened understanding and the highest places in government," she wrote, and "this is woman's hour, with all its sweet amenities and its moral and religious reforms."[23] In no uncertain terms, laws should change to reflect parity for women; suffrage should be granted if it did not cause more problems than it solved; morally bettered humans should create morally better laws; and women should have the same wage, property, custody, and other rights as men. In sum it is a "marvel," she wrote with fervor in every edition of her book, why society did not recognize the rights of women more fairly and broadly, as Christian Science and "civilization" (reforming society) did (1875:321; 1911:63).

This last passage could be read to imply that if Christian Science were to become the basis for societal regulations and mores, notably through bettering humans morally, discrimination against women would have no roots and thus gradually and eventually vanish. Similarly, her work registers ardent approval of all human rights won through what she termed the "Christianization" of humanity.

Her use of the term "reform" encompasses and links both goals: individual religious reform and human rights. *Science and Health* (1911) contains thirty-two references to "reform" and its variants, of which twenty-four (three-fourths) refer to the reformation of sinners through Christ; five refer to some type of moral reform in society, two to religious reform, and one to the "reformatory mission" of Christian Science (1911:129).²⁴

Her collection *Miscellaneous Writings* (1896) follows a similar pattern, with seventy-three references to "reform" and its variants, of which twenty-eight (over one-third) refer to the repentance and reformation of sinners. Another third is devoted to defining and discussing the spiritual nature of the "reformer," and the remaining third relates to social or institutional reform, which is regularly traced to the elevating effects of Christian Science practice. She identifies "Temperance reform" as a direct effect of Christian Science healing and speaks of "all revolutions, natural, civil, or religious, the former being servant to the latter" (1891:402).²⁵

This linkage between individual religious reform and societal reform seems to be why Eddy urged her students to keep their methods distinct from those of social reformers whose modes might work against their own. As she wrote to John and Ellen Brown Linscott, who married after John's career as an "agitator" or social activist in Frances Willard's ranks, "Christian Science cannot be carried as anti-slavery and temperance are or have attempted to be. *Agitation injures our Cause*. We should always be ... Christlike. His voice was not heard in the street."²⁶

Eddy generally admired Willard, and there is interesting evidence that in the late 1880s she attempted to get John Linscott to recruit Willard to lecture on Christian Science.²⁷ This offer did not in the end pan out (and perhaps was never made). It shows, however, that at least at this juncture Eddy represented Christian Science as the cause social reformers should support wholly, rather than vice versa. In her faith social reformers could find the personal salvation that would allow them to transform and save society as a whole; what Christian Scientists could find in social reform was valuable to a degree, but much narrower and ultimately less effective.

Accordingly, rather than signing on to the causes of social reformers, Eddy tended to appropriate their terminology for her own spiritual purposes. She refers to her lifework, using reform parlance, as "the labor of uplifting the race."²⁸ In an article titled "Reformers" (1884), she appropriates the title for anyone in this line of work, spiritually speaking. Praising William Lloyd Garrison and all who are "honest to their convictions" and singly focused on their work, the article frames Garrison's political efforts as a subset and by-product of his more important moral and perhaps even spiritual labors.²⁹

Here, the title "reformer" ultimately describes those working to eradicate sinful "error" and establish the kingdom of heaven on earth. Jesus himself "was ultra," she wrote seven years later, using the era's term for a radical reformer. He "was, is, the reformer of reformers."³⁰ Proponents of the Social Gospel considered Jesus a reformer because of his social or ethical teachings, and adherents of New Thought often saw him as a central figure revolutionizing human potential by showing humans their inner divinity.

Eddy described his teachings as inaugurating "revolutions" in different millennial terms. In an undated and untitled manuscript, she wrote,

> That which bloomed out of the life of Jesus . . . was the ensample for man, and this coincidence of the human and the divine must yet appear in our lives. It may take a longer life than that of mortals to quicken it into vitality. Buried deep it may be from human sight and lie dormant for thousands of years, like the wheat found in Egyptian tombs, but in the Father's house—the many chambers of Soul—it must sometime fully disclose its identity with the spirit of Jesus. Heaven only knows what searching methods, what agonies, what ages of crime, what revolutions, may be required for this imperishable germ of greatness and goodness, to struggle up to freedom.[31]

Just as Eddy's letter to the Linscotts positions a "Christlike" demeanor as a safeguard for the religious reform activities of the Christian Science "Cause," this passage seems to position individual religious reform (in the New Testament sense of *metanoia*) at the base of eventual societal reform, and neither sounds particularly neat or quick. This perspective might be seen to reflect Eddy's Calvinist roots. "Calvin always emphasized the gradualness rather than the suddenness of conversion," writes John Bouwsma, "and the difficulty of making progress in the Christian life."[32]

It is clear, though, that the noisome mess of both struggles would ultimately give way to the goodness that "bloomed" from the life of Jesus. The passage is one of many in which Eddy links personal and societal reform, or salvation, to a larger millennial struggle. It provides an applied understanding of how the millennialism established earlier in this book might be worked out in a praxis-oriented sense and shows how the healing "unction of primitive Christianity" was expected to allow readers to participate in the "regeneration" of atonement and "to understand wherefore Jesus suffered and triumphed," which would "revolutionize the world" and "bring in the millennium" (1875:306–7).[33]

FOR MANY FIGURES who interacted religiously with the Woman Question, either as a central focus or part of a complex of concerns, religion informed if not trumped their political interests. People such as Frances Willard, Katharine Bushnell, and Ida B. Wells-Barnett were social reformers who self-identified as Christian, as did Eddy, whereas Elizabeth Cady Stanton rejected the label. Eddy's "dissent" from Stanton's *Woman's Bible* in the mid-1890s hints at their deep differences, though in articulating a complete theology meant to reform religion itself, the two women were also unique among their cohorts. Their disparate faiths eschewed temporal means they described as undermining these ends. Comparing them briefly here brings out how each sought to achieve women's rights but defined the process and result in starkly differing terms.

Like Bushnell, both Eddy and Stanton were unique biblical exegetes, and in this they departed from the devotional feminine ideal of their time (although exegesis as they practiced it arguably included devotional elements). However, Eddy sought to explain the healing truth of the scriptures, while Stanton sought to expose them as the root of all misogyny. Like many of their contemporaries, from Theodore Parker to Horace Bushnell and Henry Ward Beecher, and like predecessors such as Mother Ann Lee, Eddy and Stanton referred to God in both masculine and feminine language. Both cited Parker as an inspiration, at least to some degree; Eddy once defended her reference to God as "Father-Mother" by writing to a student, "I heard [that] Theodore Parker sometimes employed this contested phrase in the pulpit."[34]

However, Stanton pioneered an eclectic and radical woman-centered civil religion cohering around the notion of individual sovereignty achieved through freedom from the Bible's thrall; her gendered language for God was a descriptor of a dual-sexed ultimate reality and a tool with which to express and encourage the spiritual and temporal independence of women. Eddy, in contrast, pioneered a religion meant to "reinstate primitive Christianity and its lost element of healing," within which a modicum of gendered language would help worshippers achieve this millennially significant goal.[35]

Most feminist scholars have described Eddy's "Father-Mother God" as androgynous, but rather than combining male and female sexual characteristics in one deity, she always used the phrase in metaphorical or symbolic terms. Writing that she worshipped what she could conceptualize, she notes that this was first "a loving Father and Mother" and "then, as thought ascends the scale of being," the "Love" of Paul's and her forebears' God.[36]

This implies that in Christian Science, Father and Mother are the most basic and accessible descriptions of God's relationship to creation. They can be thought of as accommodations to the human inability to grasp God's infinite nature and to the human need for intimate metaphors for God in worship, helping thought "ascend" in prayer to experience God's unsexed Being as Love itself. Thus by combining familiar and intimate names for a single, undivided and ungendered deity, she allowed worshippers to draw close to a Father-Mother God who is essentially without corporeal "body, parts, or passions," as the Westminster Creed puts it.[37]

Unlike Stanton, however, Eddy did not systematically lobby for female images of the Divine; they seem to be a by-product of her effort to describe in humanly accessible terms what she perceived divine reality to be. That reality seems even more precisely described, ontologically though perhaps not affectionally speaking, with the seven synonyms she regularly used to describe the God of the Bible: Mind, Spirit, Soul, Principle, Life, Truth, Love. These synonyms are not considered abstract but expressed intimately and individually in human experience through attributes such as the intelligence of Mind, the honesty of Truth, the comforting integrity of Principle, the tenderness of Love, and so on.

This may be why, while highly significant, Eddy's gendered God-language is relatively sparse. She refers to God as "Truth" 707 times but as "Father-Mother" only 8. "Father" appears an additional 75 times, usually in reference to Jesus's worship of God, "Mother" only 4. In fewer than 700 pages, Eddy's seven synonyms for God appear over 3,000 times, gendered names less than 100 times.

This window into ontology might also explain why, in the glossary of *Science and Health*, "God" is not defined as Father or Mother, but "Mother" and "Father" are both defined as God. God's Being is not gendered, but the terms that human beings use to refer to him/her tend to be. In Christian Science, there is no tension between impersonal and personal references to God. The synonyms describe the absolute spiritual reality of God expressed in redeemed humanity. More than one Christian Science writer compared them to the facets of a diamond, names through which the one God could be better known by humans. The term "Father-Mother" describes a particularly tender, simple, and colloquial way of understanding this caring relationship.

Both Stanton and Eddy refigured the Eve story, but in very different ways. Stanton objected to the notion of the Fall and its subsequent necessity of a male savior, which she felt to be inappropriate for women. Like many women's rights advocates who embraced Darwinism as an antidote to the Eve story, she praises Eve's "thirst for [worldly] knowledge," which she implies is the real savior of women. And like many feminist and womanist theologians today, she felt that "the differences between men and women made a belief in sin more oppressive for women."[38]

Eddy's teaching of sin and salvation retains Christ Jesus in the central salvific role, although her roughly pre-Nicene definition of Jesus as the Son of God and her definition of the Christ as an "office" of the Godhead lived fully and individually only by Jesus (also instantiated fully and systematically in Christian Science and always available, to some degree, to all people throughout time and space) are hardly orthodox. Eddy breaks from both orthodoxy and Stanton in considering Eve not innocent but honest and courageous; when her sin was discovered, she was "first to confess her fault."[39]

In contrast to Eddy's particularism, Stanton's mature theology was eclectic. She was not mystical enough to consistently or centrally embrace Theosophy, but unlike Eddy she did not oppose it wholesale. Their opposing positions are suggested in the person of Ursula Newell Gestefeld, who worked with Stanton on the *Woman's Bible* after a fiery departure from Eddy's faith in which differing views of Theosophy played a key role. Although Gestefeld's views on such matters would have meshed generally with Stanton's, their collaboration could hardly be classed a success. Gestefeld's assertion that the "male half" of humanity represents the "female half" and serves as the agent for female salvation could hardly have endeared her to the author of "The Solitude of Self," who wrote of the "importance of fitting every human soul for independent action."[40]

This, along with Gestefeld's statement, less than winning in its context, that "woman's strongest foes have been of her own sex" probably explains why Stanton shuttled her commentary to the end of the book. Just as Eddy had once objected to what she considered Gestefeld's effete "revery," which failed to produce healing results, Stanton later objected to what she considered a dreamy, apolitical religious imagination. Her theology was primarily esoteric rather than practical, and as Stanton and Eddy were both pragmatists in very different ways, neither found it convincing.[41]

Both Eddy and Stanton emerged over against Victorian gender ideals to pioneer new principles of sexual complementarity. They assigned religious dimensions to the view that men and women were naturally fitted to work together, each supplying those qualities and skills specially possessed by their sex, to aid the forward progress of humanity.

Neither subscribed to the New Thought concept of creation's "spiritual androgyny" or "sexless soul," noting instead that manhood and womanhood constituted spiritually distinct categories of some type. However, in contrast to Stanton's eternal "sex in soul," in which sex was an attribute belonging to the immaterial soul as well as to the material body, Eddy spoke of sexual complementarity on a strictly human level, notably in her writings on marriage.

What relations between the "male and female" of Genesis 1:27 might look like "in the resurrection," when "they neither marry, nor are given in marriage, but are as the angels of God in heaven" (Matt. 22:30) seems to have been a different matter for her. For Stanton, however, sexual complementarity was an eternal principle stemming from an androgynous God, both of which were meant to inform women's independence and resulting political action.

Of the few feminist theologians who have studied Eddy's thought, most have not found it "attractive or useful," as Amanda Porterfield notes.[42] As Mary Farrell Bednarowski puts it, Eddy's commitment to "the sole reality of Spirit is distinct from—opposed to, actually—contemporary women's earth-oriented theologies." Still, Bednarowski finds "instructive parallels" such as Eddy's opposition to "hierarchical dualisms"; her integral view of theology, practice, and ethics; and a focus on healing.[43]

Stanton, inversely, is today hailed as a foremother of feminist theology, though her racism and nativism complicate that relationship (while Eddy's religious commitments appear to have steered her away from Spencerian or social Darwinism). In many ways, these two were less reforming "sisters" than strangers; given the renown of both, it hardly seems accidental that they never corresponded or met.

Yet comparing these theologians helps position both on the broad field of reform, showing significant gendered elements within the revisionary work of both women to be at the service of larger and historically singular, while also essentially clashing, salvific projects.

AS THIS SUGGESTS, Eddy's take on women's rights was not only qualified by her larger soteriological commitments but also contextualized within a vast field of differing approaches to reform causes in which race, religion, reform, gender, freedom, salvation, and millennium mingled.

In 1875, the year *Science and Health* came out, a woman named Virginia Minor lost her lawsuit claiming the U.S. Constitution afforded her the right to vote, a right she needed only to claim and exercise. Her suit was part of the "New Departure" among woman suffragists, one of the legal strategies they rolled out in response to Reconstruction amendments guaranteeing African American citizenship and male suffrage, respectively, but not female suffrage. The historian Ellen DuBois shows how the New Departure "embodied a radical and democratic vision" lacking in the later, separate-amendment approach.[44]

At the heart of this vision, writes DuBois, was the argument that "the vote was already women's right; they merely had to take it." In the 1870s, this "militant and activist" message inspired hundreds of women to attempt to register to vote.[45] Freedmen's Bureau officials encouraged freedwomen to attempt voting under the Enforcement Act of 1870 (intended to give teeth to the Fifteenth Amendment), and male officials sometimes accepted their votes.

As with Minor, those who did not vote sometimes sued. A series of legal decisions, however, ruled that the Constitution did not guarantee any citizen the right to vote. Suffragists turned to the strategy of securing enfranchisement through a constitutional amendment of their own, which became a concerted national effort by the early twentieth century. DuBois finds this strategy less radical because "its goal was 'woman suffrage' not 'universal suffrage,'" which gave freer rein to "elitist and racist tendencies."[46]

Many scholars have noted the racism, overt or oblique, that often infected this effort (a problem that for Stanton and Anthony went back to 1867).[47] Claims to universality sometimes operated as flattening agents by which a dominant group imposed its vision on those it wished to free, but in this case, DuBois argues, the narrowing from universal to specific goals resulted in a loss of diverse voices.

The phrase "new departure" commonly described new ventures of all types in the era, and Eddy's work resonated with some more than others. After the free-love activist Victoria Woodhull became a female suffrage advocate in 1871, legal responses to suffragist strategies gradually shifted their focus from constitutional matters to the issue of free love.

The association of the two was not viable to Eddy. "It was about the year 1875," she wrote, "that Science and Health first crossed swords with free-love, and the latter fell hors de combat."[48] She described her book embodying a moral stance that intrinsically clashed with and defeated the free-love principles held by some radical reformers. Her description of universal spiritual rights, with women's and race rights as providential "signs following," also rested on very different grounds than New Departure universalism did.

Yet as suffragists shifted their strategies toward the particular in the 1880s, Eddy's text remained focused on universality. As New Departurists argued that women's suffrage already existed but needed to be exercised, Eddy argued that women's right "to be an heir with Christ and joint heir with Jesus" already existed but needed to be claimed. Similarly, the saving spiritual liberty of all people was intact but needed to be understood and exercised. In discussing this, she specifically invoked African American legal history, not politically, as suffragists did, but providentially.

In a passage that went through several iterations from 1875 onward, she declared that "the voice of God in behalf of the African slave was still echoing in our land, when the voice of the herald of this new crusade sounded the keynote of universal freedom," and that this freedom from sin, sickness, and death would occur "not through human warfare, not with bayonet and blood, but through Christ's divine Science" (1911:226).

Initially such passages resonated with the "baptism of blood" theology so predominant during and immediately after the Civil War, but Eddy pondered and revised, indexing this particular example on a flyleaf of her book copy in 1892 with the word "Liberty."[49] By 1907, she had moved these passages further from Civil War theology and into a new sensibility.

Throughout all renditions, the elimination of African American enslavement was the divinely wrought event representative of "all history," as it pointed to how "the might of Mind," God, could and would ensure the outcome of "right thinking" in creation (1911:245). Her theology in general portrays salvation and human progress as occurring through the increasing spiritualization of thought of all humans progressively, universally, and equally. Those on board with this definition of universality saw it rooted in spiritual rather than temporal law and playing out individually according to different cultures and customs.

Echoing earlier antislavery and abolitionist commitments, Eddy expressed a viewpoint in which social justice was a by-product of spiritual enlightenment. The liberation of African Americans from enslavement constituted foundational, important evidence that served as necessary precedent on which further "demonstrations" of freedom from tyranny of all kinds could take place. Those demonstrations would involve a "new departure" of a different type, however, one "from the old orthodox beliefs in which we were educated," as a student once wrote her.[50]

AN AVID USER OF her books' back flyleaves for notations, Mary Baker Eddy's penciled notes at the back of a copy of her book's third edition (1881) cover a variety of topics. She calculated the amount due on her board ($6.23) and resulting balance ($10.23); tried out quotations for her magazine (Thomas Jefferson, Mme. Roland, Paul); acutely marked and indexed passages about the loss of friendship, evil sometimes parading as good, and correct spiritual practice.

Her indexed list of comments at the back of the second volume includes only one obvious reference to gender ("Man the generic term," she jotted, which was less a cultural norm for her than an innovation within her religious lexicon following Genesis 1:27). She sandwiched her comment between references to "God's omnipotence" and "Gethsemane & Calvary."[51] She crossed out the quotation from the frontispiece and replaced it, with Jesus superseding Paul. The bulk of her notations, as we have seen, revolved around Jesus. This matches her book's published text, which in 1881 referred to "Jesus" and the synonym "Master" a combined 406 times and to God as "She," "Her," or "Mother" a combined 42 times.

This 1881 edition introduced a variety of new content. Robert Peel remarks that it appeared "in full battle dress," noting its expanded chapter on demonology (though just after its printing the author made a note to take out twenty of those pages) and Gilbert Eddy's pointed defense addressed to his wife's plagiarist.[52] The author's "scientific statement of being," thereafter one of her religion's central texts, appeared for the first time (1881:185; 1911:479). Importantly, it also includes Eddy's first textual references to God as "Mother," which she later developed into her trademark "Father-Mother God." Many of her contemporaries and predecessors (Theodore Parker, Horace Bushnell, Henry Ward Beecher, Elizabeth Cady Stanton, Ann Lee) referred to God in both masculine and feminine language, though Eddy always did so in purely metaphorical terms.

Eddy never lobbied for female images of the Divine, using them rather as a by-product of her effort to describe in humanly accessible terms what she perceived divine reality to be. In this context, Eddy's use of "She" and "Her" for God in one chapter was distinctive and radical but neither the edition's most outstanding nor its most enduring feature. After twelve subsequent printings, just before the next major revision in 1886, she dropped the usage without explanation.[53]

Peel suggests that the divine "She" was "disconcerting to the ear," but Eddy did not shy away from other phrasings some readers found unconventional and even heretical (a response not entirely unrelated to her status as a woman, as several authors have pointed out).[54] Still, she felt the need to defend her use of the term "Father-Mother God" by referring to Theodore Parker as precedent, suggesting such language pushed some students out of their comfort zone, and adding a bevy of divinely feminine pronouns may have seemed like asking too much of them.

Whatever the case, there is the divine "She," nonetheless. However briefly, Eddy's use of "She" for God joined other similar contemporaneous instances, yet it also carried particular significance, signaling her relationship to the intersection of the female and the Divine and to women's rights in general.

Her early, temporary use of the female pronoun for God, in context with her emphasis on Christian salvation, mirrors her relationship to the Woman Question as a whole: it is emphatic and radical, yet qualified and ultimately subsumed by her soteriology, not lost but included within it. This is why Eddy could develop and retain the term "Mother" for God but simultaneously back away from using the divine "She" with no obvious residual concerns for her readers' spiritual safety or the ultimate reform of society. Both choices preserved the ability of readers to approach God in a manner they could more readily understand and embrace, thus hastening the salvation experience by which they would revolutionize the world through Christ and bring in the millennium.

Seeking to codify Eddy's relationship to the women's movement, her student Carol Norton published the pamphlet *Woman's Cause* in 1895. He wrote that this cause "owes endless homage and gratitude" to Eddy and that to praise her work "is to add glory to the sex which she so grandly represents." After several pages of similarly admiring prose, he writes, "The work of Mrs. Eddy has opened to woman in the ministry of Christian Science, the two noblest of all avocations, philanthropy and medicine," by which they can "reform the sinner and heal the sick," and it has given "a glimpse of the resurrection state, and of the reflections of the Fatherhood and Motherhood of God."[55]

Norton alludes to a larger spiritual significance he sees in Eddy's work, a "counter current" like the "warm gulf-stream" leading to "the port of Salvation," but his main focus is on the particular significance she had for women.[56] His conclusions are interesting because they prefigure the arguments of feminists almost a century later: that the value of Christian Science for women lay in the new avocations it afforded them; in its worship of a Father-Mother God; and in Eddy herself, who was personally significant as a representative of her sex.

Writing to Eddy immediately after his book's publication, Norton hoped for its success and summarized its goals as establishing "your place and work as a culmination" of "Woman's work in religion, reformation, art literature and in the home," "your rightful place in the famous Mass. group of authors, poets, reformers," and "what your work has opened to the race." A highly favorable review of the work soon appeared, much of it describing Norton as a young man (around twenty-five) of poetic and "Puritan" extraction who had been earnestly interested in "reform work" since his early teens.[57]

Before long, however, negative reviews apparently began rolling in. A letter from Eddy cherished Norton's character and valued his commitment, thanking him "deeply for your arduous desire to help our Cause," but enumerated major concerns about this particular project. Detailing these in a later letter, she specifies the intemperate and triumphalist content of his endeavor as particularly problematic. Most centrally, however, the pamphlet "does not do historical justice" to her, "and in too many respects does lessen C. S."[58]

THIS CHAPTER HAS SOUGHT to identify and interpret the gendered significance of Mary Baker Eddy's religion in a manner that does not "lessen" it but rather shows its larger context. Eddy's writings on women's rights are multi-layered and imbued with a variety of meanings having a range of religious and social implications. Ultimately, though, her relationship to women's rights is clear and unambiguous.

Her distinctive millennial vision for what she called "the way of salvation through Christ Jesus" was the pivot point around which her gendered texts and teachings revolved, leading her (with remarkable consistency) to support what aligned with that soteriological strategy and reject what did not. She wrote ardently about securing women's rights and all human rights, but only through methods that aligned with her primary spiritual commitments.

Rather than measuring the activities of reformers against a particular standard of social justice, Eddy seems to have measured them against the totality of human salvation in revisionary Christian terms. She framed the achievement of women's societal and religious rights, like all reform causes, as a subset and extension of her brand of salvation through the atonement patterned and enabled by Jesus and in turn framed that salvation as a component of her millennialism.

Within this schema, her gendered language for God supports worshippers in grasping and living the spiritual reality that saves them and ultimately the world. Within this larger eschatological framework, Eddy's position on the Woman Question in every sense finds its proper scope and seamless significance.

Back in 1875, when her critic H. S. C. advised Eddy and all women to leave theological authorship to gentlemen, he roundly disagreed with her eschatology. Yet as with other critics, he saw that her objectionable book described an unusual type of Christianity. In the 1880s, different perceptions of her work would arise in which gender and eschatology made a less than obvious appearance.

CHAPTER ELEVEN

Naming Her Experience
(1883)

In which controversy prompts Eddy to fully blend the preexisting elements of scientific discovery and religious revelation within her narrative of religious origins, a narrative that is seen to be both strictly dated and gradual

IN 1882, a massive front-page article in the *Boston Sunday Globe* opened by citing lengthy accounts of the healings of Jesus, decrying centuries of cessationism as told by Edward Gibbon, and reporting that the new "Christian Scientists" claimed the power of Jesus's healings "is not lost, and [they] have supported that claim by inducing cures astonishingly like those quoted from the New Testament."[1]

Eddy was not consulted for the article. The reporter, who called himself a hard-boiled skeptic, instead interviewed people at Christian Science services and meetings. He recorded their beliefs, methods, and healing experiences, then followed them into their neighborhoods. Linking one healing report to another, he contacted each party and confirmed their cases. The volume of recoveries he encountered warranted a book rather than an article, he concluded. In some places, he found so many "that apothecaries have complained of a decided falling off in their business."

A "confirmed invalid" of fifteen years, herself a former skeptic, told the reporter her healing left her not only "better physically, but better morally, as though I had had a revelation. And when I came to read the Bible in the light of Mrs. Eddy's books," probably referring to the two-volume set that still made up *Science and Health*, "it had received a new and glorified meaning. Isaiah was simply grand, and Revelations [sic] a revelation indeed. I cannot doubt, in the face of my own experience, that a new light has dawned upon the world." The reporter emphasized this last phrase like a headline.

With only one exception, noted the journalist, Christian Scientists who learned about his article's publication were "averse to it." They did not care for the publicity. Undeterred, he gave accounts of people and their neighbors who confirmed healings of growths, epilepsy, bleeding lungs, curvature of the spine, a crushed foot, and so on. He related the teachings about God in *Science and Health*, describing Eddy's "platform of Christian Science" as a partly traditional, partly novel presentation of Christian metaphysics. He concluded that the Christian Science "church is built on Christ . . . thus re-establishing the Christianity of ancient prophet and apostle."

Such was the description of Christian Science in its major media debut, which both reflected and shaped public perceptions. Within the year, a lone voice emerged from the West, complicating matters. Julius Dresser had known Eddy when she sought to understand and explain the work of their erstwhile Portland doctor, Phineas Quimby. Now he was concerned that she had stolen her book title from Quimby ("Science of Health" was a phrase he had used, Dresser noted) and was not properly attributing her work to him. After learning of the concept of spiritual healing from Quimby, like others, he felt she now added her "own opinions to the grain of wisdom thus obtained, presenting to the people a small amount of wheat mixed with a great quantity of chaff."[2]

Eddy objected, and a short exchange of letters between herself and Dresser appeared in the *Post*. When one of her former students subsequently copied paragraphs verbatim from her book into his own, Dresser backed him in court, arguing that it would be impossible to plagiarize Eddy because she had already plagiarized Quimby. The court sided with Eddy and upheld her copyright. The general allegations, however, remained in circulation and were debated in polemics and biographies for over a century afterward.

Scholars by now uniformly concur that Eddy did not plagiarize Quimby. Yet Dresser himself agreed with that conclusion by 1904, at least in one venue. His concern then was "not that the exact language of Quimby is reproduced verbatim in 'Science and Health,'" he told the *New York Times*, as "Mrs. Eddy's language is presumably her own." Rather, his focus was on Eddy's claim to revelatory experience. She could not have experienced a "final revelation" in 1866, he inveighed, because that "flatly contradicted" her statements linking herself to Quimby around 1868.[3]

Phrases like "Science of Health," as we have seen, circulated among irregular curists in the 1850s, among others searching for the divine law that would ensure and explain spiritual healing. Perhaps that, and certainly the court loss, caused Dresser to emphasize other aspects of his argument to the *Times*. Unlike Dresser, Eddy had not been in Quimby's inner circle, and her work had never quite represented the doctor's work as he might have wished, even when she meant it to. Now, after her watershed year in 1872, she had moved on entirely to fully claim her own 1866 experiences, resulting in her own religious project. For anyone to grasp Eddy's work on her own terms, however, meant acknowledging these developments, including her claim to revelation.

A few things complicated this for Dresser. He did not have full access to the record of Eddy's long-term, independent, and culturally resonant quest for a divine "principle" behind physical cures; to the startlingly new revelatory sensibility that emerged in her Genesis manuscript by the late 1860s; or to her inconvenient but compelling 1872 change from seeing Quimby's practice as biblical to seeing it as mesmeric, or how this resolved long-standing questions about her time in Maine, bringing out the primacy of her own religious experience.

Yet even with such evidence at hand, it would have been difficult to reconcile with a framework assuming divine Self-disclosure to be accompanied by a static, fixed, "final" message or object that humans might physically discover, record or speak verbatim, translate, channel, or otherwise more or less immediately interpret. It was hardly Dresser's fault that such were the generally available concepts of revelation. Eddy presented a new model among world religious founders in which an experience of complete and final divine Self-disclosure resulted in her progressive human understanding and explanation of it over time. This was a radical new proposition.

The denial of special revelation as a religious teaching would have almost certainly entered in for Dresser, too. This was common among movements that sprang up in mesmeric and mesmeric-adjacent traditions in the 1880s (such as Theosophy), and it became a keynote within their opposition to Eddy's increasingly public views. If Dresser felt special revelation to be either impossible or inadvisable (which is probable for a disciple of Quimby, who left a record of anti-revelatory belief), nothing could have convinced him of the validity of a revelatory claim anyone might make.

Back in 1875, perhaps Dresser would have been mollified at least by reading Eddy's warm description of Quimby in her book's first edition: he "never studied" her own science, she wrote, "but reached his own high standpoint and grew to it through his own, and not another's progress. He was a good man, a law to himself," and though since 1872 she had considered him a mesmerist, she credited him with "growing out of" it (1875:373–74). Dresser might have disagreed with this last part, feeling it to be against Quimby's self-identity, but presumably not with the rest. The 1875 edition was already hard to find by the early 1880s, however.

It is unclear whether Dresser had read a newer edition of Eddy's book, either, or only read about it. He may have learned of her activities through the *Boston Sunday Globe* article (which would have sounded alarmingly Christian to him, perhaps the basis of his distance from her in the 1860s as well). Their last contact had been nearly two decades prior when, reeling from her accident and struggling to process her recovery experience, she had sought his help securing her path forward. After he declined, she had moved ahead on her own and by the end of the year made sense of her experience as an all-encompassing experience of the Divine revealing to her a singular discovery about God and creation, or in short, a revelatory event and new discovery.

DRESSER'S IMAGE of Eddy seems to have frozen in time well before this. Yet it was also true that in 1883, Eddy's book did not yet fully unite her claims to religious discovery and divine disclosure. Both existed but as separated threads. Back in 1872, allegations in the *Lynn Transcript* had precipitated a reckoning on her part that led her to clarify the activity of Christian Science over against mesmerism and to fully claim her own experience at the heart of her religious expression. Now in 1883, unwelcome publicity in the *Globe* and the *Post* precipitated a reckoning regarding the relationship between religious discovery and divine revelation that led her to unite her descriptions of them, fully naming and describing her experience in her book.

In her 1875 edition, her descriptions of a divinely revealed message echo the thick revelatory sensibility embodied in her late 1860s Genesis manuscript and refer to 1866 events. "We learn Truth from divine revelation and our own demonstration," she wrote, and "God revealed to us the science of being" (1875:94). Using first person plural to refer to herself, then a customary practice, she wrote about the "inspiration that opened to us the spiritual sense of the Bible," which "lifted us from disease and death" (169).

Further, "the Scriptures have both a literal and spiritual import, but the latter was the especial interpretation we received" (1875:260). "We had tried all" types of physicians "and failed to recover before learning this 'more excellent way.' . . . An accident once happening to us, would have proved fatal, but for the Truth herein stated, that saved us; hundreds of cases given over by materia medica and the minor hosts of Esculapius, we have since cured by it," she wrote, made possible by jettisoning "former beliefs." It was God, or the Principle of science, that "saved us," she reemphasized, "made us stronger in the Truth, and consequently more healthy ever since" (343).

These passages, obviously, referred to her experiences in 1866 and after. She recounted them in both phenomenal and religious terms, and they were followed by life events on a scale that was new for her: a proliferation of writings, new religious teaching, and, according to accounts by herself, her readers, and her critics, a successful healing ministry.

In addition, she referred to a phenomenal (not religious or teleological) discovery in 1864 "that science mentally applied would heal the sick" (1875:4). Based on our knowledge of Eddy's emerging independence in 1864, we can link this date to her healing of Ann Mary Jarvis. It could not have referred to

Quimby, whom she had met in 1862 and was beginning to question in 1864 (and by 1875, when she published this passage, understood as operating in a tradition different from her own).[4]

References to this revelatory disclosure and healing experience, and to this earlier, lesser or limited phenomenal discovery, coexisted throughout Eddy's first few editions without overlapping much. Their relationship initially did not seem entirely clear.

The earlier date, at least, was tentative. It seemed not much on her thought, and somehow difficult to specify, but she adjusted it to some degree. Revising it in 1878 had not been an option, as so much of the second printing was scrapped due to printer errors. Now in 1881, for no obvious reason, she modified it to "about 1864" (1881:6) and adjusted the object of the sentence (or content of her discovery at that time) to "the adaptation of metaphysics to the treatment of disease." Perhaps she revisited the many uncertainties she had felt in 1864. Whatever the case, she added a looseness to the date that shows her rethinking her discovery narrative without external prompting.

In 1883, the *Post* exchange provided plenty of prompting to prioritize this topic and speed up the process. As a result, Eddy noted the date of what she had described as divinely received and unified it with her descriptions of phenomenal discovery. Since her "discovery in 1866 of the divine science of Christian Healing," she wrote, she had "labored with tongue and pen to found this system" (1883:5–6). Having and sharing "revelations and discoveries that others have not," she had found, disturbed "the quiet surface of thought," and when this happens, "your good will be evil spoken of. This is the cross. Take it up, it wins the crown and wears it" (122).

This major discovery in the "winter of 1866" was divine with phenomenal effects (1883:6). She retained this description from then on, tweaking it a bit through its final iteration in 1907 (1907:107, 110). She also kept references to her experience with Jarvis and to earlier, more tentative events in a longer discovery process.

As always, she contended that in doing all this, she was following Jesus. "There is no question but Jesus understood Christian science, and taught the divine Principle to his students. The Bible contains it." Her goal was "to know in whom we had believed, to comprehend the sure footsteps of Truth, the way to health and holiness, to reach the Horeb height and sacred mount of revelation" (1883:86–87). Many, if not most, curative systems in the nineteenth century claimed to follow Jesus in some scientific way. Yet her particular articulation of how this worked was singular, based on her own experiences.

She used the term "Christian Science" five times in 1875 and linked "Christ healing" to salvation, Jesus, and her new discovery dozens of times. This had been clear enough to a set of clerical readers, who objected not that Eddy was unchristian but that she was an odd and unacceptable Christian. In 1881, she continued to expound at length on her system of "Christian healing." She increasingly and definitively referred to her religion as Christian Science after 1881, rather than as the Science of Life, though both terms remained in her book.

In substance, the way she presented her religion qua religion remained the same. What changed was within her discovery narrative, narrowly speaking, where two originary threads now combined in clear relationship to one another. Whatever discoveries she may have made prior to 1866, they amounted to phenomenal rather than religious observations that left teleological and other religious questions unresolved. Without events in 1866, they presumably would have remained that way, as those early experiences alone would not have produced *Science and Health*.

Dresser's complaint was that Eddy had once linked herself to Quimby after 1866, which these changes did not overtly address. Nothing was likely to convince him that Eddy was an independent agent, had been since they had known one another, and had eventually received a divine Self-disclosure. For Eddy, resolving the revelatory and phenomenal threads within her discovery narrative was key, whether or not that satisfied external concerns.

Those threads were two sides of the same coin for Eddy. If they coexisted in parallel to an extent early on, that was of no great theological import. Situationally, throughout her career, she sometimes emphasized the "scientific" identity of her text to inquirers, as in some phenomenally oriented passages in her book. To an inquirer named E. J. Smith, for example, she wrote at length in 1876 about the experiments with homeopathy that had prepared her to understand the mental nature of disease, then briefly mentioned the healing power of God he would learn about in her class.[5] An advertisement she placed in 1868 had taken the same tack.[6] In 1907, she emphasized her early medical experiments and her religion as a scientific discovery with court masters interviewing her as a defendant in a lawsuit.

Like her book overall, her early public-facing announcements were religious in nature. Several early advertisements emphasized *Science and Health* as a tome of biblical interpretation explaining the renewal of "Apostolic healing."[7] An 1868 poem published in the *Lynn Reporter* reads,

> Aid me to walk, Christ ever near
> To strengthen me.
> And fix my sight on God, the rock.[8]

As in her Genesis manuscript, she openly represented herself with a religious stance at the start of her public career. Her work overall contained an emphasis on both discovery and revelation, science and religion, and over many decades she highlighted one or the other in various situations, or both together.

Mores and propriety might partly explain why she sometimes chose phenomenal versus religious explanations. It was rather scandalous to announce she had received a divine message and would now explain it, especially as a divorced woman with few means who controversially stepped out as an author in 1875. Around this time, Eddy was "charged with rouging her cheeks and dyeing her hair, with teaching 'free love' and practicing witchcraft, with being a loose woman . . . a medium, a fraud, a termagant," probably sharpening her already strong words against the "free-love" movement led by Victoria Woodhull.[9] Conversely, some audiences might have received a religious message from a woman more readily than one intruding on scientific territory.

Eddy's concern for propriety (which as we have seen had not only reputational but personal safety dimensions) seems still to have mixed with a degree of hesitancy. Literary modesty was more seemly for an authoress, blunting the audacious and unladylike intrusions into science, theology, and medicine. She was willing to go out on a limb to champion her explanation of a man's approach to cure in the 1860s and beyond. After concluding in 1872 that her own practice should be championed, she was initially more reticent.[10]

Again, though, these factors do not necessarily furnish reasons for her to relay parts of the phenomenal and revelatory elements of her discovery narrative separately at first. Most centrally and obviously, the explanation lies in her developing understanding of her own experience.

Eddy had fully claimed her 1866 experience of divine revelation and reception by 1872, but in 1882, she was still deciding how to fully name and explain it, particularly as it related to her earlier phenomenal discoveries. Perhaps the death that year of Gilbert, her last traditional male protector, pushed her to prioritize this. Prompted uncomfortably in 1883, she finally resolved the matter. If some publicly declared that any of this excluded her from making a revelatory claim, so be it. Her focus would remain on explaining an event she hardly understood at first but that grew clearer through compounding experience.

IN THIS MANNER, Eddy came to publicly and finally identify her 1866 experience as both a historically specific moment of discovery within a longer process and an incomparable, out-of-time revelatory disclosure. This merged the original impetus of her text after 1866 with her life's ongoing growth and development, producing a book that fully named and explained both.

Her *discovery* can be thought of as a tripartite process encompassing the year she claimed to experience an unparalleled moment of discovery that was also a *revelation*. First, 1845 to 1865 were experimental years during which she gradually discovered much about the mental nature of human health and illness, years in which some events and observations held particular significance.

Religion was present but not linked to these events in a clear fashion. Second, the year 1866 encapsulated a pivotal moment known as the discovery of Christian Science, which was also God's Self-revelation to her. "The first was the enlightenment of the human understanding," she explained later; "the second was the revelation from [God], divine Mind."[11]

This combined revelation and discovery event mapped to Sunday afternoon, 4 February 1866, when she claimed to experience a divine Self-disclosure that healed her of a grave injury and that she later identified as Christian Science. It also related to an unspecified moment in the "latter part of 1866" when she claimed to gain a decisive understanding of this event and began working to capture that understanding in writing.[12] Third, between roughly 1867 and 1872 she sought to understand this revelatory discovery experience through intensive Bible study: how it related and fit into her discovery process overall, how it did and did not relate to previous experiences and explanations, how to now explain it herself in teaching and text.

In the 1880s, Eddy published early iterations of a pamphlet, *Historical Sketch of Metaphysical Healing*, with an origin narrative that names the elements of this type of tripartite process (along with many other topics), retaining parts in her book. When she released her book's major 1891 revision, she also expanded the pamphlet narrative into what can be perhaps best described as her spiritual autobiography, *Retrospection and Introspection*. This narrative is full of things she says she did not know, might still be discerning, and learned over time, which matches her sense about Christian Science in 1875: that she had "grown to its discovery" (1875:379).

Back then she had written in the first person plural or "royal we," literally not naming herself directly within her own experience. As authorial modes changed, it is fitting that by the time she completed her narrative of origination and discovery, she referred to herself in the first person singular as "I" and "myself." In the 1870s, she claimed her own experiences. During the 1880s, she fully named herself within them.

Eddy's overall narrative of religious origins is strictly dated, concise, and absolute at the same time it remains loose, lengthy, and relative. It names a specific point of emergence existing within a range. It is both gradual and sudden, both process and event. This both/and viewpoint is key to understanding her book's origins and development.

I cannot verify what revelation and discovery meant to Eddy religiously or prove with academic tools whether she experienced either. Instead, I point to these textual developments as part of the historical record of her religion. I also note that they signaled but one of many debates in the 1880s about Christian Science origins and identity, as we will soon see.

CHAPTER TWELVE

Holy and Unholy Challenges: Divine Healing and Theosophy
(1886–1890)

In which divine healers and Christian Scientists share some views and also elbow one another over actual or perceived differences; in which Eddy's Christian commitments and the esoteric convictions of Theosophists mutually repel one another; in which emergent New Thought accommodates the theosophically inflected eclectic healing views neither Christian Science nor divine healing can absorb; and in which the leading public perception of Christian Science as an unorthodox Christianity continues to morph into multiple conflicting definitions by decade's end

MOST AMERICANS in 1887 were familiar with the term "Christian Science," but no one seemed to agree on its definition, much less associate it with a single denomination. An article that year in *The Century* described the scene this way:

> To many [the words "Christian Science"] have no definite meaning, and long conversations are carried on concerning them in which the most diverse views are maintained, ending in confusion and contradiction, because those who converse have not a uniform conception of the signification of the terms. Some declare Christian Science and Mind Cure to be the same; others stoutly deny this, and seek to establish a radical distinction. Some represent Christian Science as a great advance upon ordinary Christianity; others denounce it as but refined Pantheism; while many more brand both Christian Science and Mind Cure as delusion, a reaction from the uncompromising materialism of the age.[1]

The decade had opened with far more agreement. In the early 1880s readers were split on whether Eddy's book effectively engaged the Bible, but not on whether that was its goal. The suggestion that it was mesmeric hung on in pockets, as it did with unorthodoxies of all stripes. Yet in 1882, the highest-profile media coverage of Christian Science portrayed it as a new Christian movement restoring apostolic healing.

Five years later, public understanding of Christian Science as Christian was but one of many "diverse views" in circulation, so many that conversations on the topic inevitably ended in "confusion and contradiction." Eddy still described *Science and Health* as explainer of the Bible, textbook for Christian healing, and accelerator of global salvation, a triad that centrally shaped Christian Science self-identity even as public perceptions wound about in multiple directions that continue today. She also fine-tuned her theological statements in response to this diversity of perceptions.[2]

Yet ironically, just as she noted that her book became clearer, cultural conditions touching its reception became decidedly messier. The emergence of divine healing and Theosophy were key to this situation. These new nodes on the networks of American religions exploded with heavy traffic in the 1880s, as did Christian Science.

Eddy might have echoed the divine healer A. J. Gordon when he lamented how many ministers felt "the age of miracles passed away with the apostolic period."[3] He might have echoed her when she wrote in a letter, "Our Father is everywhere present and it is His presence and power that heals . . . not the power of one mind over another."[4] This speaks to a certain connection between Christian Science and divine healing. Heather Curtis notes that "doctrinal differences aside, the fact was that at some level, faith cure and Christian Science did seem to propose a similar hermeneutics of healing."[5]

Yet those doctrinal differences were the basis of significant disagreements between the two sects. Gordon recognized Eddy's claim to produce, as his son later put it, "an inspired commentary on Jesus' words—a new revelation," but judged her claim "as pretentious as that of Swedenborg or the Utah Saints."[6] Eddy disagreed with a basis for divine healing in faith that could be reduced to belief, rather than faith that amounted to spiritual understanding of divine law.

Some unorthodoxies that Gordon associated with Christian Science, however, were actually elements Eddy objected to as well: pantheism, Theosophy, and Buddhist and gnostic influences. As we will see, her teachings on this were not entirely visible to him for the same reasons they became obscured across American culture generally.

As the 1880s opened, Theosophy was just emerging and not much in anyone's field of vision. As it came into view, Eddy first assumed those with a theosophical background would drop such enchanted interests once involved in her teachings. As the decade wore on and her understanding of Theosophy grew along with the movement itself, she identified a concentrated type of Antichrist in theosophical influence, as did Gordon.

Meanwhile, theosophically inclined inquirers into Christian Science brought their preexisting religious inclinations to bear on Eddy's teachings, which they viewed through esoteric, broadly Emersonian lenses that she and the majority of her students did not claim or embrace. Unlike Gordon, such inquirers were attracted to the unorthodoxies of Christian Science. Yet as their contact with Christian Science deepened, this gave way to the reality that though radically innovative, its theology was inflexibly Christian. As Gillian Gill writes, this group "could not understand or accept the exclusively Christian cast of her thought. They found intellectual nourishment and spiritual inspiration in Eastern religions" and decried "her refusal to place the Upanishads or the Koran on the same plane as the Gospels."[7]

Confronted with how firmly even Eddy's most unorthodox teachings were rooted in a biblical framework, the eclectically minded interested in spiritual healing could not turn to the divine healing movement. They instead built an emergent mind-cure movement into a new religious option, New Thought, which drew on theosophical and assorted traditions as well as reconstituted and advanced the mesmeric tradition Eddy had so roundly rejected. Unable to actually mix these traditions with Eddy's opposing teachings, they instead "juxtaposed" them, as we will see, in their prolific writings.

The rejection of special revelation as a valid religious tenet was a central precept in theosophical and New Thought teachings. These adherents therefore defined Eddy's work as not specially revealed to or belonging to herself. The universe owned it, they contended, and thus they freely reused and reframed her wording in plagiarisms and elsewhere.

The controversies that arose have usually been cast in scholarship in terms of personality clashes, but I emphasize here that they constituted significant theological differences. Further, New Thought and theosophically adjacent perceptions of Christian Science circulated widely and heavily influenced public thought, and this extended to the claim that Eddy herself and Christian Science were part of this eclectic pantheon, over her objections and despite the substance of her own textual and experiential religious identity.

Christian inquirers proliferated as well, such as O. P. Gifford, who championed Christian Science while conducting his own influential Baptist ministry. This group found much to align with in the new Christian Science religious tenets while remaining committed to their own denominations. Certainly dabblers and experimenters existed, as did those who were serially or simultaneously interested in any number of these phenomena at once.

Perceptions of what constituted Christian Science shifted radically from one group and individual to another. The robust cultural confusion that arose around this diversity of conflicting views was not simplistic nor minor, and it obscured basic theological points. We begin to unpack this story with a consideration of Gordon and others in his milieu.

DURING THE nineteenth century, many Protestants began to challenge cessationism, the teaching that biblical healing had ceased after the apostolic era. By the early twentieth century, a group of neo-cessationists had coalesced, notably Fundamentalists, Jehovah's Witnesses, the Churches of Christ, and old-school Presbyterians (of whom Benjamin Warfield [*Counterfeit Miracles*, 1918] became most representative). As this group took shape, however, most North American Protestants grappled not with whether Christ heals the flesh but through what means.

Liberal Protestants could no longer embrace miracles in terms of suspended physical or natural law, as they now agreed science proved those laws ascendant. Some refigured miracles in terms of the redirection of natural law. Others introduced a reworked Calvinist predestination in the form of God's foreordination of each healing event.[8] Others began to reconceive God's healing power operating specifically and only through biomedical means.

Divine healers held to yet another model that both resonated with and differed from Christian Science. Curtis notes that A. J. Gordon, who associated with the divine healer and fellow Bostonian Charles Cullis in the early 1870s and became fully committed during Dwight L. Moody's 1877 campaign, was cautious and moderate "in his attempts to articulate the tenets of divine healing."[9] He wrote his influential *Ministry of Healing, or, Miracles of Cure in All Ages* while circulating among other notables in the movement such as W. E. Boardman, Carrie Judd Montgomery, A. B. Simpson, Robert Livingston Stanton, and R. Kelso Carter.

Rather than insisting, as did others, Gordon suggested that healing was a by-product or intrinsic characteristic of the atonement of Jesus. The movement eventually came to embrace "healing in the atonement" alongside "signs-gifts" healing, or a view of healing as a special sign or gift from God. Pentecostals and charismatics would later pick up on both explanations. Both Gordon and later charismatic healers used the term "miraculous" to mean, in essence, *spiritually natural*, though they retained the word "miracle" to preserve the mystique of God's nature.

As Donald Dayton notes, divine healers sometimes saw atonement-based cures as a by-product of the second blessing, indicating its Holiness orientation.[10] Similarly, the historian Samuel S. Hill notes that Christian Science and the Holiness movement emerged as the most distinct new postbellum denominational identities, and however different, both "share the deep level of conviction that God is very near, His power so manifest and accessible. What others regarded as supernatural or miraculous seemed to Mary Baker Eddy and her followers just the way a loving, all-powerful God is and how naturally He incorporates divine power into human frailty to overcome it." In addition, "classic cosmic dualism," whether ontic or epistemic, "is dealt heavy blows by these disparate movements."[11] Such theological elements accompanied the surge in spiritual healing that came to the fore in the postbellum United States.

Both divine healers and Christian Scientists began with God's sovereignty and goodness, concluding it is always his will to heal. They defined healing in terms of natural spiritual law, not as miracle per se or supernatural intervention. Eddy defined that law in singular and specific terms. Yet for her as well, Christian healing allowed participants "to understand wherefore Jesus suffered and triumphed" (1875:306). "Atonement is oneness with God . . . whereby sickness, sin, and death, are destroyed" (296), a oneness Jesus lived for the benefit and example of others.

In practice, this required prayerfully reaching beyond the testimony of the material senses to perceive God's presence and power, until human thought and physical evidence yielded to God's will. This might take persistence, or it might happen in a moment of immediate, atoning unity with God. Christian Scientists found this approach in records of early Christian healing.[12] Divine healers counseled and required one another to "claim" healing before the physical evidence complied. "Both movements," writes Curtis, "counseled sick persons to question the reliability of sensory evidence in order to overcome illness and its effects. . . . [H]ealing required an ability to act on a belief grounded in a divine truth that lay beyond the body."[13]

The historian Robert Bruce Mullin notes the sacramental nature of Protestant healing in the nineteenth century, which he describes in Anglican terms as a priestly anointing or gift. Pamela Klassen documents how Anglicans renewed their practice of "blessed oil" healing rituals in direct response to Christian Science healing. To Gordon, oil anointing was a "sacramental profession of faith in Jesus Christ as the Divine Physician acting through the Holy Ghost."[14]

Through such practices, writes Curtis, "individuals enacted their separation from sin and sensuality, and acknowledged their consecration to God."[15] As Eddy put it, in a world "of sin and sensuality hastening to greater development of power," Christian healing brought holy consecration to individuals (1875:107; 1911:102). Both Gordon and Eddy saw the gospel of healing renewing Protestant life and securing its relevance in the modern era of science. Both made space for some persistence of Christian healing across time and space on the basis that the Holy Spirit had always existed in the world, while both still claimed restorationist goals.

Profound differences also existed. Eddy defined faith as advancing beyond belief to spiritual understanding. Gordon's *Ministry of Healing* calls physical health a sign of redemption that must precede full salvation, while Eddy classed physical health the "smallest part of Christian Science," the "buglecall" to higher attainments, and found that in some cases, the sick or atypically formed may be morally better than those who bask, self-satisfied, in perfect health.[16] "Losing a limb or injuring [bodily] structure," she wrote, "is sometimes the quickener of manliness," and someone in this position "presents more nobility than the statuesque athlete" at times (1878:88). This sentence stayed essentially the same through her final edition, which denotes "loss of a limb or injury to a tissue" (1911:127).

To some extent, faith healers and Christian Scientists held different views of the Godhead as person (or the infinite Person, as Eddy put it, not patterned after limited mortal personality). Gordon and Eddy also defined crucial terms such as "belief" and "illusion" differently from one another.

Most significantly, Eddy could not identify a fully systematic explanation of faith healing. She therefore felt it operated, like mesmerism, on "belief" or "mental blindness," which "admits Truth without understanding it" rather than saying with Paul, "I know in whom I have believed."[17] Gordon also accepted the traditional Christian doctrine of a spiritual soul in a material body, which Eddy called pantheistic. She found God, or Soul, expressed not *in* but *by* all things individually, through reflection. She therefore called Gordon's reference to a "forgiven soul in a sick body" pantheistic and unscriptural.[18] The general assessment was mutual.

At times, their disagreements were more superficial. Gordon was especially concerned that "denying the existence of matter led to antinomianism in practice," as Curtis put it, that is, to indulging in sin on the dissembling basis that it did not exist.[19] Eddy's view of matter as "the things that do appear," to be redeemed for and through the things of the Spirit that actually are, led her to a different conclusion.

Thus, according to historian Beryl Satter, "Eddy's outlook was close to the orthodox Christianity of her day: one repented of sin by recognizing one's dependence on God's power."[20] Excusing or hiding sin, she wrote in 1881, "shall be found out and punished" (1881:138). In 1886 she added, "The avoidance of justice and denial of Truth tends to perpetuate sin, invoke crime, jeopardize self-control, and mock divine mercy" (1886:466). Gordon's critique and others like it, however, probably caused her to clarify and augment such statements in her book's next editions.

PUBLIC RESPONSES to both divine healing and Christian Science often tended toward marginalization, ridicule, and dismissal, as Morton Kelsey notes.[21] A popular Methodist author, Minnie Willis Baines-Miller, wrote a best-selling novel on the "fallacy" of faith healing followed by another on the "half-truths" of Christian Science.[22] Just before the Progressive Era, mainstream Protestants began to develop their central position on the symbiotic nature of spirituality and biomedicine largely in opposition to these groups of healers and later Pentecostals.

"For all Protestants, the Bible . . . served as the standard to judge modes of Christian healing," writes Klassen, but using "the Bible as a basis for healing became newly contentious" in the quickly medicalizing twentieth century. The pace of that medicalization process, she shows, resulted in part from liberal or mainstream Protestants defining biomedicine as a divine agent in a conscious counterstrategy to the perceived heresies of divine healing and Eddy's Christian Science.[23]

The outré reputation of faith healing within the orthodox Protestant community resulted in Gordon maintaining a parallel divine healing ministry. In his role as a popular Baptist minister, he acted as superintendent at the phenomenally popular series of Monday lectures at Boston's Tremont Temple run by the Reverend Joseph Cook.

This was where Gordon and Eddy most memorably crossed paths. After Gordon issued a public letter against Christian Science in early 1885, the Christian Scientist Joshua Bailey visited him and reported to the Christian Scientist Association that he "thought he left good seed with Dr. Gordon." Instead, Cook borrowed a copy of *Science and Health*, declining an interview with its author, and roundly denounced both at a Monday lecture a few days later.

Bailey then wrote Gordon, "We, as Christians, do not wish any controversy [but] feel that your letter was unjust and did not represent at all what Christian Science is." Appealing to Gordon's Christian charity, Bailey asked "the privilege of presenting this subject just for a few moments, to the same audience before which you denounce it."[24] Gordon and Cook gave Eddy ten minutes at the next Monday lecture.

Eddy's talk in Tremont Temple, delivered on 16 March 1885, has been well-documented by biographers. In her address to the skeptical crowd, she touched on basic points clarifying Christian Science theology and practice. For someone who once had been a longtime Congregational church member and now sought to reach the clergy with her new views of God, the stony reception she received must have seemed tantamount to shunning. By all accounts, she found the experience exceptionally difficult.

In May, Gordon was arrested for speaking on Boston Common and had to bail himself out of jail, which Eddy took as vindication. An article she published at this time titled "Veritas Odium Parit" ("Truth Begets Hatred") decried what she called the "materialistic portion of the pulpit and press in 1885" and the sex-based discrimination that often fueled or thickly layered clerical rejection of her religion.[25]

During this decade, Eddy revised her book in ways that reflected her interactions and observations around faith healing. She increased passages that linked faith with understanding and augmented her description of miracles in terms of spiritual natural law. For about a decade, her book carried a brief comment differentiating Christian Science from "faith cure." After the 1900 edition, she dropped the term "faith cure" but kept the major concepts in different parts of her book.

For his part, Gordon echoed earlier clerics in nearly every respect. He accepted the fact that Christian Scientists healed but rejected their unorthodoxies. Instead of dismissing Christian Science by comparing it to Spiritualism (which by the 1880s was becoming passé), he compared it to psychological modes of healing then newly ascendant. In his 1886 piece "Christian Science Tested by Scripture," which eventually circulated in many editions, he regarded Christian Science as a form of mind cure by attributing its healing agency to the powers of the personal human mind. Psychological modes of cure were not in themselves offensive to Gordon, who noted that this principle was "beginning to be recognized as of great value by eminent physicians." (Both he and Eddy objected, however, when the Methodist minister James Monroe Buckley, editor of the *Christian Advocate* from 1880 to 1912, classed them together as varied forms of psychological healing including "animal magnetism, mesmerism, Spiritualism, Mormonism, [and] Roman Catholicism.")[26]

However he might explain Eddy's approach, however, Gordon considered her a purveyor of "false doctrines" that "entangle others." Like Eddy, and echoing Bailey's letter to him, Gordon wrote "from no love of controversy" or "personal ill-will . . . but for the warning of Christians."[27] In part, divine healers were concerned about the attraction of their members to Christian Science. "Loath to have their movement regarded as spiritually regressive," writes Curtis, they presented divine healing as the authentic healing practice against which Christian Science failed to measure up—though it might seem to embody "some finer quality of Christianity."[28]

Despite their disagreements, whether substantial or fleeting, Eddy sometimes approved of Gordon's divine healing in practice, with caveats. In 1885 she praised the sincerity and Christianity of faith-healing adherents, whose "practice is in advance of their theory."[29] In 1887, she approvingly quoted a recent sermon by Gordon in which he exhorted the church to accept scriptural teachings fully, including the duty to heal as Jesus commanded. She then threw a curveball by describing Gordon's views as "wholesome avowals of Christian Science."[30] Eddy always held that her system led the vanguard of Christianity.[31]

Dayton has noted that in comparison with other faith healers, Gordon "worked out his teachings on healing somewhat . . . in dialogue with the emerging Christian Science of Mary Baker Eddy."[32] This may be a rather polite way to put it, if we single out the Tremont Temple episode, but it is essentially accurate. For a time Eddy, too, worked out her statement of Christian Science partly in dialogue with Gordon. Their exchanges seem to have had another effect, as well. The year after their public clash, Christian Scientist Association records report her indicating, "There is a great work to be done with the clergy. They have got to be talked with lovingly."[33] She would increasingly emphasize heart-based appeals over attempts to win by argument.[34]

In keeping with this pietistic sense, Eddy wrote in the historical sketch of her religion she published around this time that "Christian Science is the most evangelical religion on earth."[35] If any "so-called evangelical church" did not see this, she explained, this was because its judgment rested on merely sensory rather than spiritual evidence.

SOME PERCEIVED differences between Christian Science and divine healing were just that: perceived, not actual. This pointed to another matter altogether.

The most ominous problem Gordon found in *Science and Health*, his son later asserted, was a link to "pantheistic and Buddhistic principles." In this, he rejoined Eddy's earlier charge of pantheism against his father's book. To illustrate his point, however, he chose a book written in the mesmeric tradition by Warren Felt Evans, citing his "Hindu metaphysics" as an example of Christian Science.[36] Evans was in fact a clairvoyant and eclectic author whose work opposed Eddy's and vice versa. The reason for the mix-up will soon become clear. In 1887, Gordon Sr. agreed with most early observers and critics that Christian Scientists "are in some way effecting marked cures; nor do we charge them with practising any wilful imposture." However, he objected to it on the basis that he classified Christian Science as an emergent and devilish form of Theosophy. Given Eddy's detailed theological track record contrary to Theosophy, the *Christian Science Journal* had curt words for Gordon on this point. It noted that when it came to Theosophy, he had "as much fellowship with it as we."[37]

This was true. The Theosophical Society was founded in New York in 1875 by esoteric spiritualists who conceived its teachings as a merging of Hermetic or occult science and religion that would show all ancient and modern beliefs, Christianity included, to be rooted in, and reducible to, occult philosophy and "pagan origins."[38] It held that Asian religions, Buddhism in particular (or more precisely an understanding of these filtered through Western lenses), best embodied grand, ancient truths. Karma and reincarnation were central tenets. Its adherents organized to varying degrees, particularly after an 1895 schism, but generally emphasized individualism over institution.

Theosophy was a major point of division between Christian Scientists and a certain type of esoteric inquirer who investigated Eddy's religion, sometimes in depth, but ultimately felt unable to stay. As I have more fully detailed elsewhere, Ursula Newell Gestefeld provides a key example.[39]

Gestefeld took an 1884 class in Christian Science from Eddy in Chicago. They maintained a warm correspondence for several months in 1886 and 1887. Gestefeld shared insights and asked for advice from her teacher; Eddy provided counsel and encouragement. As it became clear that Gestefeld's Christian commitments might be mixed with other religious interests, Eddy wished to hear what Gestefeld's "feelings are on the *Christian* side of this Cause," adding that this "is the only side—it forms the other three sides of it."[40]

Gestefeld fell silent for over three months, reticent about recently joining the Chicago Theosophical Society.[41] Eddy later noted that she found Warren Felt Evans's work "incorrect" and "disheartening," asking Gestefeld if she were willing to leave it behind while promoting Christian Science literature.[42] Gestefeld, who had been pursuing some eclectic and esoteric publishing activities throughout this period, again did not answer the query.

Soon, she began to grapple with her view of Eddy's religious role and its value. If Eddy "were wiped off the face of the earth to-morrow, Christian Science would hold the place it has won for itself," Gestefeld wrote. In response, Eddy first wrote to John Linscott (who with his fiancée, Ellen Brown, had become somewhat of a confidant, and who was then a Gestefeld associate) that she gave Gestefeld "much credit for acting up to her sense of justice" in other parts of the article.[43]

She then addressed, with deep feeling, the implication that her role as the founder of Christian Science was temporary and had already passed its usefulness. She expressed this in terms of following Jesus more closely and drinking the Communion cup more deeply than those to whom she had introduced Christian Science might comprehend. Before passing on, she hoped she might find a student who would acknowledge her as "the person whom God has appointed to do this work" and recognize "the Principle" she had given everything for. Eddy then set aside these concerns by turning Godward: "Let the human heart be still, and know that His ways are not ours, and He will do what is best for His own."[44]

Gestefeld is not incidental to this letter, but neither is she its main subject. She is a touchstone to larger religious issues. Without discussing her theosophical commitments with Eddy, they both now found these had caused Gestefeld to embrace eclectic texts and reject the idea of special religious leadership. In the theosophical view, Eddy's truth was the truth not only of Jesus but also of the mahatmas and yogis of ancient and modern times, "hold[ing] the place it has won for itself" on its own accord, incidental to the individuals involved. In the Christian Science view, it was the truth only of Jesus Christ, now articulated in the modern era by someone "whom God has appointed," Mary Baker Eddy. These differences went to the very heart of religious identity.

After this exchange, Gestefeld's theosophical commitments deepened, and Eddy no longer sought to advise or influence her. Yet the growth of the theosophical movement in the 1880s caused dynamics such as this to multiply. "Unless a great and radical change is effected by *pure* Christianity," Eddy wrote to Ellen Brown in early 1887, "our Cause will disappear and the schools of Gnosticism and Theosophy, vice and crime will take the place of Chr[istian] Sci[ence]."[45]

Several of her letters in the late 1880s issue warnings against esotericism and Theosophy in the starkest of terms. Her writings had always eschewed the various elements of these traditions, including Spiritualism, reincarnation, pantheism, and paganism (and the free-love movement that overlapped with some of these). She now began to reject not only the elements of Theosophy but also the movement itself by name much more actively.

In August 1887, Eddy published *Christian Science: No and Yes*, containing several anti-theosophical passages she had revised and refined over the past two years.[46] This was followed by *Rudimental Divine Science* in November, the same month her theosophically oriented mind-cure opponents (several from Chicago) held a convention in Boston.[47] A typical *No and Yes* passage reads, "No greater opposites can be conceived of, physically, morally, and spiritually, than Christian Science, spiritualism, and theosophy."[48] Her next major revision of *Science and Health* included three similar passages, a number that grew in subsequent editions.[49]

SIMULTANEOUSLY, in a parallel universe, the Russian émigré and undisputed theosophical leader Helena Blavatsky sharpened her teaching against special revelation in general and Christianity in particular. In the 1870s and into the 1880s, Blavatsky had occasionally allowed for revelation but in general defined a Theosophist (after Henry Vaughan) as one who "has not revelation, but an inspiration of his own." Vaughan, she taught, was also correct that "every great thinker and philosopher, especially every founder of a new religion, school of philosophy, or sect, is necessarily a Theosophist."[50]

In reducing all "great" religious persons to a theosophical framework, Blavatsky operated within her own type of particularism in which no true religion could exist outside Theosophy. In autumn 1887, she compounded this teaching by contrasting "dogma" and one of its prime examples, "Christian revelation," with "Eastern wisdom." This distinction became fundamental to theosophical teaching, which held that accepting authority from one who claimed Christian revelation was dogmatic and anathema. As the Theosophist J. J. van der Leeuw would later write, from the inception of the movement, "realization" had always predominated in Theosophy to the exclusion of "revelation." Revelation, he judged, involves a "hierarchic system" in which "the authority of superiors is not to be questioned and the slightest hint is an order not to be criticised but to be obeyed." Therefore, "we must sharply distinguish revelation from authority."[51]

In the wake of such developments, Gestefeld found that her two religious interests repelled one another absolutely and could not be reconciled. Lodged in this untenable limbo, she redoubled her focus on the theme of Eddy's expendability, arguing that it should be broadly recognized so others (notably Gestefeld herself) could take over the explanation of Christian Science identity as a theosophical teaching.

To this end, Gestefeld delivered an 1888 statement on Christian Science in a series of lectures, then sold these in pamphlets and as a book.[52] As she wrote in the leading theosophical magazine *Lucifer* later in 1888, "Instead of being the 'Buddhist,' or the 'Yoga' science," Christian Science "is the science of those sciences individually and collectively. It reveals what they conceal" and "is the interior meaning of the four gospels."[53] Like others, writes Stephen Gottschalk, she sought to "link [Eddy's] teachings with various forms . . . of Eastern religious thought" that had been "popularized" within Western culture.[54]

Gestefeld's statement roughly paralleled that of the theosophically oriented Emma Curtis Hopkins, who sought to unite Eddy's teachings with those of the esoteric Warren Felt Evans. As Catherine L. Albanese puts it, "Evans was theosophical; Eddy was not. Hopkins did not unify their teaching but rather juxtaposed it" in her most well-known work, paying only "lip service to Eddy."[55] Following theosophical logic that eschewed special divine appointments and reduced all religions to itself—that is, that saw all religions as varied subsets of theosophical truths—Hopkins ran a Christian Science institute and widely advertised her creation as Christian Science itself.

Gestefeld's book followed suit. Lifting paragraphs and sections nearly verbatim from Eddy's book, she juxtaposed them with theosophical teachings throughout. This type of plagiarism was an increasing problem for many authors, given the absence of consistent copyright law and relatively lax and shifting standards of literary "borrowing" in the nineteenth century.

The historian Meredith McGill outlines a "culture of reprinting" that made this common. As Andrew Ventimiglia shows, Eddy was at the forefront of religionists responding proactively to a copyright situation with rapidly overturning norms and shifting parts. From the time an early 1880s pamphlet "egregiously plagiarized Eddy's works" through the 1890s, he writes, she employed intellectual property and copyright law "to fight back against [excessive] quotation" by New Thought adherents who approached her teachings as "simply truths—like scientific facts" and thus not under copyright protection.[56]

Several books appeared during this time, Robert Peel writes, that either "railed against her" or else "praised her . . . and claimed her sanction for ideas and practices which she had explicitly disapproved."[57] Gestefeld's *Statement of Christian Science* did a bit of both. As she later explained in a circular, it was "not intended to supplant *Science and Health*" but was "offered as a key for those who are unable to discern its meaning." The Christian Science textbook, she judged, was too "difficult of comprehension."[58]

Others thought so too, such as the abolitionist, prison reformer, and activist Abigail Hopper Gibbons, who wrote to her friend Sally in 1888, "Do not for a moment believe that I am converted to Christian Science. No, verily. It takes those who need occupation to see '*Truth*' as they see it." Reading material was sent to her house uninvited, "by whom I cannot say," so she let the issues "drift in all directions" rather than accumulate and bother her.[59]

Given the diversity of claimants to the Christian Science name at the time, it is not possible to verify which organization supplied Gibbons with reading material, but it is clear that plenty of readers disbelieved Eddy's book. A class of testifiers in the Christian Science magazines stated they did not comprehend it at first, laid it aside or threw it down in annoyance, then returned to it later. Others like Gibbons remained annoyed or nonplussed.

Gibbons and those like her set aside Eddy's book and went on with their own projects. The theosophically minded, in contrast, exhibited a religious and personal mandate to claim it as their own. (As Blavatsky put it, "Every founder of a new religion . . . is necessarily a Theosophist.") Eddy declared Christian Science as her own religious discovery and an expression of revelatory Christianity, which Theosophists and the theosophically adjacent tended to see as myopic, needlessly proprietary, and egocentric behavior that was religiously inaccurate.

This theosophically derived characterization of Eddy circulated massively after the 1880s and became a staple in some threads of historiography in later years. Such viewpoints predominated within a vocal minority we might call Christian Science "esoteric inquirers"—those who, like Gestefeld, either casually or intensely explored Christian Science along with other religions, affiliated with it for a brief time, but ultimately could not reconcile it with preexisting commitments to mystical enchantment they chose to prioritize and develop instead.

Here was the root of A. J. Gordon's mix-up. Given their religious views regarding the reducible and interchangeable nature of all religions, esoteric inquirers into Christian Science branded their eclectic ventures with terminology from Eddy's book, which they treated as universal property without authorship rights and figured as an inspired text alongside the Upanishads, Bible, Quran, and Gita. Some favored Christian texts and traditions, but never exclusively. This became a widespread and significant source of cultural confusion.

When Gestefeld's *Statement of Christian Science* came out, Eddy jotted a few terse comments to a student who asked about it, then dropped the matter.[60] Eventually the *Christian Science Journal* published some brief letters from anonymous Christian Scientists about it. One saw "the same difference between Mrs. Gestefeld's Lectures and [*Science and Health*], that I do between the zeal of Saul and the zeal of Paul. Her lectures lack regeneration. She has not yet been to Damascus." The editors added, "Can a Theosophist be a Christian Scientist?"[61] The question, of course, was rhetorical.

The episode was not quite over, however. Gestefeld soon produced a pamphlet with a title sure to strike a chord with the widespread nativist and anti-Catholic sentiments of the era: *Jesuitism in Christian Science*. Its main argument was familiar, though buried in almost fifty pages of fiery invective: the Christian Science movement had matured beyond its "mother" and no longer needed her. To argue otherwise was "Jesuitism."[62]

Again, the piece barely registered in Eddy's correspondence.[63] She immediately drafted a few responses for publication, though, and published a few lines in the *Journal*.[64] The crux of her most urgent, and therefore probably first, draft was to "rescue" her "child," Christian Science, of which Gestefeld was making a "prey" of plagiarism and Theosophy. "Though a Christian Scientist in name," she wrote, Gestefeld "is a member of the Theosophical Society."[65] Her final critique of Gestefeld's 1888 book referred to the esoteric symbol on its cover: "She who would chain the eye of God and hold it in her hand, needs to know the lesson of the cross and crown."[66] This underscores the religious, not personal, nature of their disagreement.

Gestefeld was still a member of a local branch of the Christian Science church in Chicago, which found itself split between urging her reform and excommunication. Eddy wrote advocating the first, then the second, but withdrew when the local pastor begged her off in stinging prose.

"Rest assured that I should never have named your dealings with Mrs. Gesterfeld [sic] if it had not first been named to me," she wrote to him. "I shall take not further notice of the matter. . . . I wish her no harm." This hands-off approach is not much explored in literature on Christian Science, but it appears in many of Eddy's dealings with students and branch churches. Her final words on the episode were, "I hope this will drop now and forever and that you will retain her as a member if you think best."⁶⁷ Ultimately the Chicago church voted Gestefeld off its rolls, but she had in substance, and probably in fact, already left.

Gestefeld pursued a career in the emerging New Thought movement, which accommodated her eclectic religious leanings. She referred to Eddy and her work frequently in later years, always in deeply conflicted terms. The *Christian Science Journal* grappled with several of the larger problems raised by this episode—Theosophy, plagiarism, Eddy's leadership—in ensuing years, though rarely mentioning names. Eddy treated such topics seriously and to varying degrees in her writings, though her letters mention Gestefeld only once more, incidentally in 1893.

MOST SEPARATIONS OF this type were far less dramatic. The noted political activist, children's book author, and prodigiously butter-loving, stocking-knitting, and eclectic-leaning religionist Abby Morton Diaz called herself an "inquirer" and owned the second edition of *Science and Health*. She wrote to Eddy that she found much "narrowness" and "antagonism and bitterness" against Christian Science in some sectors, and she produced a defensive tract explaining her perceptions of the religion.⁶⁸

"You may not agree with me," she told Eddy, "but I know you will give me credit for acting up to my light, and doing as nearly right as I can."⁶⁹ Eddy wrote back using the rural folk language of her youth that occasionally surfaced: "saw you was true to my statement" to an extent, but she did in fact disagree with how the tract juxtaposed other teachings with "the great Truth I have introduced at this period."⁷⁰ She invited Diaz to take a class in 1885, but Diaz was too involved in social justice and reform work to promise regular attendance and therefore declined. She was a member of the Christian Socialist Society (which Baptist and Episcopal clergy supported as a type of applied Christianity) and lecturer for the Free Religious Association.

Quiet exchanges like theirs have not been much explored in the history of Christian Science, but they were far more common than not. Diaz is representative of a changing relationship between Christian Scientists and social reformers in 1880s. Social justice workers tended to be drawn to Christian Science for its unorthodoxy, its emphasis on a wholly loving God, and its relatively egalitarian polity. They immediately encountered Eddy's core message that their political causes were to be guided and sometimes censured by Christian Science, not vice versa. Diaz and other political activists such as Susan B. Anthony could not honestly accept this position. They backed away from Christian Science to continue on their own paths.

This increasingly meant contributing to emergent New Thought, which embraced their eclecticism. In 1886, Diaz became a contributor to *Mental Science Magazine* run by Emma Curtis Hopkins and another former esoteric inquirer into Christian Science. Diaz's first article opens by citing the Bible, Hindu and Persian passages, a French philosopher, Channing and Emerson, and an "Oriental poem." "Christianity, like other great religions, arose in the East," she wrote, and though "spiritual . . . western literalism has misinterpreted the oriental symbolism."[71]

Diaz was also disappointed in Jonathan Edwards, who "dwells gloatingly" on the punishment of sinners "roasting in literal fire." (By this period, the great love of God within Edwards's sermons, appearing regularly according to the Puritan liturgical cycle, had been largely obscured in public memory.) Eddy continued issuing statements like, "A sinner ought not to be at ease, or he would never quit sinning," thus "some mortals may even need to hear the . . . thunderbolt of Jonathan Edwards" to rouse them. Fittingly, *Mental Science Magazine* started with an image of the Christian cross on its cover but quickly dropped it, matching Diaz's approach.[72]

Neither Diaz nor Eddy sought to censure the other. They seemed to like each other enough personally and never had a falling out. Diaz never released a broad-scale plagiarism of Eddy's book or claimed to be speaking specifically for her. Eddy did not particularly follow and never spoke against Diaz's activities or publications. Like other emergent New Thoughters, however, Diaz continued juxtaposing the occasional unattributed phrase from Eddy's book with eclectic passages from other sources while rejecting the idea that Eddy had been specially appointed by God to lead Christian Science and maintain authority over its expression.[73] Unless this reached the level of extensive plagiarism or claimed her personal approval, Eddy let it go.

She also took the opportunity to clarify her teachings on Buddhism in her book. A passage briefly referring to its nontheistic nature saw few changes across editions. Another read in 1875, "The history of the Chinese empire derives its antiquity and renown from the truer idea the Buddhist entertains of God, contrasted with the tyranny, intolerance and bloodshed based on the belief that Truth, Life, and Love are in matter, and the great Jehovah formed after error's pattern of mortal man, or intelligent matter" (1875:114).

She altered these views incrementally in 1881, 1886, and 1891, arriving at the nearly final 1897 passage, "The eastern empires and nations owe their false government to the misconceptions of Deity there prevalent. Tyranny, intolerance, and bloodshed, wherever found, arise from the belief that the Infinite is formed after the pattern of mortal personality, passion, and impulse" (1897:260). These changes began during her contact with quasi-Eastern theosophical teachings and would continue into the 1890s, when Christian

Scientists themselves sometimes made choices reifying impressions that they were eclectic or theosophical.

In particular, they would broadly introduce themselves to America at the Chicago World's Parliament of Religions in 1893, forging connections with the other two major religious newcomers at the parliament, Buddhism and Vedanta. Biographers have detailed how this linked the three in public memory.[74] Eddy recognized merits in most religions and in 1893 said of Buddhism, "The true sense they entertain of humanity" is its "best part." Forgetfulness of a material sense of self, she added, is "Christ-like, for Jesus taught it."[75] The inevitable invocation of Jesus as her standard recalls how she conceived, articulated, and resolved the teaching of matter as "temporal and unreal" from within the Christian tradition. This was an interesting and singular development, yet its basis in God's sovereign allness was irreconcilable to the nontheistic Buddhist view and vice versa, limiting comparisons between views of illusion or ignorance and the pain they appear to bring. Theosophical inquirers ran up against such limitations, putting constraints on their acceptance of her book.

Eddy read somewhat on Buddhism prior to 1900 but would confirm her views in 1903, when an acquaintance sent her *The Light of Buddha* by S. Kuroda, who also authored *The Light of Dharma* and *Outlines of the Mahayana*. Printed in Japanese and English, Eddy's copy has a Mormon card from the Bureau of Information and Church Literature tucked into the front cover. She read it carefully, noting teachings on karmic causality, individuality and the five Skandhas, the Atman or Ego, differences with Brahmanism, and so on.

Next to the paragraph on transmigration or reincarnation, she marked a passage describing the Nama-rupa as "the physical element . . . the body in which the Spiritual and Conscious Being resides." She put two check marks in the margin and called this an "Error," as it saw "matter and Spirit combined." She dwelt at length on transmigration, with which she roundly disagreed. Individuality to her was eternally distinctive, reflected from an eternal God and ever unfolding, not changing from one form to another and not subject to karma, *vasanas*, maya, or bodhi as was the Alaya-vijnana or storehouse consciousness.[76] The merging of an individual into a cosmic collective consciousness was a non-option here. Even Hegel's sublation (*aufheben*), with its "determinate nothingness" and relational process of identity creation, was at odds with her view of each individual's eternally distinct identity as God's reflection.

ESOTERIC INQUIRERS were attracted initially to Eddy's anti-dogmatic and anti-creedal ethos, radical revision of Eve's fall, teaching of God's universal love, egalitarian polity, and other elements. They valued that she was a heterodox revisionary. But when they found that she defined her religion as the "true evangelical" church restored in modernity, with all that entailed, they reconsidered.[77] Truth could not certainly or safely be found in the real yet scattered merits embodied in other religious systems, Eddy taught. "There is a little truth in all creeds, isms, and ologies," an account quotes her as saying, "but if you try to find the truth in a part of the vessel, you will get cut. Study the Bible and Science and Health and leave the fragments alone."[78]

No Theosophist could support such teachings. As unorthodox as Eddy was within the Christian pantheon, she was nevertheless within it. Eddy attempted reconciliation with some of the most public of these theosophical innovators, notably Hopkins, in Christian terms they were sure to find unappealing.[79] Yet this only underscored the religious gulf between them, which both sides found too broad to bridge.

Historical studies mentioning such differences usually gloss them as personal quarrels. Yet they were deeply and unavoidably religious in nature. New Thought arose to accommodate the eclectic, theosophically inflected, esoteric religious views that Christian Science and divine healing could not. Ironically, New Thoughters, or next-generation mind curists, then reached back over Eddy to retroactively claim a founder in Phineas P. Quimby, partly based on the arguments of Julius Dresser. As they established their own healing work in the mesmeric tradition, they claimed to sandwich Eddy into it as well over her objections, following their own religious leaders on this matter.

THESE WERE NOT the only inquirers into Christian Science at the time, of course. Christian inquirers such as O. P. Gifford took a very different approach. Like Gordon, he had graduated from the Baptist-affiliated Brown University and a seminary. Gifford "won considerable fame" for his sermons and writings as pastor of Boston's Warren Avenue Baptist Church.[80]

Gordon's letter against Christian Science prompted Gifford to read Eddy's book and "decide for himself on its doctrine." It convinced him in a way the divine healing movement did not, and he decided if the majority of his congregation was interested in Eddy's faith, that was "not too bad," and he should apply for instruction in Christian Science. "Much of the prejudice against Christian Science," he wrote in 1886, echoing Diaz, "is the result of misunderstanding."[81]

His solution was quite unlike Diaz's, though. Gifford advised those who rejected *Science and Health* "through prejudice" to consider it more closely to see how the "Christian Scientist takes his place, in thought, by God's side, attempts to get the Divine point of view, judges all things from the spiritual side." He noted that those in this new sect find that "'the far-off divine event, to which the whole creation moves,' is a present accomplished fact."[82]

As a minister, Gifford was part of a trend. After releasing her book's 1886 edition, Eddy noted an increase in church members, and "six clergymen have applied to enter my next class." She had brought out its meaning far more, she judged, and the clergy now understood it better to some degree.[83] Her book had always noted that while "sage and philosopher" might be fascinated by Christian Science, "the Christian alone will fathom it" (1875:275; 1911:556). Now she became more careful in vetting the preexisting religious commitments of her students to confirm they aligned with hers enough to make their new education possible and sustainable.

Gifford remained both a high-profile Baptist minister and a consistent Christian Science supporter. He eventually championed anti-sweatshop and other labor causes in his Social Gospel ministry. Stephen Gottschalk points out that liberal ministers were more likely than conservatives to be supportive of Eddy's teaching and practice. This is true, though Eddy was neither wholly liberal nor without traditional supporters or liberal detractors. Labels for liberalism and traditionalism have also shifted enough that present-day observers would not entirely recognize their former usages.

Caveats aside, her theology resonated with the "new departure" from "the old orthodox beliefs in which we were educated," as the Christian Scientist George H. Bradford put it in an 1885 letter to her. The Congregationalist minister and Bushnell disciple Theodore Munger articulated the features of this wave of theological change in his 1883 *Freedom of Faith*, which Bradford sent to Eddy. Bradford felt she should know its main points, which no one but Munger "has so clearly and lovingly stated."[84]

These points included retaining the doctrines of the church but refiguring them for new demands and needs; recognizing revelation "not so much *from* God as *of* God, its logical attitude . . . that of seeing and interpreting"; requiring not only faith but reason, and that not as formal logic but the "full exercise of our nature"; understanding the Bible "as a *living* book," one that is "warm and vital" and speaking to humanity, its interpretation ideally bringing out the "inspiration" of the biblical writers; exposing the false division between science and religion; and engaging people's actual lives rather than only holding out ideals.[85]

Eddy's book also ticked several of these boxes for some Christian ministers who found Munger's work compelling. Every new direction of thought, argumentation, or activism in the postbellum era was called a "new departure," and Eddy had already referred to her own theology in 1884 as a "new departure of metaphysics" in which "Christ is clad with a richer illumination as our

Saviour from sickness, sin, and death," making "God's fatherliness" and His "sovereignty glorious."[86] As with social justice movements, she set up her own Bible interpretations as the standard for a new theological departure.

Ministers like O. P. Gifford did not leave their Social Gospel for her Christian Science, but they identified a standard in it they appreciated. In 1886 Gifford wrote, "Christian Science attempts the role of Paul in Athens: 'Whom therefore ye ignorantly worship, Him declare I unto you.' So long as this declaration runs along old lines, men listen; but when it touches the resurrection of the dead, some mock, others promise a new hearing, and yet others cleave and believe. So long as most men take the material point of view, and judge by sense, the few who attempt to take the spiritual point of view, and judge righteous judgment, will be despised and rejected."[87]

By 1895 Gifford was pastoring a church in Buffalo seating 1,200. When W. T. Stead published his famous *If Christ Came to Chicago* in 1894, it praised Gifford's commitment to social causes.[88] Gifford's views on Eddy's religion changed little in coming years. In 1899 the *Christian Science Sentinel* reprinted a snippet from a piece he published in the Baptist *Standard* on the serendipity of good works, including Christian healing.[89] He also contributed a paper on the "form and substance" of Christian Science to the *Chicago Standard*. This was reprinted in a critically sympathetic anthology on Christian Science with the assessments of other ministers.[90]

The following year, he contributed an article on Christian Science to a distinguished anthology titled *Theology at the Dawn of the Twentieth Century*, which centered on "the present status of Christianity and its doctrines." The anthology included four contributions on Christian Science, two by adherents and two by well-known ministerial scholars. In Gifford's entry, his view of healing aligned with Eddy's on several major points, such as the nature of miracles, body and Spirit, Jesus's role, and the place of healing within Christianity as a whole.[91]

IN THE EARLY 1880s, judging from the lengthy *Boston Sunday Globe* article of March 1882 and ministerial and lay descriptions of Christian Science, most Americans who had heard of Eddy's book understood that she thought of herself as following Jesus in a new, unorthodox, unusual way and claimed to restore apostolic healing. They might have disagreed with her, but they knew her viewpoint. The 1883 *Post* exchange questioned this, but in late 1884, Christians of many stripes were still listening to Eddy preach on Sunday afternoons at Hawthorne Hall in Boston, where Christian Scientists met on and off from the late 1870s until 1885 (when they moved to Chickering Hall until 1894, the year they completed their own church building).[92]

As Peel notes, liberal ministers such as Andrew P. Peabody, longtime Plummer Professor of Christian Morals and Preacher to Harvard University, took her pulpit when she was not available. A young man who frequented Trinity Church on Sunday mornings to hear the sermons of Phillips Brooks often listened to Eddy preach in the afternoon. Comparing the two after Easter services, he found Brooks's sermon "uplifting" and Eddy's experientially immediate: the resurrection was not only reverently remembered but right at hand.[93] The sick and disabled reported finding healing at her services, and the clergy took note.

Yet by the end of April 1885, "the Boston press was reporting that the last session of the Baptist Ministers' Meeting had been greatly disturbed over the issue of Christian Science, A. J. Gordon leading the attack against it and O. P. Gifford speaking in its defense. A week later the Congregational ministers were treated to a paper by the Reverend Stacy Fowler (subsequently published in the *Homiletic Review*) in which he took issue with everyone."[94] Fowler "pointed out the errors of those who confused Christian Science with spiritism and faith cure," though he himself neither strongly endorsed nor opposed it.[95]

Alongside Christian supporters like Gifford, esoteric inquirers such as Gestefeld and Diaz increased apace. They objected to Eddy's core teachings yet adopted some of her phraseology, often calling themselves Christian Scientists.[96] The resulting impressions of Christian Science that swirled around media outlets and lecture halls were correspondingly conflicting and diverse.

As the 1880s drew to a close, the only thing most Americans knew for sure about Christian Science was that they had no idea what it truly was or whom or what it included. This profound cultural confusion about Christian Science identity would persist, ebbing and flowing as Eddy's church expanded, and would affect its nascent historiography in equally profound ways.

Eddy responded to the situation by emphasizing and sharpening essential Christian Science teachings, making strong demands on her book. The large core group of adherents who remained in the Christian Science denomination through the 1880s welcomed her book revisions, including her anti-theosophical message. A representative 1888 letter writer from a Chicago adherent noted her Christian Science teacher had instructed her that "Theosophy and Buddhism was not what we're seeking for, but the perfect Truth as it was taught by Christ."[97]

Such adherents shared a view of Eddy as a Christian pathbreaker without peer in modern times. As Janet Colman wrote in 1888 to Eddy's future publisher, Joseph Armstrong, "In thinking of Mrs Eddy last night I saw a high mountain, with only a few common weeds on it, then I looked to the top and saw the sun shining in all its glory, with a wooden cross in the center. It showed me no matter how drear the path upward that our teacher was leading us, that there was Light at the summit, and the cross taken up and carried through every thing would bring us into the Light."[98]

Eddy was not personally in Colman's vision, which centered on the cross of Jesus. Yet in the view of Christian Scientists like Colman, Eddy and her work were leading them to take up the cross and navigate oppositions and difficulties up to Christ. Their stories come next.

FINDINGS: PART III

EDDY'S *SCIENCE AND HEALTH* conversed and interacted with many religious and cultural movements, and vice versa, while retaining its own distinct and unduplicated message. As these conversations unfolded across wider American culture in the 1880s, public perceptions of Christian Science came to diversify greatly.

Social justice reformers often envisioned Christian Science as a fascinating adjunct to their primary commitment to societal change. Eddy conversely described Christian Science as the overarching program for Christian salvation, with needed societal change as one of its effects. She sympathized with social reform efforts that aligned with her statement of salvation in Christ and left aside those that did not. Further, workers for women's and race rights invoked African American legal history to political effect, while Eddy did so to providential effect. She positioned freedom from race-based enslavement as harbinger and precursor to humanity's full spiritual freedom. This allows us to understand her relationship to women's rights, and social justice generally, as a seamless component of her religious commitments.

Eddy's book saw a huge surge in readership in the 1880s. Christian supporters and critics both increased. The Baptist pastor O. P. Gifford, for example, championed Christian Science while conducting his own influential ministry, while the well-known Baptist divine healer A. J. Gordon considered Christian Science unorthodoxies to negate any religious gains it might represent. Still, he noted in Eddy's religion its "large use of the Bible, its strenuous demand for holiness and self-abnegation in its disciples, the results apparently effected in its ministry to the sick," as his son later put it.[1] Christian Science and divine healing shared a "similar hermeneutics of healing," as Heather Curtis notes.[2] Yet they also disagreed on important theological points. Both objected to Theosophy, though the cultural misunderstandings I have detailed obscured this.

Meanwhile, theosophically inclined inquirers attracted to innovative aspects of Christian Science explored it alongside other religions, affiliating to varying degrees of intensity for a brief time. Their interest faded with the realization that although Eddy's theology was radically innovative, it was also thoroughly Christian. Theosophists rejected its exclusive use of the Christian scriptures and the concept of special revelation, leading them to class

Christian Science as yet another Christian "dogma" that was narrowly possessive and authoritarian.

Eddy rejected Theosophy as unchristian, increasingly detailing why in *Science and Health*. She called Christian Science "the most evangelical religion on earth," which was a no-go for eclectic religionists.[3] Yet Theosophy included a doctrine wherein "every great thinker and philosopher, especially every founder of a new religion . . . is necessarily a Theosophist."[4] Thus the theosophically minded rejected Eddy's claim to be, as she put it, "the person whom God has appointed" to lead Christian Science, deciding she and her teachings were instead unwitting subsets of their own tradition.

Those subscribing to this view defined Eddy's claims to authorship and authority through revelatory discovery as inherently possessive and authoritarian. Characterizations of Eddy and her work from this differing religious perspective circulated widely and became culturally and historiographically influential.

As mind cure and later New Thought emerged, they accommodated the eclectic, theosophically inflected healing views neither Christian Science nor divine healing found amenable. As Eddy had once done with Phineas Quimby, these new arrivals sought to understand her presuppositions by bringing them into their own preexisting worldview—not a Congregational one like her own, but in their case, an esoteric one that would remove her work from its Christian moorings.

Unlike Quimby, Eddy objected on religious grounds. Unlike Eddy, esotericists persisted when the combination became impossible due to mutually exclusive elements. They thus produced what Beryl Satter calls "contradictory" texts marked by "ambiguities," or what Catherine L. Albanese calls a "juxtaposition" of teachings that would not blend.[5] Satter posits such ambiguities may have contributed to New Thought's appeal among eclectic religionists of the era.

Nascent criticism of Eddy's authorial and revelatory claims from such quarters prompted her to accelerate earlier revisionary efforts of her book. In its 1875 debut, *Science and Health* had referred to the origins of Christian Science as both a phenomenal discovery and religious revelation. Yet Eddy did not seamlessly join these descriptions until 1883, when on the heels of critical press attention she called out and blended these preexisting elements within Christian Science identity. This involved reorganizing more than rewriting. It led to a final narrative of religious origins that is both strictly dated and gradual, both process and event, naming a specific point of emergence within a range of experience. Critics continued to contend that by revising her book, she voided her claims to revelation.

Critics in the 1870s had described *Science and Health* as ridiculously heterodox, or plain ridiculous, but they understood Eddy's project in Christian terms. By the early 1880s readers were split on whether her book—panned by a Swedenborgian minister, extolled by a Methodist looking for the end times—effectively engaged the Bible, but not on whether that was its goal. In 1882, the highest-profile media coverage of Christian Science portrayed it as a new Christian movement restoring apostolic healing.

Five years later, public understanding of Christian Science as Christian was one of many "diverse views" in circulation, so many that conversations on the topic inevitably ended in "confusion and contradiction."[6] Eddy still described *Science and Health* as explainer of the Bible, textbook for Christian healing, and accelerator of global salvation, a triad that centrally shaped Christian Science self-identity even as public perceptions wound about in multiple directions that continue today. She also fine-tuned her theological statements in response to this diversity of perceptions. Once again, she articulated her singular vision in ways we cannot capture using contemporary, bifurcated descriptions of Christianity in modern America.

We now turn to an in-depth view of those who accepted Eddy's description of Christian Science and used her book with the Bible to forge a new religious identity.

PART IV

Pastor
(1891–)

CHAPTER THIRTEEN

Church Body

(1891)

In which Eddy ordains her book and the Bible joint pastor of her church, and polity and practice are discussed; in which Christian Scientists engage their pastor to "demonstrate" their religion and provide the lived element by which the Bible's promises as described in Science and Health are thought to be proved; and in which the diverse backgrounds of readers are considered

"THE LONG-LOOKED-FOR, much-coveted volume of SCIENCE AND HEALTH, that is to mark an epoch in the Christian Science movement, has at last appeared," announced the *Christian Science Journal* in March 1891, and will lift up "the thought of all true Scientists" who combine their reading with "*faithful, daily effort to reduce its teachings to practice.*"[1] This rhetoric illustrates the self-conscious growth of the Christian Science organization, now marking itself in "epochs," and how reading was not an academic or abstract exercise for adherents. Reading meant absorbing spiritual truths to be applied to daily life. The distance between reading and practice was fluid.

This chapter concerns itself with how Christian Scientists used their scriptures and their sacred "textbook" in their church organization and in private worship. Eddy's 1891 edition emerged in parallel with her reorganized church, and it signaled a massive increase in adherents and their testimonial literature. We first look at church polity, Eddy's 1894 ordination of her book and the Bible as the dual pastor of her church, the development of the Christian Science Bible Lesson, and the technologies and practices people employed in accessing it. Then we turn to testimonials: how they represented healing, what they said about the Bible and *Science and Health*, and how temporal matters of social identity entered in, especially considering race.

EDDY'S THIRD MAJOR revision (1886) had sold out several times, and by 1889 subsequent printings were earning $12,000 a year (over $328,000 in 2020).[2] In her midsixties, she had finally secured a livelihood and means to fuel her church's expansion. Local churches and Sunday schools sprang up organically where students of Christian Science practiced healing work.

The National Christian Scientist Association (NCSA, for students of Eddy) and the Christian Scientist Association (CSA, for those taught by Eddy's students and their students) both formed. Eddy established the Massachusetts Metaphysical College for teaching aspiring Christian Science healers and teachers. She appointed public lecturers to travel circuits throughout the United States. In 1888, the CSA opened a reading room where the public could read, buy, and borrow the Bible, Eddy's writings, and other materials such as the *Christian Science Journal*. The following year, mother and daughter O. W. and Jessie Day of Chicago produced the first hymnal for Christian Scientists, before the composer Lyman Foster Brackett later took up the effort. They filled the volume with Protestant hymns often reworded somewhat to better fit Christian Science theology.

The church in the 1880s grew without cohesive strength, however. What Christian Science was, what and whom it included, what and whom *Science and Health* represented, what constituted efficacious practice, whether Eddy had leadership status based on a revelatory and religious discovery event: widespread disagreement and confusion around such questions resulted in a "perfect storm" of interlocking issues regarding authority, efficacy, and organization.

After a series of events showcasing these issues, in 1889 Eddy made the surprising decision to dissolve her church's half-functioning format. Her book, she noted, needed major editing and a new, more reliable platform for promotion and protection. She resigned her Boston pastorate, dissolved the CSA, and closed her college despite steadily increasing enrollment requests. On her recommendation, her then-democratic church voted to discard its congregational organization and remain incorporated as a voluntary organization.

Eddy appointed a handful of directors to ensure her church still held Sunday services and Friday evening "experience" or testimony meetings. She had earlier purchased the land for a new worship space in Boston from her church, whose treasurer had run off with previously collected building funds, and she now conveyed the land back to it through a church representative. Then she retired to her home state to begin her most comprehensive book revision to date while searching for whatever new church format might emerge. She would stay just outside Concord, New Hampshire, for over eighteen years, until 1908.

Around 1890, as adherents began to use *Science and Health* and the Bible in or as their sermons, Eddy thrilled that her book was fit to replace her as teacher, healer, and preacher.³ "I do not *want* to teach, I am *tired tired*, of teaching," she had written in 1889, and all things considered would "rather there would never be a teacher but the Bible and Science and Health."⁴ A few years earlier she had called her book the best healer and biblical interpreter and thus her movement's "only standard" in its distinctive Jesus-following efforts.⁵

It was a short step from there to calling it the most effective and "best preacher," as she wrote to students in 1890 and 1891.⁶ She would still appoint and ordain reverends for a few more years, but as she leaned more on her revised book she felt refreshed, "well and younger than ever before." She no longer colored her hair, which had gone white, "but what of that if the heart is hopeful, and not tired of the strife?"⁷ She would personally teach only one more class, in 1898.

The fourth major revision and fiftieth printing of *Science and Health* debuted in 1891, just before the reorganized First Church of Christ, Scientist, in 1892.⁸ Both seemed a world away from the 1880s.

During the 1890s, Eddy organized The Mother Church under her *Manual of The Mother Church*, with guidelines and rules she presented as just as divinely revealed to her as the teachings in *Science and Health*.⁹ The manual stipulated a five-person board of directors to administer its bylaws. These directors were answerable to Eddy personally until her passing and after that through her writings.

The idea was to establish a structure that would gradually transfer daily decision making from herself to her church while keeping her religious authority and place intact. As Eddy worked on the manual, she gradually called for several boards (of trustees, lectureship, education), a publication committee, a Sunday school superintendent, and several other appointed officers. Local churches became locally and democratically run "branches" of The Mother Church. They were to have a reading room (first called a dispensary) to sell the Bible, Eddy's book, and other Christian Science literature and to operate a public outreach ministry.

Like other denominations, Congregational churches used the word "branch" to describe outlying locales and activities under the umbrella of a central church organization, a concept that existed in the colonial era but grew exponentially after 1850.[10] This hints at the many parallels between Eddy's new church and the Congregational tradition she came from. The practice of dedicating branch church buildings after clearing debt was a cultural norm based on Bible passages and appears in the manuals of both groups.[11] Eddy's Sunday school curriculum, which centers on the Ten Commandments, the Beatitudes, and the Lord's Prayer, is distinctive but draws from Congregational models.

In the manual, Eddy also established a new iteration of the New England and specifically Congregational tradition of an annual Thanksgiving service, open to the public. Per broader Protestant tradition, she also included a historical sketch of her church. And like the Congregationalists, she required members to resolve complaints directly with one another as far as possible within their covenant relationship, referencing the same scripture (Matt. 18:15–17).

On the cover of her manual she placed a cross and crown insignia. She first used it on a sign for her Christian Scientist's home in Lynn, Massachusetts, just before it appeared on the cover of the *Manual of the Congregational Church* for the Concord and Tilton congregations in 1878.[12] The symbol did not appear on the cover when she attended (all surviving copies have blank covers, except one with a nicely preserved handwritten recipe for biscuits, circa 1850).

This was obviously a traditional Christian symbol, however, that Eddy would have known in her early worship context. During the 1880s the insignia became associated with her church. She eventually copyrighted a version encircled with gospel words and stamped it on the cover of her book. Two New Hampshire Congregational churches near her childhood homes later added cross and crown designs to their stained glass windows, which their church historians speculate may have a "connection" to her.[13] They did not embrace her biblical interpretation as readily as she had hoped, but they tended to celebrate her organizational successes.

EDDY'S REORGANIZED DENOMINATION began to build a Boston church edifice in 1894. As workers laid tiles and installed pews, she took the unusual step to "ordain the BIBLE, and SCIENCE AND HEALTH WITH KEY TO THE SCRIPTURES, Pastor over" The Mother Church. The ordination appeared as a bylaw in her newly minted manual in 1895. A man and a woman should read from this joint pastor at the podium, she noted. Either could fill the role of First Reader, reading from the Bible, or Second Reader, reading from her book (designations she would swap in 1899). "Sermons are *done*," Eddy wrote to her student Edward P. Bates in January 1895. "Bible and Text-Book teach more than sermons[;] they give lessons to be *practised*."[14]

In April, she extended the ordination to branches. Her primary interest was in supplying a reliable preacher that she considered "uncontaminated and unfettered by human hypotheses, and divinely authorized," free from personal opinions and mistakes, and that would not "mislead the thought."[15] The scholar Andrew Ventimiglia notes that "this innovation stabilized worship practice across all congregations and oriented worship around the text alone," which gave Eddy "perpetual religious control through the text" she deemed the Bible's revealed interpretation.[16]

As the historian Seth Perry has recently argued, *sola scriptura* has never truly meant the Bible alone but the Bible alongside a variety of interpretive tools and texts.[17] Eddy took this to new lengths. As she explained in 1895 to the Reverend Ruth B. Ewing, whom she had ordained not long before, "It is satisfactory to note how [this] responds to the example of our Master. Jesus was not ordained as our churches ordain ministers. . . . He preached in their synagogues by reading the Scriptures and expounding them, and God has given to this age Science and Health with Key to The Scriptures to elucidate His Word."[18]

Like her book itself, this move struck some critics as sacrilege, evidence of megalomania, or the rash and unseemly promotion of women's rights (not her main cause, as we have seen, but one that often had her sympathies).[19] Christian Scientists regularly fielded the view that this unusual pastoral arrangement meant they prioritized Eddy's book over the Bible. A director of The Mother Church, William R. Rathvon, advised New York adherent Julia C. Fremont not to worry. "The Bible predominates over Science and Health in our services" overall, he noted, so adherents should carry on and let others notice if they wished to.[20]

Others speculated that Christian Scientists might consider Eddy and Jesus to be equals. In private, Eddy indexed a passage in her book, asking, "Can he who is begotten of the beliefs of the flesh, or serves them, ever reach, in this world, the divine heights of his Master?" Then she wrote a note to herself, "Proof that I claim no place of our Master."[21] Only the Savior had a virgin birth. No one else could claim to approach his divinity. She later called personal comparisons to Jesus "abnormal" and made a rule against it in her church manual, though this did not stop some from doing so when speaking of her.[22]

Controversies aside, after the new ordination in early 1895, weekly Bible lessons always doubled as sermons each Sunday in Christian Science churches. Listening to the Sunday sermon became a culmination of weekly study. Several other denominations used publications such as the *International Sunday Bible Lesson*, which the Christian Science church adapted at first for its sermons. The church had begun publishing its own *Christian Science Bible Lessons* in 1890, initially prepared by an adherent, Frank E. Mason, who had contributed Bible lessons to the *Journal* on and off since 1888. Switching to a quarterly format, the Bible Lessons were soon published in the *Christian Science Quarterly*. They contained citations from the Bible and *Science and Health* organized under weekly themes.[23] These were not used as Sunday morning sermons until 1898, however, when Eddy chose twenty-six Bible Lesson-Sermon topics to present in something like a novel lectionary arrangement. By 1899, these took the place of the *International Sunday Bible Lessons* at Sunday evening services as well.

Bible Lesson-Sermon subjects repeated twice a year and ranged from God, synonyms for God, and Christ Jesus to less expected titles, such as one denouncing animal magnetism and the oddly prescient "Is the Universe,

Including Man, Evolved by Atomic Force?" Though the topics rotated, the cited passages were always new. An appointed Bible Lesson Committee chose them by 1906. Each Bible Lesson averaged a few dozen readings from the Bible matched with interpretive passages from *Science and Health*.

AT HOME, readers used citations in the *Quarterly* to look up each chapter and verse in the Bible and each page and line in *Science and Health*. For efficiency, they sometimes used Bibles with thumb indexes or cutaway tabs marking each chapter (these would not become available to mark pages in Eddy's book until 1940, in a set with a matching Bible). Line numbers appeared in Eddy's book in early 1902. Before then, many readers used specially fabricated bookmarks printed with line numbers, often decorated with book ads and devotional snippets. They aligned the bookmark with the text to quickly find the lines they wanted. Other readers wrote line numbers in the margins on each page of their books.[24]

Another early bookmarking technology involved winding threads through the books to mark each passage in order. Starting with the first Bible Lesson citation, the reader placed the start of a long thread in the Bible, then turned to the next citation and placed the next length of thread. After weaving the thread through all the Bible citations, they used a second thread to mark the correlative passages in *Science and Health*. By unwinding the threads, they could read the citations in order. A Christian Scientist later recalled that as a small girl, she eyed the amount of thread in the readers' hands to know how much longer she would need to sit still and listen.[25]

Around 1890, a cottage industry arose catering to a growing market of goods for Christian Scientists to complement their Bible study. A devotional calendar titled *Stepping-Stones in Truth for Christian Scientists* featured a large cross and crown design. Each week indicated the date and two passages from the New Testament, the Psalms, or Isaiah.[26] Around 1900, the John M. Tearle Company manufactured numbered tabs that readers could clip onto their book pages to mark Bible lesson passages.[27] He and his competitors offered plaques, bookmarks, jewelry, and calendars, many with a cross and crown insignia.

Tearle's rounded page clips (fabricated from rigid, coated paper) were not very popular, probably because they tore or degraded page edges. Higher-end printings in particular used strong but ultra-thin Oxford India paper. Oxford University Press reserved India paper exclusively for Bibles and Anglican Prayer Books until 1894, when it reversed an earlier decision and granted Eddy's book an exception. Her printer later recalled that this was because of "how much the circulation of Science and Health was doing to stimulate the

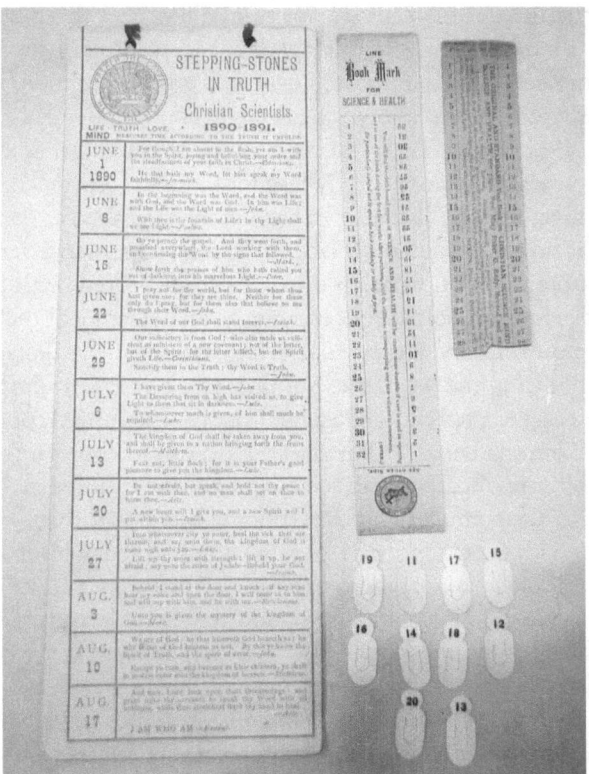

A cottage industry of practical objects and bookmarking tools for use with the Bible and Mary Baker Eddy's book arose in the 1890s. Next to the calendar are bookmarking clips to mark Bible Lesson passages and bookmarks with line numbers to find citations in *Science and Health*. Line numbers were printed directly in her book starting in 1902. *Stepping-Stones in Truth for Christian Scientists* calendar, 1890, 2009.001 FIC C; lined bookmarks, 1984.37.185 and 1984.37.186, c. 1890; Tearle clip page markers, 1984.37.343.1-.62, all in Art and Artifact Collection, Special Collections, Mary Baker Eddy Library. Photo © The Mary Baker Eddy Library. Used by permission.

demand for Bibles."[28] Christian Scientists after that could mark and read the Bible lesson-sermon using matching sets of books printed on India paper.

Readers studied their Bible lesson in these ways until 1920, when the Scott Abbott Manufacturing Company began fabricating numbered metal markers especially for use with the Christian Science pastor. These attached to thin springs encircling pages near the spine. Not everyone adopted the metal marker system right away, but it proved convenient and eventually became the standard. Studying the pastoral books in an unstructured way also remained popular.

Around the turn of the century, many families read the Bible lesson together.[29] Testimonials spoke of this as well as of reading in small groups or to a friend in need. This did not spill over into group recitation, however. In 1891 Eddy advised, "Never allow Science and Health to be read in *concert*."[30] Organizing discussions among themselves *about* Christian Science, rather than simply practicing it, apparently also took readers off track. "Assembling themselves together, and listening to each other amicably, or contentiously," she wrote, "is no aid to students in acquiring solid Christian Science."[31]

She put a premium on working directly and intimately with the pastoral books. At the time, schools taught copying as an educational tool thought to promote comprehension. Writing out each passage of the Bible Lessons by hand to read during the week was not unusual. But in her church manual, Eddy decided that elected church Readers "shall not read from copies or manuscripts, but from the books."[32] Further, she expressed concern that compilations of her writings together with the Bible would be credited to the compiler, or perceived as the compiler's product in some way rather than her own.[33]

Above all, Eddy seemed to want her own book to speak for itself. She told her student Carol Norton never to explain its meaning to anyone except for the teaching chapter, "Recapitulation," and then only in the classroom. Her students did not fully understand the "Science" behind her work, she told him, so trying to explain it tended to "ensnare the hearer in a net of human opinions."[34] Eddy also advised students against interspersing too many quotes from her in their testimonies, conversations, and publications. Instead, she wrote, let people study the books themselves and listen to them in church together, sharing their experiences with one another there. The focus again was on communion, community, and healing stemming from the unusual Christian Science pastor.[35]

TESTIMONIALS IN THE main Christian Science periodicals also highlight how readers used these books together. The sheer number of these accounts is overwhelming; over 8,700 testimonies were published in these periodicals between 1883 and 1910, a fraction of those sent in.[36] This sets them apart from other religious healing literatures, which appear in books, tracts, and magazines on a much smaller scale and often an ad-hoc basis.

Some general observations apply. As with Marietta Webb's account, adherents described physical healing as a by-product of spiritual growth rather than as an end in itself. They tended to view the spiritual growth experienced during the curative episode as the actual substance of the healing, although many (probably most) did not enter the process with that expectation. Readers used

Eddy's book in concert with the Bible to look for a satisfying way of conceptualizing and worshipping God, to experience healing, or both.

They did this in a distinctive way compared with other religions reporting healing claims. Textual Protestants nuzzled their Bibles and heard them speak through the covers.[37] Pentecostals, Anglicans, and Catholics found their Bibles, prayer cloths, and other objects literally infused with "Holy Ghost power," or in Catholic language, sanctified. New Thought and Emmanuel practitioners sought to change their thinking to change their bodies, often with the assistance of objects charged with a presumed sacred presence, and in the process they sacralized the psychological and psychologized the sacred.

Christian Scientists described a simple affection for their books, which they held and studied, often via their weekly Bible lessons. They recounted listening in an attitude of prayerful thought to hear and understand messages from God that would take root in their daily lives. They found the Holy Ghost acting and moving in the messages delivered through their books, which they recounted bringing a consciousness of holiness having practical effects. They described material and mortal thought processes of "mortal mind," like Paul's "carnal mind," yielding to God, Mind, in individualized ways to effect healing.[38]

Eddy's 1881 revision included a picture of Jesus raising a young woman from death after witnesses "laughed him to scorn" for assuring them she was "not dead, but sleepeth" (Mark 5:39–40). Eddy would write that while raising the dead was not conceivable for most followers of Jesus at their present stage of understanding, denying what the physical senses present as afflicted reality still flows naturally from the theodicy of Jesus: his acceptance of the complete and total reality of a good God, in which evil was a "liar, and the father of it" (John 8:44). Such views did not amount to a cursory or flippant rejection of materiality but to striving for redemption of its inharmonious claims by reflecting God in human thought and life.

Sometimes this might happen suddenly; other times, gradually. To expect instant human perfection, constant triumphs, and no setbacks was unrealistic. "The trials of prophet, disciple, and apostle," Eddy wrote, "await, in some form, the pioneers of Truth" (1875:305). Jesus required us to be as perfect as our Maker, but this would happen step by step. Thus "to stop eating, drinking, or being clothed materially before the spiritual facts of existence are gained step by step, is not legitimate" (1911:254). She began writing versions of this statement in 1881. Similarly, she wrote that a true Christian Scientist "never abuses the corporeal personality, but uplifts it."[39]

Like their sacred books, testimonials linked spiritual healing to spiritual growth in human consciousness, allowing adherents to perceive and experience something of spiritual reality on earth. They described this making "the

Adherents used their religious books daily. Mary Baker Eddy ordained the Bible and her book, *Science and Health*, as the joint pastor of her church in 1894. Christian Scientists consider the Bible their only scripture. Eddy's book interprets it. Here, readers hold their pastoral books. They turned to their "dual pastor" as a friend, healer, teacher, and adviser. Images from the Mary Baker Eddy Library. Top row: P01563, Laura Sargent; P00572, Margaret Easton; P00654AB, Alfred Farlow. Bottom row: P00690, Dr. and Mrs. Francis J. Fluno; P01333, Mrs. Mary C. Metcalf; P00302, George Armstrong. Portrait montage © The Mary Baker Eddy Library. Used by permission.

things that do appear," or what was apparent around the adherent on earth, whole and beautiful. As Eddy put it,

> To take all earth's beauty into one gulp of vacuity and label beauty nothing, is ignorantly to caricature God's creation, which is unjust to human sense and to the divine realism. In our immature sense of spiritual things, let us say of the beauties of the sensuous universe: "I love your promise; and shall know, some time, the spiritual reality and substance of form, light, and color, of what I now through you discern dimly; and knowing this, I shall be satisfied . . ."[40]

In January 1891, S. J. H. reported having been a long-term "invalid" with leg and eye problems, having spent six years in a "darkened room." When a Chris-

Early Christian Scientists occasionally produced devotional art in the style of the period. Here, the Bible is open to the gospel of John with Christian Science literature in the background. Oxford University Press reserved its fine India paper for Bibles and Anglican Prayer Books until 1894, when it granted Eddy's *Science and Health* an exception because its circulation greatly increased the demand for Bibles.
C. L. Hunting, *Still Life with Science and Health and Roses*, signed pastel, 2002.139, courtesy of The Mary Baker Eddy Collection and The Mary Baker Eddy Library.

tian Scientist visited, the experience was like "a 'Light shining in darkness.'" Quoting the New Testament, S. J. H. wrote that "it seemed indeed that 'I saw a new heaven and a new earth: for the first heaven and the first earth were passed away.' I feel that the Church of Christ, Scientist, of which I am now a member, is indeed the Body of Christ; and 'Our baptism is a purification from the flesh.'" S. J. H. then described taking patients and using "the Bible Lessons in our *Quarterlies*" to treat their ills.[41]

S. J. H. described the lessons bringing "a wonderful revelation of light. . . . In my study of the references given, I am always lifted above self; and often the feeling comes that angel visitants are with me. In the lesson on the raising of Lazarus, was healing for one of my patients. . . . She was resurrected from her dead beliefs, into newness of life."[42] S. J. H. seems to have perceived the role of the practitioner as a spiritual advocate for the patient. Both patient and practitioner relied on the "truth" they felt the Bible and Eddy's book contained.

The goal of such reading was to apply the "truth" to daily incidents, problems, and emergencies in order to "demonstrate" healing. Study time was part of this. An unidentified testifier wrote that working with the Christian Science Bible Lesson took about "a half hour, twice a day," throughout the week.[43] This was about average. On Sundays, wrote one adherent, focus was on "the Golden

Rule, and Lord's Prayer. We need no *ordained pastor*, as the Sunday School Quarterlies, together with the Bible and *New Book*, Science and Health, supply that need. Our Sunday morning service is a continual feast of Love. The lesson for the day is brought out clearly, and a rich experience is ours. Each listener comes prepared. . . . The Sabbath School, immediately following the morning service, is a sweet benediction."[44] Small churches regularly held Sunday school either before or after their worship service to ensure both were well staffed and everyone was able to attend.

Mrs. J. S. from New York wrote in March 1891 that she had long been "the victim of complicated diseases" that confined her to her bed, where she "suffered intensely." Then an aunt

> gave me two [Christian Science] treatments, and the third day I went to the table with the rest of my family, and ate the same that they did. In one week I was well enough to visit my neighbors, and I have continued well ever since.
>
> In my younger days, I had been a member of the church, and for years had been seeking a higher enjoyment, or knowledge of the Truth; but, never receiving any satisfaction in my search, I had become about discouraged. I think I never was truly converted until after my cure; for, after that, I read the Bible with a new light and understanding. I studied both the Bible and Science and Health; asking God for wisdom and understanding, for He has said, "all things, whatsoever ye ask in prayer, believing, ye shall receive." I now do the work for five in [the] family, and know that God is my Rock and Strong Tower.[45]

Like other testifiers, Mrs. J. S. contrasted her healing to faith cure, noting that she did not believe her recovery possible until she experienced it. Her method was individual study and prayer, in which she read the pastoral books while "asking God for wisdom and understanding." Rather than simply thinking about her texts in an abstract sense, she sought to embody and live their message.

Some testifiers reported healings in progress instead of immediate or full cures. In July 1891 M. E. W. testified that she had not had a "*perfect realization of my cure*" but had still been "led into *marvellous light*." The grippe had alleviated so she could get out of bed and "walk quite a distance."[46] She visited the practitioner who had been praying for her and bought a copy of *Science and Health* to read with her Bible.

Another 1891 testifier discussed the "depraved" husband of a "dear friend" who "abused her so many times while intoxicated" that the testifier loathed him. For unspecified reasons, the wife died. The testifier struggled with feeling the widower was "vile," then "was awakened" in the night by a message she attributed to God that she should visit for the sake of the children. She spoke to the widower "in the spirit of Truth and Love. I loaned him Science and Health. In three days he came to us with a great light in his face," having experienced a reformation of character.[47]

An ongoing thread considers what it means to be Christian. R. E. K. "*professed to believe in Christ*," he wrote, but was "in despair, without health, Spiritually a wreck." After trying magnetic healing and finding little relief, he tried Christian Science. Here, too, he "found only temporary relief" after six months. "Others had been healed, why could I not receive the blessing?" he wondered. "I was told to read Science and Health, and study. That precious book taught me, a professor of religion for twenty years, how to be a Christian."[48]

Similarly, in August 1891 J. S. wrote that despite being a longtime member of the Methodist church of Canada, until three years ago he felt spiritually unsatisfied. He "tried to live a consistent, godly life," but an "aching void" left him in a state of spiritual agony and impoverishment. Glimpses of "light, freedom and peace" were elusive. "I became wretched," he wrote, with the constant "fear of an eternal punishment, ready to engulf me. I wished I had never been born." When his health also failed, he narrowly escaped death and became completely broken down. He was hesitant to try Christian Science, but an adherent assured him he could be healed. Ten days went by with no change. Then a night of obvious change led to consistent progress, until a few weeks later "I awoke to the realization of being in *perfect health*; and never since then, February 1888, has there been even a symptom of any previous trouble."[49]

Wanting to understand this experience, he and his wife took a class in Christian Science. "Oh, how orthodox beliefs warred!" he commented. "But we were both convinced that Christian Science was Bible Truth." During the class he was healed of an addiction to occasional smoking. "We severed connection with the ism," he wrote, meaning Methodism, "and oh, what peace has since been ours. . . . [T]he former 'aching void' had also passed away. We have left all for Truth and Love, in, and with which, our every desire is satisfied."

A Cherokee woman told testifier W. F. Seaver that he could be healed of invalidism through Christian Science. Seaver went to a practitioner, then reported his healing.[50] The daughter of a Christian Science healer working in Ute communities, eleven-year-old Florence Kimball, wrote to Mary Baker Eddy from Salt Lake City in 1900, "I can see that when all the wrong thoughts about Indians are destroyed, they will not be called savages any more." Her mother, she added, said "my healing ten years ago did much to establish the work here."[51] The Christian Science magazines reprinted some reports on Indian affairs around this period, many acknowledging the injustices of Indian removal and the ongoing problem of land rights.

In 1901, Amanda James of Austin, Texas, wrote that she had long been an invalid after two successive surgeries weakened her. She had to have a companion during her husband's absences, and after a friend introduced her to Christian Science, she reported several diseases healed and others lessening. "I feel that I shall yet stand in the liberty where Christ makes free," James wrote.

> I bought "Science and Health with Key to the Scriptures," and it and my Bible are my daily companions. I use the lesson *Quarterly*, take the *Journal* and *Sentinel*, have all of Mrs. Eddy's writings. I am a colored woman, and have quite a battle to fight, but the battle is the Lord's. I have been a student of the Bible from childhood, but I never understood it in the light that I now see it, and I feel that the Bible interpreted as Science and Health interprets it, is Truth understood and not believed only.[52]

James exhibited both independence and community-mindedness, expressing gratitude for her friend, her church group, and Eddy. Like most early adherents, she felt she had entered a new world through studying *Science and Health*, one in which her Bible now made complete sense. She sought to embody what she now knew to address daily problems, from illness to racial discrimination to theological questions.

Christian Science teachings on Christ (eternally present while also historically specific) and its stance against proselytizing made it comparatively attractive to Jewish "seekers," some of whom submitted testimonials. A Russian immigrant to Canada in 1909 wrote that a practitioner relieved him from "misery and suffering," for which he thanked "that godly woman, Mrs. Eddy." Some converts were prolific and became quite prominent in the Christian Science movement.[53]

A contributor to the *Journal* in 1908 sought to explain "the rapid spread of Christian Science among the Jewish people" from her own viewpoint as a convert.[54] The number of Jews interested in Christian Science eventually became such a problem within Reform communities that Alfred G. Moses, along with Morris and Tehilla Lichtenstein, formed the Jewish Science movement as a countertrend in the early 1900s.[55]

A handful of testimonials from people identifying themselves as African American appeared in the periodicals in the decades around 1900, likely along with others from those who chose not to say so. Like James, race was part and parcel of their Christian Science experience but not the key determination. John H. Pitchford of New Orleans wrote that he suffered from "severe stomach trouble" from 1902 until 1911, when a friend told him about Christian Science healing. At the time, wrote Pitchford,

> I had been confined to my room about nine days with what the doctor called malarial fever and other complaints, and my eyes were badly

affected. My friend almost insisted on my going to see a practitioner, even though I did not care to go and thought I was not able to do so.

The practitioner asked me if I believed in Christian Science enough to lay aside all material means and trust God. I said I did, but my thought was that I would try it a few days, and if it failed to help me I would return to my medicines. She then gave me a silent treatment and had me read aloud the Lord's Prayer with its spiritual interpretation as given on page 16 of Science and Health. When I asked her what I could eat, she told me I could have anything I wanted, saying the food God provided never made any one sick. That night I slept well, a very unusual thing, and the next morning arose feeling all right. I went to work, and found that I could walk without getting tired, something I had not done for a long time.... That was the end of my illness.[56]

Pitchford went on to report several other maladies cured. He started attending Christian Science services after his healing ("never missed a meeting") and felt he had

> found the spiritual food which satisfies. In August, 1912, I bought my first copy of Science and Health, and have read it through ten times. I have come to love the Bible, which was not the case in former times. I am now a member of The Mother Church, and have had many beautiful demonstrations for myself and others. I am grateful to know that I can help others, particularly my own people (the colored race). As I have been benefited by the testimonies of others, I hope some one will be helped by mine. I am grateful to Mrs. Eddy for this Christ-teaching, and thankful to God for the spiritual understanding.

This testimony is interesting for what it includes of the practitioner's method of "silently" treating or praying for Pitchford while he read from Eddy's book. His testimony shares features with many others in this period. Pitchford was skeptical about the initial treatment, willing to try it conditionally, and found spiritual satisfaction both stemming from and superseding the healing experience. He reported gaining a newfound love for the Bible from reading *Science and Health*, followed by institutional participation and a commitment to helping others. Pitchford adds his particular gratitude that fellow African Americans would be among those he could help.

A former Baptist missionary from Florida, Anderson Jefferson, wrote in 1909 that following his Christian Science healing, several fellow African Americans became interested and hoped to form their own "society, where we can meet and go over our Lesson-Sermon."[57] Amanda James of Austin, mentioned earlier, made a similar comment.

Forming a primarily or entirely African American church may have been voluntary at times or a de facto development within primarily African American neighborhoods, but at other times it was neither. The Mother Church was open to members and attendees of any race, but following regional habits, some local churches practiced segregation. Testifiers did not mention this, probably because it was culturally assumed, perhaps out of a sense of dignity or decorum, and perhaps because they did not want to magnify a problem they felt to be resolvable through religious practice.

As Scott E. Caspar has noted, the emergence of the book trade in mid-nineteenth-century America linked literacy with the middle class.[58] Yet as the social historian Rolf Swensen shows, while in certain urban locations (Manhattan, Los Angeles, and Portland, Oregon) members of Christian Science branch churches in the long nineteenth century tended toward the middle class, overall church members came from a wide variety of income brackets and occupational backgrounds. At least one-third of his Manhattan sample and almost 40 percent of his Pacific Coast sample were clerks, artisans, or service workers. The West Coast especially included a significant proportion of members who worked in labor and craft occupations.[59] Farmers, not in his sampling, were well-represented in the Midwest.

At least some adherents used Eddy's book to learn to read. A 1901 testimonial refers to a formerly enslaved woman who "never knew how to read," but after an eye difficulty was "overcome" in "three treatments," she wanted to build on what she had learned and was "now learning to read Science and Health."[60] A visitor to the Toledo, Ohio, Dispensary had a similar experience. Dispensaries were literature distribution hubs located in urban centers that functioned something like missionary organizations; the Toledo hub had at least one "missionary" on staff.[61] Reading rooms ultimately replaced them.

A worker at the Toledo Dispensary reported that a visitor wondered if it might be possible to understand *Science and Health* "with my lack of education," commenting that the book had already brought her healing and "peace" through a practitioner's treatment. The worker told her "that worldly wisdom availeth nothing; that this Truth was for all." The visitor returned a week later feeling that "'this Book is an education of itself.'" The worker added, "Physical beliefs disappeared. In two months she studied, and is doing a beautiful work for the Master," Jesus Christ.[62]

A Mexican Christian Scientist, Susana Mendez, gave similar counsel to a patient, according to an account sent in 1901 by an English-speaking church member in Mexico City. Susana, a "sewing woman," used a Spanish-English dictionary to translate sentences and sections of Eddy's book, which she used with her Spanish-language Bible. An English-speaking Episcopalian was among her other patients. The church eventually produced a Spanish translation of Eddy's book in the 1940s. Susana and her husband, Francisco, a police officer, were apparently the first Christian Scientists in Mexico City. Francisco reportedly employed the Christian Science pastor to alleviate what he described as police corruption, "and he constantly stands up for Jesus Christ even when they make fun of him."[63]

RACED ACCOUNTS OF Christian Science practice were not tremendously common, but more so than is usually acknowledged. The primary source importance of these records is manifest. Their overall tone and content are representative of testimonials in general during this early era, and they also speak to a larger raced narrative touching on cultural reception of Christian Science practice.

In the 1890s, as in the two decades prior, many observers tended to accept accounts of Christian Science healing. In 1891, Eddy's publisher continued to field regular inquiries from ministers.[64] A general curiosity reigned. Religious critics of Christian Science were still mostly concerned with matters of teaching rather than questioning efficacy.

On one hand, high church traditions tended to find Christian Science heretical. How could its healing activities be valid without clergy or rites to convey God's sacramental graces? This was a weighty question. On the other hand, as Pamela Klassen notes in the Canadian context, "For Methodist and Anglican writers to forswear the principles behind Christian Science altogether would be to deny God's effectiveness in the world."[65] In seeking to "critique Christian Science without giving up the God-infused body," they charted a new type of *via media* that saw God in biomedical applications. Their spiritual texts served "not only as paths to devotion but also as grounds for truth claims about Christianity's essential role in the new age of medical and scientific progress."[66]

Mixed into these views, Klassen finds a steady undercurrent of grudging respect, "reluctant acknowledgments of the glimpses of truth in Christian Science." This mixture was unsettled by nature. The Protestant clergy, she concludes, "demonstrated that Christian Science had not only raised their orthodox ire but that it had also worked a transformation of their thinking. By emphasizing the 'supremacy of the spiritual,' one Methodist minister suggested, Christian Science had 'met a deep want in human experiences,' but it had also 'snatched our birthright and appropriated our heritage.'" Such rhetoric coexisted with ongoing clerical support in the manner of O. P. Gifford, though Klassen finds it commonplace.[67]

One response to these conflicting emotions was to emphasize healing as a sacramental activity dependent on the priestly office and healing oil. An Episcopal offshoot, Elwood Worcester's Boston-based Emmanuel Movement, sought to reclaim and reconstitute the sacrament of confession by refiguring it through modern psychology and a vigorous masculine image. Emmanuel techniques (rubbing, suggestion, voiced commands) recalled the mesmeric techniques Eddy had so decisively rejected. Adherents also participated in the establishment of psychotherapy and hypnotism as professional fields. Limned between older mesmeric and newer hypnosis and psychological models, Emmanuel was short-lived. It illustrates, however, how some of Eddy's liberal detractors after 1900 consciously developed movements to be in competition with hers.[68]

Another response was to racialize and feminize Christian Science rhetorically. Klassen notes that after the 1890s, liberal Protestants used racial and religious epithets to feminize and condemn Eddy's religion by aligning it with the perceived "weaknesses" of selfish and comfortable housewives, Jews, Roman Catholics, "Mohammedans," and the "Oriental." She calls this strategy "heathenizing" Christian Science. This language continued to be used by various critics in the 1880s.[69]

Christian Scientists themselves were all over the board in terms of racist theories and antiracism. Adherents such as James, McKenzie, Pitchford, and Webb considered its antiracist theology central to their practice. Yet a suffragist and recording secretary of the National American Woman Suffrage Association, Rachel Foster Avery, exhibited racist xenophobia when she sought to rid the association of a program of "Mzoomdar and all the other Orientals."[70] Avery remained a student of Christian Science into the 1890s.

In contrast, during the Boxer Rebellion in 1900 Beijing, Sarah Pike Conger sent letters to Eddy detailing how she "relied on her faith," writes Stephen Gottschalk, and afterward formed an unexpected friendship with Empress Dowager Cixi.[71] In December 1910 Christian Scientists on official church duty recorded in a logbook spending a "quiet" and "profitable" night studying the lesson-sermon on Spirit, which "seems to unfold more as the week advances." They read several "letters from China and found them very helpful in giving a broader insight into, and love for our Chinese brethren."[72]

An African American porter approached two presumably Euro-American women studying *Science and Health* on a train to Chicago in 1899 and told them he owned it too, calling it "the good little book." Turning the tables on social hierarchies, he commended them for their interest. They found this surprising but "pleasing" and reported "a very interesting conversation with him."[73]

The same year, however, Mrs. E. W. H. wrote from South Carolina that she sought to introduce Christian Science among the African American workers on her rice plantations. Her account is romanticizing and infantilizing toward employees, referring to their poverty as though it were a natural rather than constructed economic state in which she played a key part. When one man phonetically called her religion "Christian Signs," she "thought what he said beautiful."[74]

At impromptu Wednesday meetings she apparently organized and obliged her employees to attend, she thrilled at the experiences they recounted, which consisted primarily of illustrations of how recalling Christian Science group study enabled them to continue difficult work they would have abandoned previously. They signified on E. W. H.'s faith, as Charles Long would have it, playing off her religious beliefs and terms in order to undercut and invert a subordinating relationship within the available limits in an unstable Reconstruction environment.[75]

The *Journal* occasionally included news clippings or "items of interest" regarding African American experience, often emphasizing Tuskegee-style "uplift" through education, possibly a nod to Booker T. Washington's positive reception of *Science and Health* in 1891. Some mocked and upended common racial and religious prejudices. One brief morality tale, printed in September 1898, told a sly yarn about a woman who found herself in a "respectable church" where she became "inspired by the music" and began to gesticulate with abandon. "The sexton telling her to keep still, she replied that she could not, she had got religion." To this the overexcited sexton insisted, "Madam, you must keep still or go out. You ought to know that this is no place to get religion. This is a church."[76]

What at first looks like a racist trope is turned on its head. The joke is on the presumably white sexton and not the charismatic African American woman. In light of the minority status and rejection of Christian Science by the "respectable" churches, this fictional woman even reads like a metaphorical representative of Christian Science itself. Somewhat differently, the architectural historian Paul Eli Ivey argues that in the wake of the Chicago World's Fair in 1893, Christian Science architecture increasingly embodied the "city beautiful" style introduced at the fair's White City, which he casts as the new denomination making a bid for respectability.[77]

For many early Christian Scientists of every racial background, in particular the African Americans who singled out this factor as important to them, their religion continued to provide a spiritual basis for antiracism and egalitarianism. As American policies shifted in the Jim Crow era, however, and as the national interwar cultural climate slid toward the Johnson-Reed Act of 1924, the balance of raced experiences and messages within the church would soon also shift in a different, mixed direction.

Whatever their societal or personal profile, individual Christian Scientists at the turn of the twentieth century fundamentally defined themselves by what they had each seen and experienced by studying the Bible and Eddy's book. As a boggling array of conflicting definitions of their religious identity swirled around them, their testimonies show how adherents used their new dual pastor as they sought to experience healing, understand their Father-Mother God, and participate in their church organization.

CHAPTER FOURTEEN

Public Perceptions, Private Experiences

(1902–1906)

In which a bundle of contrary definitions of Christian Science continue to flow and collide across American culture, and in which people continue to use their Christian Science pastoral books together in a way that points to a relatively consistent religious identity matching some but not all elements of public discourse

IN THE YEARS BETWEEN her landmark 1891 edition of *Science and Health* and her almost finalized 1907 edition, Eddy's 1902 volume emerged to circulate widely within a cultural soup of impressions about its contents and author. Scores of notable names dotted ever-widening lists of recipients and correspondents: admirals and royalty, bishops and libraries, literary figures and innovators such as Booker T. Washington, Queen Liliuokalani, Leo Tolstoy.[1] Circulation continued to increase among the rank and file, too. Reception followed familiar patterns. Mentions of Christian Science in personal letters, media, court records, and other avenues help us reconstruct these popular cultural views.

The YMCA declined to place *Science and Health* in its library in 1896, feeling it was not mission-appropriate for a Christian organization. Conversely, the clerk of a women's prison in 1898 was grateful to have what she considered a practical statement of Christianity and signed off as a "Sister in Christ." The New Hampshire State Librarian read it and sent the publisher a long discourse of his own views on state letterhead (he found suffering and pain to be "necessary instrumentalities" of the Divine but agreed that "*Divine Man* is the only form that reveals God's creative designs fulfilled"). Differences aside, he closed gallantly with "personal regards to your lady."[2]

By the 1880s, social reformers and Eddy agreed that they sympathized with each other but held different priorities. By 1900, however, critics of women's rights grouped these high-profile public figures together. Gendered and doctrinal critiques of Eddy's work often intertwined, as in the example above, which shows a caricature of Eddy toward the back among such notables as Carrie Nation, Elizabeth Cady Stanton, Susan B. Anthony, and Dr. Mary Walker. Louis Dalrymple, "A Suggestion to the Buffalo Exposition; - Let Us Have a Chamber of Female Horrors," *Puck* 49, no. 1256 (3 April 1901), centerfold, chromolithograph, Library of Congress Prints and Photographs Division, LC-DIG-ppmsca-25513, http://loc.gov/pictures/resource/ppmsca.25513/.

Alice Weston Smith wrote from Boston in 1895 about an article on Christian Science, "Some parts I can't quite grasp and others I totally disagree with, but there is a great deal of it that I found most beautiful and true."[3] In 1898, a Vermont woman wrote to her cousin that she had "no sympathy with the teachings of 'Christian Science' falsely so called," apparently for orthodox religious reasons, but her household would still "be glad to receive you or any of the family" and try their utmost to be hospitable.[4] In 1899, a Bostonian named Louise wrote a newsy letter to her friend Herbert, including a closing jocund aside that Christian Science was obviously a "sham."[5]

In 1900, Susan Hale recalled to Caroline Weld a family she knew who "had absolutely no digestion, and suffered agonies from peritonitis, bronchitis, diagnosis, and meningitis, whenever they put food in their mouths." After meeting a Christian Science practitioner, "they used to have cucumbers and lobster salad regularly for dinner, and just telegraph afterwards to her, and she would simply fix her mind upon her Maker, and they would digest by return telegram."⁶ Hale had no further judgment or apparent interest other than this unusual observation.

In 1901, *Puck* magazine published a cartoon titled "Superstition Has Always Ruled the World." Whether early Millerites or Spiritualists, the followers of early prophets or alchemists, the dupes of "modern drug worship" or Christian Science, all were deluded. Eddy and faith healer John Alexander Dowie are portrayed collecting money; next to Eddy are *Science and Health* and a placard reading, "God Has Himself Spoken to Me."⁷ The trope of her as mercenary increased after Mark Twain satirized her work this way in 1899. Gendered critiques continued as well. In 1901, *Puck* also depicted Eddy with suffragists and other social reformers above the caption, "Let Us Have a Chamber of Female Horrors." Despite their different priorities, they were grouped together, all rendered in an unflattering style.⁸

In 1906, Caroline A. Huling told her niece that her Christian Science friends were on to something helpful, but they mistook the nature of their religion. It was "really the control of yourself and others through the exercise of a strong mentality. . . . Psychology—the scientific study of the action of the mind—is a fascinating subject."⁹

The opinions of medical professionals were similarly diverse around the turn of the century. Some physicians rejected Christian Science outright; others defended it with caveats; a few recommended their patients to it. In a highly unusual case back in 1888, an allopathic physician in Iowa, Dr. Sears, did all three. Stating his credentials, Sears called himself "one of the most *ultra* sticklers" for conventional treatment, "denouncing all the outside schools of medicine in the strongest terms."

The Christian Science healings he encountered, however, "were not by any means cases of diseased imagination, but serious cases of long standing, which had baffled the best medical skill. . . . Without going into details, I will state that some of the results were to me very wonderful." Such observations led him to experiment with giving Christian Science treatment himself. He never committed to it fully but felt he had some successes.

More typically, Sears accepted that just as physicians sometimes failed to meet their goals, so did Christian Scientists. They sometimes courted controversy, he felt, when they "rushed" into the healing work without adequate experience, "claiming for it more than they were able to demonstrate." Some practitioners were egocentric, drawing attention to themselves "instead of giving God all the glory." Yet, Sears concluded, it would not make sense for Jesus to "command his followers to heal the sick, unless he knew it to be possible, and desired them to make the effort."¹⁰

He noted that in his local Iowa newspaper, when it came to Christian Scientists, their "cases of failure are always mentioned, while the cases of cures and benefits derived are either ridiculed or ignored. Ordinary medical treatment is not always successful. I find in our beautiful cemetery many newly made graves. . . . No one would think of discarding doctors and medicines because of these failures."[11]

Other fascinated observers skipped personal experimentation but made similar comments. William Lloyd Garrison III, grandson of the abolitionist, frankly noted that he doubted Christian Science theology was logical and did not agree with its "Biblical dogmas." However, from his "own enforced observation," he cited cases of physical and moral regeneration through its practice that he led him to feel "whatever the cause of this phenomenal and widespread change, it seems to me a blessing to the world."[12]

Garrison invoked William James in finding Christian Scientists valuable because of their unusual and compelling religious practice. Like Sears, he also noted that they could fall short of their ideals and in such cases draw special scrutiny. "If all deaths resulting from regular [medical] ignorance or carelessness were exploited, as are the cases where Christian Science has failed of success," Garrison commented, "what fright would take possession of the community."[13]

One of my book's unexpected research findings, as I have noted, is that even Eddy's severest critics routinely accepted evidence that her religion healed but proposed that its curative effects rested on religiously, medically, or philosophically fraudulent grounds. Some physicians thus felt the practice should be banned, arguing that Christian Science healings were built on delusions and falsehoods.[14] In so doing, most medical, legal, clerical, and other professionals tended to grapple with evidence of Christian Science successes and failures together as a unit in the decades around 1900. As the twentieth century progressed, this gave way to an emphasis on failures alone.

Historians are not arbiters of efficacy, but some scholars of religious healing have sought to put parameters around the topic. Andrew Singleton suggests that healing groups explain curative reversals as purposive or fated, thus reinscribing faith rather than challenging it.[15] James B. Waldram, on the other hand, shows that traditional or indigenous medicine is not always culturally constructed to ensure an emic interpretation of success.[16] Not only is skepticism apparent within communities that practice traditional medicine, he notes, but all systems of medicine require a viable explanation of failure. This explanation can deflect criticism, refine healing practice, or act as a test of a healer's skill.

Waldram's sophisticated work posits that within medical anthropology, literature on traditional medicine either assumes efficacy without explaining why or assumes a biomedical framework that cannot grasp indigenous experience. He argues that efficacy can be discussed adequately only if all participants in the "sickness episode" are deeply contextualized. Religious healing is a "moving target" to academics, he concludes, inherently ambiguous and multiform to outside perspectives, and researchers need to learn to live with this.[17]

This underscores how once again, Christian Science cannot be easily categorized (or perhaps categorized at all) using conventional academic tools, in this case like other forms of religious healing. Such healing cannot be measured using biomedicine as the "arbiter of efficacy," argues Waldram, because not only does this mask biomedicine's own efficacy issues, it takes traditional medicine out of its indigenous context, an arrangement wherein biomedicine applies efficacy expectations to religious healing that it does not apply to itself.[18] James Opp similarly argues that faith healers had a different perception of the body than medicalists, which in practice constituted a form of resistance to biomedical hegemony and the medicalized, Foucauldian gaze.[19] As Waldram, Opp, and others have sought to describe the indigenous context for the religious healing traditions they have studied, so I seek to provide a semblance of indigenous context for Christian Scientists.

In the realm of divine healing, Heather Curtis registers emotive responses to failure such as bewilderment, stigmatization, and shame, as well as constructive responses such as refining theology and building faith homes where protracted healings might take place outside the glare of a critical society. Similarly, Christian Scientists sometimes responded with grief or discouragement and sometimes with reflection, study, and renewed persistence. In the early 1900s, they also built Christian Science nursing facilities staffed by Christian Science Nurses. These facilities were not tailored for protracted cases specifically but could accommodate them. In other ways Christian Science responses differed from faith healers, as literature on this topic shows.

Some Christian groups, notes Raymond J. Cunningham, cited Paul's "thorn in the flesh" as evidence that if Paul had an unhealed condition, there was no shame in today's healing Christians having one, too.[20] The rarity of true faith, he notes, is also sometimes an explanation for failure, as is God's sovereign will. This last explanation raises conflicts relating to theodicy but is nevertheless somewhat common except in Christian Science. Jonathan Baer, Opp, Ruth Harris, and Wouter Hanegraaff show how a spectrum of healers, from some faith curers to Catholics to New Agers, describe God as permitting suffering as a learning or reforming tool. New Agers, notes Hanegraaff, also believe that we manifest our own reality, including our failures (a position analogous to lack of faith among divine healers).[21]

Baer, Robert Peel, and Stephen Gottschalk all cite slow healings, as understood by divine healers and Christian Scientists, as pointing to a need for spiritual growth on the part of adherents. These healings took patience and persistence over time, which in the interim might look like failure to others and periodically even to the adherents themselves. Similarly, Thomas Csordas speaks of incremental healing, which he calls the norm among Catholic charismatics.[22] Donald W. Dayton discusses protracted healings as the norm among faith healers.[23]

Peel and Gottschalk present in different terms Christian Science healings that take place over time. Gottschalk emphasizes a necessary period of spiritual growth preceding some healings, citing the entrenched nature of carnal beliefs that Christ must root out. Peel finds that though some healings appear slow, they are actually experienced as sudden or immediate healings following a longer period of prayer.[24]

In general, Peel and Gottschalk emphasize the Christian Science dependence on Mind, God, rather than on processes within the human mind (in contrast to New Thought or New Age philosophies). They focus on its dependence on natural spiritual law rather than belief (which, as I have shown, overlaps to some degree with the approach of early divine healers). Rennie Schoepflin characterizes Christian Science as therapeutic, while Peel positions therapy as a minor subset of the healing experience whereby healing is a result but not a goal per se, a by-product of spiritual growth but not an end in itself. Peel also discusses frequent reports in Christian Science testimonials of what he calls a "flood of light and joy" accompanying physical healing; this "flood," he says, is the actual healing itself, and he notes a confluence between such descriptions and evangelical reports of being saved.[25] I also found that early Christian Science narratives of healing were dominated by statements of joy, happiness, and often glad surprise.

IT IS IMPORTANT to read passages regarding the failures of Christian Scientists in this larger context. These existed within a preponderance of healing successes acknowledged by adherents and observers alike; they received special scrutiny culturally, legally, religiously, and medically; and they were accompanied by both emic (internal) and etic (external) explanations and responses.

Christian Scientists themselves did not pretend to have a perfect track record. "I have grieved over my failure in mastery over many things," wrote E. N., "but am able to thank God also for victories over many."[26] L. H. noted, "I find it impossible to become Christlike in a day, and I find also that the greatest work is with ourselves."[27] Without the "Spirit of Love . . . even Christian Science is a failure," wrote a *Christian Science Journal* editor, lamenting the ineffectual focus he sometimes saw "upon the mere 'letter' of Science."[28]

Looking to the model of Christian healing, the prominent Christian Scientist Rev. Irving C. Tomlinson noted that the disciples of Jesus sometimes failed to cure. Speaking at the Philosophical Conference at Tufts College in 1900 hosted by Professor Herbert E. Cushman, Tomlinson said, "When Christ's students asked for the explanation of their failure" to heal, Jesus "did not ascribe it to their weak personalities, but to their lack of understanding." This was an occasion to better understand his statement, "'The Son can do nothing of himself, but what he seeth the Father do.'"[29]

In a 1905 minor edition of *Science and Health*, Eddy added a provision that if Christian Scientists experienced pain so severe they could not pray for and "treat" themselves, "and the Scientists had failed to relieve" them, they could request a physician for a painkiller until able to handle the situation effectively through prayer (the first major edition this appears in is 1907:464).[30] In 1875 and every edition after, she wrote that it is "better to call a surgeon" to set broken bones and dislocated joints until a fuller understanding of Christian Science prevailed (1875:400; 1911:401). This was considered a sign not of failure but of the gradual experience of "demonstrating" Christian Science in human life.

As Rennie B. Schoepflin points out, she also temporarily advised Christian Scientists to decline treating contagious cases until public acceptance of their methods had increased, remembering that "whether successful or not, *they are not specially protected by law.*"[31] *Puck* ran a 1902 image in which a personification of the law reprimanded a Christian Scientist for not reporting contagious diseases.[32] This problem affected pockets of the divine healing community more than it did Christian Scientists, but in some cases Christian Scientists were unclear or unwise regarding legal requirements, which dominated media attention. Public scrutiny correspondingly declined after Eddy permanently advised reporting contagious diseases and cooperating with vaccination laws.

Careful and literal obedience to public health law became ingrained in Christian Science ethics from then on. A New Hampshire woman, Mary Gove, who became a Christian Scientist around 1915, wrote in her diary in 1920 that her son "Ken seems to have a bad cold and as he wasn't a bit good tonight called Mrs. B," a local Christian Science practitioner. The following day she called Mrs. B. again and decided they would return home from their vacation "unless he is better." In her next entry, she wrote, Ken was "much better[;] decided to stay. . . . Had a lovely time." At the end of the month, she "had Ken vaccinated again, by Dr. Amsden" and several days later took him for a checkup. She made three quarts of mincemeat and two and a half quarts of crabapple jelly, then "took Ken up to Dr's & he said he was O.K. & got his vaccination card."[33]

MARY GOVE ALSO often visited friends in the hospital and had physicians in her social circle, underscoring that Christian Scientists had more regular contact with physicians than is usually assumed, a point Robert Peel observes in regard to the twentieth century.[34] In addition, Gove's family experience illustrates how early Christian Scientists responded to efficacy and legal concerns by accommodating societal expectations to a point both parties deemed reasonable, as Schoepflin brings out. Relying on Christian Science healing while accommodating public health laws became the standard. The emphasis on complying with public health codes also reflects Eddy's effort to distinguish herself from the high-profile faith healer John Alexander Dowie, who issued extreme statements against medical, legal, and clerical figures in the years around 1900. Such extremism existed in obscure pockets of Eddy's church but was not the norm. Dowie's statements prompted Eddy to issue her own supporting legal compliance, respect for physicians, and religious tolerance, even (and perhaps especially) where disagreements might occur. In sorting this out she took to her Bible, where she noted "Dowie" on a back flyleaf and indicated a psalm about turning to God for guidance.[35]

The extensive cultural confusion between Eddy's religion and other groups inhered in medical circles as much as in others, making discussions difficult to track with precision. A widely circulated book by William Archer Purrington, lecturer in the university and Bellevue Hospital Medical Center of New York and author of *A System of Legal Medicine*, sought to protect "helpless" patients by "expounding the dangerous teachings of our latter-day delusion, Christian Science," which he identified with faith cure, mesmerism, hypnotism, and vitapathy. His leading example involved a woman who "professed belief in Christian Science and mental treatment, but also in the efficacy of [physical] remedies" and who "was not a strict Eddyite but had a system and book of her own."[36]

Schoepflin zeroes in on actual Christian Scientists by reviewing the twenty-eight court proceedings involving them between 1885 and 1901. He shows that in general, questions about efficacy were handled under a medical licensing rubric. Whether they healed their patients or not, this group of practitioners were taken to court for practicing without a medical license. He contextualizes the latter trend within the increasing medicalization of healing options in America, citing the efforts of physicians to consolidate medical interests and set biomedical standards of care.

Litigants most often presented Christian Science as a renegade and "irregular" medical system disguised as a religion and lacking the proper licensing. Several states passed bills specifically designed to limit and contain Christian Science practice. Cases resulting from these laws, however, usually ended in acquittal (all but two by 1900), which led future plaintiffs to adjust their strategies. Litigation against Christian Scientists dropped off considerably between 1890 and 1930, when Schoepflin finds a gradual shift toward renewed public health concerns. Lawsuits disappeared entirely for four decades mid-century before an uptick on different grounds.[37]

In the decades around 1900, I find the same licensing-oriented rationale for early litigation as does Schoepflin, and also that courts usually acquitted on the ruling that Christian Science was a religion with a nonmedical healing practice. A random selection of transcripts and newspaper articles from historical databases shows that the question of efficacy entered and exited deliberations in sometimes surprising ways.

In an 1889 Ohio case, the appeals court set aside the matter of efficacy entirely, ruling that "what efficacy there may be in treating bodily ills through means" such as prayer, "the court is not called upon to decide." The judgment granted "perfect sincerity to a now considerable number of highly respectable persons" employing Christian Science but found it impossible to rule that Harriet Evans's practice was medical in nature, as it did not involve medicines, medical training, or physical diagnosis. Thus "it is clear that christian science is a kind of religious belief." The court did not punish those of other sects who sought healing through contact with holy relics, and if that "applies to one class, it must also apply to the other."[38] Further, the practitioner, Evans, accepted a modest donation but did not charge the patient. Most state licensing laws required a billing transaction to establish professional activity as opposed to charity. Thus her conviction was overturned.

In an 1891 case against the Christian Science practitioner James Neal, the *Kearney Daily Hub* in Nebraska reported a jury conviction following the demise of Laura Thomas. Sources disagree regarding basic facts. The *Hub* stated that home remedies were employed but not physicians; Neal claimed to be on the case for only a day following Thomas's weeks of medical care.[39] Regardless, Nebraska had recently passed a law that Christian Science be practiced as a charity and not a profession, and Neal became the test case. Amid large-font rumor (false, as it turned out) that he had skipped town on a freight train after dark, he published a notice that he would keep an office for six months in Kearney, ready for questions. He was ultimately convicted on licensing grounds, efficacy aside. He paid the judgment, he told his friend Joseph Armstrong, by securing a second mortgage on his two mules and cow. "Dear Brother," Neal wrote, "Jesus hadn't as much as a 'Jack Knife' in material things," and are "we absolutely willing to lay down all for Christ?"[40]

An appeals court in Indiana overturned a 1901 conviction, also revolving around licensing, for reasons similar to the earlier Evans decision. State senators and attorneys spoke on all sides of the issue, some lambasting and others supporting the religion and its tenets.[41] A 1905 probate court in Ohio convicted

Oliver W. Marble for lack of licensing without commenting on efficacy, as Marble's patient was apparently healthy and registered no complaints. An appeals court overturned the conviction, noting exceptions.[42] Court records sometimes include lengthy testimony from Christian Scientists, which is invariably sincere but ranges in character from mature and measured to odd and naive.

Overall, legislation defined Christian Science as medical practice only to be countered by courts unable to sustain that definition under examination, finding instead that it was a religion. These opposing legislative and judicial characterizations circulated simultaneously and widely across media outlets. Legislative efforts to legally group Christian Science with such therapies as osteopathy and chiropractic for licensing purposes were also nearly always overturned, but they also made their mark, resulting in increased public perceptions of Christian Science as a therapeutic system with a religious overlay. As the church expanded, these competing categorizations became part of its cultural backdrop.

In a typical 1901 letter, Heloise Edwina Hersey wrote her friend Helen that of all the "fads" that had "multiplied" in America, none could be counted on to "secure health"—neither "oatmeal nor blue glass, nor Swedish gymnastics nor Christian Science, nor osteopathy nor abstinence from eating of breakfast, nor dress reform, nor cold water, nor vegetarianism."[43] In contrast, as Holly Folk shows, the founder of chiropractic D. D. Palmer styled his vision for public acceptance of the "religion of chiropractic" around the successes of "Christ, Mohamed, Jo. Smith, Mrs. Eddy, Martin Luther and other[s] who have founded religions."[44]

AGAINST THIS BACKDROP, multiple authorship contentions about *Science and Health* also emerged or renewed around the turn of the century. In 1899 Mark Twain recalled Eddy's early critic H. S. C. by characterizing her book as effeminate, nonsensical "Eddygush" and a mercenary tool.[45] Twain scholars and Eddy biographers have parsed his complex love-hate relationship with Eddy and her religion.[46] By 1900 Julius Dresser's son Horatio had renewed his father's contention that Eddy's claims to revelation and discovery were bogus, and Josephine Woodbury enlisted him to cast Eddy and her book as fraudulent in the pages of Benjamin O. Flower's *Arena*.[47] Woodbury then launched a libel suit against Eddy, which Woodbury lost in 1902, attracting national publicity.

Around this time, "The Disputed Authorship of Science and Health" appeared in *Literary Digest* claiming Eddy's former editor the Unitarian John Henry Wiggin had authored her book. Like Twain, Livingston Wright argued that Eddy's feminine illogic and incompetence made it literally impossible for her to produce her own text. Like a later contention that her book was actually a Hegelian plagiarism, this view developed serious media and academic traction into the twentieth century until other scholars finally debunked it.[48]

It is difficult to imagine a male author, however marginalized by his religious innovations, continually facing the repeated contention that he could not have written his own text. Eddy's style was judged too "female"; her sales success aggressively masculine. Yet her claim to have experienced a religious revelation that constituted a new spiritual discovery and to have authored a book over time that explained it continued to be not only a gendered affront but an outrageous claim, period. Who had ever hired an editor to help them fine-tune a description of a divine disclosure? The idea that a human being using regularly available editorial processes might take years to progressively bring out a message pursuant to her divine appointment—this was a new claim among world religions.

Back in 1894, the great investigator into religious experience William James had thrown his hat in the ring. James wrote to the *Boston Transcript* regarding Christian Science and other emergent healing religions, "I assuredly hold no brief for any of these healers"; he was "unable to assimilate their theories, so far as I have heard them given," while finding them intriguing.[49] "But their facts are patent and startling," he went on, "and anything that interferes with the multiplication of such facts, and with our freest opportunity of observing and studying them, will, I believe, be a public calamity."[50]

When he published his massively influential Edinburgh lectures as *The Varieties of Religious Experience* in 1902, which defined Christian Science as a "once-born" religion in the same sunny category as positive thinking and New Thought, his liberal intellect had no particular investment in that characterization. The same could not be said of New Thought advocate and self-professed Eddy detractor Horatio Dresser, James's student and a main informant on Christian Science matters.[51]

If Eddy had a sunny outlook, it might be hinted at in a mark she left in Katharine G. Spear's Methodist *Sunshine and Love* in 1903, the year after James's *Varieties* was published. Despite the title, the book is a rather sober compilation of biblical and literary passages. An entry by the YMCA leader John R. Mott reads, "Prayer is the greatest force that we can wield. It is the greatest talent which God has given us. There is a democracy in this matter," as prayer is available to all regardless of wealth, education, ability, social position, or "our inherited characteristics."[52] It is the only entry in the book Eddy found compelling. It was characteristic of her to find "sunshine and love" in the democracy of prayer as a force.

On 30 June 1903, the *Boston Journal* filled its front page with photographs of the 12,000 Christian Scientists Eddy welcomed to her home, Pleasant View, outside Concord. Calling the event an unparalleled and "remarkable religious pilgrimage," the newspaper showed her on her balcony addressing the crowd. The picture would become iconic, circulating widely for over a century among media outlets and adherents. Outside the public eye, Eddy wrote in the back of her copy of *Science and Health* on or near this date, "for all at P.V.," and indicated a passage about how to demonstrate "the facts of Soul [God], in Jesus's way."[53]

Eddy was using the 1902 revision of her book at the time. In addition to making some capitalization changes, she had omitted the index in favor of a concordance produced by an adherent, Albert Conant.[54] She had shifted the chapters into their final order, with "Prayer" placed first and a new testimonial section called "Fruitage" last. Though she would replace all the testimonies to match her revised text in 1907, she found one especially meaningful in the 1902 edition. It described her book as "the grandest conception of God, the most intelligent explanation of Christ's life, his teachings, and his works, and the highest ideal of manhood ever brought to our consideration, and for the first time in our lives did we seem to get that spiritual food, that bread from heaven, for which we had hungered."[55]

This echoed Marietta Webb's description. "The Bible and 'Science and Health with Key to the Scriptures' are my daily guides, the heavenly manna on which I feast and live," she declared.[56] Such accounts invoke the immanence and presence of God without the sense of divine absence felt by many Protestants of the era, signaled by the Nietzschean vision of an unsustainable Christianity folding in on itself. They recall Friedrich Schleiermacher's "absolute dependence on God," but Christian Science practice did not especially resonate with that pole of modernity, either, particularly its distinction between feeling and action.

Amid conflicting descriptions of Christian Science, using adherent books as artifacts of religious history helps us map its vernacular practice and draw its contours from the inside out.

WILLIAM MCKENZIE'S 1894 COPY of *Science and Health with Key to the Scriptures* is a remarkable artifact of early Christian Science history. A Presbyterian minister and professor with degrees from Knox College at the University of Toronto and Auburn Theological Seminary in New York, Reverend McKenzie was teaching on the faculty at Rochester University when Mary Baker Eddy's biblical exposition won him over. Wrestling with his conscience, he gradually changed allegiances.

He began an 1896 letter to her, "God is restoring to me the 'joy of His Salvation.' Like a new revelation is coming to me some vision of the impact of the crucifixion: I see it as a consummation of meekness wherein God became All-in-all, & so to enemies & cruel ones there was no answer but only love from the heart of Jesus." He went on to reveal that "in my own thought I unearthed much of that desire for knowledge in order to *know* instead of *do*, a sort of intellectual avarice: also a hidden love of distinction & honor from men. I can see how these conditions of mind have in them the elements of unfaithfulness, & I am earnestly seeking humility." He closed by noting that his congregation of Christian Scientists in Toronto was "growing in grace, honesty, gentleness," and love.[57]

Eddy wrote on the envelope with emphasis, "*Best*." She invited him to Boston soon after. He used the same book for personal study for many years, including while serving on teams assisting her with the 1902 and 1907 revisions. Daisette Stocking, a Christian Scientist from Cleveland, had introduced him to the religion and gifted him with *Science and Health*. When the two decided to marry in 1901, she wrote to her "Laddie" on stationery headed with a large picture of the marriage of the Lamb that she overdrew in ink, "So it has come from God to us both. How wonderful is Love's mystery, faithful heart, and how graciously we are allowed to enter." William wrote to her around this time that staying single may serve a purpose as well as marrying, but "we do not wish to lose the hallowing influences of the relation of man & woman."[58] They soon had a son, Guilford Stuart.

In McKenzie's copy of Eddy's book, each page is laden with marginalia inscribed with his signature purple pen, its impossibly tiny nib carving out hundreds of Bible references, related Hebrew and Greek word roots, personal notations, and at least one joke. People often pasted illustrations or snippets of text into their books. In William's, a portrait of Jesus is pasted on a front flyleaf, an illustration of the Annunciation and a copy of the Beatitudes to the back of the title page. Daisette wrote an inscription about Saul of Tarsus becoming Paul the Apostle when he "beheld the way," and "the *man* was changed." The inscription reads as a reference to their shared perception of William's experience "coming into" or "finding" Christian Science, phrases Christian Scientists often used in lieu of traditional conversion language.[59]

A testimony McKenzie helped select for the 1907 edition of Eddy's book indicated, "When I reached the place where Mrs. Eddy says she found this truth in the Bible, I began comparing the two books" (1907:642; 1911:642). This was common, and McKenzie did it on a massively detailed and educated scale. On almost every page of *Science and Health*, he noted the chapter and verse of a scripture Eddy alluded to or quoted. He often indicated his feelings or insights.

On a typical span of five pages, he wrote fourteen Bible references. "Humanity advances out of material sense into spiritual understanding slowly," Eddy wrote, "because unwillingness to learn clogs the footsteps and loads Christendom with chains" (1894:261). McKenzie found corroboration in

Proverbs 29:1 and Amos 8:10. On the first three pages of her exegesis of the book of Revelation, he found relevance and supporting insight in passages from Psalms, John, and Luke. In a single sentence about how "to misunderstand Paul, was to be ignorant of the divine idea he taught," McKenzie jotted references to Jeremiah, 1 Samuel, 1 John, and Micah.

Underneath the reference to misunderstanding Paul, he wrote, "If an ambassador arrived with the King's message travel-stained, some would refuse to hear[,] saying He has mud on his cloak, His hat is gone, He has lost a shoe in a mudhole, He drinks water—We want one who drinks red wine, rides a horse & has gorgeous dress; and does not come in haste." The surrounding context makes clear McKenzie's commentary relates not only to Paul but to how he saw Eddy as the messenger of Christian Science.

Moving on to her interpretation of the twenty-third psalm, he wrote underneath, "*To see* is to dwell in the Temple of which the Lamb is the Light; to realize the 'unselfish Love that goes out in divine pity to the blindness of the world.'" Under Eddy's exegesis of Revelation 12:9, which "shows how the Lamb slays the wolf" (1894:559), McKenzie wrote "Rev 12:11" and compared this "divine method of warfare in Science" shown in the Apocalypse to "I Sam 7:10." He added in the margin, "The shield of faith quenches the ignited shafts of the Evil one; that in our sense of love as power, & Good as our trust prevents any kindling of indignation or response to malice."

At the start of the book, he indicated something of his view of the Bible and *Science and Health* by marking the passage, "When a new spiritual idea is borne to earth, the prophetic Scripture of Isaiah is renewedly fulfilled . . ." (1894:3). McKenzie noted Isaiah chapter 9, verse 7, and wrote in response, "The writings of them of old time, & the compilations & letters of the later writers had little chance of accuracy" (as evinced by manuscript damage, loss, and multiple subsequent translations). "The later revelation," he wrote, has much "care in revision & exactness."[60]

McKenzie became devoted to Eddy and her message, Peel notes, after his first visit with her on Christmas Day in 1894.[61] One of his notations indicates what he attributed this to. "The manifestation of God through mortals," Eddy wrote in her 1894 version of *Science and Health*, "is as light passing through the windowpane. The light and glass never mingle, only the glass is less opaque than the walls. The mortal mind through which Truth appears most vividly is that one which has lost much materiality, error, in order to become a better transparency for Truth" (1894:191). McKenzie marked the passage by carefully noting Acts 9:10 and Luke 12:38 in the margin. He underlined the phrase "transparency for Truth" and wrote beside it, "Concord, transparency / Xmas 1894."

The question of whether someone else could have discovered, articulated, and founded Christian Science seems to have been moot in this scenario as, historically speaking, someone else did not. Thus to adherents, Eddy and Christian Science were inseparable, even as they were qualitatively and quantitatively not the same thing. This was the basis for their appreciation and affection for both, individually and together.

The sheer volume of McKenzie's notations is as interesting as their specificity. They also show the particular cast of his spirituality. As for the joke, it appears under Eddy's consideration of angels. "Angels are not etherealized human beings," she wrote, "evolving animal qualities in their wings; but they are celestial visitors, flying on spiritual, not material, pinions" (1894:194). She still appreciated the symbolism of the traditional depiction of angelic wings in artwork, as did McKenzie. He wrote jokingly in the margin, "A child accustomed to the household use of turkey wings" in feather dusters once asked, "Auntie, are angel wings good to dust with?"

After the publication of new editions or minor printings, early readers often manually updated and changed their books to reflect revisions. McKenzie fixed typos, crossed out revised words and phrases, and inserted replacements.[62] This was possible between 1891 and 1911, when new editions contained relatively few revisions compared to prior years. Although it became impractical after a while, readers often related warmly to their *Science and Health* copies as close friends, like their Bibles, and were slow to trade them in. Dozens of archival photographs show readers fondly carrying or holding their Bibles or Eddy's book in their laps as prized possessions.

Like McKenzie, adherents often packed their Bibles and copies of the Christian Science textbook with notations. They used their books together, constantly referencing the Bible while reading Eddy's book. Some left *Science and Health* blank, perhaps to preserve a valued copy, but more often they heavily marked the margins, flyleaves, and endpapers with personal and inspirational commentary, teaching notes, scriptural references and quotes, line numbers, doodles or humor, and notes and dates of insights linked to specific passages, patients, or events.

The adherent Ellen C. Jones stuffed the flyleaves and other pages of her Christian Science textbook with a hodgepodge of writing and pasted clippings, unconcerned with perfection. She wrote in a loose style with black, blue, and brown pen, sometimes pencil. "Judas betrayed him / Peter denied him / Thomas doubted him / the other 12 forsake him & fled," she noted. She marked pages she found helpful in treating "coughs and colds" and other diseases such as rheumatism and consumption. A handmade, short index lists "Why healing was lost, sickness not imaginary, the Comforter, the story of error, matter, the Adam dream, casting pearls, Why Jesus struggled on Calvary, qualifications for church membership," and other items of note. In the margins throughout her book, she made notes summarizing pages and adding Bible references.[63]

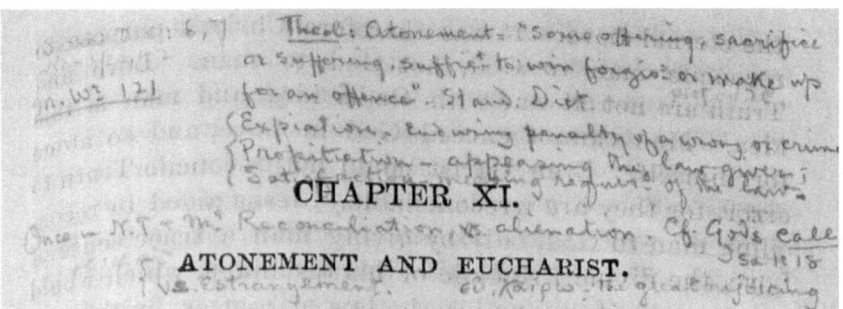

CHAPTER XI.

ATONEMENT AND EUCHARIST.

CHAPTER III.

FOOTSTEPS OF TRUTH.

REMEMBER, Lord, the reproach of Thy servant; how I do bear in my bosom the reproach of all the mighty people; wherewith Thine enemies have reproached, O Lord, wherewith they have reproached the footsteps of Thine anointed. — PSALMS.

THE best sermon is the practice of Truth, and its demonstration through the destruction of sin, sickness, and death. Knowing that one affection will be supreme in us, and take the lead in our lives, Jesus said, "No man can serve two masters."

To build aright, we must first tear down. Truth makes a new creature, wherein old things pass away and "all things are become new." Passions, selfish-

<small>Practical preaching.</small>

Christian Scientists often filled their pastoral books with notes, marks, pasted snippets, biblical quotes, and doodles. These recorded what they described as divine inspiration or answers to prayer. With his tiny purple pen, the former Presbyterian minister William McKenzie packed his copy of *Science and Health* with Bible references and passages. At the start of Eddy's chapter "Atonement and Eucharist," he wrote relevant theological and dictionary definitions and compared New Testament terms, once in the original Greek. On the first page of the chapter "Footsteps of Truth," he found resonance with passages in the biblical books Joshua, I Kings, Psalms, and Proverbs. Notes by McKenzie in Mary Baker Eddy, *Science and Health with Key to the Scriptures* (Boston: E. J. Foster-Eddy, 1894). Photograph by David Brooks Andrews. Courtesy of Ralph Byron Copper Private Collection.

Public Perceptions, Private Experiences

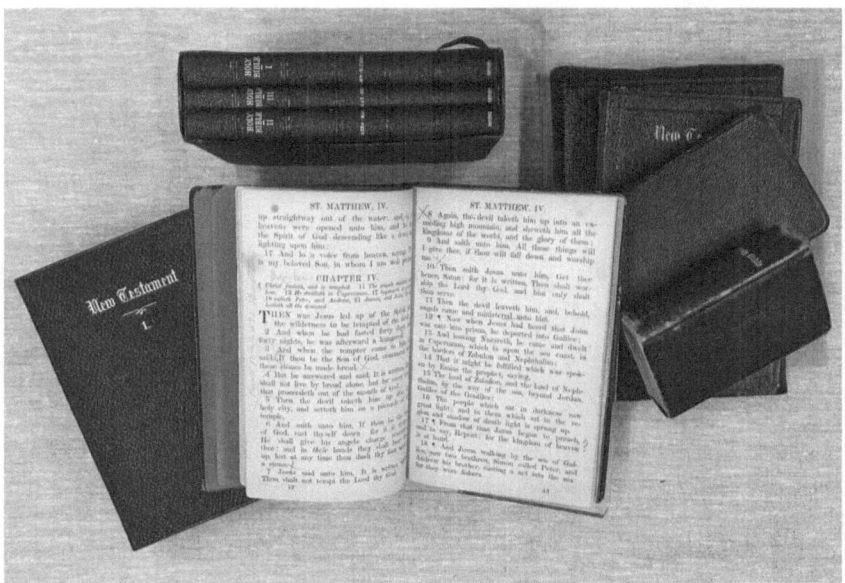

Eddy owned dozens of Bibles. Her notes in them indicate she began each morning by opening the scriptures at random and reading and reflecting, often teaching her household from the text. She made notations about chapters and verses that answered her specific questions and needs. This New Testament edition is bound in four volumes and open to the gospel of Matthew, where Eddy noted the verses she read. She often used an *X* for emphasis. The question mark might indicate a translation question, an exegetical query, or a note to herself about whether to include a verse in a text or a teaching session. Image from the Mary Baker Eddy Collection, B00017.A–C, © The Mary Baker Eddy Library. Used by permission.

Like Americans generally at the time, adherents had their books rebound when the covers wore out or a signature fell loose. Mrs. G. S. Adams, C.S.B. (a teacher of Christian Science), wrote notations for the bookbinder in her volume. Like McKenzie, Adams also went through her copy of *Science and Health* and added the book, chapter, and verse of every scriptural passage Eddy referenced, almost 700 in all. She copied dozens of Bible quotations onto the back flyleaves (at least fifteen from the New Testament on one page). She indexed several passages she connected to such topics as "Identity, Nature and Beauty," "Philosophy of Christian Science," "Healing through Mind [God]," "Liberation," and "Mark 9:23 If thou canst believe all things are possible to him that believe[th] Luke 20_18."[64]

Sue Mims of Atlanta, Georgia, pasted Webster's definition of God into her volume.[65] Rev. Irving Tomlinson put squiggly peacock blue vertical marks throughout his book, sometimes including dates of events or insights he associated with a passage. He used another edition so heavily that his thumb wore a groove into the pages.[66] The spine of Ella Rathvon's small suede book is worn shiny from her hands holding the book. She pressed two small yellow flowers into it and noted the dates of insights and experiences related to her study.[67]

Martha Wilcox did most of her heavy underlining in the chapter "Christian Science Practice," on healing sickness.[68] John Henry Keene, Esq., kept a sheet of paper inside the cover listing books on religion from the early nineteenth century. Baptists, Unitarians, and Roman Catholic texts appear under the title "Thoughts on true and false religions," which seemed to encompass Keene's feelings about Eddy's book. He noted that one page contained a description of how to be "thoroughly healed," indexed "C. S. Revelation" on another, found one passage "queer," and decorated the margins throughout with question marks.[69]

Joseph G. Mann, who maintained buildings and grounds at Eddy's home, marked his copy of *Science and Health* with spare efficiency. Next to a passage about the new birth, he commented that he read it in Boston with a friend before returning to Eddy's home at Pleasant View during a difficult time in 1902 (probably the Woodbury lawsuit). In the margin by Eddy's exegesis of Genesis 1:20, he wrote, "Afterwards I referred to this and understood it better." By a passage about Jesus waiting until flesh yielded to Spirit, he wrote simply, "waited."[70]

A book owned by Calvin A. Frye, Eddy's longtime secretary, contains short, imperative, sometimes funny notes in the margins. "Look here!" and "Important!" appear, as does "Pause and reflect" and a double exclamation point. Dated notations mark passages he or Eddy found helpful on various occasions. Frye created a doodle of a grinning, puckish face next to a passage about Christian love.[71]

The Reverend George Tomkins, DD, started as assistant pastor to the renowned Charles H. Spurgeon of London's large Baptist Tabernacle and eventually weathered controversy over his Christian Science branch church readership. He pasted a red-and-white illustration from another denomination's devotional publication (perhaps Roman Catholic, as the women are clothed in habits) of the gospel account of Jesus healing a girl.

On the same page he pasted lines from Eddy titled "What Our Leader Says" (advice so popular it was made into plaques) and a clipping (possibly from a Baptist periodical) of the scripture Jeremiah 33:3, "Call unto me, and I will answer thee, and show thee great and mighty things, which thou knowest not." Tomkins wrote scriptural references, pasted notices about himself as a Christian Science lecturer, quoted the Edinburgh hymnist Horatius Bonar, copied verbatim a letter he had received from Eddy onto a flyleaf and pasted the envelope into the book, and wrote personal notations. The interior of the book is full of cross-referenced page numbers, notes, and exclamation points.[72]

Readers thought and conversed about what they read and let ideas develop. Anna H. Knox wrote to Mary Armstrong with her understanding so far of the first few verses of John 8, in which Jesus wrote on the ground while liberating an adulterous woman. "Do I get the right thought?" Knox asks. "What was it Jesus was writing on the ground? I know there is more in these few verses to be brought out but I do not get it."[73] A response has not survived.

In an article draft, Lewis C. Strang discussed the need for students to have their own revelations showing them what the original revelation of Christian Science meant and how to individually employ it. This religion teaches all who study it "to think," Strang wrote, no matter what their station in life, and usually one of their first revelations is that "however complicated one's mental processes may have been before he touched the hem of Christian Science," Paul was right that "the wisdom of this world is foolishness with God."[74] Students could then flesh out and fill in the completed contours of Eddy's discovery with their own continually new insights and experiences, moving into ever-new territory.

Eddy encouraged students to gain such insights of their own having a practical quality, as opposed to dreamy imagination.[75] Laura Lathrop wrote to her about the deep struggle she had had with loneliness when her work in New York separated her from her adult son and friends who were at Eddy's home. Her study and prayer on the matter would be hard to put into words, wrote Lathrop, but "the revelation of this morning was the outcome of it." In this experience, "God revealed Himself to me in a fuller way than ever before.... I had felt forlorn and forsaken.... But now I know that I am" cared for and satisfied.[76]

CHRISTIAN SCIENTISTS used their pastoral books together and engaged with them often and intimately, as if in conversation. They asked questions, reflected on their reading, and recorded highly individualized messages tailored to the needs and occasions in their lives. They commemorated these in their books with notes, marks, pasted snippets, and doodles.

This opens a window for us onto adherent spirituality and provides important evidence in understanding Christian Science identity. For readers like this, using their religious books as their pastor was an interactive experience.

They found validation and new significance for Bible texts in *Science and Health* and noted how, where, and why. They considered God to be speaking to them directly through these texts, revealing constantly new messages that opened up their own specifically important niches in life.

McKenzie's particular niche included working on a team to help finalize edits to Eddy's textbook. By 1906, she was ready for her penultimate round of revisions.

CHAPTER FIFTEEN

Final Words

(1907)

In which Eddy mostly completes her book and
writes something like a benediction in it

"SEE SCRIPTURE QUOTATIONS in this edition M. B. G. Eddy's last book Oct. 7. 1908," reads the first flyleaf notation in her library copy. She then jotted the first part of 1 Corinthians 1:27, "For God hath chosen the foolishness of" this world to confound the wise. On a back flyleaf, she simply wrote "Excellent," as if her final commentary on the whole book.[1]

A few more Bible quotations follow. A passage from Isaiah begins, "The spirit of the Lord God is upon me; because the Lord hath anointed me to preach good tidings unto the meek; he hath sent me to bind up the brokenhearted, to proclaim liberty to the captives, and the opening of the prison to them that are bound," and so on. Cross referencing this to a page in her book, Eddy put a big black X next to the paragraph beginning, "Jesus taught the way of Life by demonstration, that we may understand how this divine Principle heals the sick, casts out error, and triumphs over death. Jesus presented the ideal of God better than could any man whose origin was less spiritual" (1908:25). The final scripture she copied into her book reads, "Jeremiah 33.6 'Behold, I will bring it health and cure, and I will cure them, and will reveal unto them the abundance of peace and truth.'"

That was it. Written in private, with no plans to make them public but with a sense that they held historic meaning, these were the last notations Eddy made in her textbook. Getting there involved a publicly raucous and privately difficult 1907, however, that looked to be about anything but peace or truth. It also involved resolving long-standing problems in book production.

IT TOOK MARY BAKER EDDY until 1906–7 to establish a system of proofing, editing, revising, and printing her book that worked well. Until then, publishers and readers regularly pointed out that the printing plates were decrepit, the type was worn out, the production of the book was sometimes substandard, and the proofreading was lacking.[2] Proofing standards for her book had improved considerably in 1902, when she asked William McKenzie to pore over and standardize all its scriptural quotations and offer minor but helpful general grammar advice.[3]

Workflow problems persisted, however. Eddy made edits by hand in copies of her book, and heading into her eighty-fifth year, she often had to make the same edit more than once, point it out to her production team, and then check that the change made it into print. Finding duplicate edits became much easier when she realized in 1907 that she could use Conant's concordance as a cross-reference tool.[4]

It might seem odd that a book considered a sacred text by its publishers and circulating copies in the tens of thousands by 1907 would have such production struggles. Yet despite the church's growth, it was still a young and chronically understaffed organization. Eddy's publisher at the time, Joseph Armstrong, also served simultaneously as manager of the Christian Science Publishing Society and member of the Christian Science Board of Directors. (After 1907, these job functions were assigned to separate people.)

Armstrong shopped for furniture for a new appointee when another church officer was "in a dilemma" and out of time, found practical items for the First Reader on request, lined up soloists for Sunday services (at least once including Eddy's printer William Dana Orcutt, who was "a very fine singer"), and settled bills.[5] "I don't like this dinkey little thing," Armstrong wrote on a soloist's two-inch bill in a tiny envelope, then paid it. Papers suggest he may have settled some bills out of his own pocket when time was short, lines of compensation were unclear, or communication gaps arose between Eddy's organizational staff in Boston and her household staff in Concord.[6]

His responsibilities hardly ended there. Armstrong played a central role in building The Mother Church edifice, then wrote a book on the topic. He handled all communications, ordering, billing, and tracking for printings of the denomination's textbook; fielded copyright and plagiarism issues, which the church now sought to resolve through communication with authors rather than lawsuit; and personally placed *Science and Health* with dozens of institutions. He processed receipts and fielded letters from Chicago, New York, Oskaloosa. Most of the letters in his files begin with "Dear Brother" or "Dear Sister."

This correspondence with other church members covered a vast range of issues. Church officers often declined to dictate to corresponding members a specific course of action, instead sending questioners to the Christian Science pastor and church bylaws to make their own decisions.[7] They generally told this to inquirers directly, rather than through a secretary, though this was time consuming. F. R. Comstock of Connecticut wrote that his branch church had begun filling Wednesday testimony meetings with readings from the joint pastor, leaving only five minutes for testimonies, because "the people would not take an active part in the service and it would drag."[8] Whatever Armstrong's response, Comstock later wrote back thanking him and reporting that meetings were again running on the level, with more group participation.

All of Eddy's church officers were multitasking at a similar rate. Among other things, this meant a limited pool of resources for the work of book revision and production, which always seemed to fall outside day-to-day operations. According to the letters and memoirs of her household staff and her own written schedules, she kept the longest hours of any of them, and she often cited heavy work and little time as a barrier to overcome in working on her book. "The burden of doing [is] not as much as having to remember how much is left undone," she once wrote in a note to herself in her Bible.[9]

THIS WAS HARDLY the most of her worries in 1907, however, when a lawsuit culminated against Eddy, then age eighty-six, to end her personal and financial autonomy and place her under legal guardianship. Known as the "Next Friends suit" after the ironically dubbed "next friends" in whose name the suit was brought by the *New York World*, the interested parties informally active behind the scenes were actually the lawyer Frederick Peabody and his client Josephine Woodbury, who had lost a libel case against Eddy in 1902.

Scholars have well established the parameters of the Next Friends case. Most recently, David Holland has traced the contention of the plaintiff's lawyer, Senator William E. Chandler of New Hampshire, that Christian Science was a species of insanity, not religion. He sought to establish "Eddy's delusions and claimed that her religious teachings were proof of her insanity," as Peter A. Wallner notes.[10]

Chandler's papers and those of Eddy's counsel Frank A. Streeter not only lay out this strategy in detail but illustrate the stunning cultural reach of the suit. Financially backed and sensationally promoted by the *New York World* (which hoped to capitalize on the mixture of notoriety, popularity, confusion, controversy, and sheer name recognition by then surrounding Eddy and her new sect), the Next Friends suit could be considered the largest national media spectacle at the opening of the twentieth century. Streeter hired a New York City newspaper clipping service to supply him with coverage of the suit nationwide. The results filled twenty-two giant scrapbooks over a span of thirteen months with approximately 2,800 articles having eye-popping headlines.[11]

Eddy's book was at the center of the plaintiff's strategies. The counselors sought to "take this book upon the stand and read passages from it," particularly early editions, alleging its author had a "number of delusions about the inspiration of Science and Health."[12] Chandler's team homed in on Eddy's claims to divine inspiration and her innovative terminology (showing particular interest in her use of "animal magnetism" as a synonym for evil) as alleged proof of insanity.

Like other court actions, they also sought to characterize her work as only incidentally and opportunistically Christian. "Eddyism," wrote one adviser, was "primarily and essentially a system of medical practice—This is what it was for 13 years, and that only, from 1866 to 1879. Then the religious side came out but only as a subsidiary matter.... As a matter of fact," he continued, most Christian Scientists are only trying to reduce "doctors bills" or acquire "money as Healers."[13] Both rationales occasionally appeared in adherent documents, though very rarely, and almost never as primary considerations.

Chandler began the case frankly hoping to reallocate Eddy's "millions" but gradually became invested in Peabody's viewpoint and looked forward to seeing Eddy "break down" under examination.[14] His descriptions of her as a woman, and generally as a person, were extreme. His papers are full of expositions regarding what Eddy's book *really* meant and why she *really* wrote it, which he expounded on as he crafted his aggressive litigation strategy.

Gender was not at the heart of this suit, but neither was it a side matter. As Aimee Semple McPherson later put it while under public and legal attack for entirely different reasons, "Were I a man I would be stoned.... With a woman, however, it is different; an attack on your character is the first thing the devil thinks of." Parallels between Eddy and McPherson are limited, particularly after the midpoint of their respective biographies, but Matthew Avery Sutton notes that "McPherson's success spawned powerful opposition," as did Eddy's. A particularly dogged critic gave his "'calm, unbiased judgement ... that outside of perhaps Mrs. Eddy, there has not been so dangerous a religious teacher in the United States in the past two hundred years.'"[15]

Yet the same critic also denounced McPherson alongside Charles T. Russell and Joseph Smith. Concerns with religious heterodoxy were partly gendered but had a broad reach. He ended "with a six-point comparison between what the Bible taught and what McPherson preached," concluding she was in the wrong in every case.[16] Opponents of new religious expressions commonly used such point-by-point comparisons as a tool meant to discredit those they disagreed with. Several circulated for decades regarding Eddy's work.

As the Next Friends suit played out, the *Boston Transcript* covered what it called Peabody's parallel "attack on Christian Science" before the state legislature in 1907.[17] The proceedings show a representative cross-section of the character of public discourse on Christian Science at the time.

Dr. Edward H. Adams invoked the *New York World*'s media coverage to testify that he found it true until proved false that Eddy was insane, incapacitated, and impersonated by one of her followers and that her whole life was a "gigantic fraud." Others, such as the president of Harvard University, he noted, agreed. Rabbi Charles Fleischer volunteered to speak on behalf of Eddy's counsel, as it "rather sickened him to hear an attack on Christian Science as a religion," though he thought in general medical supervision may be in the public interest.

William Lloyd Garrison III commented that he was under medical treatment and "unable to accept" the religious teachings of Christian Science, yet as we have seen, observing its successes compelled his support. In a wider sense, he invoked Christian Science in his fight against what he called "paternalism" and "monopoly" in the medical system (one of his many social interests). He cited William James to place Christian Scientists among "thinkers outside the recognized organizations" who were valuable precisely because they did "not bear the impress of some medical institution." Because "the whole face of medicine changes from one generation to another, in consequence of widening experience," he noted, and "we look with a mixture of amusement and horror at the practice of our grandfathers, we cannot be sure how large a proportion of our present practice will awaken similar feelings in our posterity. . . . Our State needs the assistance of every type of mind, academic and nonacademic, of which she possesses specimens. . . . Each is necessarily partly perceptive and partly blind."[18]

Like James, Garrison frankly noted he could make neither heads nor tails of Christian Science and cast himself as an agnostic supporter of the sect. As an investment banker and lawyer, Garrison had clear limits on his radicalism, yet the religion's underdog status appealed to him. If the Christian Science Church should "arrive at a time when its strength should lead it to decree all other practice unlawful," he would oppose that just as vigorously. "Institutions perish; human rights are imperishable." Eventually, however, Garrison parted ways with Eddy over his Quaker pacifist commitments.[19]

Like Eddy's earliest critics, Peabody's statement to the committee also "'did not deny that there were cures in Christian Science,'" but he sought to discount their legitimacy. He urged "a competent body to consider the worth of Christian Science treatment from a medical standpoint" and portrayed Christian Scientists as irrational and confused. He closed out the proceedings by drawing laughs at the Christian Scientists' small numbers and presumably irrational commitments.[20]

Peabody frequently landed the last laugh in 1907. As the suit progressed, he and Chandler coordinated with *McClure's* magazine as it produced an essay tailored to aid their litigation against Eddy. The later reticent Willa Cather wrote

Chandler of her plan "to submit to you the proofs" of her article, and "I shall ask you to cut out any statement . . . which might be detrimental" to his client's interests. Citing Peabody's advice, she offered to send Chandler any resources "that could be of use to you," adding, "please do not hesitate to command us."[21] They discussed exchanging key sources with Peabody as intermediary.

McClure's attributed the polemical series and subsequent book to Georgine Milmine. It set the tone for one type of Eddy biography throughout the twentieth century and beyond. Another type, represented by Sibyl Wilbur (a professional reporter and a Catholic) and initially published in *Human Life* magazine, was mild but rather awestruck and not particularly compelling literature. Eddy politely but rather tepidly endorsed Wilbur's work. Scholarly biographies would later generate quantities of research on the place of the primary sources both efforts produced and the complex interests at work in their production.[22]

As *Human Life* and *McClure's* duked it out in the court of public opinion, public support appeared in the form of the notable journalist Arthur Brisbane, who interviewed Eddy and published a complimentary piece in the reputable *Cosmopolitan* magazine. Mark Twain's *Christian Science* also appeared in 1907, formalizing his long-running public caricature of Eddy as a money-grubbing fake with an interesting if laughable religion (as I noted earlier, several scholars have shown his private views were more complex). Such opposing characterizations deeply influenced cultural views about Christian Science.

The Next Friends suit, *McClure's*, the state legislature, and so on: the Peabody-Woodbury duo orchestrated a sober circus of anti-Eddy events around 1907. Streeter's papers include an interesting affidavit recording Peabody's frank intent to destroy Eddy's religion through litigation, which he and Woodbury conceived as a multipronged effort.[23] As a full slate of highly competent and reputable medical and judicial professionals joined the proceedings to handle evidence and examine Eddy, Chandler and his correspondents increasingly assumed they would handily win the case, as "all sane people find Christian Science ridiculous."[24]

When the court's medical and psychological team found Eddy sane and competent, however, sympathy for her stretched well beyond her religion's ranks for a time. The tide of public opinion briefly but dramatically shifted in her favor. In terms of legal precedent, David Holland argues that in rebutting Chandler's contention that Christian Science was a species of insanity, not religion, the presiding judge Edgar Aldrich employed a broad definition of religion whereby "religion became increasingly sequestered from the secular affairs of the state, simultaneously protected and marginalized—indeed, protectable because marginal. Christian Science, with its balance of normalcy and strangeness, abetted such a conclusion." Ultimately, Holland argues, the process of defining "religion" in this way rendered that process more secular. This conclusion meshes with increasingly secular processes of defining religion in general.[25]

PRIVATELY IN 1907, Eddy undertook her final substantial book revision. Her overhauled 1891 edition was the last she had extensively rewritten, and her edits after that had been contained but theologically significant enough to warrant a new copyright in 1902. Now in 1907 she made many small changes to significant phrases and some chapters, notably the teaching chapter "Recapitulation," and took out the last copyright on her book within her lifetime.

Several long-standing book production problems were streamlined and resolved. Five years earlier Eddy was still filling the flyleaves of her book copies with printing corrections to be made. Multiple copies and rotating help meant some were not picked up immediately. "See cloth bound book. I have corrected this before," she wrote on one typical page. On another, "*awful mistakes.*"[26] Now she and her household staff rounded up and triple-checked all the book copies in which she had made edits, flagged dozens of small changes, and ensured they went to the printer. She had constructed her book in chapters and parts, not finalizing the chapter order until 1902. In the middle of 1907, she finally read the entire book from cover to cover in its conclusive format for the first time (1911:xii).

Eddy directed the testimonies at the end of her book be replaced to accompany her revisions and appointed a team including William McKenzie, William McCrackan, and Professor Spence Lowell to handle this and other matters, sending them detailed instructions. She also asked them to do a final check on scriptural quotations and grammar, sending their edits to her for approval. Their syntax suggestions were minor and technical, and she accepted all or most.

In a typical example, McKenzie recommended changing the phrase "willing our neighbor should see" to "willing to have our neighbor see," noting that the first "cannot be grammatically analyzed." At least one scriptural question was outsourced to the Bible scholar James Hardy Ropes, a Congregational minister and Harvard professor, who vetted and approved the scholarship behind Eddy's exegesis of Matthew 10:28.[27]

Though straightforward, this editorial process was not without its dramas. The team worked at McKenzie's office at 1010 Massachusetts Avenue, where a fire broke out; smoke affected some pages, but none were lost.[28] Near the end of the year, a Christian Scientist in Washington, D.C., produced new printing plates and in the process added another line number on several pages, which was typographically cumbersome and confusing. After he shuttled the plates up to Boston by train, Eddy's regular printer, John Wilson, found them faulty for additional reasons and had to make new ones. The complications and extra expense were eventually sorted out.

By 1908, Eddy had finally produced a book she deemed nearly finished. She read through it carefully, leaving a handful of markings. "Super," she enthused about a few passages, using a new word for the first time.[29] She had vigorously crossed out a portrait of herself as a younger woman on the frontispiece of a 1907 copy, and 1908 printings carried a contemporary white-haired portrait she found satisfactory.

Two small but very significant pencil edits appear in her 1908 copy: she crossed out the chapter title "Christian Science and Spiritualism," changing it to "Christian Science versus Spiritualism," and likewise changed the chapter title "Animal Magnetism" to "Animal Magnetism Unmasked." Her publisher, now Allison V. Stewart, oversaw a streamlined production and distribution process that found him keeping far fewer and less detailed records than his predecessor, Armstrong. The cascade of small and large book production annoyances prior to 1907 had been fixed to a point of satisfaction.

In contrast to her earlier copies of *Science and Health*, which she used both as working documents to mark up changes for her printer and for her own spiritual study, Eddy used her 1908 copy primarily to take historical notes. "Nov 26 Newspaper to be published," she wrote on a flyleaf, confirming plans that were finally underway. The first copy of her newspaper the *Christian Science Monitor* had gone on sale the day before; in her Bible, she opened to and marked a passage in Isaiah.[30] The paper was a conscious antidote to the type of sensationalistic journalism that had turned the machinery of the Next Friends suit.

She also added the scriptural passages noted in the first pages of this chapter, which appear something like a benediction and a summary. Throughout the difficulties of 1907 and into 1910, Eddy continued her lifelong practice of daily Bible study. She owned forty-one Bibles, and combined with Bible commentaries, these made up the vast majority of her personal library. Her annotations confirm that she began each morning by opening the scriptures at random, reading and reflecting, often teaching her household from the text. These could be quite specific. In the summer of 1907, when the court returned a judgment in her favor in the Next Friends suit, she opened to a passage in Proverbs about wise counsel that also seemed to speak to the security of her family moving forward.[31]

The last Bibles she used, from 1908 to 1910, overflow with marginal and flyleaf notes, sometimes written by a household assistant. Several passages stood out as her "favorite" at various times. Sometime in 1908, she found "wonderful love and mercy" in Psalm 103 and felt Hebrews 10:36 was *"consoling, read it."*[32]

That passage reads, "For ye have need of patience, that, after ye have done the will of God, ye might receive the promise." Such notes are representative of hundreds more. During just part of 1909, she marked over 100 passages. In what appears to be her last Bible, gifted by a student that year, she found Luke 21 "prophetic of these days" and Luke 22 "emphatic of the *present*."[33]

Eddy's Bible and personal notes in 1908 had a contented, refreshed feel, speaking to all kinds of ways she was leaving 1907 behind. Her handwriting during the height of the lawsuit had been almost illegible, but now it was clearly legible, only slightly shaky with age, sometimes surprisingly youthful looking. She used her 1908 copy of *Science and Health* through 1910, when she pasted a clipping about herself from *Life* magazine onto a front flyleaf.[34] The clipping shows no volume or issue number, but the article marked her birth date, offered her "felicitations," and noted that she had been "more maligned than any woman has ever been that we can now recall, and, on the other hand, more exalted."

The snippet complimented her public response to adversity. "She has made the doctors sit up and be more careful; she has attracted crowds of worshipers, and she still remains with us in undiminished glory. Every effort to dislodge her has only resulted in disaster." This must have been a hugely gratifying assessment to Eddy, especially considering the range of innovative and ongoing attempts to "dislodge" her. None culminated again during her lifetime, but several would challenge her leadership and religious vision after 1910.

"Madam," the *Life* piece ended, "you have established a true claim upon our respect," adding, "however much we may disagree with your views." Agreement aside, respectful civility from nonsectarian quarters became more common for a few years after Eddy's exoneration in the Next Friends suit. They were the norm immediately after her death, when an exceptional volume of high-minded public tributes poured in.

As Klassen notes, however, after the tributes subsided the media occasionally complimented Eddy's popularity but "most references to her were not so kind and were often expressed in quite violent language."[35] Eddy's last few years coincided with a window of broad cultural acceptance and media civility that would soon largely close down.

CHAPTER SIXTEEN

Into the Twentieth Century

(1911)

In which Eddy has finished her book, and
in which we return to Marietta Webb

IN DECEMBER 1910, a few weeks after Mary Baker Eddy passed on at her home in Chestnut Hill, Massachusetts, the Christian Science Board of Directors purchased the three most recent published sets of her writings from her household estate. She had assigned her writings to her church for custodial care, and these copies formed what became known as the textual "Standards for All Time."[1] Employees put them into three separate padlocked copper boxes, and for the next sixty-one years, until 1971, archivists opened these annually to check, repair if necessary, and air the books. The preservation system was then updated and changed, and the copper boxes are now artifacts in the church's archives.

Eddy clearly considered her book done. She had finalized its content gradually and decisively over decades, even identifying small matters of grammar and syntax essential to her meaning and laboring over them extensively. She continued reading and checking printings regularly after 1908 but made few edits, writing what amounted to a benediction in the last copy of her book containing her notations. Then she left the tasks of implementing her final directions and minor copyediting to her students, as she always had.

With that, the story of the Christian Science dual pastor—the Christian Bible together with Eddy's book—opened into the great drama of the twentieth century. The final, "authorized" edition of *Science and Health with Key to the Scriptures* used by readers today came out in 1911, incorporating all of Eddy's late 1910 edits. Several printings of her book were in circulation in 1910. Since none after 1907 had been dated or numbered, her church began to find and compare them to the Standards copies in an effort to identify them.[2] The work of helping Eddy produce her book had been all-absorbing for her staff, and some tentatively began to research its technical and textual development.[3]

Between 1911 and 1914, the publisher of her writings fixed a handful of minuscule typographical issues (removing extra spaces, making a line flush with the margin). No matter how small, they were copiously cross-checked against Eddy's final notes. The publisher implemented the two chapter title edits she had made earlier. He also felt it practical to remove a note (which had appeared without line numbers) from her preface that she was no longer taking patients. Following her prior practice, he removed a testimony from a testifier who no longer practiced Christian Science. Finally, he complied with her written request to remove her picture from the frontispiece.

Religious portraiture carried different weight and meaning in 1910 than in decades prior. Its popularity had waned as the novelty of reproductive media and photographic imagery wore off, and Eddy's decision might have reflected this. Further, a "shift in the modern consciousness of the self occurred in the late nineteenth and early twentieth centuries—from character as the dominant construct of personal identity to personality," writes the visual historian of religion David Morgan.[4]

Citing Warren Sussman, Morgan notes that religious portraiture began to reflect this new emphasis on personality, which celebrated psychologized views that turned away from traditional Christian virtues such as "moderation, self-restraint, even self-denial" to focus on energy, dominance, power, consumption, and acquisition.[5] Consciously or not, but in keeping with her religious views, Eddy opted out of this modernist shift from "character" to "personality" by dropping her portrait. Her book still meshed with modernity in other ways, not least in its emphasis on subjective experience.

With a handful of exceptions, Christian Scientists understood that Eddy had gotten her book to the state she wanted it, that she had designated her church as its custodian, and that this involved executing her final written instructions and resolving small proofing and other issues. A few fetishized whatever 1910 printing of Eddy's book they owned at her passing and declined to accept any textual changes after that date, even forming micro-breakaway movements. Conversely, another small group favored the initial 1875 edition, disagreeing with Eddy's view that her book became more accurate with her edits over time. A few also disagreed with Eddy's view that she had finalized her text and began to edit it on their own.

For the most part, however, readers used her book as she completed it. She once implied that since she had worked out her book's revealed message in its original English, its original meaning was clear and stood as she finished it. Anyone who does not understand this "mixes translation with revelation[.] The former may, does mistake," she wrote, but "the latter cannot."[6] Translations might include mistakes that need to be corrected, but not an original work as the author completed it.

Foreign-language translations therefore were done with care and appeared as the church globalized. In 1910 Eddy had authorized the translation of her book into German, which appeared in 1912. Translations into French (1917) and Spanish (1947) followed, then dozens more as the decades advanced: Russian, Indonesian, Japanese, to name a few. Over a century later an Igbo translation would appear, reflecting the growth of Christian Science in Africa.

Dozens of official editions of the Christian Science pastor, the Bible and *Science and Health* together in a set, came into print over the ensuing decades. In the first half of the century alone, in addition to editions in other languages, new editions appeared for the visually impaired (1914), soldiers, for their small vest pockets (1917–20), Braille readers (1924), Sunday school students (1936), and those who wanted a thumb index to match their Bibles (1940). Huge editions appeared for First and Second Readers to use at the lecterns of large church sanctuaries and auditoriums.

In 1941, William Dana Orcutt published a subscription-only run of a massive art book edition, for which he invented the Laurentian font and formulated a new red ink. Orcutt never became a Christian Scientist but credited his professional success to Eddy's encouragement, and he considered the volume his lifework and masterpiece.[7] In 1942, the church established publishing control over a facsimile of Eddy's signature by stamping it on a small edition, after which the facsimile appeared on several books. Her church pursued a series of copyright and trademark actions, sometimes winning and sometimes losing.[8]

Privately, the adherent Dorothy Whitley marked her Bible Lesson in 1950 with metal markers and used erasable blue chalk to indicate which passages to read. She indexed a front flyleaf in her Bible with the Ten Commandments of Moses, the Beatitudes in Matthew 5, and passages in Deuteronomy and the Psalms.[9] In the summer of 1952, the poet Sylvia Plath lay in the sun with her Christian Scientist date on an island off Cape Cod as they read *Science and Health* to each other. Months earlier, she could barely stifle her mockery after attending a Christian Science lecture as a campus news reporter at Smith College. Now she poked fun at her Sunday school teacher's appearance and thick Massachusetts accent, yet also seriously grappled with Christian Science theology, deciding in her journal that she agreed with some points yet overall disagreed with its construct at war with her own "tribe" of relativist materialists.[10]

"Now that I ponder over it," Plath wrote in her journal, "I do see a sudden neat edifice of logic, and I do agree with some of their generalizations in spite of the fact that I am philosophically at the other end of the pole,—a 'matter worshiper.'" Her deep affection for the Christian Scientists she lived with as a babysitter, the Cantors, led her to settle on an intellectual relativism in which no religious construct could be proven more or less "real" than her own philosophical materialism, for better or for worse. "Paradoxically," she wrote, all are "'true' although mutually exclusive at the same time."[11]

Typically for Plath, she came to adore the Cantors and maintained a friendship with them for years afterward. She found them cultured and lively, contentedly read the Bible Lesson with them, and wrote to her mother, "I never have felt so happy, rich (spiritually) and loving." The following winter, as she mused over her Fulbright application, graduate schools, and marriage, she chastised herself for not studying harder over the summer. "I suppose, though," she concluded, "that learning to get along with farm hands and Christian Scientists is at least, if not more, important than learning about Kant's categorical imperative."[12]

In 1954, after Plath returned to Smith College from McLean Hospital, she wrote to matriarch Margaret Cantor, "I appreciated your last wonderful letter—it simply exuded love and strength. . . . Even though I steeled myself for all sorts of little awkwardnesses and problems in my coming back, I was met by such love and warmth that I still can hardly believe it." She mentioned Mary Baker Eddy, quoted *Science and Health*, and thanked Margaret "for having faith that the 'real me' was there" during her bout with mental illness. Plath's honesty about her relativistic materialism led her to limit her interest in Christian Science, but the warmth remained. She later told her mother she hoped to have the reception of her wedding to Ted Hughes "at Mrs. Cantor's place . . . *with* alcohol in spite of her Christian Science!" though the logistics did not work out.[13]

Over the course of her acquaintance with Christian Scientists, Plath's feelings ranged from contempt to awe, skepticism to attraction, intellectual mockery to intellectual grappling, delighted acceptance to materialistic disagreement. This combination of feelings characterized, to some extent, midcentury America's entire relationship with Christian Science. That larger story, however, will have to wait.

THIS BOOK CLOSES as it opened, with the story of Marietta Webb. In 1893, she and her family lived on Northampton Street in Boston's South End, just in from the corner of Columbus Avenue and Chester Park (soon renamed Massachusetts Avenue). It was a neighborhood in transition, racially and economically mixed. Elegant homes still lined nearby Chester Square. A few decades earlier, the wealthy had begun transitioning down the road to the Back Bay neighborhood, a shift Henry James chronicled in *The Bostonians*.[14]

Four days after Webb delivered her son, Orlando, a streetcar line replaced the old horsecar route in the neighborhood. Another soon followed to the corner where The Mother Church sat at the crossroads between the older and newer neighborhoods, making it easy for Webb to attend her first Christian Science testimony meeting in 1897.[15]

At 1010 Massachusetts Avenue, 2.7 miles and a world away from Northampton Street, the Canadian immigrant William McKenzie was by 1900 settling into a new brick apartment building, the Cantabrigia. Joseph Harmon, an African American butler a few years his junior, collected wages from McKenzie. By then, Webb had relocated to California with her family. For at least a year beginning in 1897, however, Webb and McKenzie—we have no record concerning Harmon—reached for hymnals not far from one another on the church's curved oak pews.

They could not see the eighty-first edition of *Science and Health* laid in the church's New Hampshire granite cornerstone in the spring of 1894, but they read the inscription dedicating the building to Mary Baker Eddy, the "Discoverer" of Christian Science—a title Eddy privately noted God had "christened" her with in 1892 while reading the Psalms in Concord, New Hampshire. Up the marble stairs in a rounded sanctuary the scholar Jeanne Halgren Kilde has described as "maternal," Webb and McKenzie listened to the same sermon, then passed one another in the small lobby on the way out.[16]

In 1907, they metaphorically crossed paths again when McKenzie served on the team Eddy had formed to select testimonies of Christian Science healing for her book's final chapter. These included Webb's account of Orlando's healing, which Eddy approved for publication. Webb and McKenzie were part of a small group who not only read and used but directly contributed to the production of *Science and Health*. In a particular and rare way, Webb's identity and life was inscribed into her religious text, and vice versa.

Webb indicated that she valued Christian Science for a satisfying view of God and the healing she credited to it, not for reasons rooted in race or gender. Yet she was a Christian Scientist *as* an African American woman, not *despite* this fact.[17] She would have approvingly read the *Christian Science Journal*'s 1902 summary of McKenzie's lecture on Christian Science and freedom at Boston's Symphony Hall.

Citing Booker T. Washington's *Up from Slavery*, McKenzie noted that enslaved Americans at the close of the war experienced a "new hope . . . that liberty was coming to them here, in this world." Echoing Eddy's stance in *Science and Health*, he added, "Like these slaves we have been singing of liberty to come" from every type of tyranny still in existence, whether physical, moral, or mental. He denounced the "horrors of slave-pens" and "hideous agonies of the slave-ship."[18]

William P. McKenzie, a former Presbyterian minister from Toronto, assisted Eddy in copyediting later editions of her book. He kept copious Bible notes in his own copy. McKenzie and his wife, Daisette, became residents of Cambridge, Massachusetts, where they helped form a Christian Science branch church. The Cambridge "Blue Book" reported on their work and travels. Portrait of William P. McKenzie, P01304, courtesy of the Mary Baker Eddy Collection and The Mary Baker Eddy Library.

Webb also would have been pleased to know that in January 1911, a group of African American pilgrims to the grave of the antislavery leader Charles Sumner quietly filed by Eddy's receiving tomb and "requested the privilege" of paying their respects, the first group to do so.[19]

Six months after this event, Webb applied to list her business card as a Christian Science practitioner in the *Journal*. Her application was stamped and accepted without incident. So was her application to advertise as a Christian Science Nurse. In 1914, however, she found in her mailbox a survey from her church's "Card Department" asking all advertised practitioners several questions for administrative purposes. One line read, "What is your nationality (or color)?" She filled in the blank with subversive and accurate dignity by writing, "Purely American, Natural color."[20]

Marietta T. Webb credited her son's healing experience, her own feeling of spiritual satisfaction, and her renewed love for the Bible to Christian Science. In 1907, Eddy permanently included Webb's testimony in the last chapter of *Science and Health*. Webb later become a well-known Christian Science practitioner in Los Angeles. This portrait is after a photograph of Webb featured in an *Ebony* magazine article about African American Christian Scientists. Simeon D. Youngmann, sketch of Marietta T. Webb, pencil on paper, 2020. Courtesy of the author.

Thus an organizational tilt came into view that would last for decades. Los Angeles had been less than 1.7 percent African American when Webb moved there just before 1900, and she probably attended services with European Americans in one of two Christian Science churches on the west side, perhaps with Orlando but not Hiram. He survived a house fire while she was at church, which she credited to a "sweet peace" that "stole over" her during silent prayer, a distinctive practice preceding the Lord's Prayer at Christian Science Sunday services and midweek testimony meetings.[21]

Webb published an ardent account of this experience in the *Christian Science Sentinel*. Everywhere we go, she concluded, "we are made to feel our color," yet she felt through Christian Science, "man is not only learning what the true love of God is . . . but he is getting out of his old prejudiced self, into the spiritual sense of man's union with God."[22]

In 1910, her testimony had been in *Science and Health* for three years. She was by then widowed and began maintaining a rotating cast of relatives and boarders at her home, notably migrating Virginians and her Massachusetts siblings.[23] Los Angeles Christian Science churches more than tripled by 1912, another Christian Science Nurse became active in the city, and Christian Science practitioners increased eightfold, outpacing the city's percentage of growth for the decade by more than double. Webb was among them.

Around this time, race became a newly visible topic within the church. In 1919, The Mother Church initiated a study on several aspects of church life. The question of racial segregation was one of several submitted by members. In 1920, the investigating committee found that it "believes that the race question is slowly being solved on the basis of Christian Science." This very "complex" matter must "be approached with courage, hope and love," it stated, and "some degree of consideration should be given to custom, condition and environment."[24]

Therefore, the report continued, segregation "in Christian Science churches must be a question for local determination. When both the white man and his darker skinned brother understand enough of Christian Science," any differences between them "will disappear. In working out this demonstration all need to be charitable, unselfish, forbearing, and kind." Finally, "immediate change" might not always be realistic, "but it would seem that patience and the demonstration of the higher and better qualities of character are more essential than the correction of social inequalities" in the shorter term.[25]

A period of high-profile organizational strife known in newspapers as the Great Litigation (1919–20) occurred simultaneously to the committee report.[26] Following the state supreme court decision upholding Eddy's *Manual of The Mother Church* as arbiter of church affairs, with its directors tasked with bylaw administration, branch churches began to show new levels of concern with strict organizational compliance and to reconsider the nature of their democratic structure. Further, as new expressions of institutionalized racism evolved and became entrenched in legal codes across the United States, the Christian Science practice of carefully complying with the law and seeking to reasonably accommodate cultural expectations entered uncharted territory. These cultural and internal developments introduced a situation on race that some adherents welcomed, some resisted, and others experienced as a dilemma.

The Mother Church was neither bureaucratically inclined nor quite authorized to enforce policies regarding segregation. Yet in the 1920s, the *Journal* unsystematically but increasingly began to denote African American practitioners and branch churches with predominantly African American congregations with the word "colored" or a small *c*. In 1922, the prominent African American newspaper the *Kansas City Sun* simultaneously championed the Christian Science textbook for its theology of racial equity and criticized the new church policy.

A church official responded with a letter to the editor, which was excerpted at the back of the *Christian Science Sentinel* and presented less as an announcement of policy than a piece of media commentary. Yet it still carried considerable weight. The piece affirmed that the Christian Science Church "does not discriminate" based on race, "yet it does not attempt to change" segregation laws and customs, instead deferring to local branches on the matter.[27]

Several Christian Science congregations either initiated or accelerated informal segregation throughout the 1920s and 1930s. Webb would have witnessed a similar trend among other churches not "born into" the practice, such as those with Pentecostal roots. In the 1920s, she moved from her modest home and purchased a large triplex further east, in South-Central Los Angeles. A few miles north, in Echo Park, Aimee Semple McPherson's Angelus Temple and its satellite branches were largely segregated despite their emergence from the Pentecostal mixed-race hubbub of Azusa Street.

Christian Science origins partook of a different kind of hubbub, discussed thoroughly in this book, but still quietly attracted a mixture of races. According to Paul E. Ivey, a Christian Science weekly published by and for African Americans may have existed as early as 1895.[28] The Mother Church opposed extremes like those seen at Angelus Temple, which once endorsed the Ku Klux Klan even while supporting large congregations of people of Latin American descent. Yet its mixed messages on race still pushed in opposing directions.

In June 1934, Marietta Webb became a founding member of a culturally influential African American congregation on the east side of Los Angeles. She had been able to sidestep the "colored" designation by her *Journal* listing for several years, partly by claiming "Indian" heritage (which was not uncommon) but more crucially by insisting that Eddy had "regarded her as [a] 'Child of God' and not a colored 'Child of God.'"[29] Now disagreements centering on democracy and personality arose within her new branch church.

Members disagreed on whether they wanted an entirely African American or a mixed church, but they became especially split about rule-following and democratic procedure. At a 1934 meeting where police deployed to prevent public disturbance, a development churches in white communities almost certainly would not have experienced, a majority voted that compliance with the new *Journal* designation was necessary for membership. African American media covered the situation nationally. Calling Webb a "world known church worker," a community newspaper reported that "she would continue in the work of the church and a group of real friends had banded themselves to work by the rules of the church. In all probability, meetings will be held at her home."[30] The designation affected Webb's practitioner listing in 1935.

Meanwhile, at the branch church in Cambridge attended by William and Daisette McKenzie, events unfolded that indicate why some in Webb's church preferred an entirely African American congregation. A man described by his daughter as a "devoted Christian Scientist" brought her to the Cambridge Reading Room in the early 1930s to buy her the Bible and *Science and Health*. She was experiencing a "physical problem," and the European American attendant met this African American family with "a cold stare and barely audible 'good morning,'" showing them the books "in silence." The young woman told her father that "I didn't think I wanted to have anything to do with Christian Science if that was an example of what Christian Scientists are like. He told me not to let that person's problem be my problem: that Christian Science is the absolute Truth. He said that I was coming into Christian Science to learn more about the Truth and to receive a healing. He immediately engaged a wonderful practitioner from Cambridge Church, and I am very grateful to say I received my healing."[31]

The practitioner might have been one of the McKenzies or Mabel Adams, an African American member of the Cambridge church. A few years later, Adams withdrew her membership to attend a Christian Science church in the Roxbury neighborhood, which was then on the cusp of becoming predominantly African American following the Great Migration. When she reapplied at Cambridge in 1940, the membership committee supported her application, but the branch's board denied it. "Mrs. Adams's response to the denial was gracious. Encouraged and supported by a white member who was also a *Journal*-listed practitioner, she reapplied and was admitted" in early 1945, remaining a member for over fifty years.[32]

In 1946, in response to objections, a church administrator clarified that designating *Journal* listings as African American was for advertising purposes and not segregation, ostensibly a convenience for African Americans wishing to find accommodating worship experiences.[33] Yet it cut both ways. Christian Scientists had deeply mixed reactions to the policy, which would continue eleven more years.

As the experiences here show, Christian Scientists opposing this practice felt it undercut the radical Christian theology of love and liberation they found in Eddy's book. That cut both ways, too: the theology undercut the practice. During these years, the *Journal* and *Sentinel* never published discernibly racist content, continuing to run antiracist articles and essays. A representative article in the early 1950s notes that "the essential dignity and worth of the individual are an integral part" of the Christian message; thus we must "spurn national and racial hatreds."³⁴ Such reader-submitted content was not uncommon, and church officers readily published it, even while experiences like Mabel Adams's played out in various locales.

Like Adams and her supporters, Marietta Webb continued her Christian Science practice. She maintained her ministry as a Christian Science practitioner for the next four decades. Shortly before her death in 1952, *Ebony* magazine featured her achievements and photograph in a story about African American Christian Scientists, whose numbers had "burgeoned."³⁵

As for Orlando, he served in France during the Great War, married, divorced, and worked as a skilled mechanic, private chauffeur, and airport custodian.³⁶ His 1917 draft registration lists him as medium height and medium build with no physical defects.³⁷ Above his impeccable signature, his 1942 draft registration shows him employed at North American Airport in Inglewood.³⁸ He remained exceptionally close to his mother and died in California in 1979.

Christian Science identity in the twentieth century involved a vastly different social, legal, scientific, political, medical, and religious context than the one I have explored throughout this book. That context and identity will need to be detailed elsewhere. By necessity, however, it will capture the diversity of ways Christian Scientists sought to use what Eddy called their "dual pastor": the Bible together with her interpretive book, *Science and Health with Key to the Scriptures*.

FINDINGS: PART IV

"JESUS' WORK was done for *me*," Eddy wrote in a private note to herself while reading her own book in 1894.[1] She had wanted to call her church the "Church of Christ" when it organized back in 1879, but the name was taken by other restorationist congregations, so she settled on the Church of Christ (Scientist). In the early 1890s, she removed the parentheses and called it The First Church of Christ, Scientist, or The Mother Church.

Her landmark 1891 edition of *Science and Health* emerged in tandem with a reorganized church that would literally give it a platform from which to speak. Seeking to set a standard for preaching, she ordained the scriptures and her interpretative book as joint pastor in the 1894 church building that adherents raised in Boston and also in localized branch churches.

"Students" of Christian Science studied the Bible and their "textbook" throughout the week on their own and also used the new Bible Lesson-Sermons. Testimonials describe how they applied what they read to experience healings of illnesses and other problems. Scholars of religious healing refer to it as sometimes observable but never knowable outside the event itself. However their phenomena might be explained academically, testimonials constitute a significant body of primary sources about this religion that illuminate life and worship within the early Christian Science organization.

Like Eddy, testifiers linked a full understanding of her metaphysics to experience. They described their "demonstrations" of God's healing love as variously gradual or immediate, dramatic or prolonged, and always as by-products of spiritual growth rather than ends in themselves (although many, perhaps most, did not enter the curative process with that expectation). Testifiers were usually of European descent, but significant racial diversity existed. They were inevitably readers, educated or not, who described embodying what they read in uncommon ways, making them a distinct sort of "people of the book."

Public controversies, and the grains of truth these often contained, continued to shape diverse public views of Christian Science. Legislative efforts to define Christian Science as a medical system were countered by judges and juries who found it to be a religion. Yet both perceptions persisted. Concerns about efficacy were generally indistinguishable from those over religious doctrine, legal code compliance, civic responsibility, reasonableness, and "sanity."

Observers tended to grapple with evidence of Christian Science healing successes and failures together as a unit.

Sometimes commentators supported the new religion or felt neutral, fascinated, or curious. Some who opposed it remained collegial. Those who did not often used feminized and racialized rhetoric to undercut its perceived denominational gains. Amid such developments, around 1900, critics of *Science and Health* renewed authorship and authority contentions. These were also often expressed in gendered terms. Each event and characterization that entered public memory helps us to understand shifting perceptions of Christian Science from varying vantage points.

Privately, artifacts and portraits give us glimpses of adherents' spirituality. Christian Scientists handled their religious books daily, filling their copies of *Science and Health* with Bible citations, pasting in cards, supplying pictures. They indexed passages they described as meaningful in daily life and sometimes left clues regarding their views of their religious founder, whom they considered the leader of the Christian vanguard. For her part, Eddy used copies of her own book not only for proofing and editing but increasingly for spiritual study, especially after producing the 1891 edition. She also took daily notes in her Bible regarding scriptures she credited with guidance in varied situations. She eventually owned a library of dozens of heavily marked copies of the scriptures.

In 1908, Eddy called her last substantial book revision, completed in 1907, "excellent" and "super" as it stood, requiring only a handful of final edits. She wrote scriptural passages in her copy, which appear something like a benediction and a summary of her work. A cascade of book production issues had been addressed, and in 1910 she sent final changes to the printer to produce a final 1911 edition. Eddy's last few years coincided with a window of broad cultural acceptance and media civility that continued into the second decade of the twentieth century before beginning to reverse. Both threads persisted and continue to coexist.

As Christian Science entered the new century, early and sometimes radical openness on race matters within its organization gave way to mixed messages during the interwar years, mirroring national patterns, before gradually opening up again well into the twentieth century. The Mother Church found racial inequality to have no spiritual basis and believed it was "being solved on the basis of Christian Science," continuing to publish antiracist articles in its magazines. It also deferred to branch locales that accommodated segregation, and for some years it specially denoted African American listings in its *Journal*. Local branch churches recorded race-based experiences ranging from individual discrimination to support. Congregations of African American Christian Scientists tended to be culturally influential and, like predominantly

European American groups, wrestled with individualized matters of polity, practice, and spirituality.

The evidence in this part of the book allows us to further parse Eddy's singular contribution to Christian theology, measure its wide impact on American culture, and begin to establish a vernacular history of Christian Science as a lived religion. We now turn to conclusions.

Christian Science Identity

"A FACT FOR [William] James was never ontologically permanent," writes Krister Dylan Knapp, because "it could be modified or even erased as new data poured in, making it a fluid rather than a static concept."[1] Thus James characterized his own definitions of religion and related phenomena as provisional, always subject to the flow and logic of new data. This data must arrive from both external and internal quarters, he held, as subjective experience is critical to knowledge formation.

The flood of new and newly contextualized data in this book, culled from a wide range of external and internal points on the cultural spectrum, shows that in the aftermath of the American Civil War, Eddy's *Science and Health* emerged to describe a distinctive expression of Christianity with a restorationist, revelatory, healing rationale. It tracked across multiple nodes on the vast networks making up American religion and culture, conversing and interacting with many while retaining its own singular teachings and message. It claimed to explain the divine law or Christian Science that animated the healings of Jesus and could now be validated and proved in modernity via a new system of applied Christian metaphysics.

Christian Science was and is not the once-born, nominally Christian, Hindu-inflected subset of mind cure or New Thought that James provisionally described it to be. Nor was it the medical system with a Christian overlay postulated by legislatures and litigants (though not upheld in courts); nor was it the esoteric, theosophically adjacent religion that emergent New Thought adherents wished to find and went on to independently construct; nor was it a type of Christianity already then existing. At every turn, Christian Science texts and lives confounded such descriptions.

It is ironic, and thus quintessentially modern, that James would introduce a definition of Christian Science that initially obscured its identity and also a method or set of intellectual commitments that now helps to clarify it. His focus on process and data in making meaning of religion—on "'religious experience'" as not "a fixed and stable set of experiences" but the dynamic process of "how people decide on the meaning and significance of their experiences," as Ann Taves puts it—is one I have sought to invoke in this book.[2]

James also argued that whether or not we agree with a particular religion's precepts, our basic descriptions of it should at least be recognizable to those who currently practice it. His emphasis on the fluidity of facts and the inherent scholarly value of first-person representations are not only presciently current but useful in parsing the many data points in this book.

In seeking to analyze the experiences of claimants to Christian Science, James gathered data not only from Horatio Dresser but within a cultural scene marked by "confusion and contradiction, because those who converse have not a uniform conception of the signification of the terms."[3] It makes sense that James found himself "unable to assimilate their theories, so far as I have heard them given," although like every other religious expression, he found them infinitely intriguing.[4] Were he here today, I like to think his flexible and open intellect would be interested in my book's findings.

In these pages, I have described in detail the cultural conditions and historical events that led to a gradual proliferation of perceptions about Christian Science contrary to its textual, practical, and theological identity. Sometimes this was a matter of taking the part as the whole so that an actual minority aspect of Christian Science experience became magnified as if representative. At other times, such perceptions were flatly contrary to Christian Science experience. Such characterizations have usually said more about the culture that produced them than about Christian Science identity itself. Simultaneously, initial views of it as a new Christian expression grew and persisted.

These insights help explain the taxonomic difficulties and persistent core tensions that have marked scholarly efforts to classify Christian Science. In preparing this book, I reviewed twenty-eight influential scholarly surveys, chapters, and other works mentioning Christian Science. I found that scholars have consistently identified it in three ways: as a new form of unorthodox Christianity with an indeterminate theology; as a "metaphysical" system of some type grouped with eclectic or esoteric movements; and as a type of religious or spiritual healing. Sometimes these descriptors appear singly; sometimes they overlap. We have often grouped Christian Science with other American innovators on the Christian spectrum such as Shakers, Mormons, Seventh-Day Adventists, and Pentecostals. We have often agreed that Christian Science is not New Thought but have remained largely uncertain whether and how these two religions are related.

Most fundamentally, what we have meant by these three descriptors—*Christian*, *metaphysical*, and *healing*—has varied widely. On the one hand, it is obvious to many that any religion with the term "Christian" in its name and calling itself a Church of Christ is, in a basic sense, a Christian religion. On the other hand, perceived tensions between core elements of Christian Science identity, notably its Bible-based piety and its traditionally unfamiliar metaphysics, have at times appeared to push Christian Science outside the Christian pantheon. Its early textual history, previously so murkily charted, has raised classifying questions as well. Further, Christian Science often bridged or occupied territory outside most options historians have mapped out for Christianity in the long nineteenth century, making it difficult to pin down in a scholarly sense.

The solution, I have proposed in this book, is to gain a deeply contextualized view of Christian Science as a radical theology of practical Christian metaphysics with a central concern for the survival of Christianity in modernity through the "proof" of healing. Its metaphysics did not engage esoteric, "energetic," or other enchanted concerns prized by some other movements but foreign to Christian Science textual and practical identity. Neither were its metaphysics resolved in wholly traditional Christian fashion. Instead, they represent a new type of applied Christian metaphysics inhabiting new space on the map of American religions.

To argue these points with integrity has required examining the textual and experiential origins of this religion and its identity to a depth not previously executed. This, in turn, has meant gaining a newly detailed historical appreciation of the development of Mary Baker Eddy's *Science and Health* as a religious text. To understand how her book functioned as a sacred text, as opposed to a scripture, interpreting the Bible in the lives of those who used it, has required us to examine previously open questions about authorship, reception, circulation, practice, and overarching religious identity within a wide cultural milieu and historical context.

We have needed to peel back the layers of Eddy's experience as a religious founder and leader by tracing in detail her earliest life and writings, charting how her dual claim to discovery and revelation always coexisted and intertwined, and seeing how they were always her own not only in terms of language and organizational development but in terms of her singular religious explanations and claims. In America, it is notable that many unorthodox and nontraditional Christian expressions—or better, many innovative, novel, distinctive Christian expressions (to use terms describing what they do and are, rather than what they are not)—have existed outside commonly mapped territory.[5] One point of this book is that our map of nineteenth-century religiosity should expand to accommodate such expressions. This grouping of distinctive Christian religions sits in a field of religiosity so diverse that it might be most accurately conceived in terms of networks with nodes. Some networks and some nodes have been historically more prominent than others. Yet in strictly bifurcated, triangulated, or other geometrically delimited models, there is always an overemphasis or underemphasis, someone or something who is left out. Instead, every spectrum of American religion sits on a node within intertwined networks having various paths of communication.

Sometimes new nodes appear, historically speaking, as in the case of Christian Science, which spooled off of Congregational Christianity and tracked across multiple nodes, joining with none, on the way to forming its own. As with other emergent Christian expressions in modernity, when we separate out its innovative features as if they are distinct from its overall Christianity, we obscure rather than illuminate its identity. These are new expressions of an ancient religion, not entirely new religious movements.

Eddy, her book, and its readers charted a religiously independent course while in intimate conversation with contemporary cultural and religious movements as diverse as divine healing, mesmerism, Darwinism and natural science, the women's movement, the antislavery and abolitionist movements and their postwar legacies, Theosophy, Buddhism, New Thought, Christian orthodoxy, Christian liberalism, and so on. *Science and Health* described a new form of Christianity that interacted with many traditions in ways that were both subtle and decisive, formative and tangential. It overlapped with some, conversed with others, contested or rejected still others, always remaining distinct.

As modernity fades and terms such as "conservative" and "liberal" lose meaning, with new categories emerging on postmodern spectrums with many points around and in between, Christian Science continues to make sense to us academically only as we see it inhabiting its own singular, fully Christian node on a historically rich network of currently charted options. It is a distinctive type of Christianity needing its own category, a new taxonomic location.

When James penned his *Varieties of Religious Experience* in 1902, he unwittingly became the most influential historiographer of Christian Science in the decades since. Robert Peel noted over sixty years ago that "the point William James was to miss" in *Varieties* was that Eddy "chose the cross and crown—crucifixion and resurrection, trial and victory—as the symbol of Christian Science."[6] In his influential 1973 work, Stephen Gottschalk wrote that Christian Science can be best understood as a *"pragmatic interpretation of Christian revelation,"* invoking a loose and generic rather than a Pierce-specific sense of American pragmatism.[7]

More condensed studies have agreed, such as David Weddle's contention that Eddy "intended Christian Science to be the movement that would both restore primitive Christianity and also advance Christian understanding into the promised age of redemption" and that "the usual claims for the authority of *Science and Health* based on the coherence of its metaphysics and the efficacy of its healing practice are fully intelligible only when placed in the wider context of the mythic vision of Christian history, shared by Eddy and her students in a community of interpretation."[8] Catherine Albanese's widely used introductory history of American religions currently brings out that "Christian Science taught a broad interpretation of Christian revelation, expounded a metaphysical system to help modern people understand it, and practiced healing as the logical outcome of its beliefs about Christ and the world."[9] A genre of similar descriptions exist, many instances of which are cited in this book.

Such definitions stand out for their closeness to relevant primary sources, and I have built on them here. What I have added is a study of the genesis, development, and uses of Eddy's text and its lived aspects among adherents that resolves open questions about the scope and accuracy of such explanations in comparison with others, provides a critical mass of evidence to back this up, and pins down the meaning of terms such as "restorationist" and "metaphysical" in historical context. I then advance a similar definition I find to be most comprehensive and historically true.

Speaking about the cultural and religious significance of *Science and Health*, Paul Gutjahr once hoped for a study that provides "the reader a sense of the book's importance and place in the life of this religious tradition in particular, and in American culture in general."[10] I hope this book provides that. At the very least, it sketches out why public descriptions of Christian Science have so often differed from this religion's own identity as indicated by its primary sources. At most, it establishes that Eddy's book articulated a novel type of Christianity, creating the new religious identity lived by adherents populating this study.

Science and Health with Key to the Scriptures is a book Mary Baker Eddy wrote interpreting the Bible, titled to this end, and which she referred to in its own pages as fulfilling and explaining biblical promises. She paired her book with the Bible as pastor of her Church of Christ, Scientist, where the Bible opens and closes each service and makes up a majority of readings overall. This pastoral coupling sold massive amounts of Bibles into the twentieth century.

Eddy took almost daily notes in one of her forty-one personal Bibles as she wrote her book, a book in which she referred to the Bible on nearly every page. In their own copies of her book and their first-person accounts, adherents referred to *Science and Health* as drawing them to the Bible and enabling them in the modern era to fulfill the commands and promises of Jesus. They spoke of Eddy as their "Leader" to the one Christ of the New Testament scriptures. Hers was and is not a book that is Christian adjacent, with some Christian themes or a partial Christian orientation. It represents a new Christian identity.

That some people at some points, occasionally even adherents, found this unusual Christian identity inconvenient, inexplicable, outrageous, or unpopular does not change its textual and historical existence. Neither does it negate the majority of adherents who cohered around it or the observers and advocates who recognized its particular form of Christian expression, whether or not they were sympathetic.

If we respond to the historically lived content of Mary Baker Eddy's Christian Science claims to revelation and discovery by acknowledging this religion's fully Bible-centered identity from its inception, in conversation with every imaginable aspect of modernity with the purpose of preserving and extending Christian healing in the present era, we begin to carve out a space for its identity. To encompass this identity, our map of American religion should expand to accommodate the possibility of a distinctive, anti-mesmeric, revelatory, restorationist statement of applied Christian metaphysics that its adherents historically expressed in experiences they called healing.

Christian Science does not sit easily within our predominantly dichotomous map of nineteenth-century religious options, and from its modern emergence through the present postmodern era, it can best be seen as one node in a network of Christian expressions, whether innovative or orthodox. This network in turn sits in a field of religious networks, each carrying varied weight and with nodes containing full spectrums of religious experience in varying degrees of conversation, often contestation, and sometimes combination with one another. In this way, once again, the outliers of American religion reveal its unexpected boundaries in new ways that reconceive its nature and overall patterns.

APPENDIX

Major Copyrighted Editions and Content Revisions of *Science and Health with Key to the Scriptures* by Mary Baker Eddy

IN ARCHIVAL PAPERS related to *Science and Health,* and in my book, sometimes the word *edition* refers to a major content revision the author made. Sometimes it refers to a numbered printing.

Mary Baker Eddy called the 1891 edition of *Science and Health* her "fourth" edition or major content revision (Eddy to Nixon, 1891, L04140, MBEC). She seems to have referred to the book in its fourth edition until 1902, when she revised her book's content extensively for the last time. She made smaller but significant changes in 1907 and indicated her book was almost complete by 1908. She made a few brief changes through late 1910 that were printed in the final 1911 volume.

However, until 1907, Eddy's publisher numbered each of her book's many printings and called them "editions." Nine of these are major: Eddy took out a new copyright for all nine—occasionally in the calendar year prior to printing—due to significant (though sometimes small) changes. The other 400-plus numbered editions, a.k.a printings, are minor: they contain nominal changes, usually minuscule typesetting or copyediting corrections.

The last numbered printing was the 418th in 1906. From 1907 onward, the publisher left off numbering and identified printings by year.

Major Edition © Year	Extensive Content Revision	Printing Number(s)	Full Citation and Notes
1875	N/A	1st	Mary Baker Glover, *Science and Health* (Boston: Christian Scientist Publishing Company, 1875). Printed by W. F. Brown & Co., Boston. Many printer errors. Per standard practice, Brown probably threw out the manuscript after setting type. Eddy wrote "Key to the Scriptures" on her copy's title page.
1878		2nd	Mary Baker Glover Eddy, *Science and Health*, vol. 2 (Lynn, Mass.: Asa G. Eddy, 1878). Printed by Rand, Avery, & Co., Boston. Many more printer errors. Most revisions that Eddy drafted did not make it into print. Only volume 2 could be salvaged for release. Subsequently used with the first edition as volume 1. Picture of Noah's ark stamped on cover.
1881	First	3rd–5th	Mary B. Glover Eddy, *Science and Health*, 2 vols. (Lynn, Mass.: Asa G. Eddy, 1881). Printed by John Wilson & Sons, University Press, Cambridge, Mass. Printed correctly and completely. The cover showed a cross and crown, which appeared through the final edition. New chapter, "Recapitulation," included material revised from the author's 1870s *Science of Man*. Chapter "Creation" refers to God as "She" (through 1885).
1883	Second	6th	Mary Baker G. Eddy, *Science and Health with a Key to the Scriptures*, 2 vols. (Boston: By the author, 1883). Printed by John Wilson & Sons, University Press, Cambridge, Mass. Added subtitle, "with a Key to the Scriptures." Added new section matching subtitle containing one untitled chapter and a brief Bible dictionary, some of it revised from the author's 1860s Genesis manuscript.

Major Edition © Year	Extensive Content Revision	Printing Number(s)	Full Citation and Notes
1886	Third	16th–24th	Mary Baker G. Eddy, *Science and Health with Key to the Scriptures* (Boston: By the author, 1886). Printed by John Wilson & Sons, University Press, Cambridge, Mass.
			Finalized subtitle, "with Key to the Scriptures." Converted existing "Key" content to a "Glossary" and added exegesis of Genesis. Added chapter "Prayer and Atonement." This material edited from earlier writings or moved from other parts of the book. Added new exegesis of Saint John's book of Revelation. Professional copyediting. Index added.
1890 (printed 1891)	Fourth	50th–65th	Mary Baker G. Eddy, *Science and Health with Key to the Scriptures* (Boston: By the author, 1891). Printed by John Wilson & Sons, University Press, Cambridge, Mass.
			Most substantial revision. Chapters arranged close to their final order. Chapter "Prayer and Atonement" divided into two chapters (titled "Prayer" and "Atonement and Eucharist") and moved from back to front part of book. New chapters added incorporating earlier drafts and material from existing chapters: "Science, Theology, Medicine," "Christian Science and Spiritualism," "Christian Science Practice," "Teaching Christian Science." Chapter "Reply to a Clergyman" edited and renamed "Some Objections Answered." Eleven-page allegory illustrating Christian Science healing dropped. Marginal headings added. Many 1886 copyedits revised or removed. Many significant wording changes and theological refinements.

(continued)

Major Edition © Year	Extensive Content Revision	Printing Number(s)	Full Citation and Notes
1894		81st–91st	Mary Baker G. Eddy, *Science and Health with Key to the Scriptures* (Boston: E. J. Foster-Eddy, 1894). Printed by John Wilson & Sons, University Press, Cambridge, Mass.
			Allegory illustrating Christian Science healing restored. A few other smaller changes. Author ordained the Bible and her book "dual pastor" of The Mother Church from this year on.
1901 (printed 1902)		226th–262nd	Mary Baker G. Eddy, *Science and Health with Key to the Scriptures* (Boston: Joseph Armstrong, 1902). Printed by John Wilson & Sons, University Press, Cambridge, Mass.
			Last substantial revision prior to final edition. Chapter order finalized. Chapter "Prayer" moved to first place and a final chapter of testimonials, "Fruitage," added. Separate comprehensive concordance (published in 1903) replaced index. Line numbers added to each page. Reflects capitalization Eddy finalized in 1901: seven synonyms for God capitalized, all attributes of God lowercased. Marginal headings edited, scriptural references standardized copyediting.
1906 (printed 1907)		N/A	Mary Baker G. Eddy, *Science and Health with Key to the Scriptures* (Boston: Joseph Armstrong, 1907). Printed by John Wilson & Sons, University Press, Cambridge, Mass.
			In final chapter, "Fruitage," all testimonials but one replaced with those referring to most recent version of Eddy's book. Many small changes to chapters, especially "Recapitulation." Last edition to receive a copyright in the author's lifetime. At author's request, subsequent printings identified by year of publication instead of number. Eddy considered her book almost complete by 1908.

Major Edition © Year	Extensive Content Revision	Printing Number(s)	Full Citation and Notes
1910 (printed 1911)	Final	N/A	Mary Baker G. Eddy, *Science and Health with Key to the Scriptures* (Boston: Allison V. Stewart, 1911). Printed by William Dana Orcutt, Plimpton Press, Norwood, Mass. Includes small but important changes indicated by the author through 1910. Chapter "Animal Magnetism" retitled "Animal Magnetism Unmasked." Chapter "Christian Science and Spiritualism" retitled "Christian Science versus Spiritualism." Per her October 1910 request, the frontispiece including her portrait was removed. A few other small changes according to her directions were cross-checked, completed by 1914, and protected under her existing copyrights. Printings from 1914 to the present are identical. Eddy extended her 1875 copyright in 1903. From 1917 to 1934, her 1875 and 1890–1906 copyrights were extended and transferred to the Trustees under the Will of Mary Baker G. Eddy.

NOTES

Abbreviations

AAC	Art and Artifact Collection, Special Collections, Mary Baker Eddy Library, Boston
AIB	Autographed and Inscribed Books, Special Collections, Mary Baker Eddy Library, Boston
BA	Boston Athenaeum
CJ	*Congregational Journal*
CSA	Christian Scientist Association
CSJ	*Christian Science Journal* (1883–)
CSS	*Christian Science Sentinel* (1898–)
GFC	Grimes Family Correspondence, New Hampshire Historical Society, Concord
GFP	Garrison Family Papers, Sophia Smith Collection, Special Collections, Smith College, Northampton, Mass.
GMS	Mary Baker Eddy, "The Bible in Its Spiritual Meaning" [a.k.a. Genesis manuscript], Mary Baker Eddy Collection, c. 1867–1969, Special Collections, Mary Baker Eddy Library, Boston
HPCW	Historical Periodicals Collection, American Antiquarian Society, Worcester, Mass.
JFSR	*Journal of Feminist Studies in Religion*
LT	*Lynn (Mass.) Transcript*
LYM	Longyear Museum, Chestnut Hill, Mass.
MBEC	Mary Baker Eddy Collection, Special Collections, Mary Baker Eddy Library, Boston
MBEL	Mary Baker Eddy Library, Boston
MEHS	Maine Historical Society, Portland
NAWLD	North American Women's Letters and Diaries, alexanderstreet.com
NHHS	New Hampshire Historical Society, Concord
ORT	Organizational Records of the First Church of Christ, Scientist, the Mary Baker Eddy Library, Boston
RF	Reminiscence File, Special Collections, the Mary Baker Eddy Library, Boston
SC	Special Collections
SF	Subject File, Special Collections, the Mary Baker Eddy Library, Boston
SSC	Sophia Smith Collection, Special Collections, Smith College, Northampton, Mass.
TC	*The Congregationalist*
WECP	William E. Chandler Papers, New Hampshire Historical Society, Concord

A Restoration Story and a New History

1. Marietta T. Webb, Councilmanic District 10, Los Angeles, Los Angeles Township, Los Angeles, Calif., citing enumeration district 60–813, sheet 17A, line 26, family 354, NARA digital publication T627, Sixteenth Census of the United States, 1940, https://familysearch.org/ark:/61903/1:1:K9ZS-6BJ; Records of the Bureau of the Census, 1790–2007, RG 29, roll 415; United States Federal Census for Boston, Suffolk County, Mass., 1880, familysearch.org, p. 718; Marietta Thomas Webb, 8 December 1951, California Death Record, State of California Department of Health Services, Center for Health Statistics, Sacramento. The death index lists Webb's birth name, Jones.

2. Marietta T. Webb, "Long before I Heard of Christian Science," *CSS* 24, no. 5 (1906): 299.

3. Hiram Webb, Military Correspondence, District of Columbia, United States, NARA microfilm publication M1902, roll 12, District of Columbia Freedmen's Bureau Field Office Records, 1863–1872, https://familysearch.org/ark:/61903/1:1:Q2QV-TTNS, FHL microfilm 2,424,787.

4. Hiram Webb, 1893, Massachusetts Births, 1841–1915, https://familysearch.org/ark:/61903/1:1:FX6T-4DB.

5. M. Webb, "Long before I heard of Christian Science," 299. See W. M. Byrd and L. A. Clayton, "Race, Medicine, and Health Care in the United States: A Historical Survey," *Journal of the National Medical Association* 3 suppl. (2001): 11S–34S; and Anthony W. Neal, "Boston's Black Medical Community Thrived in the Mid-nineteenth Century," *Bay State Banner*, 4 April 2012, https://www.baystatebanner.com/2012/04/11/bostons-black-medical-community-thrived-in-the-mid-19th-century/.

6. M. Webb, "Long before I Heard of Christian Science," 299.

7. M. Webb, "Long before I Heard of Christian Science," 300. Webb also read Mary Baker Eddy (hereafter Eddy), *Miscellaneous Writings*.

8. Marietta T. Webb, "The Protecting Power of Truth," *CSS* 2, no. 12 (1899): 195–96.

9. Curtis, *Faith*, 24, notes that she is not "competent to judge these matters." In *Spirit Cure*, Williams sets aside efficacy and instead cites historical accounts in Porterfield's *Healing in the History of Christianity* and Candy Gunther Brown's *Testing Prayer*. These strategies are Jamesian; in *William James*, 4, Knapp notes that James "was not a believer or a seeker"; neither was he "a skeptic nor a debunker." Taves, *Religious Experience Reconsidered*, xii, says her "goal is . . . not to debunk or explain away" the claims of religious groups "but to learn about the interactive process" constituting them.

10. See Moore, *Religious Outsiders*. For the centrality of religious dissent to the definition and protection of American identity, see Freeman, *Undomesticated Dissent*.

11. See Grant A. Wacker, "The Holy Spirit and the Spirit of the Age in American Protestantism, 1880–1910," *Journal of American History* 72 (1985): 45–62, in which he argues "that boundary markers between presumably liberal and conservative groups were often much more fluid than would be the case" later on; Pietsch, *Dispensational Modernism*; and R. Robins, *A. J. Tomlinson*, which depicts early Pentecostalism as a form of "plainfolk modernism" that should not be read through the lens of later fundamentalist controversies. I thank an anonymous press reader for astute comments pointing me to these references.

12. Gottschalk, *Emergence*.

13. Ventimiglia, *Copyrighting God*, 133.

14. Grant Wacker, introduction to Aamodt, Land, and Numbers, *Ellen Harmon White*, ix, xiii.

15. Squires, *Healing the Nation*, 6.

16. Gottschalk, *Rolling Away*, 124.

17. Peel, *Years of Authority*, 184.

18. Taves, *Revelatory Events*, 1.

19. Stephen J. Stein, "American Bibles: Canon, Commentary, and Community," *Church History* 64, no. 2 (June 1995): 177.

20. Paul C. Gutjahr, "The State of the Discipline: Sacred Texts in the United States," *Book History* 4 (2001): 335. Also see Gutjahr, *Oxford Handbook*.

21. See, e.g., Stein, "American Bibles," 171, citing Wilfred Cantwell Smith; and Elizabeth Schüssler Fiorenza, "Powerful Words," in Wimbush, *Theorizing Scriptures*, 265.

22. Eddy, "Teachers SS Lessons," n.d. [est. 1890–1891], A10433, MBEC.

23. Eva Payne, "God Works through Strength, Not through Weakness: Laura Lathrop and Christian Science in New York City, 1880–1910," unpublished paper, Harvard Divinity School, 2009.

24. Curtis, *Faith*, 20.

25. Eddy, *Manual*, 17.

Chapter One

1. On stereotyped Bibles in America, see Gutjahr, *American Bible*, 13, 29, 30, 206n107. Also see Goff, Farnsley, and Thuesen, *Bible in American Life*. The Baker family Bible and other artifacts mentioned in this chapter are held at LYM.

2. *Yankee Farmer* 3, no. 3 (1837), SC, MEHS; *Yankee Farmer* 2, no. 1 (1836), SC, MEHS. The second joke appeared in dozens of New England newspapers of the era.

3. For an overview of New England domestic life, see Nylander, *Our Own Snug Fireside*. All early Baker family artifacts are held at LYM.

4. For a history of early American atheists, see Schmidt, *Village Atheists*.

5. Rev. Richard S. Rust, obituary of Abigail Baker, in Stearns, *Genealogical and Family History*, 118.

6. *Manual of the Congregational Church*, back pages. Eddy later suggested her first profession of faith may have been at a revival at Old North Church, Concord, in 1834 (Peel, *Years of Discovery*, 293).

7. Untitled, *Granite Monthly* 7, no. 1 (1883): n.p.

8. *Minutes of the Fifty-Ninth Annual Meeting*, 29; *Addresses at the Semi-centennial Anniversary*, 9.

9. *Seventy-Fifth Anniversary*, 9, 25. Also see *Addresses at the Semi-centennial Anniversary*, 9; and W. H. J., "Obituary, Rev. Enoch Corser," *Congregational Quarterly* 40, no. 1 (1869): 287.

10. See Eddy, *Retrospection*, 13. This statement is uncorroborated and far removed from events but meshes with the cultural state of predestination at the time.

11. *Addresses at the Semi-centennial Anniversary*, 13, 4, 15.

12. *Addresses at the Semi-centennial Anniversary*, 8.

13. *Addresses at the Semi-centennial Anniversary*, 8.

14. Albert Baker, "Temperance," LYM.

15. Thayer, *Congregationalism in New Hampshire*, 12–14.

16. Many publications, such as Cogswell, *Christian Philanthropist*, linked the coming millennium to atonement for slavery. Cogswell also argued that African physiology was not inferior and called slavery "unjust, sinful, and infamous" and a "detestable crime" (198). On the arrest, see Corbin Curtice in *Addresses at the Semi-centennial Anniversary*, 9–10.

17. "Anti-slavery," *New Hampshire Observer* 18, no. 4, whole no. 888 (1836): 2.

18. Rufus A. Putnam, "Slavery Subject," *New Hampshire Observer* 18, no. 10, whole no. 894 (1836): 2.

19. "Antislavery," *New Hampshire Observer* 18, no. 11, whole no. 895 (1836): 2.

20. Brother John to Sister, 17 February 1837, 1962.017, GFC.

21. Cyrus W. Wallace, "Church Action on Slavery," *CJ* 3, no. 8, whole no. 112 (1843), 1; P., "Southern Slaveholders," *CJ* 3, no. 5, whole no. 109 (1843): 2. For a later example, see "Rev. Henry Ward Beecher's Lecture on Slavery," *TC* 6, no. 7 (1854): 26.

22. Thayer, *Congregationalism in New Hampshire*, 12–14.

23. *Addresses at the Semi-centennial Anniversary*, 10.

24. Eddy, "Our National Thanksgiving Hymn" (7 December 1865), *Poems*, 78.

25. Thayer, *Religious Conditions*, 12. The ubiquitous Congregational minister and state historian Nathaniel Bouton, who pastored the Bakers when they attended church in Concord, noted in 1833 that free public education in New Hampshire reflected the "civil and religious polity" of its first European settlers, who came first for religious liberty, second and "subsidiar[il]y . . . *to educate their children*." Bouton, *History of Education*, 3, emphasis his. Bouton later reiterated that "New England owes her intellectual and moral glory, primarily to her religion, secondarily to her schools," 30.

26. See, e.g., Hosmer, *Young Lady's Book*.

27. *Daily Courier* (Portland, Maine), 8 March 1830. Earlier, Ann Greene Chapman (Notebooks and Diary, 1813, SC, BA) noted that in a stagecoach as in public generally, "a woman is under great disadvantages as she cannot join in the conversation."

28. This view lingered into the twentieth century. A popular 1910 sexual education book (Lowry, *Confidences*, 55) declared that "the modern athletic girl glories in her strength" and "in her strong, well-trained body," but the title of a 1919 physical exercise chart speaks for itself: "Chart C: Overcoming Weaknesses of Women," Olympian System of exercises, Health Collection, Sophia Smith Collection, Special Collections, Smith College, Northampton, Mass.

29. Russell, *President's Address*, 11; Bissell, *Physical Development*, 42.

30. For a classic study, see Gould, "Women's Brains," in *Panda's Thumb*, 152–55. Gill discusses the effect of this cultural assumption on Eddy's education in *Mary Baker Eddy*, 35–36. See also Eddy, *Retrospection*, 10.

31. See Peel, *Years of Discovery*, 27–28; and Gill, *Mary Baker Eddy*, 18. Also on Eddy's childhood, see R. Thomas, "With Bleeding Footsteps," 19–47; and Kennedy, *Mrs. Eddy*, 13–34.

32. "Untitled," *Granite Monthly* 7, no. 1 (1883): n.p. My thanks to Heather Frederick for recommending this source. Also see Sanborn, *Analytical Grammar*.

33. On Sarah Bodwell, see Smaus, *Mary Baker Eddy*, 78, 89, 90, 94, 100; and Peel, *Years of Discovery*, 64. Also see Abraham Bodwell, "Woodman Sanbornton Academy," *Repository and Observer* (Concord, N.H.) 9, no. 15 (April 6, 1827), n.s. no. 41 (October 3, 1827), 2.

34. Eddy, "Resolutions for the Day," *Poems*, 32; N. Brown, *The Apocalypse*, QJ 378 C 6725-b, SC, MEHS; Ann Greene Chapman, Notebooks and Diary, 1813, SC, BA. Reverend Brown preserved Black's ladylikeness by issuing her poem under his name before reading it to a large audience of men at Waterville (later Colby) College in Maine, though Black autographed copies for admirers. Chapman's preacher was the renowned William Ellery Channing.

35. Mullen, *Chance of Salvation*, 268.

36. See Peel, *Years of Discovery*, 44–46; Gill, *Mary Baker Eddy*, 44; Thomas, "With Bleeding Footsteps," 22–82, 101–20; Kennedy, *Mrs. Eddy*, 72–73.

37. Eddy to Daniel Patterson, 29 April 1853, L08900, MBEC, SC, MBEL.

38. Hodgkiss, *From Lesion to Metaphor*, 14. Hodgkiss focuses on the European context,

which in the nineteenth century had broad transatlantic influence. The meaning of hypochondria, like neuralgia, considerably evolved.

39. Charles M. Parsons, "Neuralgia; Its History, Nature, and Temperament," *American Journal of the Medical Sciences* 56 (October 1854): 427.

40. George C. Peavey to Bartholomew Van Dame, 2 April 1842, M.1956.008, Papers of Bartholomew van Dame, NHHS; Sarah Grimes Smith to Almira Grimes, 14 November 1861, M.1962–017.(M), GFC; Sarah Grimes to unknown, 19 April 1853, GFC.

41. Hodgkiss, *From Lesion to Metaphor*, 14.

42. See Laycock, *Essay on Hysteria*. In early literature, neuralgia and hysteria were occasionally theorized as secondary symptoms of one another based on their common nervous nature.

43. Napheys, *Physical Life of Woman*, 29, 26.

44. Hysteria took on new definitions and diagnostic meanings with the advent of psychology and persisted into the twentieth century, like other claims of female weakness, only to become widely debunked for its misogynistic elements. For a classic "hystery" of sexism and racism around the womb in America, see Barker-Benfield, *Horrors of the Half-Known Life*. Characterizations of Eddy as "hysterical" emerged in 1906 when, notes Gill, authors at *McClure's* magazine read "clinical accounts then recently reported on hysteria in French asylums" and began "grafting" them onto her biography. Gill, *Mary Baker Eddy*, 47. This assessment matches my own research.

45. "Spinal Institution," *TC* 6, no. 1 (1854): 4.

46. Parsons, "Neuralgia," 427.

47. Corban Curtice in *Addresses at the Semi-centennial Anniversary*, 16. Corser was never formally installed as pastor; though no reason is given, hiring details in country churches often could not be arranged to mutual satisfaction (salary, firewood, parsonage, and so on). Corser tutored students largely to supplement his meager salary.

48. *Addresses at the Semi-centennial Anniversary*, 9.

49. Peel, *Years of Discovery*, 68; Gill, *Mary Baker Eddy*, 58; also Thomas, "With Bleeding Footsteps," 45–49; and Kennedy, *Mrs. Eddy*, 35–36.

50. Peel, *Years of Discovery*, 68.

51. Peel, 75; Kennedy, *Mrs. Eddy*, 59–70.

52. Many publications such as Cogswell, *Christian Philanthropist*, linked the coming millennium to atonement for slavery. Also see Faust, *This Republic*; Foner, *Fiery Trial*; Noll, *Civil War*; Miller, Stout, and Wilson, *Religion*; Rable, *God's Almost Chosen Peoples*; and Stout, *Upon the Altar*.

53. Livermore, *Testimony*, 138, 143, discusses Bible passages such as Jesus's parable of the woman hiding leaven in three measures of meal. "Men are asleep, as on the top of a mast— they dream vain dreams," Livermore writes. "The woman has not taken the leaven."

Chapter Two

1. See Nord, *Faith in Reading*; and Casper et al., *Industrial Book*.

2. Brontë, *Jane Eyre*, 3.

3. Peel, *Years of Discovery*, 95; Thomas, "With Bleeding Footsteps," 22–82; Kennedy, *Mrs. Eddy*, 72–73.

4. Peel, *Years of Discovery*, 83.

5. See T. Thomas, *Elizabeth Cady Stanton*.

6. See Eddy, *Poems*, 15–16; and Peel, *Years of Discovery*, 102–3. Her grieving poems are not

unlike items such as "Dying Girl," *TC* 6, no. 8 (1854): 32, or "Gather Ripe Fruits, O Death," in *CJ* 3, no. 2, whole no. 106 (1843): back page.

7. Eddy, marginal mark in *Festival of Sons of New Hampshire*, B00299A, MBEC.

8. Gill, *Mary Baker Eddy*, 613n17; *Longyear Quarterly News*, Autumn 1983, 315. Thanks to Cindy Safronoff.

9. By the 1850s, heroic treatments (counterirritants, cupping, leeching) and bed rest were losing favor among physicians specializing in spinal neuralgia compared with lifestyle changes that would allow patients "to lead a comparatively active and happy life," managing their chronic pain and weakness through regular hours, exercise, and diet; the careful concern of employers; avoiding stresses that "are a frequent exciting cause" of the disease; and maintaining "cheerful employment of the mind and feelings." Charles M. Parsons, "Neuralgia; Its History, Nature, and Temperament," *American Journal of the Medical Sciences* 56 (October 1854): 433, 446.

10. Nora Unwin, Mary Baker Eddy House at North Groton (engraving), 2004.031, NHHS.

11. Eddy, notations in Tolstoy, *The Kreutzer Sonata*, 8, B00305, MBEC.

12. Peel, *Years of Discovery*, 140.

13. Parsons, "Neuralgia," 427.

14. Starling, *Noble Deeds of Woman*, xv, xvi.

15. Peel, *Years of Discovery*, 141.

16. John Grimes to Sister, 28 October 1857, 1962.01, GFC.

17. Amy Mecklenburg-Faenger, "Trifles, Abominations, and Literary Gossip: Gendered Rhetoric and Nineteenth-Century Scrapbooks," *Genders* 1 (February 2012), https://www.colorado.edu/gendersarchive1998–2013/2012/02/01/trifles-abominations-and-literary-gossip-gendered-rhetoric-and-nineteenth-century. Also see Tucker, Ott, and Buckler, *Scrapbook in American Life*.

18. Horton, *Directions for the Sick*.

19. C. Brown, *Healing Gods*, 164. The American Medical Association eventually formed in response to the American Institute of Homeopathy, outrunning it by the 1880s.

20. David Nartonis, "How Homeopathy Came to New Hampshire," *Historical New Hampshire* 64, no. 1 (Summer 2010): 31.

21. Wight, *Address*, 6.

22. Nartonis, "How Homeopathy Came to New Hampshire," 33.

23. O. A. Woodbury, "Homoeopathy: The Only True Medical Practice," *Homeopathic Advocate and Guide to Health* 1, no. 5 (1851): 66.

24. See Le Bosquet, *Congregational Manual*.

25. Mary to Ester, 14 August 1854, 1995.008(M), White Family Papers, NHHS. For the role of women as homeopathic pioneers, see Kirschmann, *Vital Force*; and N. Robins, *Copeland's Cure*. Hedrick, *Harriet Beecher Stowe*, cites Donegan, *Hydropathic Highway*, who also characterizes hydropathy as a secular mimic of perfectionist piety. Both, says Hedrick, were "narrowly focused on the self" (173). She also cites Cayleff, *Wash and Be Healed*, who argues that the sensuousness of the physical experience of water cure provided relief and release to the women at these resorts. Finally, see Weiss and Kemble, *Great American Water-Cure Craze*.

26. Peel, *Years of Discovery*, 99, 111.

27. Parker Pillsbury to Armenia White, 19 January 1859, 2014.059.001.007.003, White Family Papers, NHHS. In later years, White and Eddy engaged the same lawyer, Frank Streeter, on different matters.

28. "The New Hydropathic Cook Book," *TC* 6, no. 2 (1854): 8.

29. Hedrick, *Harriet Beecher Stowe*, 173.

30. Clifton Springs Water-Cure, *Report of the Addresses*, n.p. (the source for the quotes in the next paragraph too).

31. Upham, *Elements of Mental Philosophy*, was the standard textbook on moral science at the time. Also see Alexander, *Outlines of Moral Science*; Beattie, *Elements of Moral Science*; and Wayland, *Elements of Moral Science*. Also see Riskin, *Science and Sensibility*; and Roberts, "Science of the Soul."

32. Hedge, *Sick Woman*, 6.

33. Untitled, *Millennial Star* 11, no. 10 (1849): 153. Primarily for British Mormons, this periodical was discontinued in 1970 during internal "correlation."

34. Untitled, *CJ* 3, no. 3, whole no. 107 (1843): n.p.

35. Clifton Springs Water-Cure, *Report of the Addresses*, 6–7.

36. Woodbury, "Homoeopathy," 66.

37. See Paretsky, *Words, Works, and Ways of Knowing*.

38. "Minutes of Doings and Speeches at Meeting of Church in Shelburne, Ma., Dec. 27, 1843," 8, Congregational Library and Archives, Boston (also the source for the quotes in the next few paragraphs). My thanks to Cristina Prochilo, archivist at the Congregational Library and Archives, for pointing out this document, and to Brett Grainger for generously sharing his transcript.

39. See Porter, *Spirit Rappings*; and A. Putnam, *Mesmerism*, 1, 36.

40. Bushnell, "Unconscious Influence," in *Sermons*, 193. I thank Margaret Bendroth for recommending this title and supplying a copy.

41. Knapp, *William James*, 11.

42. See Ogden, *Credulity*. Also see Taves, *Fits*.

43. For an exploration of the relationship between religion, stage performance, clairvoyance (or clairaudience), and reputation, see Schmidt, *Hearing Things*, for example 159, 163, 173, 225.

44. For the participation of religious ministers in this endeavor, see Taves, *Fits*, 131; and, e.g., George C. Peavey to Rev. Bartholomew Van Dame, 2 April 1842, M.1956.008, Papers of Bartholomew Van Dame, NHHS.

45. Bushnell, *Nature and the Supernatural*, 321, 318.

46. Corban Curtice in *Addresses at the Semi-centennial Anniversary*, 19, italics his.

47. Frank T. Daniell to Cousin, 3 July 1858, 1962.017, GFC. Cousin Frank added he meant no offense, respected all who love God, and for fun, "I have invested 13 cts. in fire works and intend to make something of a display on the 'Glorious Fourth.'"

48. See Eddy, marks in Messenger, *Time of the End*, B00236, MBEC.

Chapter Three

1. Eddy, "The Heart's Unrest," 13 December 1861, A09001, MBEC.

2. John Abbott to Rebecca S. Abbott, 31 January 1863, Fogg Collection, MEHS.

3. Daniel Patterson to Eddy, 2 April 1853, L16248, MBEC.

4. Jim Burgess, personal communication, 16 December 2011, Manassas National Battlefield Park Archives, Va.

5. McPherson, *Battle Cry of Freedom*, 147, 413.

6. Eddy to Benjamin F. Butler, 12 August 1861, V03472, MBEC. Eddy received an undated reply from Butler's camp. See Peel, *Years of Discovery*, 145; and Kennedy, *Mrs. Eddy*, 104–5.

7. Eddy to James Patterson, 12 May 1862, F00043, MBEC.

8. Faust, *This Republic*, 132.

9. Eddy to Patterson, 12 May 1862.

10. Patterson was first incarcerated at Richmond but by April had been transferred to North Carolina's Salisbury prison, which then was at just over half capacity with a 2 percent death rate, compared to over 25 percent in 1864, when the prison was vastly overcrowded. Salisbury Confederate Prison Archives, N.C., http://www.salisburyprison.org/PrisonHistory .htm (accessed 26 August 2011).

11. Peel, *Years of Discovery*, 335n69. There are even records of "town ball" (baseball) games played at Salisbury in the spring of 1862, the first allegedly played in the South. Salisbury Confederate Prison Archives, www.salisburyprison.org/PrisonHistory.htm (accessed 28 November 2011).

12. Prison camps filled after Bull Run in late August and Antietam on 17 September. According to Sue Curtis, personal communication, 4 September 2011, Salisbury Confederate Prison Archives, there were "more civilians at the [Salisbury] Prison between June 1862 [and] Oct[ober] 1864 and [they] probably were treated the worst."

13. Eddy to Phineas P. Quimby, 29 May 1862, V03341, MBEC.

14. John 8:32. All scripture references are from the King James Version.

Chapter Four

1. Thanks to Bill Barry at MEHS for noting this. For Portland as a center of social reform, see Pritchard, *Jeremiah Hacker*. Also see Marsha Robinson, "Frances Ellen Watkins Harper," in Price and Talbot, *Maine's Visible Black History*, 265–66, 356.

2. See Dominic, *Down from the Balcony*.

3. Dominic, 1. Portland's fifteen churches are shown on Samuel H. Colesworthy, "Plan of Portland, 1852," Map Folder or MaineMemory.net #176, SC, MEHS.

4. *Decision of the Council*, M347.9p837, SC, MEHS.

5. See Pritchard, *Jeremiah Hacker*.

6. In *Protestants and Pictures*, 123, 127, David Morgan writes, "Antebellum religious life in the United States was strongly colored by the early republic's radical evangelical egalitarians, who were steeped in revival and a fiery rhetoric attacking traditional church polity. . . . The evangelical belief in access to the Bible assumed that the Bible could be successfully interpreted by anyone who genuinely tried to understand it." William Miller's focus on prophetic scripture responded to "the rationalistic claim that scripture was historically false and its prophecies were obscure or mystical."

7. Neck chain and collar, 1860, 82, SC, MEHS.

8. See Sons of Temperance Sash, 1850, 2002.062.010; Cork Total Abstinence Society Medal, 1850, 2007.400.004; *The Genius of Temperance* lithograph, 1850, 2008.311; and Young Temperance Volunteers Diploma, 1865, 2003.267.001, all in MEHS.

9. Embroidered bookmarks, 2001.319.002b and 751-67-2, MEHS.

10. *Daily Press* (Portland, Maine) 1, no. 165 (1862): 1. This newspaper had the largest daily circulation then in Portland.

11. "Mrs. Manchester," *Daily Evening Courier* (Portland, Maine) 3, no. 116 (1863): 2.

12. Eddy, marks and notations, in Alger, *Friendships of Women*, 114, B00107, MBEC. Eddy enthused over the "beautiful" account of the mourning widower who built the Taj Mahal for his dead bride and marked the passage on 114, "Prudery is the parsimony of a shriveled heart, and is scarcely worthy of respect." She sympathized with the description of "platonic love" between friends, writing "true" and "grand" and "I believe it" next to several descriptions of deeply felt friendship.

13. For a gendered discussion of this topic, see Haynes, *Riotous Flesh*.

14. "Dr. Stackpole," *Daily Evening Courier* 3, no. 116 (1863): 4.

15. "Mrs. S. B. Brown, a doctor who can cure all who are diseased," Broadside 307 (1863), SC, MEHS; "Mrs. Manchester," *Daily Evening Courier* 3, no. 116 (1863): 2.

16. Quimby's papers are held at the Library of Congress and Boston University's Mugar Memorial Library with a third, lesser collection at Harvard's Houghton Library. His seventy letters, fewer than ten in his own hand, are housed at Boston University. About two hundred pages of his original manuscripts exist, a fraction of the total, and consist of fragments in note form. His copyists and patients, notably the sisters Ware, redacted them with aplomb. Julius Dresser's son, Horatio, later heavily altered them prior to publishing his versions in the earliest anthology of Quimby papers in 1922. More recent compilations of these papers by Ervin Seale, Erroll Stafford Collie, and Alan Anderson are not heavily altered, but controversies regarding the influence of early copyists and patients (including Eddy) on the manuscripts have proved impossible to resolve historically. For such reasons, Quimby's papers need to be approached carefully. For a detailed description of the state of Quimby's papers in their original and published forms, see the introduction to Keith McNeil, *The Phineas Quimby–Mary Baker Eddy Debate*, 2016, at https://ppquimby-mbeddydebate.com/.

17. See Phineas P. Quimby, untitled, November 1859, 171:1, Howard Gotlieb Archival Research Center, Mugar Library, Boston University.

18. Electromagnetic machine, 1993.039.14.01, NHHS; advertisement for Richardson's Magneto-Galvanic Batteries, Broadside, 1881, S1997.553.38, NHHS.

19. *Daily Press* 1, no. 165 (1862): 1. Quimby's first exam cost $2.00 for rural folk and $2.50 for city patients, roughly equivalent to $50–60 in 2020. Subsequent sittings at his residence were half that.

20. "To The Sick," c. 1860, SF Quimby, Phineas P: Published/Printed Items.

21. See, e.g., Quimby, November 1859.

22. Eddy to Phineas P. Quimby, 1 January 1863, V03343, MBEC.

23. Eddy to Phineas P. Quimby, 31 January 1863, V03344, MBEC.

24. Eddy to Phineas P. Quimby, 10 March 1863, V03345, MBEC. Explaining her nephew's delay, Eddy wrote, "This is the period of excitement in N. Hampshire and the ballot box controls, hence, he cannot visit you until next week."

25. L. Brown, *Salisbury Prison*, 70; Sue Curtis, personal communication, 4 September 2011, Salisbury Confederate Prison Archives.

26. Eddy to James Patterson [attributed], n.d. [probably June–September 1863], LYM. Eddy used the Elizabethan spelling of "diverse" found in the King James Bible.

27. Eddy to Phineas P. Quimby, 31 March 1864, V03347, MBEC. This letter and Eddy to Quimby, 1 January 1863, answer Gill's speculation (*Mary Baker Eddy*, 48) that Eddy may have been "anorexic" with evidence that she desired to eat and enjoyed it when possible but was often too ill.

28. Eddy to Phineas P. Quimby, May 1864, V03351, MBEC (the source of the quotes in the next paragraph too).

29. Eddy to Phineas P. Quimby, 27 May 1864, V03352, MBEC. Eddy possibly composed this before Eddy to Quimby, May 1864, but it is not probable based on context.

30. Eddy to Quimby, 27 May 1864; Eddy to Phineas P. Quimby, 24 April 1864, V03350, MBEC.

31. Ann Mary Jarvis is often called Mary Ann in biographies. She went by her middle name (letters address her as "Mary"). The Warren census in 1850 and 1860 shows her family. According to Patricia Cline Cohen, whom I thank for this information, the 1850 census estimated Ann M. Jarvis to be twenty years old and living with her father, Robert W., a "cordwind" (probably a cordwainer, a leather shoemaker) born in England; her mother, Hannah;

three brothers; and four sisters. The 1860 census omits both parents and four of the eight children, matching accounts of the family's devastation by tuberculosis.

32. Eddy to Quimby, 31 March 1864.
33. Eddy to Quimby, 31 March 1864.
34. Eddy to Phineas P. Quimby, 10 April 1864, V03349, MBEC.
35. In place of endnotes, I use in-text citations for *Science and Health* throughout.
36. Eddy to Quimby, 31 March 1864 (the source of the quotes in the next two paragraphs too).
37. Eddy, "The Heart's Unrest," 13 December 1861, A09001, MBEC.
38. Eddy to Quimby, 24 April 1864 (the source of the quotes in the next three paragraphs too).
39. Eddy to Quimby, 10 April 1864.
40. Mary M. Patterson [Eddy], "The South and the North," *Waterville (Maine) Mail*, 9 September 1864.
41. Eddy to Quimby, 1 January 1863.
42. "Anecdote of Rev. Antoinette Brown," *TC* 18, no. 2 (1866): 4.
43. Phineas P. Quimby to an unknown patient, n.d. [c. 1862], http://www.ppquimby.com/. The letters on this site are based on originals held at Howard Gotlieb Archival Research Center.
44. Phineas P. Quimby, untitled or "Science, Woman, and the Spiritual Rib," August 1860, http://www.ppquimby.com/articles/science_woman_the_spiritual_rib.htm.
45. Susannah B. Quimby to Julius Dresser, n.d. [c. 1875–1883], in Anderson, *Healing Hypotheses*, 366 (the source of the quotes in the next paragraph too).
46. Gill, *Mary Baker Eddy*, 136.
47. Keith McNeil, personal communication, 13 January 2012.
48. The self-identified Quimby apologist Deb Whitehouse also notes this in her review of Gill, *Mary Baker Eddy*, in *Journal of the Society for the Study of Metaphysical Religion* 5, no. 1 (1999): 75–79.
49. Quoted in Gottschalk, *Rolling Away*, 72.
50. Eddy to Quimby, 24 April 1864. A few weeks earlier Eddy had written, "I thoroughly wish we understood as a people, the *True American idea*." Eddy to Quimby, 10 April 1864, emphasis hers.
51. Keats, *Endymion*, 3.
52. Eddy to Quimby, 10 April 1864.
53. Faust, *This Republic*, 204, notes that historians long thought of Emily Dickinson as isolated and removed from national matters, but four newspapers arrived at her home daily replete with the same wartime imagery that filled her poems, almost half of which she wrote during war years.
54. From the time of Daniel's return, notes Peel, he and Mary can be thought of as "moving in different directions" (*Years of Discovery*, 174).
55. Eddy to Phineas P. Quimby, 29 July 1865, V03356, MBEC.
56. *Lady's Book of Etiquette*, 14.

Chapter Five

1. *Lynn (Mass.) Weekly Reporter* 13, no. 10 (3 February 1866).
2. Peel, *Years of Discovery*, 195–97; Gill, *Mary Baker Eddy*, 161; R. Thomas, "With Bleeding Footsteps," 114–20; Kennedy, *Mrs. Eddy*, 130–32. Also see Myra Smith Reminiscences,

1 January 1907, 29 October 1911, and 7 November 1911, RF. Smith, the Pattersons' household helper, recalled Eddy losing her faith in homeopathy by the time she moved to Rumney in 1861.

3. See Mary Patterson to Julius Dresser, 15 February 1866, L07796, MBEC; Julius Dresser to Mary Patterson, 632.64.008, 2 March 1866, MBEC.

4. Faust, *This Republic*, 268.

5. See T. Hunter, *To 'Joy My Freedom*; Foner, *Fiery Trial*, 336; Samuel S. Hill, "Religion and the Results of the Civil War," in Miller, Stout, and Wilson, *Religion and the American Civil War*, 362.

6. Patterson provided about $200 in annual alimony for a few years, equivalent to about $3,200 in 2020. See Eddy to Charlotte Penniman Mulliken, 6 July 1869, L08866, MBEC.

Findings: Part I

1. Clifton Springs Water-Cure, *Report*.
2. Hedge, *Sick Woman*, 6.
3. See Gill, *Mary Baker Eddy*; Gottschalk, *Rolling Away*, 168–93.

Chapter Six

1. She wrote her first texts between late 1866 and 1869, completing the Genesis manuscript (hereafter GMS) near the end of that time. See Eddy to Charlotte Penniman Mulliken, 6 July 1869, L08866, MBEC.

2. The GMS was possibly but not certainly intended as the first installation of a book to be titled "The Bible in Its Spiritual Meaning." The Matthew manuscript may have come first but is a much shorter "teaching manuscript" and not meant as part of a book. Among Eddy's few early writings, the GMS stands out for its length, tone, and purpose.

3. R. Thomas, *"With Bleeding Footsteps,"* 127.

4. Eddy, GMS, 143, 521, A09000, MBEC.

5. Eddy, 247 (Gen. 17:19), 370 (Gen. 28:12).

6. Eddy, 403 (Gen. 31:24).

7. Eddy, 489–90 (Gen. 42:23), 564 (Genesis 49:16).

8. Eddy, "Introduction," GMS, 023.

9. Eddy, 125 (Gen. 5:3).

10. Eddy, GMS, 395 (Gen. 30:43).

11. Eddy, 372–73 (Gen. 28:18).

12. Eddy, 551 (Gen. 48:14).

13. Eddy, 557 (Gen. 49:2).

14. Eddy, 399 (Gen. 40).

15. Eddy, "The Higher Criticism," *CSS* 10, no. 16 (1907): 310. See also Alfred Farlow, "Christian Science and the Higher Criticism," *CSS* 8, no. 30 (1906): 470.

16. Eddy, GMS, 179 (Gen. 9:17).

17. The best scholarly discussion of Eddy's theodicy is Stephen Gottschalk, "Theodicy after Auschwitz and the Reality of God," *Union Seminary Quarterly Review* 41, nos. 3–4 (1987): 77–91.

18. Eddy, GMS, 002.

19. Eddy, GMS, 002.

20. Keith McNeil, *The Phineas Quimby–Mary Baker Eddy Debate*, 2016, at https://ppquimby-mbeddydebate.com/. Eleven manuscripts of this work exist, making it difficult to track and

study. Early biographers often confused it with a Quimby piece that shared one of its three names, a contention recent authors sometimes repeat. When the documents are laid next to one another, properly dated and attributed, it is clear they share no actual wording or material. See SF Eddy, Writings: Science of Man, and SF Wentworth, Sally. Also see Gottschalk, *Rolling Away*, 82; Milmine, *The Life*, 166; Peel, *Years of Discovery*, 230–34; R. Thomas, "With Bleeding Footsteps," 133, 149; and Seale, *Phineas Parkhurst Quimby*.

21. See Bancroft, *Mrs. Eddy as I Knew Her*.

22. Mss.L391, Margaret Urann Collection, Family Papers, 1828–1966, BA. The sum of $109 in 1872 is equivalent to $1,698 in 2020; $40.50 in 1872 is equivalent to $846 in 2020.

23. Peel, *Years of Discovery*, 252.

24. Samuel Stewart, pastor of Second Congregational Church (Unitarian), Lynn, recalled Eddy telling him his sermons had assisted her in writing *Science and Health* (hereafter *S&H*). Reminiscences of Samuel Stewart, 2 May 1914 and 25 November 1915, RF. O'Brien, *Life of Mary Baker Eddy*, 188, also writes that Eddy and Kennedy rented a pew at a (Congregational) Unitarian church.

25. See Eddy, *Science of Man*, 8, A10066, MBEC. Also see her "Science and Philosophy," *CSJ* 4, no. 9 (1886): 209.

26. See Tyndall, *Prayer-Gauge Debate*. For discussions of Tyndall, see Mullin, *Miracles*; Ostrander, *Life of Prayer*; and Frank M. Turner, "Rainfall, Plagues, and the Prince of Wales: A Chapter in the Conflict of Religion and Science," *Journal of British Studies* 13, no. 2 (1974): 46–65.

27. Ostrander, *Life of Prayer*, 19.

28. Holy Bible, B00031, MBEC.

29. Holy Bible, B00032. Eddy would later paste into this Bible her 1877 marriage certificate to Asa Gilbert Eddy, signed by 1872 student Miranda Rice as a witness.

Chapter Seven

1. Eddy, marks in Barnes, *Scenes and Incidents*, 32, 35, 37, B00146, MBEC.

2. Gottschalk, *Rolling Away*, 73; W. W. Wright, "Moral Science alias Mesmerism," *LT* 5, no. 4 (27 January 1872).

3. Gottschalk, *Rolling Away*, 73.

4. Mrs. Mary M. B. Glover (Eddy), "To the Public. Moral Science and Mesmerism," *LT* 5, no. 5 (3 February 1872).

5. Peel, *Years of Trial*, 48. Also Gill, *Mary Baker Eddy*, 188–93 and 201–8; Gottschalk, *Rolling Away*, 90, 267n381; and R. Thomas, "With Bleeding Footsteps," 141–48 and 159–62.

6. Charles Fox Parham, for example, "repented" of studying to become a doctor in order to accept God's healing grace alone. See Jonathan R. Baer, "Redeemed Bodies: The Functions of Divine Healing in Incipient Pentecostalism," *Church History* 70, no. 4 (December 2001): 756.

7. Curtis, *Faith*, 114; also see 12.

8. Baer, "Redeemed Bodies," 756.

9. Baer, 756.

10. As Peel puts it, "Increasingly she was to see all evil as hypnotic in nature, a temptation to accept as actual and inevitable what was . . . perceptual and contingent" (*Years of Trial*, 35).

11. Taves, *Fits*, 213. In the 1890s a medical researcher in the tradition of Scots surgeon James Braid would examine hypnotism and suggestion for their potentially therapeutic uses, citing as an "example of the malicious aspect of suggestion" the same case Eddy would add to her book in 1886, in which Oxford experimenters produced the death of a blindfolded felon by trickling warm water over his wrist and convincing him it was his own blood. The

researcher concluded that such cruel uses of suggestion were amply balanced by its "influence for good," a point with which Eddy forcefully disagreed. D. Crosby, *Some Remarks*, 11–12, 612.8217.C949, NHHS. Braid's research became foundational to psychological theories of hypnosis and suggestion.

12. Quimby saw Deity as "potentially *within* the human mentality" more than a "force or power exterior to it," writes Gottschalk in *Rolling Away*, 71.

13. Notes in Eddy's 1872 teaching manuscript signal a permanent change to this policy. At least three versions and twenty copies exist of *Science of Man*. Prior to 1872, Eddy's manuscript had permitted students to "rub [the] heads" of patients (A11351), as a copy in Sally Wentworth's handwriting put it. A new version of the manuscript in 1872 replaced these instructions with the sentence, "Rubbing the head has no virtue" (A10064, A10065, A10860). That same year, Daniel Spofford wrote in his copy, he crossed out head-rubbing passages "by instruction of M. B. G." [Mary Baker Glover Eddy] (A11316). George Barry's copy dates this change to March 1872 (A11352). All in MBEC.

14. Taves, *Fits*, 212, 218–19.

15. Gottschalk, *Rolling Away*, 73–74.

16. Homestead, *American Women Authors*, notes that the husbands of nineteenth-century American women owned the copyrights to the published works of their wives. No documentation suggests this motivated Eddy's divorce, but owning her own book was one result. For Homestead's brief mention of Eddy, see 118.

17. She retained this basic description in 1883 and 1886 and in her volume *Retrospection and Introspection* after 1891.

18. According to Margaret Bendroth, personal communication, April 2017, Congregational churches held a wave of centennial and semi-centennial celebrations as they sought to solidify their presence, history, and identity.

19. Holy Bible, B00001, MBEC. Eddy added the scriptural passage from Psalms, sans punctuation, "I hate vain thoughts but thy law do I love" (Ps. 119:113).

Chapter Eight

1. *TC* 17, no. 4 (1875): 28 (the source of the quotes in the next few paragraphs too).

2. Eddy, "A Correction," *The First Church of Christ, Scientist, and Miscellany* (hereafter *Miscellany*), 217–18.

3. In other words, her aim was practical religion instead of religious pragmatism. Leslie Crecelius makes a similar point in an unpublished paper cited in Robert Peel, "Christian Science and Value Clarification," *Voices: Journal of the American Academy of Psychotherapists* 13, no. 3 (Fall 1977): 62–65. Eddy further linked comprehension of her religion to experience in *Rudimental*, 6: "The proof of what you apprehend in the simplest definite and absolute form of healing, can alone answer this question of how much you understand of Christian Science Mind-healing."

4. Eddy, *S&H* 1875, B00427. She also recorded her intention to use this subtitle in Eddy to Daniel H. Spofford, 14 April 1877, L07816. Both in MBEC. For the "keys of the kingdom," see Matt. 16:19.

5. Hatch, *Democratization*; Hughes, *Reviving*, 26. Also see Hughes, *American Quest*.

6. Hughes, *Reviving*, 30.

7. See Eddy, "Message for 1901," in *Prose Works*, 6. She called her idea different from traditional "theology, which reckons three as one and the infinite in a finite form," whereas Christian Science "reckons one as one and this one *infinite*" (emphasis hers).

8. Hall, *Worlds of Wonder*, 7, notes that Christians preached universal salvation, free will,

prophecy over priesthood, and other radical ideas in modern Europe and perhaps gained their "widest hearing in the period of the English Civil War."

9. See Reminiscence of Anna B. White Baker, 54, RF.

10. Eddy, marks in Phipps, *True Christian Baptism*, B00204, MBEC. The title page reads, "Sold at Friend's Book Store, No. 304 Arch St."

11. See Eddy, notations in Stevens, *Messages of Paul*, B00299, MBEC. Eddy marked a few pages, including page 98, about "gifts of God which surpass the power of the *senses* and the capacity of the mind to imagine and know. This philosophy speaks of a revelation to the heart of man, by the divine Spirit, of things which wholly surpass human knowledge" (her underline).

12. Ernst van den Hemel, "Things That Matter: The *Extra Calvinisticum*, the Eucharist, and John Calvin's Unstable Materiality," in Houtman and Meyer, *Things*, 63.

13. D. Morgan, *Protestants and Pictures*, 298. Also see Eggleston, *Christ in Art*.

14. See Mary A. Batchelder, portrait of Jesus, oil on canvas, 0.1043, AAC. Batchelder was an artist and Christian Scientist from Boston. Also see Eddy, "Card," *CSJ* 3, no. 2 (1885): 40; and John Sartain, *Our Saviour from the Only Authentic Likeness of Our Saviour Cut on an Emerald by Command of Tiberius Caesar*, Library of Congress Prints and Photographs Division, LC-DIG-pga-08227, pga 08227, http://hdl.loc.gov/loc.pnp/pga.08227.

15. Eddy, *Retrospection*, 22.

16. See Eddy, *Miscellany*, 318. The clergyman, John Henry Wiggin, was also her editor through most of the 1880s.

17. Mullin, *Miracles*, 2.

18. Rev. Jesse H. Jones, "Miracles," *TC* 55, no. 10 (1870): 74 (the source of the quotes in the next paragraph too).

19. Roberts, *Darwinism and the Divine*, 64.

20. See Hamlin, *From Eve to Evolution*.

21. See Paretsky, *Words, Works, and Ways of Knowing*.

22. Roberts, *Darwinism and the Divine*, 64.

23. Dan Cohen, "Searching for the Victorians," DanCohen.org, 4 October 2010, https://dancohen.org/2010/10/04/searching-for-the-victorians/.

24. Kern, *Mrs. Stanton's Bible*, 69.

25. Adams, *Elements of Christian Science*, HPCW; "Three Graces of Christian Science," *Little's Living Age* 42 (1854): 25–28, HPCW, Series 4; "Three Graces of Christian Science," *Household Words: A Weekly Journal Conducted by Charles Dickens* 9, no. 14 (1855): 317–20, HPCW, Series 4; "An Oration Delivered on the Public Square at New Haven, at the Request of the Citizens," *Church Review* 4, no. 3 (1851): 384–98, HPCW.

26. Nicolaas Grönum, "Abraham Kuyper's Christian Science and Empirical Science—Different Yet Similar: An Investigation into Epistemological Structures," *In die skriflig: Tydskrif van die Gereformeerde Teologiese Vereniging* 48, no. 1 (2014): e1; Eaton, *Permanence of Christianity*, 221.

27. "St. John's School," *Edgefield Advertiser*, 15 March 1854, 3; "Glenn Springs Female Institute," *Abbeville (S.C.) Press and Banner*, 12 January 1854, 3; "The Young Ladies' Institute," *Wheeling (W.Va.) Daily Intelligencer*, 7 March 1870, 2.

28. Wayland, *Elements of Moral Science*, 110. Wayland was a Baptist minister and president of Brown University whose book ran in six editions over four decades. Typical descendants of this early text include Bain, *Mental and Moral Science*, and D. Putnam, *Elementary Psychology*.

29. Payne, *Elements of Mental and Moral Science*, 14, 82. Other examples in this genre include Alexander, *Outlines of Moral Science*; Dagg, *Elements of Moral Science*; and Stinson, *Ethica*.

30. *Evening Telegraph* (Philadelphia), 14 (1871): 8, Chronicling America: Historic American Newspapers, Library of Congress.

31. See "Cather's Character and Cather's Cuisine," *Brooklyn Daily Eagle*, 14 February 1871, 2; and "A Divine Dejeuner," *New York Herald*, 15 December 1870, 2.

32. In 1831, Bowdoin professor Thomas Cogswell Upham published his *Elements of Mental Philosophy*, generally considered the first American textbook in psychology, although psychology did not emerge as a distinct discipline until later in the century.

33. Eddy's first statement about her "moral science" in the *LT* is Mary M. B. Glover, "Letter to the Editor," 20 January 1872; the second is "To the Public," 3 February 1872.

34. "Miracles?," *Boston Sunday Globe*, 26 March 1882, 1.

35. See, e.g., "Science of Health and Happiness," *Water-Cure Journal and Herald of Reforms* 10, no. 2 (1850): 73, HPCW; Quimby also used this phrase one time.

36. H. Hunter, *Sacred Biography*, 60.

37. Rom. 11:33.

38. Ps. 19:12.

39. See "A Discourse," *Times-Picayune*, 25 September 1853, 1; "New Year's Eve of an Unhappy Man," *The Advocate*, 24 January 1861, 1. The 1850s saw similar groupings in multiple states as well as in Waterford, Ireland.

40. "Little Robie's Memorial," *TC* 24, no. 7 (1872): 49.

41. A New Hampshire Baptist wrote an 1850 poem in a letter to her minister using the term "all in all" for God, Susan M. Perkins to Rev. Bartholomew Van Dame, 14 January 1850, Papers of Bartholomew Van Dame, NHHS. An 1866 medical address urged physicians, like everyone committed to all deemed right and good, to be "seekers for truth," not an uncommon phrase; Buck, *Annual Address*, 5.

42. Scott E. Casper, "Introduction," in Casper et al., *Industrial Book*, 4–5.

43. See Loughran, *Republic in Print*.

44. See Loughran, 1.

45. Peel, *Christian Science*, covers Alcott and Eddy in detail.

46. Shepard, *Journals of Bronson Alcott*, 464.

47. Peel, *Years of Discovery*, 223, and *Christian Science*, 53. Eddy sent Whittier a copy of her "Questions and Answers" manuscript in 1872 and wrote a friend that he had praised parts of it. See Eddy to Sarah Bagley, 31 January 1872, L08301, MBEC. Eddy also later recalled that Whittier recovered from an illness following her visit. LYM owns the copy of *S&H* Eddy inscribed to Whittier. Thanks to Research and Collections assistant Kelly Byquist, LYM.

48. "'Science and Health.' The Wonder of the Age!," Bro.1.416 [1875/6], SC, BA. Also see K., "Wonderful Discovery Concerning Man," Bro.3.51 [1875/6], SC, BA; Isa. 30:8.

Chapter Nine

1. "Printer's Mistakes," *Drum Beat* 7 (29 February 1864): 3, HPCW.

2. "Mistakes—Reporters or Printers?," *Printers' Circular* 10, no. 12 (1876): 319, HPCW.

3. Anonymous, "The Song of the Printer," in MacKellar, *Manual of Typography*, xii. By 1895 this well-known poem had been eulogized in A. K. H., "A Printer's Lament," HPCW.

4. "Mistakes of Printers," *New Hampshire Journal of Education* 1, no. 6 (1857): 188, HPCW.

5. Archival objects relating to Eddy's first edition are the plates from which a chapter was printed, a printing bill, and book copies, which are rare and poor quality like paper stock generally in the nineteenth century. W. F. Brown presumably tossed the original manuscript after setting type. Authors made subsequent edits and revisions in the published book, which

printers then used as "manuscripts" to alter type for the next imprint. Authors who wanted to delete a line or who were compelled to replace a line of misprinted text had to replace it with a line or word of exactly the same number of characters or less. Gouges, grooves, and scrapes on the 1875 printing plates indicate this. This spared the time and expense of entirely resetting the plates. For a technical description of this process, see Romano, *Machine Writing and Typesetting*.

6. The 1875 edition errata list includes sixty-seven misprints in 456 pages, but based on additional corrections Eddy made in her copy, that number can be more than doubled.

7. The 1878 edition errata list shows thirty-one misprints in 171 surviving pages, but as I note, the list itself contained errors.

8. Eddy, *S&H* 1878:165, B00432, MBEC.

9. Rand, Avery printed the book title as "Metaphysics versus Physiology."

10. See F. Crosby, *Into Light*; and Boardman, *Catalogue*.

11. Eddy to Elizabeth Newhall, 6 July 1877, L02551, MBEC.

12. Eddy to Daniel Spofford, 22 October 1876, L07810, MBEC. Her second edition was labeled "Volume II." Either volume 1 was lost, or the 1878 edition was meant to be read in combination with the 1875 edition as a de facto first volume.

13. Eddy to A. Bronson Alcott, 14 January 1876, L05660, MBEC.

14. Eddy, "Science and Health," *New York Weekly Sun*, 20 January 1876. This letter was probably also printed in the *Boston Daily Journal* on 20 January 1876.

15. "Incapacity of Language for the Expression of Feeling," *Christian Palladium* 6, no. 18 (1838): 279–80, HPCW. The *Palladium* began in western New York as an outgrowth of Charles G. Finney's 1830–31 *Great Revival* and was, like *Herald of Gospel Liberty*, a leading revivalist periodical.

16. "Language Inadequate," *American Scrapbook and Magazine of United States Literature* 2, no. 31 (1862): 76, HPCW.

17. H. A. L., "Words Are Inadequate," *Printers' Circular* 6, no. 6 (1871): 249, HPCW.

18. D. P. H., "Essays on Language and Its Expression, No. 1," *Browne's Phonographic Monthly* 1, no. 2 (1875): 20–21, HPCW. For a description of phonography in its social context, see Guarneri, *Utopian Alternative*, 286.

19. See, e.g., "Tower of Babel," *Youth's Companion* 17, no. 20 (1843): 79, HPCW.

20. "Thesaurus of English Words and Phrases," *Godey's Lady's Book* 84, no. 502 (1872): 385, HPCW.

21. H. Smith, *Horace Bushnell*, 35. Today this elicits secular postmodern theories, in which the temporal sign represents the fixed signified, though the extent and significance of such a parallel is another matter. Gill, feminist Eddy biographer and translator of the French feminist and postmodernist Luce Irigaray, likens Eddy's style, though not her theology, to Irigaray in *Mary Baker Eddy*, 219.

22. Bronson A. Alcott to Eddy, 17 January 1876, SF Alcott, A. Bronson.

23. Quoted in Peel, *Years of Trial*, 9–10 and 317n21 (an "undated letter, apparently spring of 1876").

24. H. S. C., "Science and Health by Mary Baker Glover," c. 1875, 10, 2, 7, 8, 2, 10, SF Eddy, Writings: *S&H*, Public Reception. This is the source of H. S. C.'s quotes in the next paragraph and later in the chapter too. Peel (*Years of Trial*, 8–9 and 317n16) attributes the H. S. C. manuscript to Silver and vice versa. Additionally, the author he renders "A. S. C." is now thought to be "H. S. C."

25. Rev. Mr. Silver [attributed], "Science and Health," c. 1875, 7–9, SF Eddy, Writings: *S&H*, Public Reception. This is the source of the quotes in the next paragraph too. Eddy's views on marriage resonated with those of Ellen Harmon White to some extent.

26. An 1889 minor edition further identifies Letts as a U.S. minister posted to Haiti. It is not clear whether this was a religious or political role.

27. Eddy, "Science and Health."

28. Quoted in Peel, *Years of Trial*, 9–10.

29. Eddy, "Science and Health."

30. Silver, "Science and Health."

31. Eddy, "Science and Health."

32. CSA, meeting minutes, vol. 2, no. 2 (June 1886), EOR11, ORT; Eddy to Edward H. Hammond, 22 March 1886, L04552, MBEC.

33. Peel, *Years of Trial*, 9.

34. See Twain, *Christian Science*.

35. Peel, *Years of Trial*, 8.

36. H. S. C., "Science and Health by Mary Baker Glover."

37. See David Weddle, "The Christian Science Textbook: An Analysis of the Religious Authority of Science and Health by Mary Baker Eddy," *Harvard Theological Review* 84, no. 3 (1991): 274; see also 281.

38. See Rowe, *God's Strange Work*.

39. See "Millerism and Insanity," *CJ* 3, no. 6, whole no. 110 (1844): 2.

40. Eddy, notation in B00017.B, c. 1900, MBEC. See Luke 17:20.

41. See Cohen, *Calculating People*.

42. For more on the Kelloggs and Adventism, see B. Wilson, *Dr. John Harvey Kellogg*.

43. See Bodwell, *Sermon*, 11–12. "According to the best calculations, which can be made from Scripture, the Millennium will commence about the year 1866," preached Bodwell. "In a little more than fifty years, we expect that the reign of universal righteousness and peace will commence." The Baker family heard Bodwell preach occasionally at the Sanbornton Square church. See Smaus, *Mary Baker Eddy*, 77, 87; Peel, *Years of Discovery*, 64.

44. See Moorhead, *American Apocalypse*. For popular apocalyptic themes in ensuing years, see Moorhead, *World without End*.

45. John F. Wilson, "History, Redemption, and the Millennium," in Hatch and Stout, *Jonathan Edwards*, 132.

46. J. Wilson, 132. Wilson differs from Goen by finding greater precedent for Puritan millennialism prior to Edwards in elements of the Westminster Confession, Savoy Declaration, Cambridge Platform, and Saybrook Platform.

47. Marsden, *Jonathan Edwards*, 89. Marsden adds that Edwards shared a general Protestant anti-papalism that saw "the Church of Rome as the Antichrist" and that he "followed those who said that A.D. 606 marked the Pope's ascendancy," meaning "the decisive blow against papal power was likely to occur around 1866."

48. J. Wilson, "History, Redemption, and the Millennium," 135.

49. J. Wilson, 138.

50. Lord, *Millennium*, 7, 13 (the source for the quotes in the next few paragraphs too).

51. Eddy, untitled, n.d., A10624, MBEC. A passage with similarities in *Christian Science: No and Yes* (hereafter *No and Yes*), 8, suggests dating the manuscript c. 1890 or 1891. It resonates with earlier passages, however, such as *S&H* 1875:3.

52. Eddy, notation in *S&H*, c. 1876:282, B00428A, MBEC. The printing bill for Eddy's first edition is dated 30 October 1875, but the *CSS* noted almost sixty years later that its "heaviest sales" occurred in fall 1876 ("Item of Interest," *CSS* 36, no. 6 [1933]: 111). Spofford contracted to handle its sales and marketing in April 1876, and that fall Eddy wrote him that her book was about to encounter the world. Thus in her calculation, she used that year rather than the date of publication.

53. Eddy, notations in Messenger, *Time of the End*, B00236, 119, 171, 179, MBEC. Based on context and handwriting, it is possible but not probable that she marked this book closer to 1856 than 1875.

54. Eddy, "Questions and Answers," *Miscellany*, 239.

55. Eddy, "Message to the Mother Church for 1900," *Miscellany*, 6.

56. Maria Louise Baum to Eddy, 17 August 1906, L10466, MBEC.

57. Eddy, "Prophecy," n.d., A10269, MBEC. This document also noted that after 1875, the year of her book's publication, "the next jubilee was to be celebrated at Christ's coming."

58. See Eddy to George H. Prescott, 15 August 1877, L11167, MBEC. Eddy told Prescott the present period was "the six thousandth one" connected with the "sixth seal" in John's revelation. See also *S&H* 1886:511, 1881:14; and Eddy, *Retrospection*, 70.

59. Stein, *Shaker Experience*, 71.

60. *Shaker Manifesto* 9, no. 1 (1879): 16, 17.

61. Stein, *Shaker Experience*, 71, 72.

62. Eddy, *Retrospection*, 70.

63. The work of carrying and delivering a divine message, as opposed to being or personifying that message, has interesting parallels with social activists of the era who were driven by religious motives. Patricia A. Schechter astutely reads the title "Mother" given to Ida B. Wells-Barnett in Christian terms. Through the Virgin Mary's body came salvation in Jesus; through Wells-Barnett's body came racial justice in Jesus's name; thus her activity was described as "mothering" the anti-lynching cause. See Schechter, *Ida B. Wells-Barnett*.

64. For book inscriptions, see Finding Aid, Mary Baker Eddy Book Collection, MBEC.

65. See Holland, *Particular Universe*.

Findings: Part II

1. Quoted in Gottschalk, *Rolling Away*, 73.

Chapter Ten

1. Material in this chapter modifies and expands on my article "Mary Baker Eddy, the 'Woman Question,' and Christian Salvation: Finding a Consistent Connection by Broadening the Boundaries of Feminist Scholarship," *JFSR* 28, no. 2 (2012): 5–25. My thanks to *JFSR* for permission to reprint portions of this article here.

2. Eddy, notations in *S&H* 1881, B00433, vol. 2, MBEC. Quotation marks have been standardized from the original.

3. Susan Lindley labeled Eddy's multivalent views "ambiguous" in "The Ambiguous Feminism of Mary Baker Eddy," *Journal of Religion* 64, no. 3 (1984): 318. For a full review of feminist scholarship in relation to Mary Baker Eddy, see Amy B. Voorhees, "Mary Baker Eddy, the 'Woman Question,' and Christian Salvation." Key studies are Susan M. Setta, "Denial of the Female—Affirmation of the Feminine: The Father-Mother God of Mary Baker Eddy," in Gross, *Beyond Androcentrism*, 289–304; Margery Fox, "Protest in Piety: Christian Science Revisited," *International Journal of Women's Studies* 1 (1978): 401–16; Mary Farrell Bednarowski, "Outside the Mainstream: Women's Religion and Women Religious Leaders in Nineteenth-Century America," *Journal of the American Academy of Religion* 48 (1980), 207–31; Hansen, "Woman's Hour"; Jean MacDonald, "Mary Baker Eddy and the Nineteenth Century 'Public' Woman: A Feminist Reappraisal," *JFSR* 2, no. 1 (1986): 89–111; Ann Braude, "The Perils of Passivity: Women's Leadership in Spiritualism and Christian Science," in Wessinger, *Women's*

Leadership, 55–67; Gill, *Mary Baker Eddy*; Bednarowski, *Religious Imagination*; Rosemary Hicks, "Religion and Remedies Reunited: Rethinking Christian Science," *JFSR* 20, no. 2 (2004): 25–58; and Gottschalk, "Woman Goes Forth" in *Rolling Away*, 168–93.

4. Alger, *Friendships of Women*, 9.

5. Eddy, "Womans Bible," n.d. (c. 1895), A10873, MBEC.

6. See William V. Alexander to Alfred Farlow, 24 June 1910, L16129, SC, MBEL.

7. Eddy to the Christian Science Board of Directors, 15 November 1904, L00864, MBEC.

8. Eddy, *Manual*, 45. Robert Peel writes that this bylaw was designed to stem "activities which would drain the movement's energies away from . . . Christian healing and regeneration" (*Years of Authority*, 226). Jeanne Halgren Kilde notes that in 1908 Eddy closed the "Mother's Room" in the original edifice of the Mother Church, a room readied for her sole use, because the gendered controversies it provoked took attention away from more important religious concerns ("Material Expression and Maternalism in Mary Baker Eddy's Boston Churches: How Architecture and Gender Compromised Mind," *Material Religion* 1, no. 2 [2005]: 164–97).

9. See Daisette D. S. McKenzie, "The Writings of Mary Baker Eddy," in *We Knew Mary Baker Eddy*, 123.

10. Harriet H. Robinson to Eddy, 14 January 1887, L17368, MBEC. The sum of $5 in 1887 is equivalent to about $135 in 2020.

11. "The truth is," Anthony wrote to Stanton in 1897 after a visit from the theosophist Annie Besant, "I can no more see through Theosophy than I can through Christian Science, Spiritualism, Calvinism or any other of the theories, so I shall have to go on knocking away to remove the obstructions in the road of us mortals while in these bodies and on this planet." Harper, *Life and Work of Susan B. Anthony*, 918.

12. See *CSS* 2, no. 15 (1899): 245.

13. Susan B. Anthony to Eddy, 19 June 1903, in Holland and Gordon, *Papers of Elizabeth Cady Stanton and Susan B. Anthony*, series 43.

14. Hicks, "Religion and Remedies Reunited," 55.

15. This is not listed on the errata sheet for the first edition, but such sheets were always incomplete. It is possible, for example, that the word "not" was inserted by mistake or as a misprint of "now." Regardless, the main point stands regarding the consistency of Eddy's views in this case.

16. Eddy, *Miscellaneous Writings*, 388.

17. See Hamlin, *From Eve to Evolution*; and Taylor and Weir, *Let Her Speak*. I thank Anne Braude for the second recommendation and for the observation that Eddy is usually left out of such studies. Also see Joy A. Schroeder, "African American Women Interpreting the Bible in the Nineteenth Century," The Bible and Interpretation, August 2014, http://www.bibleinterp.com/articles/2014/08/sch388026.shtml#sdfootnote3anc.

18. Eddy to Clara Louise Burnham, 4 February 1907, L08342, MBEC; Eddy, "Men in Our Ranks," *Miscellany*, 355.

19. Eddy, "Man and Woman," 26 August 1915, A10142B, MBEC. This piece was copyrighted on 19 December 1900 but never published. It probably entered the church archives in 1915 when Eddy's former longtime secretary Calvin A. Frye deposited a copy.

20. Eddy to Edward A. Kimball, 19 November 1892, L07411, MBEC.

21. Note by Eddy, written on Edward A. Kimball to Eddy, 14 November 1892, L16694, MBEC.

22. Another reason for this ardent approach was more personal, notably Eddy's lack of legal rights to retrieve her son when family members placed him in a neighbor's home during her

widowhood and illness. Gill, *Mary Baker Eddy*, 87–92; Peel, *Years of Discovery*, 96–99. See also Eddy, *Retrospection*, 20.

23. Eddy, *No and Yes*, 45. A similar passage is in her "Veritas Odium Parit," *Miscellaneous Writings*, 245.

24. This phrase first appeared in 1891, "reformatory efforts" in 1875, and "reformatory purpose" in 1886.

25. This passage remains in all subsequent editions. See also Eddy, "Pond and Purpose," *Miscellaneous Writings*, 206.26. Quoted in Peel, *Years of Authority*, 89 (emphasis in original). Eddy cited the same scripture passage and underscored a similar message in an 1895 letter to the Readers of The Mother Church, writing, "'His voice was not heard in the streets.' It is not Christlike to act in any worldly way to promote anything. 'His ways are not as ours.'" Peel, *Years of Authority*, 123; see also 417n132.

27. See Eddy to John F. Linscott, 11 August 1887, L11037, and 23 October 1893, V01257, MBEC. Eddy's views about Willard mark another difference from Stanton, who deplored the merging of Christian temperance and suffrage interests.

28. Eddy, "Injustice," *Miscellaneous Writings*, 236.

29. Eddy, "Reformers," *Miscellaneous Writings*, 237.

30. Eddy, "Message to the Mother Church for 1901," *Prose Works*, 23; *Miscellany*, 288.

31. Eddy, untitled, n.d., A10624, MBEC. A passage with similarities in *No and Yes*, 8, suggests dating the manuscript c. 1890 or 1891.

32. Bouwsma, *John Calvin*, 11. For more on the link between Christian Science and Calvinism, see Johnsen, "Christian Science and the Puritan Tradition"; Taves, *Fits*; Gottschalk, *Rolling Away*; and Albanese, *Republic*.

33. The basic message remains in *S&H* 1911:34.

34. Eddy to Septimus J. Hanna, n.d., L09535, MBEC. See also Eddy to Frank L. Phalen, 13 May 1898, L13288, MBEC. For the Baker family's earlier (and less approving) view of Parker, whose meeting Mary's brother Samuel once attended, to their dismay, see Daniel Patterson to Eddy, 17 February 1857, L16251, MBEC.

35. Eddy, *Manual*, 17.

36. Eddy, "Christian Science in Tremont Temple," *Miscellaneous Writings*, 96.

37. Donaldson, *Westminster Confession of Faith*, 6.

38. Stanton, *The Woman's Bible*, 1:25; Pellauer, *Toward a Tradition*, 125. For another feminist theologian who argues that the doctrine of sin is more oppressive to women, see Serene Jones, *Feminist Theory and Christian Theology*. On women's rights advocates who embraced Darwinism as an antidote to the Eve story, see Hamlin, *From Eve to Evolution*.

39. On Christ as an "office" of the Godhead, see Eddy, "Message to the Mother Church for 1900," *Prose Works*, 5; "Message to the Mother Church for 1901," *Prose Works*, 4; and *S&H* 1911:331. On Eve's moral strength, see *S&H* 1911:533.

40. Gestefeld in Stanton, *The Woman's Bible*, 1:143; Stanton, "The Solitude of Self" (speech presented at the Annual Convention of the National Women's Suffrage Association, January 18, 1892), quoted in Dubois, *Elizabeth Cady Stanton and Susan B. Anthony*, 248. Gestefeld's theology is discussed in Griffith, *Born Again Bodies*, 83–86, and Satter, *Each Mind*, 126–34. Later tensions in Gestefeld's thought, writes Satter, "all help explain why some women were drawn to the contradictory and nonconfrontational doctrines of New Thought" (134). Similarly, Emma Hopkins's "ambiguities . . . may have been the key to her importance" (81).

41. Gestefeld in Stanton, *The Woman's Bible*, 1:143; Eddy to Ursula N. Gestefeld, 2 July 1884, L14278, MBEC.

42. Amanda Porterfield, "Mary Baker Eddy," in Toulouse and Duke, *Makers of Christian Theology*, 306.

43. Bednarowski, *Religious Imagination*, 158.

44. Ellen DuBois, "Taking the Law into Our Own Hands: *Bradwell, Minor*, and Suffrage Militance in the 1870s," in Hewitt and Lebsock, *Visible Women*, 21.

45. DuBois, "Taking the Law," 23. See also Allison Sneider, "Woman Suffrage in Congress: American Expansion and the Politics of Federalism, 1870–1890," in Baker, *Votes for Women*, 77–89.

46. DuBois, "Taking the Law," 34.

47. See "Woman's Suffrage: George Frances Train, Elizabeth Cady Stanton, and Susan B. Anthony at Steinway Hall," *New York Times*, 15 December 1867. Several articles in Baker's *Votes for Women* address the problem of racism within many women's rights efforts. Also see Terborg-Penn, *African American Women*; Kern, *Mrs. Stanton's Bible*; and Ginzberg, *Elizabeth Cady Stanton*.

48. Eddy, "Wedlock," *Miscellaneous Writings*, 285.

49. Eddy, notation in *S&H* 1892:122, B00452, MBEC.

50. George H. Bradford to Eddy, 30 January 1885, L17345, MBEC.

51. Eddy, notations in *S&H* 1881, B00433, vol. 2, MBEC.

52. Peel, *Years of Trial*, 87.

53. One reference to God as "Himself or Herself" remains in Eddy's "Science and Philosophy," *Miscellaneous Writings*, 367. For the original context, see *CSJ* 4, no. 12 (1887): 288.

54. Peel, *Years of Trial*, 92.

55. Norton, *Woman's Cause*, 48, 51.

56. Norton, *Woman's Cause*, 55.

57. Norton to Eddy, 26 September 1895, L16535, MBEC; *Current Literature* 18 (July–December 1895): 474. Norton was interested in reform work from the age of fourteen, noted the reviewer, and at sixteen gave his "maiden speech . . . before the Y. M. C. A. in the interest of the White Cross work, when he took the ground that the law of purity is equally binding upon man and woman."

58. Eddy to Augusta E. Stetson and Norton, 5 December 1895, V01412, MBEC. Also see Eddy to Stetson and Norton, 16 February 1896, V01424, MBEC. In sum, Eddy pointed out the problem of "love of doing good that mistakes its aim." This might be seen as her main critique of temporal social reform work in general.

Chapter Eleven

1. "Miracles?," *Boston Sunday Globe*, 26 March 1882, 1 (the source of the quotes in the next few paragraphs).

2. A. O. [Julius Dresser], "The Founder of the Mental Method of Treating Disease," *Boston Post*, 8 February 1883.

3. For biographical treatments of Eddy, Quimby, and Dresser's initial plagiarism concern, see Gill, *Mary Baker Eddy*, 136–46; Gottschalk, *Rolling Away*, 68–77; Peel, *Health and Medicine*, 7–9; R. Thomas, "With Bleeding Footsteps," 82–113; and Keith McNeil, *The Phineas Quimby–Mary Baker Eddy Debate*, 2016, at https://ppquimby-mbeddydebate.com/.

4. Messenger, *Time of the End*. The year 1864 was also the time Eddy identified a desire to write out the "model" of her own career, if only she were well enough, and it may have been significant to her at some point that according to "most prophetic interpreters," that year might inaugurate the millennial period.

5. Eddy to Eldridge J. Smith, 12 May 1876, L02043, MBEC.

6. *Banner of Light*, 4 July 1868, SF Eddy, Writings: *S&H*, Publication and Sale, Circulars. Eddy was staying with the family of Captain Webster in Amesbury at the time.

7. See "'Science and Health.' The Wonder of the Age!," Bro.1.416 [1875/6], SC, BA; and K., "Wonderful Discovery Concerning Man," Bro.3.51 [1875/6], SC, BA.

8. Mary M. Patterson [Eddy], "Poetry," *Lynn Reporter* 17, no. 14 (1868): 1. Eddy later titled it "Christ My Refuge." A revised version of it remains a staple of Christian Science hymnody.

9. Peel, *Years of Trial*, 14. Also see Safronoff, *Crossing Swords*.

10. See *S&H* 1875:171 and 1881:170; 1875:13, 1878:53, and 1881:17.

11. Irving C. Tomlinson, 9 September 1907, A11887, MBEC. In this dictation to Tomlinson, Eddy noted that she told court masters in a 1907 lawsuit "that the discovery that the unmedicated pellet produced same effect as the medicated pellet was the falling apple which led to the discovery of C.S. . . . My recovery from a fall in Lynn when I opened the Bible and read there of the healing dated the discovery of C.S. The first was the enlightenment of the human understanding, the second was the revelation from this divine Mind."

12. Eddy, *Historical Sketch*; *Retrospection*, 24.

Chapter Twelve

1. "'Christian Science' and 'Mind Cure,'" *Century: A Popular Quarterly* 34, no. 3 (1887): 418.
2. "'Christian Science' and 'Mind Cure,'" 418.
3. A. Gordon, *Ministry of Healing*, 1.
4. Eddy to George B. Wickersham, 19 March 1885, L07907, MBEC.
5. Curtis, *Faith*, 100.
6. E. Gordon, *Adonirum Judson Gordon*, 134.
7. Gill, *Mary Baker Eddy*, 340.
8. On the development of Protestant prayer at the intersection of miracles and natural law at the turn of the twentieth century, see Ostrander, *Life of Prayer*. On American Christianities, miracles, and healing, see Klassen, *Spirits of Protestantism*; Mullin, *Miracles*; Curtis, *Faith*; and Opp, *Lord for the Body*.
9. Curtis, *Faith*, 88.
10. See Dayton, *Theological Roots*, 128–29.
11. Samuel S. Hill, "Religion and the Results of the Civil War," in Miller, Stout, and Wilson, *Religion and the American Civil War*, 373–74.
12. E.g., Matt. 9:24; Acts 20:9–12.
13. Curtis, *Faith*, 100–101. Descendants of divine healers in the postwar faith healing revival counseled the same approach. "No matter how you feel," preached William Branham, "it ain't what you feel; it's what you believe. Jesus never did say, 'Did you feel it?' He said, 'Did you believe it?'" (Branham, "The Deep Calleth to the Deep," 1954, William Branham archival videos). He further noted, "It's not a mind reading; it's not psychology. . . . I will grant you this. It is psychology in this way. . . . 'Psyche,' of course means 'mind.' And it's the mind of Christ that the human being has the privilege to enter in, and know the mind of Christ. . . . Hallelujah. My, what a—a reality. . . . Oh my. I get to shouting" (Branham, "The Angel of God," William Branham archival videos). Branham worked within the charismatic shouting tradition, and he felt the Holy Ghost power to be signaled and transferred by a physical presence in his right hand. However, his reasoning here shared similarities with that of Christian Scientists.
14. Klassen, *Spirits of Protestantism*, 20; Curtis, *Faith*, 120; and A. Gordon, *Ministry of Healing*, 39. Also see Mullin, *Miracles*.
15. Curtis, *Faith*, 120. Emergent Pentecostals would later find healing agency in oil anointing, not only a declaration of faith. See Wacker, *Heaven Below*; and C. Brown, *Word in the World*.

16. Eddy, *Rudimental*, 2.
17. Eddy, *Historical Sketch*, 15.
18. Eddy, *No and Yes*, 29.
19. Curtis, *Faith*, 99.
20. Satter, *Each Mind*, 64.
21. Kelsey, *Healing and Christianity*, 265.
22. Baines-Miller, *My Cousin and Mrs. Cherry's Sister*.
23. Klassen, *Spirits of Protestantism*, 60, 72.
24. CSA, meeting minutes (1885), EOR10.02, 62, ORT.
25. Eddy, "Veritas Odium Parit," *Miscellaneous Writings*, 245.
26. A. J. Gordon, "Christian Science Tested by Scripture," *Triumph of Faith* 6 (1886): 276–80; Curtis, *Faith*, 98.
27. Gordon, "Christian Science Tested by Scripture," 276.
28. Curtis, *Faith*, 77, 99–100.
29. Eddy, *Retrospection*, 54.
30. Eddy, *No and Yes*, 42.
31. As she would put it from 1891 on, "Christian Science and Christianity are one" (*S&H* 1891:371).
32. Dayton, *Theological Roots*, 128.
33. CSA, meeting minutes (2 June 1886), ORT.
34. See, for example, Dr. Alfred Baker's note, "Mother said, 'Take a cell out of the brain and put a fibre more into the heart'" (A. Baker, obstetric notes, 1900, 23, MBEC); Eddy's comment, "Jesus was his own interpreter, his heart revealed his head, and interpreted his power" (Eddy, "Stray Thoughts," n.d., A10556, MBEC); and her advice to a student to feel increasing warmth in his work, and "this will do more than homilies or the absolute letter of C.S. to open the heart of the world.... And I have learned from bitter experience that the head instructed before the heart is ready, costs me and our Cause dangerous difficulties and sore defeats" (Eddy to Edward A. Kimball, 15 October 1893, L07433, MBEC).
35. Eddy, *Historical Sketch*, 12–13.
36. E. Gordon, *Adonirum Judson Gordon*, 136.
37. "Rev. A. J. Gordon," *CSJ* 5, no. 3 (1887): 157.
38. Campbell, *Ancient Wisdom*, 29.
39. Amy B. Voorhees, "Understanding the Religious Gulf between Mary Baker Eddy, Ursula N. Gestefeld, and Their Churches," *Church History* 80, no. 4 (December 2011): 798–831.
40. Eddy to Ursula N. Gestefeld, 28 July 1886, L12898, MBEC.
41. Gestefeld joined the International Theosophical Society through a Chicago lodge on 8 May 1886 and resigned from the society on 13 September 1895 after it split into factions. I thank the Theosophical Society of Pasadena, California, for these dates.
42. Eddy to Ursula N. Gestefeld, n.d. (probably early 1887), F00420, MBEC. This letter was probably a follow-up to Eddy's 16 January 1887 letter.
43. Ursula N. Gestefeld, "Christian Science: Its Origin," *Religio-Philosophical Journal* 41–42 (1887): 8, Newberry Library, Chicago; Eddy to John F. Linscott, 16 June 1887, L11035, MBEC.
44. Eddy to Linscott, 16 June 1887.
45. Eddy to Ellen Brown [Linscott], 8 March 1887, L11008, MBEC. Gottschalk discusses the pervasive nature of such writings in *Rolling Away*, 140–41.
46. Eddy developed *No and Yes* from a March 1885 *Journal* article, also published as a pamphlet, titled "Defence of Christian Science," *CSJ* 2, no. 16 (1885), 1–3.
47. See "Mental Healing Conference," *Esoteric* 1, no. 2 (1887): 60–61; also Gottschalk, *Emergence*, 98–156. Participants advertised the conference topic as "Christian Science." It

appeared to be associated with Eddy, leading O. P. Gifford to submit an address. Once he learned its nature, however, he disassociated himself. His address was not theosophically oriented.

48. Eddy, *No and Yes*, 13.

49. See *S&H* 1891:111, 129, 139.

50. Blavatsky, "The Arya Samaj," in *Modern Parnarion*, 188 (this article was probably first published late 1870s), and "What Is a Theosophist?," in *Modern Parnarion*, 262 (the article was first published October 1879).

51. Helena P. Blavatsky, "The History of a Planet," *Lucifer* 1, no. 1 (1887): 21; J. J. van der Leeuw, "Revelation or Realization: The Conflict in Theosophy," 1930, Alpheus, http://www.alpheus.org/html/source_materials/krishnamurti/leeuw.html).

52. Gestefeld, *Statement of Christian Science*. See also L17835, MBEC.

53. Gestefeld, "Christian Science," *Lucifer* 3, no. 14 (1888): 164. *Lucifer* endorsed not only Theosophy but a free love. Gestefeld's writings objected to the second.

54. Gottschalk, *Rolling Away*, 141.

55. Albanese, *Republic*, 318.

56. McGill, *American Literature*; Ventimiglia, *Copyrighting God*, 120. For more context, see Greene, *Trouble with Ownership*; Homestead, *American Women Authors*; Macfarlane, *Original Copy*; Mazzeo, *Plagiarisms*; and Rose, *Authors and Owners*.

57. Peel, *Years of Trial*, 227–28. See also Peel, 134–35; Gill, *Mary Baker Eddy*, 314; and Eddy, "Vainglory," *CSJ* 5, no. 8 (1887): 379, and "Things to Be Thought Of," *CSJ* 5, no. 12 (1888): 595. Sometimes Eddy's most faithful students copied her words verbatim as their own; see Gill, *Mary Baker Eddy*, 340; Peel, *Years of Trial*, 201; and Gottschalk, *Emergence*, 113.

58. Gestefeld, advertisement, *CSJ* 6, no. 11 (1889): 583. The *CSJ* reprinted Gestefeld's advertising circular.

59. Abigail Hopper Gibbons to Sally Thayer, 15 February 1888, in Emerson, *Life of Abby Hopper Gibbons*, 261.

60. See Eddy notation on Mary Hinds Philbrick to Eddy, 24 May 1888, MBEC.

61. *CSJ* 6, no. 7 (1888): 345.

62. Gestefeld, *Jesuitism*, 41.

63. See Eddy to Malinda J. Lancaster, 7 November 1888, L04539, and Eddy to Ellen Brown Linscott, 9 November 1888, L11018, MBEC.

64. Eddy, "Jesuitism in Christian Science," *CSJ* 6, no. 8 (1888): 427–28. A third unpublished fragment also exists; possibly it was initially part of one of the other two drafts.

65. Eddy, 427. As she wrote more urgently in an unpublished draft, "The premise of Truth she sinks in [is] the rerobed dreams of theosophy and pagan theology," creating a "mad meadley [sic]." Eddy, untitled, n.d., A10164, MBEC.

66. Eddy, "Jesuitism in Christian Science," 428.

67. Eddy to George B. Day, 18 March 1889, L14736, MBEC.

68. See Diaz inscription in Eddy, *S&H*, 2nd ed., B00431, MBEC; A. M. Diaz to Eddy, 18 January [1885], IC662(c), MBEC.

69. A. M. Diaz to Eddy, 18 January [1885].

70. Eddy to A. M. Diaz, 20 January 1885 (archivist estimate), V00862, MBEC.

71. Abby M. Diaz, "God-Life in the Soul," *Mental Science Magazine and Mind-Cure Journal* 2, no. 4 (1886): 73, 74.

72. Diaz, 74; Eddy, "Message for 1901," *Prose Works*, 15.

73. See "The Life Work of Mrs. Abby Morton Diaz," 13 June 1903, Abby Morton Diaz Papers, Sophia Smith Collection, Special Collections, Smith College, Northampton, Mass.

74. Gottschalk, *Rolling Away*, 134–146; Peel, *Years of Authority*, 51–58.
75. Eddy to Margaret Easton, 7 February 1893, L04690, MBEC.
76. Eddy, notations and marks in Kuroda, *Light of Buddha*, B00219, MBEC.
77. Eddy, "Bible Lesson," *CSJ* 2, no. 7 (1884): 4. The text of the lesson was John 14:12.
78. Bogue, *Miscellaneous Documents*, 70, quoted in Gottschalk, *Emergence*, 119.
79. Eddy asked Hopkins and her partner, Mary Plunkett, why they continued to spread rumors, declared her Christian love for them, and invited them to reform and join forces with her again. A friend recently "spoke very encouragingly of you both," she wrote, "and it may give me great hope" (Eddy to Emma Curtis Hopkins and Mary Plunkett, 22 August 1887, V01015, MBEC). The word "may" is in superscript, inserted after completing the sentence. Hopkins had denied spreading rumors the year before in an emotive, mystical letter mixing reconciliation and reserve (see Harley, *Emma Curtis Hopkins*, 23).
80. "Biography of Rev. O. P. Gifford," in White, *Our County and Its People*, 2:459–60.
81. CSA, meeting minutes (1885), EOR10.02, 62, 59, 60, 62, ORT; O. P. Gifford, "The Point of View," *CSJ* 3, no. 12 (1886): 223. This record suggests such interactions with the clergy marked the genesis of a formative Committee on Publication within the church and an early iteration of a directorial board (a meeting participant "reported progress and suggested a Board of Directors to take charge of business").
82. Gifford, "The Point of View," 223.
83. Eddy to Edward H. Hammond, 22 March 1886, L04552, MBEC.
84. George H. Bradford to Eddy, L17345, MBEC.
85. Munger, *Freedom of Faith*, 7, 10, 11, 17.
86. Eddy, *Miscellaneous Writings*, 234, and "Christian Science," *CSJ* 1, no. 6 (February 1884): 2.
87. O. Gifford, "Point of View," 223–24. Something of Gifford's approach to religious readership is hinted in J. L. Withrow and O. P. Gifford, "How Much Do I Study the Bible, and How? Responses to This Question from Working Pastors," *Biblical World* 3, no. 4 (1894): 262. Gifford wrote, "I assume that the text I have tells what the writer did," and he therefore sought "to find just what the writer said, and what he meant when he said it." This experiential approach was well matched to *Science and Health*.
88. Stead, *If Christ Came to Chicago*. Gifford and the Reverends Lyman Abbott and Washington Gladden endorsed Stead's work. The Christian Science hymnal later included Gladden's hymns; Eddy cited Abbott in her *Christian Science vs. Pantheism*.
89. O. P. Gifford, "By the Way," *CSS* 1, no. 53 (1899): 11.
90. O. P. Gifford, "Its Form and Substance," in *Searchlights on Christian Science*, 114–26.
91. O. P. Gifford, "Exposition of Christian Science," in J. Morgan, *Theology at the Dawn of the Twentieth Century*, 365–79. Contributors on Christian Science are Gifford; the First Reader of a prominent Chicago church; Edward A. Kimball, C.S.D.; and president of Brown University, the Reverend W. H. P. Faunce, D.D., LL.D.
92. Christian Scientists in Boston held their Sunday services at Hawthorne Hall, 2 Park Street, from 1879 into 1880 and from 1883 to 1885 (excluding summer recess). Between those dates, services were held either at Eddy's home in Lynn or at her Massachusetts Metaphysical College in Boston. In 1885, the group moved to Chickering Hall, where they stayed until early 1894. When the hall underwent renovation, they moved to Copley Hall, Clarendon Street, from March to December 1894. They held their first Sunday service in the newly completed edifice of The Mother Church on December 30, 1894.
93. Peel, *Years of Trial*, 154; also see Peel, *Christian Science*, 105.
94. Peel, *Years of Trial*, 157; also see Peel, *Christian Science*, 118, 130.

95. Peel, *Years of Trial*, 158.

96. In *Each Mind*, 2, Satter notes her numbers are difficult to verify but estimates that by the end of the 1880s, adherents belonging to Eddy's church constituted about 20 percent of the total number of people referring to themselves as Christian Scientists. As Eddy's denomination expanded institutionally in the 1890s and beyond, the term became firmly associated with her church once more, but cultural confusion about its teachings persisted to a significant degree.

97. Phebe L. Haines to Eddy, 24 October 1888, MBEC.

98. Janet Colman to Joseph Armstrong, 15 April 1888, SF Armstrong, Joseph Papers: Correspondence 1888.

Findings: Part III

1. E. Gordon, *Adoniram Judson Gordon*, 135.
2. Curtis, *Faith*, 100.
3. Eddy, *Historical Sketch*, 12–13.
4. Blavatsky, "What Is a Theosophist?," in *Modern Parnarion*, 262.
5. Satter, *Each Mind*, 134; Albanese, *Republic*, 318.
6. "'Christian Science' and 'Mind Cure,'" 418.

Chapter Thirteen

1. Fiat Lux [Lanson P. Norcross], "The New Book," *CSJ* 8, no. 12 (March 1891): 509. The two biographers to consider Eddy's landmark 1891 edition are Peel, *Years of Trial*, 288, and Gottschalk, *Rolling Away*, 114.

2. The 1886 revision sold more quickly than it could be stocked. "Dear Sister," wrote Calvin Frye to a fellow church member, "Have been out of books, sent yours to-day." Calvin Frye to Mary M. W. Adams, 5 August 1886, L13564, SC, MBEL.

3. See Eddy to Joseph S. Eastaman, 15 February 1891, L03475, MBEC.

4. Eddy to Lizzie L. and John P. Filbert, 8 March 1889, L12782, MBEC.

5. Eddy to Wickersham, 19 March 1885, and Eddy to Ellen Brown Linscott, 12 September 1887, L11013, MBEC.

6. Eddy to Hannah A. Larminie, 8 April 1890, L04501, MBEC. Eddy wrote, "I believe it will be shown us that Science and Health is the best preacher with a student that loves and understands it." To Emilie B. Hulin on 1 April 1891, L08688, MBEC, she wrote that her "book is the present preacher of the gospel of Truth and Love."

7. Eddy to George B. and Elizabeth C. Wickersham, 17 July 1891, L07926, MBEC.

8. Eddy called the 1891 edition her "fourth" edition or major revision (Eddy to William G. Nixon, 1891, L04140, MBEC.). It was technically the forty-ninth printing, but the numbering skips to an even fifty for this landmark revision. Since printings and editions were conflated, the book was known as the "fiftieth edition."

9. The final edition (89th) of the *Manual* was issued on 17 December 1910. Like *S&H*, its printings were numbered as editions. Eddy revised it piecemeal and situationally.

10. Congregational Year-Books during this period (e.g., 1875) list hundreds of Sunday schools operating as "branches" of a parent church. I thank Rick Taylor, American Congregational Association board member, for noting this usage on 7 June 2013.

11. Also see "Church Debts," *TC* 27, no. 46 (1875): 364, which calls debt "sometimes, no doubt, a necessity" but as a rule not advisable for churches. For additional similarities, see Barton, *Historical Address*, 26.

12. *Manual of the Congregational Church*, cover.

13. The Sanbornton Congregational Church added a stained glass cross and crown window in 1903, which its local historian notes is rendered "in the style which is utilized in the Church of Christ, Scientist's symbol" and may have a "connection" to Eddy, for example a tribute or nod to her religious roots (Mildred Blaisdell Sanborn Shaw, "History of the Memorial Stained Glass Windows: Congregational Church, Sanbornton, New Hampshire" [by the author, 1995], 23). The Sanbornton Bridge (later Tilton) Congregational Church also added a stained glass cross and crown window in the twentieth century. Its congregational historian made a similar speculation on a tour of the church in 2013.

14. Eddy, *Manual*, 2nd ed. (1895), 20 (for the final version, see Eddy, *Manual*, 89th ed. [1913], 60); Eddy to Edward P. Bates, 13 January 1895, L08165, MBEC. When her directors extended her the invitation to become pastor a few months later, she responded they could make her pastor emeritus if that would be a "comfort," but "through my book your text book I already speak to you each Sunday." Eddy to the Christian Science Board of Directors, March 1895, L02662B. Stephen Stein notes she had already commented to a friendly clergyman that "those who look for me in person, or elsewhere than in my writings, lose me instead of find me" (Eddy, "Letter to a Clergyman," *Miscellany*, 118; Stephen J. Stein, "American Bibles: Canon, Commentary, and Community," *Church History* 64, no. 2 [June 1995]: 170).

15. Eddy to Caroline W. Frame, 21 September 1891, L12815, MBEC. The recurring "Explanatory Note" she placed in the *Quarterly* to precede each Lesson-Sermon underscores this point. It notes that "the Scriptural texts, and their correlative passages . . . corroborating and explaining the Bible texts in their spiritual import . . . constitute a sermon undivorced from truth, uncontaminated and unfettered by human hypotheses, and divinely authorized." For this quote and a discussion of its significance for Christian Science Sunday services, see Cecil E. Benjamin, "The Explanatory Note," *CSS* 20, no. 6 (1917): 105; and Archibald McLellan, "The Sunday Services," *CSS* 19, no. 28 (1917): 550.

16. Ventimiglia, *Copyrighting God*, 137.

17. See Perry, *Bible Culture and Authority*.

18. Eddy to Ruth B. Ewing, 18 March 1895, L08514, MBEC.

19. Among many scholars to note that the cause of women's rights was not central for Eddy, yet one that often had her sympathies, are Rosemary Hicks, "Religion and Remedies Reunited: Rethinking Christian Science," *JFSR* 20, no. 2 (2004): 25–58; Gill, *Mary Baker Eddy*; Jeanne Halgren Kilde, "Material Expression and Maternalism in Mary Baker Eddy's Boston Churches: How Architecture and Gender Compromised Mind," *Material Religion* 1, no. 2 (2005): 164–97; and Amy B. Voorhees, "Mary Baker Eddy, the 'Woman Question,' and Christian Salvation: Finding a Consistent Connection by Broadening the Boundaries of Feminist Scholarship," *JFSR* 28, no. 2 (2012): 5–25.

20. William R. Rathvon to Julia C. Fremont, 4 February 1910, V04308, SC, MBEL.

21. Eddy, notation in S&H 1896, B00460 (A100a), MBEC. Eddy turned to her own book increasingly for inspiration and guidance as she aged. She distinguished between what she considered its revealed contents and her own "human opinions."

22. Eddy, *Manual*, 41.

23. Thanks to A. J. Kiser for information about the *International Sunday Bible Lesson*.

24. S&H line bookmarks, 1984.37.185 and 1984.37.186, c. 1890, AAC.

25. Thanks to the late Stephen Howard, who recounted to me his interview with a senior adherent who recalled observing this bookmarking method as a young girl.

26. Calendar, 1890, 2009.001 FIC C, AAC.

27. Tearle page clips, 1984.37.343.1–.62, AAC.

28. Orcutt, *Mary Baker Eddy and Her Books*, 60–65. Also see E. P. Bates, "Wonderful India Paper!," *CSJ* 13, no. 13 (1896): 476.

29. H. H., testimonial, *CSJ* 22, no. 8 (1904): 516.
30. Eddy to Augusta E. Stetson, 1 December 1891, L04236, MBEC.
31. Eddy, *Miscellaneous Writings*, 156.
32. Eddy, *Manual*, 20. Also see Eddy, "Teachers SS Lessons," n.d. [est. 1890–1891], A10433, MBEC.
33. Eddy, "Advice to Students," *Miscellany*, 300.
34. Eddy to Carol Norton, 4 November 1891, L02347; also see Eddy to Septimus J. Hanna, 23 March 1892, L04927, MBEC. She told Hanna, "Those who talk little if any between the lines" of her book do the best at teaching it.
35. See Eddy to Septimus J. and Camilla Hanna, 30 December 1893, L04995 ("The letter *killeth*; it is the spirit, understanding, behind the words which maketh alive"), and Eddy to Alfred Farlow, 2 February 1901, L01674 ("'Few and far between' must my works be quoted," she would conclude in 1901. "A word to the wise is *sufficient*."), both MBEC.
36. I did not read or include in my totals testimonials from the *Herald of Christian Science*, published in a variety of languages other than English starting in 1903.
37. On textual Protestants, see Pamela Klassen, "Textual Healing: Mainstream Protestants and the Therapeutic Text, 1900–1925," *Church History* 75, no. 4 (2006): 809–48.
38. Regarding Christian Science treatment, see Gottschalk, *Emergence*; Peel, *Spiritual Healing* and *Health and Medicine*; and Schoepflin, *Christian Science on Trial*.
39. Eddy, *Retrospection*, 76.
40. Eddy, *Miscellaneous Writings*, 87.
41. S. J. H., testimonial, *CSJ* 8, no. 10 (1891): 457.
42. S. J. H., 457.
43. Anonymous, testimonial, *CSJ* 9, no. 1 (1891): 82.
44. Anonymous, "A Demonstration," *CSJ* 9, no. 1 (1891): 18.
45. J. S., testimonial, *CSJ* 8, no. 12 (1891): 545.
46. M. E. W., testimonial, *CSJ* 9, no. 4 (1891): 170.
47. Anonymous, "Extracts from a Private Letter," *CSJ* 9, no. 1 (1891): 37–38.
48. R. E. K., testimonial, *CSJ* 8, no. 11 (1891): 500.
49. J. S., testimonial, *CSJ* 9, no. 5 (1891): 210 (also the source for the quotes in the next paragraph). This was not the same J. S. who submitted the earlier testimony.
50. W. F. Seaver, *CSS* 13, no. 4 (1910): 73.
51. Florence Kimball, *CSS* 2, no. 33 (1900): 541.
52. Amanda James, testimonial, *CSJ* 19, no. 4 (1901): 256–57.
53. James Friedman, *CSS* 12, no. 4 (1909): 77.
54. Isador Jacobs, "Christian Science from the Jewish View-point," *CSJ* 26, no. 4 (1908): 212.
55. Umansky, *From Christian Science to Jewish Science*. Jewish Science became institutionalized in 1922. Umansky argues that it carried broad cultural influence.
56. John H. Pitchford, *CSS* 18, no. 39 (1916): 774 (also the source for the next quotes in the next paragraph).
57. Anderson Jefferson, *CSS* 11, no. 34 (1909): 677.
58. See Scott E. Casper, introduction to Casper et al., *Industrial Book*, 4–5. Casper lists several themes, including class issues and controlling and characterizing the expansion of the book trade in its industrial era.
59. Rolf Swensen, "A Metaphysical Rocket in Gotham: The Rise of Christian Science in New York City, 1885–1910," *Journal of Religion and Society* 12 (2010): 1–24, and "Pilgrims at the Golden Gate: Christian Scientists on the Pacific Coast, 1880–1915," *Pacific Historical Review* 72 (2003): 229–62.

60. Dayton O. Herald, "Christian Science Healing," *CSS* 3, no. 50 (1901): 799.

61. Church officer Joseph Armstrong wrote to Mary L. Twichell, 12 April 1904, "Dear Sister . . . The Mother Church can send missionaries but does not send practitioners to take charge of the work and organize churches." SF Armstrong, Joseph Papers: Correspondence 1904.

62. Anonymous, "Toledo Dispensary," *CSJ* 9, no. 2 (1891): 78.

63. Edward C. Butler, *CSJ* 19, no. 6 (1901): 381.

64. William Nixon wrote to Eddy, 22 October 1891, IC220, MBEC, "Not a month passes hardly that I do not receive a communication from some pastor." Most were positive.

65. Klassen, *Spirits of Protestantism*, 78.

66. Klassen, 92, 78.

67. Klassen, 76.

68. On the Emmanuel Movement, see S. Gifford, *Emmanuel Movement*; and Klassen, *Spirits of Protestantism*, 78–82.

69. Klassen, *Spirits of Protestantism*, 76.

70. Kern, *Mrs. Stanton's Bible*, 205, 268n122. The National American Woman Suffrage Association merged two branches of the suffrage movement previously split over the Fifteenth Amendment, the American Woman Suffrage Association and the National Woman Suffrage Association, under temperance leader Frances Willard.

71. Gottschalk, *Rolling Away*, 380. Also see Chang, *Empress Dowager Cixi*; and Hayter-Menzies, *Empress and Mrs. Conger*. Conger was wife to the American minister in China, Edwin H. Conger.

72. Charles A. Blake, Jonathan R. Irving, Roderick McLennan, and William W. Slocumb, 8 December 1910, EOR 24, ORT.

73. Anonymous, *CSS* 1, no. 23 (1899): 15.

74. E. W. H., "Work among the Colored People," *CSS* 1, no. 39 (1899): 14.

75. Long, *Significations*.

76. Anonymous, *CSJ* 16, no. 6 (1898): 403.

77. Ivey, *Prayers in Stone*; also Gottschalk, *Rolling Away*, 133–45. For interpretations of the 1893 World's Fair in Chicago, see Cronon, *Nature's Metropolis*; Pacyga, *Chicago*; and Seager, *World's Parliament*.

Chapter Fourteen

1. See SF Eddy, Writings: *S&H*, Distribution.

2. Letters in SF Kinter, George H.

3. Alice Weston Smith to Mrs. Frederic Dexter, 22 May 1895, *Alice Weston Smith*, 154, NAWLD.

4. C. A. Castle to Mary Warren, 9 December 1898, SF CS Practice: Public Reception of.

5. Louise Imogen Guiney to Herbert E. Clarke, 23 June 1899, *Letters of Louise Imogen Guiney*, 2, NAWLD.

6. Susan Hale to Caroline Weld, 4 February 1900, *Letters of Susan Hale*, 351, NAWLD.

7. Samuel D. Ehrhardt, "Superstition Has Always Ruled the World," *Puck* 49, no. 1258 (10 April 1901), centerfold, Library of Congress Prints and Photographs Division, LC-DIG-ppmsca-25518, ppmsca 25518 //hdl.loc.gov/loc.pnp/ppmsca.25518.

8. Louis Dalrymple, "A Suggestion to the Buffalo Exposition; - Let Us Have a Chamber of Female Horrors," *Puck* 49, no. 1256 (3 April 1901), centerfold, chromolithograph, Library of Congress Prints and Photographs Division, LC-DIG-ppmsca-25513, ppmsca 25513 //hdl.loc.gov/loc.pnp/ppmsca.25513.

9. Caroline A. Huling to Niece, c. 1906, *Letters of a Business Woman*, 35, 255, NAWLD.

10. R. Sears, *Times-Republican* (Marshalltown, Iowa), 16 October 1888; and "Defense by an Allopathic Physician," *CSJ* 6, no. 9 (1888): 481. The *CSJ* editors judged Sears's remarks "not wholly accurate" regarding Christian Science practice but "worth printing."

11. "Defense by an Allopathic Physician," 480.

12. Archibald McLellan, "Editor's Table," *CSJ* 25, no. 1 (1907): 56, 57, GFP.

13. McLellan, 58.

14. See, e.g., Hogg, *Christian Science Unmasked*.

15. Andrew Singleton, "'Your Faith Has Made You Well': The Role of Storytelling in the Experience of Miraculous Healing," *Review of Religious Research* 43, no. 2 (December 2001): 121–38.

16. James B. Waldram, "The Efficacy of Traditional Medicine: Current Theoretical and Methodological Issues," *Medical Anthropology Quarterly* 14, no. 4 (December 2000): 603.

17. Waldram, 603, 619.

18. Waldram, 608. Also see Mark Nichter, "Ethnomedicine: Diverse Trends, Common Linkages," in *Anthropological Approaches to the Study of Ethnomedicine*, ed. Mark Nichter (Amsterdam: Gordon and Breach, 1992), 223–59.

19. Opp, *The Lord for the Body*, 9.

20. Raymond J. Cunningham, "From Holiness to Healing: The Faith Cure in America, 1872–1892," *Church History* 43, no. 4 (December 1974), 499–513.

21. See Jonathan R. Baer, "Redeemed Bodies: The Functions of Divine Healing in Incipient Pentecostalism," *Church History* 70, no. 4 (December 2001): 756; Opp, *The Lord for the Body*; Ruth Harris, "The Cures," chapter 9 in *Lourdes*, 288–319; Hanegraaff, *New Age Religion*.

22. See Csordas, *The Sacred Self*; *Language, Charisma, and Creativity*.

23. See Dayton, *The Theological Roots of Pentecostalism*.

24. See Gottschalk, *Emergence*; and Peel, *Spiritual Healing* and *Health and Medicine*.

25. Schoepflin, *Christian Science on Trial*, 60; Peel, *Health and Medicine*, 29. Peel argues that while Christian Science theology is not therapy per se, its practice involves therapeutic elements. Schoepflin focuses only on the latter argument.

26. E. N., "Questions and Discussions," *CSJ* 7, no. 9 (1889): 466. E. N. added that she wished a word could be said to "check the tendency to dress" according to "fashions" and "exhibition," which causes believers to ask, "'Can this be *coming of Christ in the Spirit?*'"

27. L. H., "I Was Called," *CSJ* 9, no. 4 (1891), 173.

28. "Fifth Annual Meeting of the N. C. S. A.," *CSJ* 8, no. 1 (1890): 3–39.

29. Irving C. Tomlinson, "The Lecture at Tufts College," with contributions from Herbert E. Cushman, *CSS* 2, no. 27 (1900): 433.

30. This change dates to 1905. Regarding a related item in the 27 May 1905 *CSS*, see William Lloyd Memo in SF Eddy, Writings: *S&H*, Revision.

31. Eddy, *Miscellany*, 266–68, quoted in Schoepflin, *Christian Science on Trial*, 182.

32. Udo J. Keppler, "The Law Cannot Be 'Removed' by Christian Science," *Puck* 52, no. 1342 (19 November 1902), cover, Library of Congress Prints and Photographs Division, illus. in AP101.P7 1902 (Case X) [P&P], LC-DIG-ppmsca-25689. Christian Scientists later worked to secure exceptions and accommodations to some public health laws, with mixed results.

33. Harold and Esther Gove Diaries, 1920, NHHS.

34. Peel, *Spiritual Healing*, makes this point by examining medically verified testimonials.

35. Eddy, notation in Holy Bible, n.d., B00016, MBEC. Eddy wrote "8 Psalm 27 Dowie" immediately following an entry dated July 1903.

36. Purrington, *Christian Science*, 3–5.

37. Schoepflin, *Christian Science on Trial*, finds twenty-eight court cases involving Christian

Science between 1885 and 1901, nine from 1902 to 1925, none from 1926 to 1966, and ten from 1967 to 1990.

38. Harriet O. Evans v. State of Ohio, 9 Ohio Dec. 222 (1899), Court of Common Pleas of Ohio, Hamilton County, Supreme Court of Ohio Law Library, Columbus.

39. "Verdict of Censure," *Kearney (Neb.) Daily Hub*, 21 September 1891, 3; see also Reminiscence of James Neal, RF.

40. James Neal to Joseph Armstrong, 11 December 1891, SF Armstrong, Joseph Papers: Correspondence 1891–1893. Neal wrote that he paid $10.50 for the mules "like any fool farmer . . . but before I gave up—I got a second Mtgr [mortgage] on the two mules and our cow, all he has to secure $50.00 of the Judgment." See also Reminiscence of James Neal, RF.

41. See "Legislation in Indiana," *CSS* 3 (1901): 477–80; and "The Indiana Bill," *CSS* 3 (1901): 492–94. My thanks to Kelly Byquist for these citations.

42. State v. Marble, 28 February 1905, 70 L.R.A. 835, Supreme Court of Ohio, Supreme Court of Ohio Law Library.

43. Heloise Edwina Hersey to Unknown [Helen], c. 1901, *To Girls*, 214, NAWLD.

44. Folk, *Religion of Chiropractic*; D. D. Palmer to P. W. Johnson, 4 May 1911, Joseph C. Keating's History of Chiropractic Archive, http://www.chiro.org/Plus/History/ (accessed 8 January 2019).

45. Mark Twain, "Christian Science and the Book of Mrs. Eddy," *Cosmopolitan* 27, no. 6 (1899): 585–94. Also see Twain, *Christian Science*; and "Mark Twain on the Authorship of 'S&H,'" *Literary Digest* 34, no. 7 (1907): 255–56.

46. See Gottschalk, *Rolling Away*, 44–50; Hamlin Hill's commentary in the 1996 edition of Twain, *Christian Science*; and Squires, *Healing the Nation*, 99–100.

47. Peel, *Years of Authority*, 151, 232–33. The junior Dresser championed the word "indebtedness" to describe his theory, urging her, "I advise you to make a clean breast of it." This word would predominate in later historiography.

48. On Wiggin, see Gill, *Mary Baker Eddy*, 332–36; Gottschalk, *Rolling Away*, 117, 141, 150, 264; Peel, *Years of Authority*, 19, 27, 102, 196, 269; R. Thomas, *"With Bleeding Footsteps,"* 136, 301–2; and Kennedy, *Mrs. Eddy*, 340–42. Regarding the Hegelian thread, see Haushalter, *Mrs. Eddy Purloins from Hegel*; Thomas C. Johnsen, "Historical Consensus and Christian Science: The Career of a Manuscript Controversy," *New England Quarterly* 53, no. 1 (March 1980): 3–22; and Moehlman, *Ordeal by Concordance*.

49. Quoted in Peel, *Christian Science*, 137. See also James, *Varieties of Religious Experience*, 106.

50. William James, letter to the *Boston Transcript* (1894), quoted in Peel, *Christian Science*, 137. See also James, *Varieties of Religious Experience*, 106.

51. Peel, *Years of Authority*, 151.

52. Spear, *Sunshine and Love*, 68, B00294, MBEC.

53. Eddy, notation in *S&H* 1903 (263rd), B00475, MBEC.

54. Eddy found it a hassle to attend to a concordance while also revising her book and was pleased to have Conant complete this oft-requested and rather herculean task, eventually paying him $5,000 (about $153,000 in 2020) for rights to the completed product in 1903. See Eddy to Albert F. Conant, 22 April 1903, in SF Eddy, Writings: *S&H*, Concordance. She constantly sent him updated material and approved his copy. The arrangement of references in it make the volume as much a thought piece as a word retrieval tool.

55. Eddy, clipping pasted into *S&H* 1902, 624, B00474, MBEC.

56. Marietta T. Webb, "The Protecting Power of Truth," *CSS* 2, no. 12 (1899): 195–96.

57. William McKenzie to Eddy, 22 June 1896, L16455, MBEC.

58. Letters in SF McKenzie, William P. and Daisette Stocking: Letters Between.

59. William McKenzie, notations in Eddy, *S&H* 1894 (85th ed.), Ralph Byron Copper Private Collection, Boston (also the source in the next several paragraphs). The 85th edition was actually a printing of the most recently revised 81st edition.

60. The scripture McKenzie cites is actually Isaiah 9:6, suggesting he made some notations from memory.

61. Peel, *Years of Authority*, 74.

62. See, e.g., William B. Johnson to Joseph Armstrong requesting a 350th edition to update his 308th edition, 1905, in SF Eddy, Writings: *S&H*, Items of Interest, Publication and Sale, General.

63. Ellen C. Jones, notations in Eddy, *S&H* 1910, 201454930, AIB.

64. G. S. Adams, notations in Eddy, *S&H* 1888 (36th ed.), L18300, AIB.

65. See Sue Mims, notations in Eddy, *S&H* 1891 (63rd ed.), L18301, AIB.

66. See Irving Tomlinson, notations and marks in Eddy, *S&H* 1902 (231st ed.), L18389, and 322nd ed. (1904), L18402, AIB.

67. See Ellen [Ella] Rathvon, wear marks on Eddy, *S&H* 1909, L18412, AIB.

68. See Martha Wilson [Wilcox], marks in Eddy, *S&H* 1909, L18415, AIB.

69. John Henry Keene, notations in Eddy, *S&H* 1902, L18396, AIB.

70. Joseph G. Mann, notations in Eddy, *S&H* 1902 (231st ed.), L18394, AIB.

71. Calvin A. Frye, notations in Eddy, *S&H* 1895 (93rd ed.), B00457, AIB. The passage by his doodle reads, "Love for God and man is the true incentive to both healing and teaching."

72. See George Tomkins, notations, marks, and ephemera in Eddy, *S&H* 1900 (180th ed.), L18380, AIB. For more on Tomkins, see Peel, *Years of Authority*, 429n71.

73. Ann H. Knox to Mary Armstrong, c. 1899, SF Armstrong Papers.

74. Lewis C. Strang, draft, 10 March 1906, V03784, SC, MBEL. Eddy wrote notes of particular approval on Strang's draft.

75. See, e.g., Eddy to Pamelia J. Leonard, 5 July 1895, V01362, and Eddy to Gestefeld, 2 July 1884, L14278, MBEC.

76. Laura Lathrop to Eddy, 21 June 1903, MBEC.

Chapter Fifteen

1. Eddy, notation in *S&H* 1908, B00482, MBEC (the source for the next paragraph too). She may have very lightly used B00483 after or concurrent to B00482, but B00482 is the last copy of her book she checked, edited, and consistently used.

2. A typical example is Charles Rodolph to Calvin Frye, 1896, SF Eddy, Writings: *S&H*, Revisions. Rodolph wrote from Omaha, Nebraska, "I enclose a list of seeming errors in capitalization, punctuation, etc." Frye wrote on the back of his letter, "Transferred these corrections & sent to Wilson Oct. 13, 1896." Not all Rodolph's comments were relevant or accurate, especially his notes on capitalization, but many were.

3. See SF Eddy, Writings: *S&H*, box 95. She did, however, slightly modify some KJV passages at the start of some chapters to reflect Christian Science theology.

4. See SF Eddy, Writings, *S&H*, Concordance: Eddy to Albert F. Conant, 20 December 1907.

5. E. B. Hulin to Joseph Armstrong, 12 August 1895; Joseph Armstrong to Bro. Kinter, 4 November 1904; Joseph Armstrong to Eddy, 25 November 1904, all in SF Armstrong, Joseph Papers: Correspondence 1894–96 and 1904.

6. Armstrong earned a healthy salary for his multiple roles, but like many others in the young Christian Science organization, his move from the world of business and farming into

Christian Science came at a financial cost. Well-known practitioners such as James Neal and Stephen Chase wrote to him frankly about how they were addressing financial struggles in the 1890s, as did others in later years. Like Eddy had, many first-generation Christian Scientists sorted through this issue.

7. As Eddy once wrote to her church's reader Septimus J. Hanna, "Do not answer questions to the public unless you can answer them *simply* and in perfect accord with God's revelation in S. &H." Mary Baker Eddy to Septimus J. Hanna, 17 October 1899, L05266, MBEC.

8. SF Armstrong, Joseph Papers: Correspondence.

9. Eddy, notation in Holy Bible near Matt. 7:3, B00017.A, MBEC.

10. Wallner, *Faith on Trial*; Peel, *Years of Authority*, 280–91; also David F. Holland, "On the Volatile Relationship of Secularization and New Religious Movements: A Christian Science Case," in Hempton and McLeod, *Secularization and Religious Innovation*, 117; Gill, *Mary Baker Eddy*, 509–22; Gottschalk, *Rolling Away*, 31–38; Peel, *Years of Authority*, 280–91, 295; and Kennedy, *Mrs. Eddy*, 444–53.

11. See Scrapbooks of Frank R. Streeter, 289.51.S9155, v.1–32, NHHS.

12. Dr. Hopkins to Chandler, 19 July 1907, and Hopkins to Chandler, 11 July 1907, WECP.

13. Hopkins to Chandler, 21 July 1907, WECP.

14. Chandler to Slaght, 10 July 1907, WECP.

15. Sutton, *Aimee Semple McPherson*, 133, 19.

16. Sutton, 19.

17. "At Christian Science: Attack Is Directed by F. W. Peabody; He Urges Laws to Restrict Practice; W. L. Garrison and Others Make Defense; They Argue That Present Law Is All Right," *Boston Transcript*, Monday, 18 February 18, 1907, GFP (the source for the next few paragraphs too).

18. "Address of Wm. Lloyd Garrison," n.d., GFP, 6–7.

19. Archibald McLellan, "Editor's Table," *CSJ* 25, no. 1 (1907): 56–59, GFP. Garrison was also active in an early version of the anti-vaccination movement, unlike Christian Scientists, who did not participate in this movement, though some were not vaccinated. A Quaker and pacifist, Garrison spoke at a massive peace event hosted by Christian Scientists. He parted ways with Eddy after she turned to her Bible, landed on a passage in Isaiah, and interpreted it to mean that at our present stage in human history we must both pray for peace and arm our navies, though war was inherently evil (see Eddy notation in Holy Bible: "Chap. 45. 22 Isaiah (Peace Conference)," B00010, MBEC.). See William Lloyd Garrison, "Christian Science and War," *Evening Post*, 29 April 1908, 8, GFP.

20. "At Christian Science," GFP.

21. Willa Gilbert Cather to William E. Chandler, 16 July 1907, 1926.006, WECP. Also see Wallner, *Faith on Trial*, 216. Cather's involvement has been discussed by scholars and polemicists for the past fifty years. See Stewart Hudson's introduction to a 1971 edition of Milmine, *Life*, from Baker Book House; Gill, *Mary Baker Eddy*, 567; Gottschalk, *Emergence*, 160, and *Rolling Away*, 258–62; and Squires, *Healing the Nation*, 132–133.

22. See Gill, *Mary Baker Eddy*; Gottschalk, *Rolling Away*; all of Peel's work; and Squires, *Healing the Nation*.

23. Affidavit of Charles H. Copeland, notarized 7 June 1907, Frank R. Streeter Papers, NHHS.

24. Hopkins to Chandler, 11 July 1907, WECP. Given his dismissal of "M. A. M.," it is interesting that near the end of the suit Chandler feared unspecified people were "working against him" mentally (William E. Chandler to Dr. H. R. Burton, 23 July 1907, 1926.006, WECP).

25. Holland, "On the Volatile Relationship," 117.

26. Eddy, notations in *S&H*, B00472, 1902 (226th ed.), MBEC.

27. James H. Ropes to Howard D. Kenyon, SF Eddy, Writings: *S&H*, Items of Interest, Publication and Sale, General, Physiology. The Massachusetts Historical Society holds the Ropes Papers.

28. News of the fire is in a note on the back of their edited pages. See SF Eddy, Writings: *S&H*, Revisions for 1907.

29. Eddy, notations in *S&H*, B00482, 1908, 70, 100, MBEC. The word "super" was then newly popular.

30. Eddy, notations in *S&H*, B00482, 1908, flyleaf. In the Bible, she marked Isaiah 62:7–12. Both in MBEC.

31. She marked Proverbs 1:2–5, 14–19, 28, 29, Holy Bible, MBEC.

32. Holy Bible, B00007, MBEC.

33. Holy Bible, B00018, MBEC.

34. Eddy, clipping in *S&H*, B00482, 1908, MBEC.

35. Klassen, *Spirits of Protestantism*, 74.

Chapter Sixteen

1. See SF Eddy, Writings: *S&H*, Standards for All Time.

2. See box 534668, folder number 344023, MBEC. Through autumn 1907, Eddy's publisher Joseph Armstrong had taken precise notes detailing how many books he ordered. After that, his successor, Allison Stewart, took less precise notes. Despite efforts to determine how many printings took place between 1907 and 1911, no one knows for sure. It may have been as many as 550. Many books were indistinguishable save minuscule printing differences.

3. Charles H. Welch, "Items of Interest about *Science and Health with Key to the Scriptures*," 1916–1919, MBEC; Harry I. Hunt, "The Story of Our Textbook," *CSS* 27, no. 39 (1925): 763–64; Irene K. MacDonald, untitled, n.d. [1943], box 95, MBEC. MacDonald's useful and surprisingly (for the time) accurate technical review of the editions of *S&H* before 1910 and from 1911 to 1943, placed in the contexts of bookmaking and publication, was the basis of her term paper for a class on the history of books and printing, School of Library Service, Columbia University.

4. D. Morgan, *Protestants and Pictures*, 10.

5. D. Morgan, 340.

6. Eddy to Julia Field-King, 22 October 1897, F00536, MBEC.

7. Eddy, *S&H*, 1941, SC, BA. See Orcutt, *Mary Baker Eddy and Her Books*.

8. E.g., C. S. Norwood, 10 March 1931, in SF Eddy, Writings: *S&H*, Misc.

9. Bible and *S&H* with metal markers, inscribed by Dorothy Whitley, 1950, ORT.

10. Sylvia Plath to Aurelia Schober Plath, 13 December 1951, in Steinberg and Kukil, *Letters*, 1:500. I thank Karen V. Kukil for pointing out to me Plath's letters and journal entries regarding Christian Science.

11. Sylvia Plath, journal entry, 25 July 1952, in Kukil, *Journals*, 120–21.

12. Sylvia Plath to Aurelia Schober Plath, 28 August 1952, in Steinberg and Kukil, *Letters*, 501; Sylvia Plath, journal entry, January 22, 1953, in Kukil, *Journals*, 167.

13. Sylvia Plath to Margaret Cantor, 15 February 1954, in Steinberg and Kukil, *Letters*, 686–87; Sylvia Plath to Aurelia Schober Plath, 21 September 1956, in Steinberg and Kukil, *Letters*, 1247.

14. See Seasholes, *Gaining Ground*, for a meticulous history of land reclamation projects throughout Boston history. Seasholes mentions the Christian Science church on 200 and 229.

15. Chester Park had several segments. Near the Webbs' home, it was called West Chester Park. By 1893, streetcars in Boston had not been segregated for many years. Conveniently for Webb, in 1897 a line ran in front of her house and jogged up the Providence Railroad tracks to the corner of Massachusetts and Huntington Avenues, the location of The Mother Church. Thanks to WardMaps, LLC, and especially to Thomas Athearn of the Boston Street Railway Association for neighborhood details.

16. Eddy notation in Holy Bible, B00016: "My name as I read P[salm] 76 was given to me[:] Discoverer." Also, Eddy back flyleaf notation in *S&H*, 2 April 1892, B00450, "Concord N. H. April 2 1892 / I was spiritually Christened *Discoverer* of Christian Science." Both MBEC. Kilde, "Material Expression and Maternalism."

17. Cressler, *Authentically Black*, shows in his study of black Catholics that authentic religious identity and authentic black identity can take many forms and are not mutually exclusive regarding denominations that do not usually identify as historically African American.

18. See William P. McKenzie, "Christian Science and the Freedom of Man, *CSJ* 20, no. 3 (1902), 130–48.

19. Charles A. Blake, Jonathan R. Irving, Roderick McLennan, and William W. Slocumb, 6 January 1911, EOR 24, ORT. On 31 December 1910, a group of armed men phoned the receiving tomb where these men were on duty and threatened to enter it by force, illustrating why guards were assigned watch until Eddy's heirs could agree on burial details.

20. Marietta Webb, "Blank for Card Department," 14 April 1914, MBEC.

21. Marietta T. Webb, "The Protecting Power of Truth," *CSS* 2, no. 12 (1899): 195.

22. Webb, 195.

23. See Hiram Webb, obituary, *Los Angeles Times*, 29 August 1904, microfilm page 842 of 1275. In addition to various boarders, Webb's brother Randall Jones and sister Corinda, Corenda, or Coranado Jones Norrington appear on various census records at Webb's Los Angeles address.

24. *Report to the Members*, 19, 20.

25. *Report to the Members*, 20.

26. See Christian Science Publishing Society, *Proceedings in Equity*. The Massachusetts Supreme Court decided in 1922 that Eddy intended the board of directors of The Mother Church to execute the church's bylaws as found in the *Manual*, including those bylaws governing the church's board of trustees.

27. Charles A. Starks, "Christian Science and Race Prejudice," *Kansas City Sun*, 4 March 1922; Clifford P. Smith, "Christian Science," *Kansas City Sun*, 18 March 1922; Clifford P. Smith, untitled, *CSS* 24, vol. 33 (15 April 1922): 555–56. Also see *Report to the Members* and "Annual Meeting of the Mother Church: Church Welfare Committee," *CSS* 21, vol. 41 (1919): 805.

28. Paul E. Ivey, personal correspondence, 22 September 2017. See A. Gilbert Bells, "The Black Press in Illinois," *Journal of the Illinois State Historical Society* 68, no. 4 (1975): 347. This information also appears in an endnote in Ivey's dissertation.

29. "Founder of Church Refuses to Have Col. Placed after Her Name; She Is Ousted," *Atlanta World*, 12 January 1934. Also see "Christian Science Leader Is Ousted," *New Age Dispatch* (Los Angeles), 12 January 1934.

30. "Police Called to Keep Order in Christian Science Church Meet," *California Eagle*, 12 January 1934; "Founder of Church Refuses to Have Col. Placed after Her Name; She Is Ousted."

31. First Church of Christ, Scientist, Cambridge, "Addendum: Progress in Healing Racial Prejudice," *Historical Sketch*, II–39.

32. "Addendum," II-40.

33. Ivey, personal correspondence, 22 September 2017. This information also appears in an endnote in Ivey's dissertation.

34. Vivienne Allen, "Man's Inviolate Dignity," *CSJ* 71, no. 7 (1953): 368–69. Allen may have been the singer and actress whose circuit overlapped with Christian Science converts such as Kay Kyser; see Serrano, *Puerto Rican Women*, 111; and "Oklahoma," *Billboard* 58, vol. 26 (June 29, 1946): 55.

35. "Christian Science: Despite Lack of Emotionalism, Church Makes Long Strides in Enlisting Negroes," *Ebony*, November 1950, 58–63.

36. Orlando Webb, San Pedro and Wilmington, California, City Directory, 1914, page 2270; Orlando Webb, Los Angeles Assembly District 72, Los Angeles, California, 1920, Roll T625_112, page 8B; Orlando Webb, Census Enumeration District 338, Los Angeles, California, 1920, roll 144, page 4A; Orlando Webb, Census Enumeration District 0291, Los Angeles, California, 1930, FHL microfilm 2339879, roll T627_415, page 17A; Orlando Webb, Census Enumeration District 60-813, Los Angeles, California, 1940. All records from Ancestry.com.

37. Orlando Webb, Registration State California, Registration County Los Angeles, roll 1530907, Draft Board 08, Ancestry.com.

38. Orlando Webb, World War II Draft Cards (4th Registration) for the State of California, Records of the Selective Service System, 1926–1975, RG 147, National Archives at St. Louis, St. Louis, Missouri, Ancestry.com.

Findings: Part IV

1. Eddy, notation in *S&H*, B00454 (81st), MBEC.

Christian Science Identity

1. Knapp, *William James*, 13.

2. Taves, *Revelatory Events*, 1.

3. "'Christian Science' and 'Mind Cure,'" *Century: A Popular Quarterly*, 34, no. 3 (1887): 418.

4. Quoted in Peel, *Christian Science*, 137. See also James, *Varieties of Religious Experience*, 106.

5. For a study of other boundary-pushing revelatory claims in early American history, see Holland, *Sacred Borders*.

6. Peel, *Christian Science*, 126.

7. Gottschalk, *Emergence*, 275.

8. David Weddle, "The Christian Science Textbook: An Analysis of the Religious Authority of Science and Health by Mary Baker Eddy," *Harvard Theological Review* 84, no. 3 (1991): 297, 276, 275.

9. Albanese, *America*, 235.

10. Paul C. Gutjahr, "The State of the Discipline: Sacred Texts in the United States," *Book History* 4 (2001).

BIBLIOGRAPHY

Primary Sources

ARCHIVES

Bethesda, Md.
  United States National Library of Medicine
    History of Medicine Division Collection
Boston, Mass.
  Boston Athenaeum
    Margaret Urann Collection, Family Papers, 1828–1966
    Special Collections
  Congregational Library and Archives
  Howard Gotlieb Archival Research Center, Mugar Library, Boston University
  Mary Baker Eddy Library
    Organizational Records of the First Church of Christ, Scientist
    Special Collections
      Art and Artifact Collection
      Autographed and Inscribed Books
      Historical Photographs Collection
      Mary Baker Eddy Collection
      Reminiscences File
      Subject File
  Massachusetts Historical Society
  Ralph Byron Copper Private Collection
Chestnut Hill, Mass.
  Longyear Museum
Chicago, Ill.
  Newberry Library
Columbus, Ohio
  Supreme Court of Ohio Law Library
Concord, N.H.
  New Hampshire Historical Society
    Frank R. Streeter Papers
    Grimes Family Correspondence
    Harold E. and Esther Gove Diaries, 1914–1972
    Papers of Bartholomew Van Dame
    Scrapbooks of Frank R. Streeter
    White Family Papers
    Whittle Family Papers
    William E. Chandler Papers

Manassas, Va.
   Manassas National Battlefield Park Archives
Northampton, Mass.
   Sophia Smith Collection, Special Collections, Smith College
      Abby Morton Diaz Papers
      Garrison Family Papers
      Health Collection
      Women: Position and Progress Collection
Pasadena, Calif.
   Theosophical Society Archives
Portland, Maine
   Maine Historical Society
      Fogg Collection
      Special Collections
Sacramento, Calif.
   State of California Department of Health Services, Center for Health Statistics
      California Death Index, 1940–1997
Salisbury, N.C.
   Salisbury Confederate Prison Archives
Washington, D.C.
   Library of Congress
      Chronicling America: Historic American Newspapers
      Prints and Photographs Division
Wenham, Mass.
   Jenks Library, Gordon College
      Adoniram Judson Gordon Papers
Worcester, Mass.
   American Antiquarian Society
      Historical Periodicals Collection

ELECTRONIC SOURCES

Alexanderstreet.com
   North American Women's Letters and Diaries
Alpheus.org
Ancestry.com
   Census Enumeration District 338, Los Angeles, California, 1920
   Census Enumeration District 0291, Los Angeles, California, 1930
   Census Enumeration District 60-813, Los Angeles, California, 1940
   Los Angeles Assembly District 72, Los Angeles, California, 1920
   Registration State California, Registration County Los Angeles, roll 1530907, Draft Board 08
   San Pedro and Wilmington, California, City Directory, 1914
   World War II Draft Cards (4th Registration) for the State of California, Records of the Selective Service System, 1926–1975, RG 147, National Archives at St. Louis, St. Louis, Missouri
Chiro.org
   Joseph C. Keating's History of Chiropractic Archive, http://www.chiro.org/Plus/History/

Familysearch.org
    District of Columbia Freedmen's Bureau Field Office Records, 1863–1872
    Sixteenth Census of the United States, 1940
    Massachusetts Births, 1841–1915
    Records of the Bureau of the Census, 1790–2007, RG 29
    United States Federal Census for Boston, Suffolk County, Mass., 1880
YouTube
    William Branham archival videos, Freddy 7700, https://www.youtube.com/user
        /freddy7700/feed, accessed January 16, 2019

PERIODICALS

Abbeville (S.C.) Press and Banner
The Advocate (Buffalo, N.Y.)
American Journal of the Medical Sciences
American Scrapbook and Magazine of United
    States Literature
Atlanta World
Banner of Light
Baptist Standard
Bay State Banner
Biblical World
Billboard
Book History
Boston Daily Journal
Boston Evening Transcript
Boston Globe
Boston Post
Boston Sunday Globe
Brooklyn Daily Eagle
Browne's Phonographic Monthly
California Eagle (Los Angeles)
Century: A Popular Quarterly
Chicago Standard
Christian Metaphysician
Christian Palladium
Christian Science Journal (1883–)
Christian Science Bible Lessons
    (January–April 1890)
Christian Science Quarterly (April 1890–)
Christian Science Sentinel (1898–)
Church History
Church Review
The Congregationalist
Congregational Journal
Congregational Quarterly
Cosmopolitan
Current Literature: A Magazine of Record and
    Review

Daily Courier (Portland, Maine)
Daily Evening Courier (Portland, Maine)
Daily Press (Portland, Maine)
Drum Beat
Ebony
Edgefield (S.C.) Advertiser
Esoteric
Evening Post (New York)
Evening Star
Evening Telegraph (Philadelphia)
Genders
Godey's Lady's Book
Granite Monthly
Great Revival
Harvard Theological Review
Herald of Christian Science (1903–)
Herald of Gospel Liberty
Historical New Hampshire
Homoeopathic Advocate and Guide to Health
Household Words: A Weekly Journal
    Conducted by Charles Dickens
Human Life
In die skriflig: Tydskrif van die Gereformeerde
    Teologiese Vereniging
International Journal of Women's Studies
Journal for the Scientific Study of Religion
Journal of American History
Journal of British Studies
Journal of Feminist Studies in Religion
Journal of Religion
Journal of Religion and Society
Journal of the American Academy of Religion
Journal of the Illinois State Historical Society
Journal of the National Medical Association
Journal of the Society for the Study of
    Metaphysical Religion
Kansas City Sun

Kearney (Neb.) Daily Hub
Literary Digest
Little's Living Age
Longyear Quarterly News
Los Angeles Times
Lucifer
Lynn (Mass.) Transcript
Lynn (Mass.) Weekly Reporter
Material Religion
McClure's
Medical Anthropology Quarterly
Mental Science Magazine and Mind-Cure Journal
Millennial Star
New Age Dispatch (Los Angeles)
New England Quarterly
New Hampshire Journal of Education
New Hampshire Observer
New York Herald
New York Times
New York Weekly Sun
Pacific Historical Review
Printers' Circular
Religio-Philosophical Journal
Review of Religious Research
Repository and Observer (Concord, N.H.)
Shaker Manifesto
Times-Picayune (New Orleans)
Times-Republican (Marshalltown, Iowa)
Triumphs of Faith
Union Seminary Quarterly Review
Voices: Journal of the American Academy of Psychotherapists
Water-Cure Journal and Herald of Reforms
Waterville (Maine) Mail
Wheeling (W.Va.) Daily Intelligencer
Yankee Farmer
Youth's Companion

WORKS BY MARY BAKER EDDY

"The Bible in Its Spiritual Meaning" [a.k.a. Genesis manuscript]. Mary Baker Eddy Collection, c. 1867–1969, Special Collections, Mary Baker Eddy Library, Boston.
Christ and Christmas. Boston: Christian Science Publishing Society, 1891.
Christian Healing: A Lecture. Cambridge, Mass.: John Wilson and Son, 1881.
Christian Science: No and Yes. Boston: By the author, 1887.
Christian Science vs. Pantheism. Boston: Christian Science Publishing Society, 1898.
The First Church of Christ, Scientist, and Miscellany. Boston: Christian Science Publishing Society, 1913.
Historical Sketch of Metaphysical Healing. Boston: By the author, 1885.
Manual of The Mother Church. 2nd ed. Boston: The Barta Press, 1895.
Manual of The Mother Church. 89th ed. Boston: Christian Science Publishing Society, 1913.
Matthew manuscript. Mary Baker Eddy Collection, c. 1867, Special Collections, Mary Baker Eddy Library, Boston.
Miscellaneous Writings, 1883–1896. Boston: Christian Science Publishing Society, 1896.
The People's Idea of God: Its Effect on Health and Christianity. 4th ed. Cambridge, Mass.: John Wilson and Son, 1889.
Poems. Boston: Christian Science Publishing Society, 1910.
Prose Works. Boston: Christian Science Publishing Society, 1925.
Pulpit and Press. Concord, N.H.: Republican Press Association, 1895.
Retrospection and Introspection. Boston: A. V. Stewart, 1891.
Rudimental Divine Science (Rudiments and Rules of Divine Science). 1887. Reprint, Boston: J. Armstrong, 1901.
Science and Health, 1875–1911. See appendix.
Science of Man [or "The Soul's Inquiries of Man"]. Mary Baker Eddy Collection, 1870, Special Collections, Mary Baker Eddy Library, Boston.
Unity of Good (Unity of Good and Unreality of Evil). 1888. Reprint, Boston: Christian Science Publishing Society, 1908.

BOOKS AND ARTICLES

Adams, William. *The Elements of Christian Science, a Treatise upon Moral Philosophy and Practice.* Philadelphia: Richard McCauley, 1870.

Addresses at the Semi-centennial Anniversary of the Congregational Church of Northfield and Tilton, New Hampshire, July 18th, 1872. Tilton, N.H.: Chas. F. Hill, 1873.

Alexander, Archibald. *Outlines of Moral Science.* New York: Charles Scribner, 1852.

Alger, William Rounsvelle. *The Friendships of Women.* 10th ed. Boston: Roberts Brothers, 1882.

Atkinson, Caroline. *Letters of Susan Hale.* Boston: Marshall Jones Co., 1918.

Bain, Alexander. *Mental and Moral Science: A Compendium of Psychology and Ethics.* London: Longmans, Green, and Company, 1868.

Baines-Miller, Minnie W. *Mrs. Cherry's Sister: or Christian Science at Fairfax.* New York: Eaton and Mains, 1901.

———. *My Cousin, the Doctor.* New York: Eaton and Mains, 1891.

Bancroft, Samuel Putnam. *Mrs. Eddy as I Knew Her in 1870.* Boston: Geo. H. Ellis, 1923.

Barnes, Albert. *Scenes and Incidents in the Life of the Apostle Paul.* Philadelphia: Zeigler, McCurdy and Co., 1869.

Barton, Walter. *Historical Address.* Lynn, Mass.: J. F. McCarty and Bro., 1882.

Beattie, James. *Elements of Moral Science.* Philadelphia: Mathew Carey, 1806.

Bissell, Mary Taylor. *Physical Development and Exercise for Women.* New York: Dodd, Mead, and Co., 1891.

Blavatsky, Helena P. *A Modern Parnarion: A Collection of Fugitive Fragments.* 1895. Reprint, Los Angeles: Theosophy Company of Los Angeles, 1981.

Boardman, Samuel Lane. *Catalogue of That Portion of the Private Library of Samuel Lane Boardman Relating to American and Local History, Biography etc., to Be Sold by Auction.* Boston: W. F. Brown, 1883.

Bodwell, Abraham. *A Sermon, Delivered at the Request of the Female Cent Society, in Sandbornton [sic], New-Hampshire, December 23, 1812.* Concord, N.H.: George Hough, 1813.

Bouton, Nathaniel. *The History of Education in New-Hampshire: A Discourse, Delivered before the New-Hampshire Historical Society, at Their Meeting in Concord, June 12, 1833.* Concord, N.H.: Marsh, Capen and Lyon, 1833.

Brontë, Charlotte. *Jane Eyre.* 1847. Reprint, New York: Penguin Books, 1985.

Brown, Newton. *The Apocalypse: A Poem.* Augusta, Maine: Luther Severance, 1836.

Buck, William D. *Annual Address before the New Hampshire Medical Society.* Manchester, N.H.: C. F. Livingston, 1866.

Bushnell, Horace. *Nature and the Supernatural as Together Constituting the One System of God.* 1858. Reprint, London: Alexander Strahan, 1867.

———. *Sermons for the New Life.* New York: Charles Scribner's Sons, 1907.

Christian Science Publishing Society, Board of Trustees. *Proceedings in Equity, 1919–1921.* Boston: Christian Science Publishing Society, 1922.

Clifton Springs Water-Cure. *Report of the Addresses and Sermon at the Dedication of the Clifton Springs Water-Cure.* Geneva and Canandaigua, N.Y.: National New Yorker Press, 1857.

Cogswell, William. *The Christian Philanthropist, or, Harbinger of the Millennium.* Boston: Perkins and Marvin, 1839.

Crosby, Dixi. *Some Remarks on Hypnotism: Presented to the New Hampshire Medical Society at Its Annual Meeting.* Concord, N.H.: Republican Press Association, 1893.

Crosby, Frederick K. *Into Light, and Other Poems.* Boston: W. F. Brown, 1876.

Dagg, J. L. *The Elements of Moral Science.* New York: Sheldon, 1860.
Decision of the Council in the Trial of Rev. W. P. Merrill, Published by Minority of the Church. Portland: Brown Thurston, 1861.
Dickerson, K. *The Philosophy of Mesmerism, or Animal Magnetism, Being a Compilation of Facts.* Concord, N.H.: Morrill, Silsby and Co., 1843.
Donaldson, James. *The Westminster Confession of Faith and the Thirty-Nine Articles of the Church of England: The Legal, Moral, and Religious Aspects of Subscription to Them.* New York: Longmans, Green, 1905.
Du Bois, W. E. B. *The Quest of the Silver Fleece.* Chicago: A. C. McClurg & Co., 1911.
Eaton, John Richard Turner. *Permanence of Christianity: Considered in Eight Lectures Preached before the University of Oxford in the Year 1872.* New York: E. P. Dutton, 1879.
Eggleston, Edward. *Christ in Art.* New York: J. B. Ford and Company, 1875.
Emerson, Sarah Hopper, ed. *Life of Abby Hopper Gibbons: Told Chiefly through Her Correspondence.* Vol. 2. New York: G. P. Putnam's Sons, 1896.
Festival of Sons of New Hampshire. Boston: J. French, 1850.
Gestefeld, Ursula N. *Jesuitism in Christian Science.* Chicago: By the author, 1888.
———. *Ursula Gestefeld's Statement of Christian Science, Comprised in Eighteen Lessons and Twelve Sections.* New York: By the author, 1888.
———. *The Woman Who Dares.* New York: Lovell, Gestefeld, 1892.
Gordon, A. J. *The Ministry of Healing, or, Miracles of Cure in All Ages.* Chicago: Fleming H. Revell, 1882.
Gordon, Ernest B. *Adoniram Judson Gordon: A Biography.* New York: Fleming H. Revell Company, 1896.
Guiney, Grace, ed. *Letters of Louise Imogen Guiney.* Vol. 2. New York: Harper and Row, 1926.
Harper, Ida Husted, ed. *The Life and Work of Susan B. Anthony: Including Public Addresses, Her Own Letters and Many from Her Contemporaries during Fifty Years.* Vol. 2. Indianapolis: Bowen-Merrill Company, 1898.
Hedge, Frederic Henry. *The Sick Woman: A Sermon for the Time.* Boston: Prentiss and Deland, 1863.
Hersey, Heloise Edwina. *To Girls, a Budget of Letters.* Boston: Athenaeum Press, 1901.
Hogg, Wilson. *Christian Science Unmasked.* Syracuse: A. W. Hall, 1892.
Holland, Patricia G., and Anna D. Gordon, eds. *Papers of Elizabeth Cady Stanton and Susan B. Anthony.* Wilmington, Del.: Scholarly Resources, Inc., 1991 [microfilm].
Horton, Freeman. *Directions for the Sick during Homeopathic Treatment.* Weare, N.H., c. 1850. S1996.523.57, New Hampshire Historical Society, Concord.
Hosmer, William. *The Young Lady's Book; or, Principles of Female Education.* Auburn, N.H.: Derby and Miller, 1852.
Huling, Caroline A. *Letters of a Business Woman to Her Niece.* New York: R. F. Fenno and Company, 1906.
Hunter, Henry. *Sacred Biography, or, the History of the Patriarchs.* Hallowell, Maine: Glazier, 1828.
James, Henry. *The Bostonians.* London: Macmillan and Co., 1886.
James, William. *The Varieties of Religious Experience: A Study in Human Nature.* New York: Random House, 1902.
Keats, John. *Endymion: A Poetic Romance.* London: Taylor and Hessey, 1818.
Kuroda, S. *The Light of Buddha.* Osaka, Japan: Dairoku-Kyoku-Kyomusho, 1903.
The Lady's Book of Etiquette and Manual of Politeness. Boston: G. W. Cottrell, 1860. 395 H3323, New Hampshire Historical Society, Concord.

Laycock, Thomas. *An Essay on Hysteria: Being an Analysis of Its Irregular and Aggravated Forms*. Philadelphia: Haswell, Barrington, and Haswell, 1840. W6 P3 v.91, History of Medicine Division Collection, United States National Library of Medicine, Bethesda, Md.

Le Bosquet, John. *Congregational Manual*. Boston: Otis, Broadstreet and Co., 1841. 285.8 L448, New Hampshire Historical Society, Concord, and 1978.011, Whittle Family Papers, New Hampshire Historical Society, Concord.

Livermore, Harriet. *A Testimony for the Times*. New York: By the author, 1843.

Lord, Nathan. *The Millennium: An Essay Read to the General Convention of New Hampshire, 1854*. Hanover: Dartmouth Press, 1854.

Lowry, E. B. *Confidences: Tales from a Young Girl Concerning Herself.* 1910. Reprint, Chicago: Forbes & Co., 1919.

MacKellar, Thomas. *A Manual of Typography*. 15th ed. Philadelphia: MacKellar, Smiths, and Jordan, 1885.

Manual of the Congregational Church of Tilton and Northfield. Tilton, N.H.: Charles F. Hill, 1878.

Meehan, Michael. *Mrs. Eddy and the Late Suit in Equity*. Concord, N.H.: By the author, 1908.

Messenger, Frank M. *The Time of the End: A Book of Revelation*. Boston: J. P. Jewett and Company, 1856.

Minutes of the Fifty-Ninth Annual Meeting of the General Association of New-Hampshire. Concord: McFarland and Jenks, 1868.

Morgan, J. Vyrnwy, D.D., ed. *Theology at the Dawn of the Twentieth Century: Essays on the Present Status of Christianity and Its Doctrines*. Boston: Small, Maynard and Company, 1900.

Munger, Theodore T. *The Freedom of Faith*. Boston: Houghton, Mifflin and Company, 1883.

Napheys, Geo. H. *The Physical Life of Woman: Advice to the Maiden, Wife, and Mother*. 5th ed. Philadelphia: George MacLean, 1871. Health Collection, Sophia Smith Collection, Special Collections, Smith College, Northampton, Mass.

Norton, Carol. *Woman's Cause*. Boston: Dana Estes, 1895.

Payne, George. *Elements of Mental and Moral Science*. New York: Leavitt, Lord, and Co., 1835.

Phipps, Joseph. *True Christian Baptism and Communion*. Philadelphia: Caxton Press of Sherman and Co., 1872.

Porter, James. *The Spirit Rappings, Mesmerism, Clairvoyance, Visions, Revelations, Startling Phenomena, and Infidelity of the Rapping Fraternity Calmly Considered, and Exposed*. Boston: James P. Magee, 1853.

Purrington, William Archer. *Christian Science: An Exposition of Mrs. Eddy's Wonderful Discovery, Including its Legal Aspects*. New York: E. B. Treat and Company, 1900.

Putnam, Allen. *Mesmerism, Spiritualism, Witchcraft, and Miracle: A Brief Treatise*. Boston: Bela Marsh, 1858.

Putnam, Daniel. *Elementary Psychology; or, First Principles of Mental and Moral Science*. Boston: A. S. Barnes & Co., 1889.

Report to the Members of the Mother Church of the Committee on General Welfare. New York: Federal Printing Company, 1920.

Russell, Moses W. *The President's Address to the New Hampshire Medical Association*. Concord, N.H.: Republican Press Association, 1892.

Sanborn, Dyer H. *An Analytical Grammar of the English Language*. Concord, N.H.: Marsh, Capen, and Lyon, 1836.

Searchlights on Christian Science: A Symposium. New York: Fleming H. Revell Company, 1899.

Seventy-Fifth Anniversary of the Congregational Church of Northfield and Tilton, New Hampshire. Concord, N.H.: Republican Press Association, 1897.

Shepard, Odell, ed. *The Journals of Bronson Alcott*. Port Washington, N.Y.: Kennikat, 1966.

Smith, Alice Weston. *Alice Weston Smith, 1868–1908: Letters to Her Friends and Selections from Her Note-books*. Boston: Addison C. Getchell and Son, 1908.

Smith, William, ed. *A Dictionary of the Bible*. Vols. 1–4. Boston: By the author, 1884.

Spear, Katharine. *Sunshine and Love*. New York: Eaton and Mains, 1903.

Starling, Elizabeth. *Noble Deeds of Woman; or, Examples of Female Courage and Virtue*. Boston: Phillips, Sampson and Company, 1850.

Stanton, Elizabeth Cady. *The Woman's Bible*. 2 vols. New York: European Publishing Company, 1895–1898.

Stead, W. T. *If Christ Came to Chicago: A Plea for the Union of All Who Love in the Service of All Who Suffer*. London: Review of Reviews, 1894.

Stearns, Ezra, ed. *Genealogical and Family History of the State of New Hampshire*. New York: Lewis Publishing Company, 1908.

Stevens, George Barker. *The Messages of Paul*. New York: Charles Scribner's Sons, 1901.

Stinson, John Harrison. *Ethica: An Outline of Moral Science, for Students and Reflecting Men*. New York: A. B. Kitsn, 1860.

Thayer, Lucius Harrison. *Congregationalism in New Hampshire during the Nineteenth Century*. 1909. [S.l.] : [s.n.], [1909], New Hampshire Historical Society, Concord.

———. *The Religious Conditions of New Hampshire during the Period 1750 to 1800*. 1909. [S.l.] : [s.n.], 1909, New Hampshire Historical Society, Concord.

Tolstoy, Leo. *The Kreutzer Sonata*. New York: Pollard, 1890.

Twain, Mark. *Christian Science*. New York: Harper Brothers, 1907.

Tyndall, John. *The Prayer-Gauge Debate*. Boston: Congregational Publishing Society, 1876.

Upham, Thomas Cogswell. *Elements of Mental Philosophy*. Boston: Wells and Lilly and Hilliard, Gray and Co., 1831.

Van Dame, Bartholomew. *New and Latest Collection of Hymns*. Lee, N.H., 1831.

Wayland, Francis. *The Elements of Moral Science*. Boston: Gould, Kendall, and Lincoln, 1835.

We Knew Mary Baker Eddy. 1943. Reprint, Boston: Christian Science Publishing Society, 1979.

White, Truman C., ed. *Our County and Its People: A Descriptive Work on Erie County, New York*. Vol. 2. Boston: Boston History Company, 1898.

Wight, Nahum. *An Address Delivered at the Annual Meeting of the New Hampshire Medical Society*. Concord, N.H.: Republican Press Association, 1875.

Wright, Livingston. *How Rev. Wiggin Rewrote Mrs. Eddy's Book*. Reprinted from the *New York World*, 1936.

Secondary Sources

BIOGRAPHIES OF MARY BAKER EDDY

Ferguson, Isabel, and Heather Vogel Frederick. *A World More Bright: The Life of Mary Baker Eddy*. Boston: Christian Science Publishing Society, 2013.

Gill, Gillian. *Mary Baker Eddy*. Reading, Mass.: Perseus Books, 1998.

Gottschalk, Stephen. *Rolling Away the Stone: Mary Baker Eddy's Challenge to Materialism.* Bloomington: University of Indiana Press, 2006.
Kennedy, Hugh A. Studdert. *Mrs. Eddy: Her Life, Her Work, and Her Place in History.* San Francisco: Farallon Press, 1947.
Milmine, Georgine. *The Life of Mary Baker Eddy and the History of Christian Science.* New York: Doubleday, Page, 1909.
O'Brien, Sibyl Wilbur. *The Life of Mary Baker Eddy.* New York: Concord, 1908.
Peel, Robert. *Mary Baker Eddy: The Years of Authority.* New York: Holt, Rinehart, and Winston, 1977.
———. *Mary Baker Eddy: The Years of Discovery.* New York: Holt, Rinehart, 1966.
———. *Mary Baker Eddy: The Years of Trial.* New York: Holt, Rinehart, and Winston, 1971.
Powell, Lyman Pierson. *Christian Science: The Faith and Its Founder.* New York: G. P. Putnam's Sons, 1907.
———. *Mary Baker Eddy: A Life Size Portrait.* New York: Macmillan, 1930.
Smaus, Jewel Spangler. *Mary Baker Eddy: The Golden Days.* Boston: Christian Science Publishing Society, 1966.
Thomas, Robert David. *"With Bleeding Footsteps": Mary Baker Eddy's Path to Religious Leadership.* New York: Knopf/Random House, 1994.

BOOKS AND DISSERTATIONS

Aamodt, Terrie Dopp, Gary Land, and Ronald L. Numbers, eds. *Ellen Harmon White: American Prophet.* New York: Oxford University Press, 2014.
Albanese, Catherine L. *America: Religions and Religion.* Belmont, Calif.: Wadsworth Publishing, 1999.
———. *A Republic of Mind and Spirit: A Cultural History of American Metaphysical Religion.* New Haven, Conn.: Yale University Press, 2007.
Anderson, Alan C. *Healing Hypotheses: Horatio W. Dresser and the Philosophy of New Thought.* New York: Garland, 1993.
Baker, Jean. *Votes for Women: The Struggle for Suffrage Revisited.* Oxford: Oxford University Press, 2002.
Barker-Benfield, Graham John. *Horrors of the Half-Known Life: Aspects of the Exploitation of Women by Men.* New York: Harper and Row, 1976.
Barlow, Philip L. *Mormons and the Bible: The Place of the Latter-Day Saints in American Religion.* New York: Oxford University Press, 1991.
Barnes, Linda L. and Susan S. Sered, eds. *Religion and Healing in America.* New York: Oxford University Press, 2005.
Bednarowski, Mary Farrell. *New Religions and the Theological Imagination in America.* Religion in North America. Bloomington: Indiana University Press, 1989.
———. *The Religious Imagination of American Women.* Bloomington: Indiana University Press, 1999.
Bogue, Martha Harris. *Miscellaneous Documents Relating to Christian Science and Its Discoverer and Founder Mary Baker Eddy.* Providence, R.I.: Carpenter Foundation, 1961.
Bouwsma, William J. *John Calvin: A Sixteenth-Century Portrait.* New York: Oxford University Press, 1988.
Braden, Charles. *Christian Science Today: Power, Policy, Practice.* Dallas: Southern Methodist University Press, 1958.

———. *Spirits in Rebellion: The Rise and Development of New Thought*. Dallas: Southern Methodist University Press, 1963.
Braude, Ann. *Radical Spirits: Spiritualism and Women's Rights in Nineteenth-Century America*. Boston: Free Press, 1989.
Brown, Candy Gunther. *The Healing Gods: Complementary and Alternative Medicine in Christian America*. New York: Oxford University Press, 2013.
———. *Testing Prayer: Science and Healing*. Cambridge, Mass.: Harvard University Press, 2012.
———. *The Word in the World: Evangelical Writing, Publishing, and Reading in America, 1789–1880*. Chapel Hill: University of North Carolina Press, 2004.
Brown, Louis. *The Salisbury Prison: A Case Study of Confederate Military Prisons*. Rev. and enlarged. Wilmington, N.C.: Broadfoot, 1992.
Bushman, Richard L. *Joseph Smith: Rough Stone Rolling*. New York: Vintage, 2007.
Campbell, Bruce F. *Ancient Wisdom Revived: A History of the Theosophical Movement*. Berkeley: University of California Press, 1980.
Casper, Scott E., Jeffrey D. Groves, Stephen W. Nissenbaum, and Michael Winship, eds. *The Industrial Book, 1840–1880*. Vol. 3 of *A History of the Book in America*. Chapel Hill: University of North Carolina Press, 2007.
Cayleff, Susan E. *Wash and Be Healed: The Water-Cure Movement and Women's Health*. Philadelphia: Temple University Press, 1987.
Chang, Jung. *Empress Dowager Cixi: The Concubine Who Launched Modern China*. New York: Anchor Books, 2014.
Cohen, Charles L., and Paul S. Boyer, eds. *Religion and the Culture of Print in Modern America*. Madison: University of Wisconsin Press, 2008.
Cohen, Patricia Cline. *A Calculating People: The Spread of Numeracy in Early America*. Chicago: University of Chicago Press, 1982.
Consor, Walter H., Jr., and Sumner B. Twiss, eds. *Religious Diversity and American Religious History: Studies in Traditions and Cultures*. Athens: University of Georgia Press, 1997.
Cressler, Matthew J. *Authentically Black and Truly Catholic: The Rise of Black Catholicism in the Great Migration*. New Nork: New York University Press, 2017.
Cronon, William. *Nature's Metropolis: Chicago and the Great West*. New York: W. W. Norton, 1991.
Csordas, Thomas J. *Body/Meaning/Healing*. New York: Palgrave, 2002.
———. *Language, Charisma, and Creativity: The Ritual Life of a Religious Movement*. Berkeley: University of California Press, 1997.
———. *The Sacred Self: A Cultural Phenomenology of Charismatic Healing*. Berkeley: University of California Press, 1994.
Curtis, Heather D. *Faith in the Great Physician: Suffering and Divine Healing in American Culture, 1860–1900*. Baltimore: Johns Hopkins University Press, 2007.
Danky, James P., and Wayne A. Wiegand, eds. *Print Culture in a Diverse America*. Madison: University of Wisconsin Press, 1998.
———. *Women in Print: Essays on the Print Culture of American Women from the Nineteenth and Twentieth Centuries*. Madison: University of Wisconsin Press, 2006.
Dayton, Donald W. *The Theological Roots of Pentecostalism*. Metuchen, N.J.: Hendrickson, 1987.
Dominic, Randolph P., Jr. *Down from the Balcony: The Abyssinian Congregational Church of Portland, Maine*. Portland, Maine: By the author, 1982.
Donegan, Jane B. *Hydropathic Highway to Health: Women and Water Cure in Antebellum America*. New York: Greenwood Press, 1986.

Dorrien, Gary. *Idealism, Realism, and Modernity, 1900–1950.* Vol. 2 of *The Making of American Liberal Theology.* Louisville: Westminster John Knox Press, 2003.

———. *Imagining Progressive Religion, 1805–1900.* Vol. 1 of *The Making of American Liberal Theology.* Louisville: Westminster John Knox Press, 2001.

DuBois, Ellen Carol, ed. *Elizabeth Cady Stanton and Susan B. Anthony: Correspondence, Writings, Speeches.* New York: Schocken Books, 1981.

Faust, Drew Gilpin. *This Republic of Suffering: Death and the American Civil War.* New York: Knopf, 2008.

First Church of Christ, Scientist, Cambridge, Mass. *Historical Sketch of the First Church of Christ, Scientist, Cambridge, Massachusetts.* Cambridge, Mass.: By the author, 2000.

Folk, Holly. *The Religion of Chiropractic: Populist Healing from the American Heartland.* Chapel Hill: University of North Carolina Press, 2018.

Foner, Eric. *The Fiery Trial: Abraham Lincoln and American Slavery.* New York: W. W. Norton, 2010.

Freeman, Curtis W. *Undomesticated Dissent: Democracy and the Public Virtue of Religious Nonconformity.* Waco: Baylor University Press, 2017.

Frerichs, Ernest S., ed. *The Bible and Bibles in America.* Atlanta: Scholars Press, 1988.

Genette, Gérard. *Paratexts: Thresholds of Interpretation.* Translated by Jane E. Lewin. Cambridge: Cambridge University Press, 1997.

Gifford, Sanford. *The Emmanuel Movement (Boston, 1904–1929): The Origins of Group Therapy and the Assault on Lay Psychotherapy.* Boston: Francis Countway Library of Medicine, 1996.

Ginzberg, Lori. *Elizabeth Cady Stanton: An American Life.* New York: Hill and Wang, 2009.

Goff, Philip, Arthur Emery Farnsley, and Peter Johannes Thuesen. *The Bible in American Life.* New York: Oxford University Press, 2017.

Gottschalk, Stephen. *The Emergence of Christian Science in American Religious Life.* Berkeley: University of California Press, 1973.

Gould, Stephen J. *The Panda's Thumb.* New York: W. W. Norton, 1980.

Greene, Jody. *The Trouble with Ownership: Literary Property and Authorial Liability in England, 1660–1730.* Philadelphia: University of Pennsylvania Press, 2005.

Griffith, R. Marie. *Born Again Bodies: Flesh and Spirit in American Christianity.* Berkeley: University of California Press, 2004.

Gross, Rita M., ed. *Beyond Androcentrism: New Essays on Women and Religion.* Missoula, Mont.: Scholars, 1977.

Gross, Robert A., and Mary Kelley. *An Extensive Republic: Print, Culture, and Society in the New Nation.* Chapel Hill: University of North Carolina Press, 2010.

Guarneri, Carl J. *The Utopian Alternative: Fourierism in Nineteenth-Century America.* Ithaca: Cornell University Press, 1994.

Gutjahr, Paul C. *An American Bible: A History of the Good Book in the United States, 1777–1880.* Stanford: Stanford University Press, 1999.

———, ed. *The Oxford Handbook of the Bible in America.* New York: Oxford University Press, 2017.

———, ed. *Popular American Literature of the Nineteenth Century.* New York: Oxford University Press, 2001.

Gutjahr, Paul C., and Megan L. Benton, eds. *Illuminating Letters: Typography and Literary Interpretation.* Amherst: University of Massachusetts Press, 2001.

Hall, David D. *Cultures of Print: Essays in the History of the Book.* Amherst: University of Massachusetts Press, 1996.

———. *Worlds of Wonder, Days of Judgment: Popular Religious Beliefs in Early New England.* Cambridge, Mass.: Harvard University Press, 1990.

Hamlin, Kimberly A. *From Eve to Evolution: Darwin, Science, and Women's Rights in Gilded Age America*. Chicago: University of Chicago Press, 2014.

Hanegraaff, Wouter. *New Age Religion and Western Culture: Esotericism in the Mirror of Secular Thought*. Albany: SUNY Press, 1996.

Hansen, Penny. "Woman's Hour: Feminist Implications of Mary Baker Eddy's Christian Science Movement, 1885–1910." PhD diss., University of California–Irvine, 1981.

Harley, Gail. *Emma Curtis Hopkins: Forgotten Founder of New Thought*. Syracuse: Syracuse University Press, 2002.

Harrell, David E., Jr. *All Things Are Possible: The Healing and Charismatic Revivals in Modern America*. Bloomington: Indiana University Press, 1975.

Harris, Ruth. *Lourdes: Body and Spirit in the Secular Age*. New York: Penguin, 1999.

Hatch, Nathan O. *The Democratization of American Christianity*. New Haven, Conn.: Yale University Press, 1989.

Hatch, Nathan O., and Harry S. Stout, eds. *Jonathan Edwards and the American Experience*. New York: Oxford University Press, 1988.

Haushalter, Walter Milton. *Mrs. Eddy Purloins from Hegel: A Newly Discovered Source Reveals Amazing Plagiarisms in Science and Health*. Boston: A. A. Beauchamp, 1936.

Haynes, April R. *Riotous Flesh: Women, Physiology, and the Solitary Vice in Nineteenth-Century America*. Chicago: University of Chicago Press, 2016.

Hayter-Menzies, Grant. *The Empress and Mrs. Conger: The Uncommon Friendship of Two Women and Two Worlds*. Hong Kong: Hong Kong University Press, 2011.

Hedrick, Joan D. *Harriet Beecher Stowe: A Life*. New York: Oxford University Press, 1995.

Heelas, Paul. *The New Age Movement: The Celebration of the Self and the Sacralization on Modernity*. Oxford: Blackwell, 1996.

Hempton, David, and Hugh McLeod, eds. *Secularization and Religious Innovation in the North Atlantic World*. Oxford: Oxford University Press, 2017.

Hewitt, Nancy, and Suzanne Lebsock, eds. *Visible Women: New Essays on American Activism*. Bloomington: University of Indiana Press, 1993.

Higginbotham, Evelyn Brooks. *Righteous Discontent: The Women's Movement in the Black Baptist Church, 1880–1920*. Cambridge, Mass.: Harvard University Press, 1993.

Hodgkiss, Andrew. *From Lesion to Metaphor: Chronic Pain in British, French and German Medical Writings, 1800–1914*. Atlanta: Rodopi, 2000.

Hodgson, Peter J. *A Most Agreeable Man: Lyman Foster Brackett*. Chestnut Hill, Mass.: Longyear Museum Press, 2003.

Holland, David. *A Particular Universe: Ellen White, Mary Baker Eddy and the Nineteenth-Century United States*. Cambridge, Mass.: Harvard University Press, forthcoming.

———. *Sacred Borders: Continuing Revelation and Canonical Restraint in Early America*. New York: Oxford University Press, 2011.

Homestead, Melissa J. *American Women Authors and Literary Property, 1822–1869*. New York: Cambridge University Press, 2005.

Houtman, Dick, and Birgit Meyer, eds. *Things: Religion and the Question of Materiality*. New York: Fordham University Press, 2012.

Howsam, Leslie. *Cheap Bibles: Nineteenth-Century Publishing and the British and Foreign Bible Society*. New York: Cambridge University Press, 2001.

Hughes, Richard T. *Reviving the Ancient Faith: The Story of Churches of Christ in America*. Grand Rapids, Mich.: Eerdmans, 1996.

———, ed. *The American Quest for the Primitive Church*. Urbana: University of Illinois Press, 1988.

Hughes, Richard T., and R. L. Roberts. *The Churches of Christ*. Westport, Conn.: Greenwood Press, 2001.

Hunter, Tera W. *To 'Joy My Freedom: Southern Black Women's Lives and Labors after the Civil War*. Cambridge, Mass.: Harvard University Press, 1997.

Ivey, Paul Eli. *Prayers in Stone: Christian Science Architecture in the United States, 1894–1930*. Urbana: University of Illinois Press, 1999.

Johnsen, Thomas C. "Christian Science and the Puritan Tradition." PhD diss., Johns Hopkins University, 1983.

Jones, Serene. *Feminist Theory and Christian Theology: Cartographies of Grace*. Minneapolis: Fortress Press, 2000.

Kelsey, Morton. *Healing and Christianity*. Minneapolis: Augsburg Books, 1985.

Kern, Kathi. *Mrs. Stanton's Bible*. Ithaca: Cornell University Press, 2001.

Kirschmann, Anne Taylor. *A Vital Force: Women in American Homeopathy*. New Brunswick, N.J.: Rutgers University Press, 2003.

Klassen, Pamela. *Spirits of Protestantism: Medicine, Healing, and Liberal Christianity*. Berkeley: University of California Press, 2011.

Knapp, Krister Dylan. *William James: Psychical Research and the Challenge of Modernity*. Chapel Hill: University of North Carolina Press, 2017.

Kukil, Karen V., ed. *The Unabridged Journals of Sylvia Plath, 1950–62*. New York: Anchor Books, 2000.

Laderman, Carol, and Marina Roseman, eds. *The Performance of Healing*. New York: Routledge, 1996.

Lincoln, C. Eric, and Lawrence H. Mamiya. *The Black Church in the African-American Experience*. Durham: Duke University Press, 1996.

Long, Charles H. *Significations: Signs, Symbols, and Images in the Interpretation of Religion*. Philadelphia: Fortress Press, 1986.

Loughran, Trish. *The Republic in Print: Print Culture in the Age of U.S. Nation Building, 1770–1870*. New York: Columbia University Press, 2007.

Macfarlane, Robert. *Original Copy: Plagiarism and Originality in Nineteenth-Century Literature*. New York: Oxford University Press, 2007.

Marsden, George M. *Jonathan Edwards: A Life*. New Haven, Conn.: Yale University Press, 2003.

Mazzeo, Tilar J. *Plagiarisms and Literary Property in the Romantic Period*. Philadelphia: University of Pennsylvania Press, 2006.

McClenon, James. *Wondrous Healing: Shamanism, Human Evolution, and the Origin of Religion*. DeKalb: Northern Illinois University Press, 2002.

McCrackan, William D. *Mary Baker Eddy and Her Book: Science and Health with Key to the Scriptures*. Tamworth, N.H.: M. E. Starr, 1925.

McGill, Meredith L. *American Literature and the Culture of Reprinting, 1834–1853*. Philadelphia: University of Pennsylvania Press, 2002.

McGuire, Meredith. *Ritual Healing in Suburban America*. New Brunswick, N.J.: Rutgers University Press, 1988.

McKim, Donald K. *Introducing the Reformed Faith: Biblical Revelation, Christian Tradition, Contemporary Significance*. Louisville: Westminster John Knox Press, 2001.

McPherson, James M. *Battle Cry of Freedom: The Civil War Era*. 2nd ed. New York: Oxford University Press, 2003.

Miller, Randall M., Harry S. Stout, and Charles Reagon Wilson. *Religion and the American Civil War*. New York: Oxford University Press, 1998.

Moehlman, Conrad Henry. *Ordeal by Concordance: An Historical Study of a Recent Literary Invention*. New York: Longmans, Green, 1955.
Moore, R. Laurence. *Religious Outsiders and the Making of Americans*. New York: Oxford University Press, 1986.
Moorhead, James H. *American Apocalypse: Yankee Protestants and the Civil War, 1860–1869*. New Haven, Conn.: Yale University Press, 1978.
———. *World without End: Mainstream American Protestant Visions of the Last Things, 1880–1925*. Bloomington: Indiana University Press, 1999.
Morgan, David. *Protestants and Pictures: Religion, Visual Culture, and the Age of American Mass Production*. New York: Oxford University Press, 1999.
———. *Religion and Material Culture: The Matter of Belief*. New York: Routledge, 2010.
———. *Visual Piety: A History and Theory of Popular Religious Images*. Berkeley: University of California Press, 1998.
Mullen, Lincoln A. *The Chance of Salvation: A History of Conversion in America*. Cambridge, Mass.: Harvard University Press, 2017.
Mullin, Robert Bruce. *Miracles and the Modern Religious Imagination*. New Haven, Conn.: Yale University Press, 1996.
Noll, Mark A. *The Civil War as a Theological Crisis*. Chapel Hill: University of North Carolina Press, 2006.
Nord, David Paul. *Faith in Reading: Religious Publishing and the Birth of Mass Media in America*. New York: Oxford University Press, 2004.
Numbers, Ronald L., and Darrel W. Amundsen, eds. *Caring and Curing: Health and Medicine in the Western Religious Traditions*. Baltimore: Johns Hopkins University Press, 1986.
Nylander, Jane C. *Our Own Snug Fireside: Images of the New England Home, 1760–1860*. New York: Alfred A. Knopf, 1993.
Ogden, Emily. *Credulity: A Cultural History of US Mesmerism*. Chicago: University of Chicago Press, 2018.
Opp, James. *The Lord for the Body: Religion, Medicine, and Protestant Faith Healing in Canada, 1880–1930*. Montreal: McGill-Queen's Press, 2005.
Orcutt, William Dana. *Mary Baker Eddy and Her Books*. Boston: Christian Science Publishing Society, 1950.
Ostrander, Richard. *The Life of Prayer in a World of Science: Protestants, Prayer, and American Culture, 1870–1930*. New York: Oxford University Press, 2000.
Pacyga, Dominic A. *Chicago: A Biography*. Chicago: University of Chicago Press, 2009.
Paretsky, Sara. *Words, Works, and Ways of Knowing: The Breakdown of Moral Philosophy in New England before the Civil War*. Chicago: University of Chicago Press, 2017.
Peel, Robert. *Christian Science: Its Encounter with American Culture*. New York: Holt, 1958.
———. *Health and Medicine in the Christian Science Tradition: Principle, Practice, and Challenge*. New York: Crossroad Press, 1988.
———. *Spiritual Healing in a Scientific Age*. San Francisco: Harper and Row, 1987.
Pellauer, Mary D. *Toward a Tradition of Feminist Theology: The Religious Social Thought of Elizabeth Cady Stanton, Susan B. Anthony, and Anna Howard Shaw*. Brooklyn, N.Y.: Carlson Publishing, 1991.
Perry, Seth. *Bible Culture and Authority in the Early United States*. Princeton: Princeton University Press, 2018.
Piepmeier, Alison. *Out in Public: Configurations of Women's Bodies in Nineteenth-Century America*. Chapel Hill: University of North Carolina Press, 2004.
Pietsch, B. M. *Dispensational Modernism*. New York: Oxford University Press, 2015.

Porterfield, Amanda. *Healing in the History of Christianity.* New York: Oxford University Press, 2005.

Price, H. H., and Gerald E. Talbot, eds. *Maine's Visible Black History: The First Chronicle of Its People.* Gardiner: Tilbury House Publishers and the University of Southern Maine, 2006.

Pritchard, Rebecca M. *Jeremiah Hacker: Journalist, Anarchist, Abolitionist.* Philadelphia: Frayed Edge Press, 2019.

Rable, George C. *God's Almost Chosen Peoples: A Religious History of the American Civil War.* Chapel Hill: University of North Carolina Press, 2010.

Raboteau, Albert J. *Canaan Land: A Religious History of African Americans.* Oxford: Oxford University Press, 2001.

Radway, Janice, and Carl Kaestle, eds. *Print in Motion: The Expansion of Publishing and Reading in the United States, 1880–1945.* Vol. 4 of *A History of the Book in America.* Chapel Hill: University of North Carolina Press, 2009.

Riskin, Jessica. *Science and Sensibility: The Sentimental Empiricists of the French Enlightenment.* Chicago: University of Chicago Press, 2010.

Roberts, Jon H. *Darwinism and the Divine in America: Protestant Intellectual and Organic Evolutionism, 1859–1900.* Madison: University of Wisconsin Press, 1988.

———. "The Science of the Soul": *American Protestant Thinkers and the Sanctity of Mind, 1607–1940.* Forthcoming.

Robins, Natalie. *Copeland's Cure: Homeopathy and the War between Conventional and Alternative Medicine.* New York: Knopf, 2009.

Robins, R. G. *A. J. Tomlinson: Plainfolk Modernist.* New York: Oxford University Press, 2004.

Romano, Frank. *Machine Writing and Typesetting: The Story of Shales and Mergenthaler and the Invention of the Typewriter and the Linotype.* Salem, N.H.: Gama, 1986.

Rose, Mark. *Authors and Owners: The Invention of Copyright.* Cambridge, Mass.: Harvard University Press, 1993.

Rowe, David L. *God's Strange Work: William Miller and the End of the World.* Grand Rapids, Mich.: William B. Eerdmans, 2008.

Safronoff, Cynthia. *Crossing Swords: Mary Baker Eddy vs. Victoria Claflin Woodhull and the Battle for the Soul of Marriage.* Seattle: This One Thing, 2015.

Satter, Beryl. *Each Mind a Kingdom: American Women, Sexual Purity, and the New Thought Movement, 1875–1920.* Berkeley: University of California Press, 1999.

Schechter, Patricia A. *Ida B. Wells-Barnett and American Reform, 1880–1930.* Chapel Hill: University of North Carolina Press, 2001.

Schmidt, Leigh. *Hearing Things: Religion, Illusion, and the American Enlightenment.* Cambridge, Mass.: Harvard University Press, 2000.

———. *Village Atheists: How America's Unbelievers Made Their Way in a Godly Nation.* Princeton: Princeton University Press, 2016.

Schoepflin, Rennie B. *Christian Science on Trial: Religious Healing in America.* Baltimore: Johns Hopkins University Press, 2003.

Seager, Richard Hughes. *Buddhism in America.* New York: Columbia University Press, 1999.

———. *The World's Parliament of Religions: The East/West Encounter, Chicago, 1893.* Bloomington: Indiana University Press, 1995.

Seale, Ervin, ed. *Phineas Parkhurst Quimby: The Complete Writings,* Volumes 1–3. Camarillo, Calif.: DeVorss, 1988.

Seasholes, Nancy. *Gaining Ground: A History of Landmaking in Boston.* Cambridge, Mass.: MIT Press, 2003.

Serrano, Basilio. *Puerto Rican Women from the Jazz Age: Stories of Success.* Bloomington, Ind.: AuthorHouse, 2019.

Sheils, W. J., ed. *The Church and Healing.* Studies in Church History 19. New York: Oxford University Press, 1982.

Shulman, David, and Guy G. Stroumsa, eds. *Self and Self-Transformation in the History of Religions.* New York: Oxford University Press, 2002.

Smith, H. Shelton. *Horace Bushnell.* New York: Scribner, 1965.

Squires, Ashley. *Healing the Nation: Literature, Progress, and Christian Science.* Bloomington: Indiana University Press, 2017.

Stein, Stephen J. *The Shaker Experience in America: A History of the United Society of Believers.* New Haven, Conn.: Yale University Press, 1994.

Steinberg, Peter K., and Karen V. Kukil, eds. *The Letters of Sylvia Plath, Volume 1: 1940–1956.* London: Faber and Faber, 2017.

Stout, Harry S. *Upon the Altar of the Nation: A Moral History of the Civil War.* New York: Viking, 2006.

Sutton, Matthew Avery. *Aimee Semple McPherson and the Resurrection of Christian America.* Cambridge, Mass.: Harvard University Press, 2009.

Tate, Claudia. *Domestic Allegories of Political Desire: The Black Heroine's Text at the Turn of the Century.* New York: Oxford University Press, 1992.

Taves, Ann. *Fits, Trances, and Visions: Experiencing Religion and Explaining Experience from Wesley to James.* Princeton: Princeton University Press, 1999.

———. *Religious Experience Reconsidered: A Building-Block Approach to the Study of Religion and Other Special Things.* Princeton: Princeton University Press, 2011.

———. *Revelatory Events: Three Case Studies of the Emergence of Spiritual Paths.* Princeton: Princeton University Press, 2017.

Taylor, Marion Ann, and Heather E. Weir. *Let Her Speak for Herself: Nineteenth-Century Women Writing on Women in Genesis.* Waco: Baylor University Press, 2006.

Terborg-Penn, Rosalyn. *African American Women in the Struggle for the Vote, 1850–1920.* Bloomington: University of Indiana Press, 1998.

Thomas, Tracy A. *Elizabeth Cady Stanton and the Feminist Foundations of Family Law.* New York: New York University Press, 2016.

Toulouse, Mark G., and James O. Duke, eds. *Makers of Christian Theology in America.* Nashville: Abingdon Press, 1997.

Tucker, Susan, Katherine Ott, and Patricia Buckler, eds. *The Scrapbook in American Life.* Philadelphia: Temple University Press, 2006.

Tweed, Thomas A. *The American Encounter with Buddhism, 1844–1912.* Wilmette, Ill.: Baha'i Publishing Trust, 1985.

———. *Retelling U.S. Religious History.* Berkeley: University of California Press, 1997.

Umansky, Ellen M. *From Christian Science to Jewish Science: Spiritual Healing and American Jews.* New York: Oxford University Press, 2005.

Ventimiglia, Andrew. *Copyrighting God: Ownership of the Sacred in American Religion.* New York: Cambridge University Press, 2019.

Wacker, Grant. *Heaven Below: Early Pentecostals and American Culture.* Cambridge, Mass.: Harvard University Press, 2001.

Wallner, Peter. *Faith on Trial: Mary Baker Eddy, Christian Science, and the First Amendment.* Concord, N.H.: Plaidswede Press, 2014.

Walton, Michael Thomson. *Genesis and the Chemical Philosophy: True Christian Science in the Sixteenth and Seventeenth Centuries.* Brooklyn: AMS Press, 2011.

Washington, Margaret. *Sojourner Truth's America*. Chicago: University of Illinois Press, 2011.
Weedon, Alexis. *Victorian Publishing: The Economics of Book Production for a Mass Market, 1836–1916*. Burlington, Vt.: Ashgate, 2003.
Weiss, Harry B., and Howard R. Kemble. *The Great American Water-Cure Craze: A History of Hydropathy in the United States*. Trenton, N.J.: Past Times Press, 1967. 615.853.W432, New Hampshire Historical Society, Concord.
Wessinger, Catherine, ed. *Women's Leadership in Marginal Religions: Explorations outside the Mainstream*. Urbana: University of Illinois Press, 1993.
Williams, Joseph. *Spirit Cure: A History of Pentecostal Healing*. New York: Oxford University Press, 2013.
Wilson, Brian C. *Dr. John Harvey Kellogg and the Religion of Biologic Living*. Bloomington: Indiana University Press, 2014.
Wimbush, Vincent, ed. *Theorizing Scriptures: New Critical Orientations to a Cultural Phenomenon*. New Brunswick: Rutgers University Press, 2008.
Wosh, Peter J. *Spreading the Word: The Bible Business in Nineteenth-Century America*. Ithaca: Cornell University Press, 1994.

INDEX

abolitionism, 7; Congregationalism on, 20, 21–22; Eddy on, 126. *See also* antislavery; slavery
Adams, Edward H., 211
Adams, G. S., 203
Adams, Mabel, 225, 226
Adventism, 28, 45, 100, 232. *See also* Seventh-Day Adventists; White, Ellen Harmon
African Americans: after Civil War, 58; as Christian Scientists, 180–82, 184–85, 219–26; as Congregationalists, 44; liberation from enslavement of, 119, 126–27, 220; religious identity of, 277n17. *See also* Webb, Marietta T.
Albanese, Catherine L., 150, 162, 235
alcohol consumption, 19–20
Alcott, Bronson, 91, 95, 96
Aldrich, Edgar, 212
American Bible Tract Society, 28–29
American Book Trade Association, 91
American Journal of Medical Sciences, 25
American Medical Association, 1
American religiosity, networks and nodes of, 5–6, 12, 107, 140, 231, 233–34
Anglicans, 143, 172, 175, 177, 183
animal magnetism, 36–38, 74, 108, 171–72, 210. *See also* mesmerism
Anthony, Susan B.: on Eddy and Christian Science, 115–16, 153; racism and, 126; on truth and religious theories, 261n11
antislavery: Congregationalism on, 20–21, 33; Eddy's "moral suasion" on, 7, 21; in Portland, Maine, 44–45. *See also* abolitionism; slavery
apostolic Christianity: Campbell on, 81; as form of restorationism, 4, 6, 9, 105, 109; forms of healing in, 35, 75, 136, 140, 142, 158, 163

Armstrong, Joseph, 159, 195, 208, 209, 274n6, 276n2
Armstrong, Mary, 205
athleticism, 246n28
authorship controversies, 96–99, 132, 196–97
Avery, Rachel Foster, 184

Baer, Jonathan, 73
Bailey, Joshua, 145
Baker, Abigail Ambrose, 17, 18, 29
Baker, Albert, 20, 23, 26, 101
Baker, George, 26
Baker, Mark, 17, 18, 29–30, 58
Baker, Mary Ann, 17
Baker, Mary Morse. *See* Eddy, Mary Baker
Baker, Samuel and Mary Ann, 44
Bancroft, Samuel Putnam, 69
baptism, 81–82, 109
Baptists, 19, 80, 141, 145, 156–58, 161, 181, 204
Barnes, Albert, 71
Bartlett, John, 29
Bartlett, Julia A., 83
Bates, Edward P., 170
Baum, Maria Louise, 105
Beaumont, William, 32
Bednarowski, Mary Farrell, 124–25
Beecher, Henry Ward, 39, 122, 127
Beecher, Lyman, xii
Benton, George, 87
Bible: as gifts among Christian Scientists, 70, 77, 215; as joint pastor of Christian Science, 170–72; owned and marked by Eddy, 70, 203; volume of references to *Science and Health*, 89. *See also* Christian Science; Eddy, Mary Baker; *Science and Health with Key to the Scriptures* (Eddy)

"The Bible in Its Spiritual Meaning" (Eddy), 65, 108, 253n2. *See also* Genesis, Eddy's manuscript on
biblical interpretation, overview, 8–9, 175, 207. *See also* Christian Science; Eddy, Mary Baker; pastoral books; *Science and Health with Key to the Scriptures* (Eddy)
Bida, Alexandre, 83
Black, Persis Sibley, 24, 246n34
Blavatsky, Helena, 149–50
Bodwell, Abraham, 23–24, 100
Bodwell, Sarah, 23
Bok, Edward, 115
book industry. *See* printing and publishing technologies
bookmarking tools, 172, 173
Book of Mormon, 9. *See also* Mormonism
Boston, Massachusetts, 158–59, 184
The Bostonians (James), 219
Boston Journal, 197–98
Boston Post (publication), 132, 134, 135, 158
Boston Sunday Globe (publication), 10, 89, 131, 158
Boston Transcript (publication), 210
Bouton, Nathaniel, 246n25
Brackett, Lyman Foster, 168
Bradford, George H., 157
Brisbane, Arthur, 212
Brooks, Phillips, 159
Brown, Candy Gunther, 32
Brown, W. F., 94
Brown (later Blackwell), Antoinette, 53
Buckley, James Monroe, 146
Buddhism, 140, 147–48, 155, 234
Burritt, Elihu, 106
Bushnell, Horace, 37, 38, 77, 81, 96, 122
Bushnell, Katharine, 121

Caesar, Tiberius, 83
calendars, 172, 173
Calvin, John, 82, 101
Calvinism, 17, 18, 19, 121, 142, 261n11
Campbell, Alexander, 80, 81
Canada, 1, 179, 180, 183
cartoon, *188*
Caspar, Scott E., 182
Cather, Willa, 211–12

Catholicism: black identity and, 277n17; Christian Science and, 184; on healing and miracles, 85, 146, 191–92; religious objects of, 35, 175, 204
The Century (publication), 139
cessationism, 85, 142
Chandler, William, 209–12
Channing, William Ellery, 81, 154, 246n34
Chapman, Ann Greene, 24, 246n27
Chase, Stephen, 275n6
Cheney, Russell, 29, 30
Cherokee, 179
child custody rights, 29–30, 261n22
China, 184
Christian liberalism, 70, 142, 145, 157, 184, 234, 244n11
Christian Moral Science Association, 88
Christian orthodoxy, 23, 35, 144–45, 232–33, 234
Christian Palladium (publication), 95
Christian Science: overview of, 3–8, 161, 227–29, 231–36; on animal magnetism, 36–38, 74, 108, 171–72, 210; Baptists and, 141, 145, 156–58, 161, 181, 204; Bible as joint pastor of, 170–72; Bible Lesson, 171–74; church polity, 167–72, 208–9, 223, 268n96, 277n26; *vs.* divine healing, 73–74, 143–47, 161, 191–92, 234; Episcopalians or Anglicans and, 172, 177, 182–84; esotericism and, 11, 37–38, 124, 141, 147–56, 159, 162, 232–33; failures of healing and, 191–94; Gifford on, 156–58, 266n47; God in, 66–68, 74, 79, 99, 107, 116–17, 122–23, 134, 143–44, 175, 181, 198; historiography of, 11–12, 151, 159, 162, 234; hymnal of, 168; James on, 231–32; libel suit against, 196; litigation on medical licensing and efficacy against, 194–96; mesmerism and, 38, 71–76, 234; metaphysics and, 6, 9, 13, 78–80, 91–92, 109, 132, 157, 227, 231, 233; Methodists and, 102, 145, 146, 163, 179, 183, 197; moral science, as term for, 24, 34, 77, 87–89, 109, 257n33; The Mother Church, 2, 169–71, 182, 208, 220, 223–24, 261n8; with network and nodes of religiosity, 5–6, 12, 107, 140, 231, 233–34; Next Friends suit on,

209–13, 214; origins of, 2, 10, 12–13; Pentecostals or Holiness and, 4, 80, 142, 145, 224, 232; Plath on, 218–19; public definition of, 139; public perceptions of, 187–92, 196; Quakers and, 81, 92, 211, 275n19; religious and cultural context of, 10–11; as restorationist, 6, 9, 13, 80–82, 109, 227, 231, 236; roots in Congregationalism, 18–19, 169, 234; science of the soul, as term for, 34, 89; Shakers and, 4, 106–7, 232; Spiritualism and, 37–38, 146; Swedenborgians and, 97, 163; as term, 87–89, 109, 135–36, 227; testimonies of healing in, 2–3, 92, 131–32, 159–60, 174–86; Theosophy and, 10–11, 139–41, 147, 149–56, 159, 161–62, 234. *See also* Eddy, Mary Baker; *Science and Health with Key to the Scriptures* (Eddy)

Christian Science (book by Twain), 212

Christian Science Bible Lessons, 171–74

Christian Science Journal (publication), 147, 153, 167, 180, 225

Christian Science Monitor (publication), 214

Christian Science: No and Yes (Eddy), 149

Christian Science Publishing Society, 208

Christian Science Quarterly (publication), 171, 172, 180, 269n15

Christian Science Sentinel (publication), 3, 116, 158, 180, 222, 224, 225

"Christian Science Tested by Scripture" (Gordon), 146

Christian Scientist Association (CSA), 168

Christ in Art (Eggleston), 83

chronic pain. *See* neuralgia

Churches of Christ, 80, 142. *See also* Disciples of Christ

Church of Christ (Scientist), 227. *See also* Christian Science

Church of Jesus Christ of Latter-Day Saints. *See* Mormonism

church polity, 167–72

Civil War, 22, 39, 42–43, 58. *See also* wartime experiences

Clifton Springs, 34, 35, 47, 59

Colman, Janet, 159

Comstock, F. R., 209

Conant, Albert, 198, 208, 273n54

Conant, Liba, 19

concordances, 70, 198, 208, 273n54

Concord Congregational Church, 170

Conger, Sarah Pike, 184

Congregationalism, 18–19, 33, 38, 100, 169, 234. *See also* Sanbornton (later Tilton) Congregational Church, New Hampshire

The Congregationalist (publication), 20, 78, 85

Congregational Journal, 35

Cook, Joseph, 145

copying passages, 174

copyright: of Eddy, 69, 89, 90, 170, 208, 213, 218; marriage and rights of, 255n16; Ventimiglia on, 7, 150–51. *See also* plagiarism

Corser, Enoch, 19, 23, 26, 247n47

Cosmopolitan (publication), 212

Cott, Nancy, 114

Crafts, Hiram, 69

creation story, 84–85, 117. *See also* Genesis, Eddy's manuscript on

C.S. *See* Christian Science

Csordas, Thomas, 192

Cullis, Charles, 142

Cunningham, Raymond J., 191

Curtice, Corbin, 26

Curtis, Heather, 12, 73, 140, 142, 143, 144, 161, 191

Darwinism, 77, 85–86, 123, 125, 234. *See also On the Origin of Species* (Darwin)

Day, Jessie and O. W., 168

Dayton, Donald, 142, 147, 192

debt, 30, 31, 45, 169, 268n11

devotional art, 175, 177

devotional books. *See* pastoral books

Diagram Showing the Convergent Endings of the Chief Prophetic Periods in Messenger, *Time of the End*, 103

Diaz, Abby Morton, 153–54

Dickinson, Emily, 55, 252n53

Disciples of Christ, 27. *See also* Churches of Christ

dispensary, 169

"The Disputed Authorship of Science and Health" (*Literary Digest*), 196

divine healing: and Christian Science, 73–74, 143–47, 161, 191–92, 234; cultural emergence of, 140–43; in postwar revival period, 264n13. *See also* healing beliefs and practices
"divine infinite calculus," as term, 106
Divine Love, as term, 90
Dowie, John Alexander, 73, 189, 194
Dresser, Annetta, 58
Dresser, Horatio, 196, 197, 232, 251n16, 273n47
Dresser, Julius, 58, 132–34, 136, 156
Dr. W. T. Vail's Hydropathic Institute, 43
DuBois, Ellen, 125, 126
Duncan, Elizabeth Patterson, 30

Eaton, John Richard Turner, 87
Ebony (publication), 222, 226
Eddy, Asa Gilbert, 92, 127, 137
Eddy, Mary Baker: accident and recovery of, 57–58, 61, 71–73, 77, 132–34, 137; on antislavery and abolitionism, 7, 20–21, 22; on baptism, 81–82, 109; biographical overview, 6; on Buddhism, 155; Colman on, 159–60; on Darwinism, 85–86; death of, 216; on descriptive terms for work, 87, 88–89, 263n4; Diaz and, 153–54; on divinity of Jesus Christ, 171, 175; divorce of, 31, 76, 137, 255n16; early life of, 17–22; early understandings of healing, 51–55, 59–60, 264n11; education of, 22–24; on evil, 51, 127, 175, 210, 254n10, 275n19; family and wartime experiences of, 42, 55–56, 58; financial situation of, 29, 55–56, 58, 168; as founder of Christian Science, 2, 135; gendered attacks against, 99, 196–97, 210; gendered theology of, 113–14, 116, 122–25, 127–28; Gestefeld and, 124, 148–53; Gordon and, 140–47; illnesses of, 7, 24–26, 30–31, 43, 48–50, 59, 247n38, 248n9; on language and expression, 95–96; marriages and family life of, 26–31, 41–42, 49, 92, 253n6, 261n22; McKenzie and, 198–201, 208; on metaphysics, 6, 9, 13, 78–80, 91–92, 109, 132, 157, 227, 231, 233; on millennialism and millennium, 103–6, 129–30; Next Friends suit against, 209–13, 214; on paganism, 147, 149, 266n65; paid work of, 29, 168; on pantheism, 78–79, 81, 140, 144; plagiarism accusations against, 127, 132–34; portraits of, 58, 214, 217; public lectures by, 51, 52, 145; on Quimby's work, 51, 52–54, 60, 68, 74, 76, 108; response to early *Science and Health* criticism, 97–99; retirement and final revisions by, 168; on revelation and discovery, 76, 134–38; on sacrament, 82–83; scrapbooking by, 31–32; on Second Coming and prophetic tradition, 103–6, 107; on sin and reformation, 119–21; student teaching by, 69–70, 74, 75, 88, 89, 90; on Trinity, 81, 109; on women's rights, 10, 114–19, 122, 124–25. *See also* Christian Science
—writings: "The Bible in Its Spiritual Meaning," 65, 108, 253n2; *Christian Science: No and Yes*, 149; Genesis manuscript, 65–70, 74, 108, 117, 136, 253n2; *Historical Sketch of Metaphysical Healing*, 138; *Manual of The Mother Church*, 169, 170, 223, 277n26; *Miscellaneous Writings*, 120; poetry by, 24, 30, 41, 70, 90; "Questions and Answers," 69; "Reformers," 120; *Retrospection and Introspection*, 138; *Rudimental Divine Science*, 149; *Science of Man*, 69; "The Soul's Inquiries of Man," 69; "Standards for All Time," 216; "Veritas Odium Parit," 146. See also *Science and Health with Key to the Scriptures* (Eddy)
"Eddygush," as term, 99, 196
education, 22–24, 174, 246n25
Edwards, Jonathan, 100–101, 105, 154
Eggleston, Edward, 83
Emmanuel Movement, 184
end-time rhetoric, 27; millennialism, 99–106, 129–30, 247n52, 259n46; Millerism, 27, 28, 100. *See also* Second Coming of Christ
Endymion (Keats), 54–55
Enforcement Act (1870), 125
Episcopalians. *See* Anglicans
error, as term, 90
esotericism *vs.* Christian Science, 11, 37–38, 124, 141, 147–56, 159, 162, 232–33

evangelicalism, 28–29
Evans, Harriet, 195
Evans, Warren Felt, 147, 148, 150
evil: Eddy on, 51, 127, 175, 210, 254n10, 275n19; and interpretations of Genesis, 117; McKenzie on, 200; of mesmerism, 38, 72, 73–74. *See also* sin
E. W. H., 184–85
Ewing, Ruth B., 171

faith cure, as term, 146
Faust, Drew Gilpin, 42, 58
feminism: and Eddy, 113–14; historiography of, 114. *See also* women's rights and equality
financial situation: of Christian Science church, 169, 268n11; of Christian Science practitioners, 274n6; of Eddy, 29, 55–56, 58, 168; of Patterson, 30, 31
Finney, Charles Grandison, 28
The First Church of Christ, Scientist, Massachusetts. *See* The Mother Church
First Congregational Church, Lynn, Massachusetts, 70
Fleischer, Charles, 211
Folk, Holly, 196
food reforms, 32. *See also* healing beliefs and practices
Fowler, Stacy, 159
Foye, William, 44
Freedom of Faith (Munger), 157
Fremont, Julia C., 171
Frye, Calvin A., 204, 261n19
Fulton, Robert, 67
Fundamentalism, 5, 67, 85, 142

Garrison, William Lloyd, III, 120–21, 190, 211, 275n19
gendered attacks against Eddy, 99, 196–97, 210. *See also* women's rights and equality
gendered theology, 113–14, 116, 122–25, 127–28. *See also* women's rights and equality
Genesis, Eddy's manuscript on, 65–70, 74, 108, 117, 136, 253n2. *See also* creation story; *Science and Health with Key to the Scriptures* (Eddy)
German criticism, 77

Gestefeld, Ursula Newell, 124, 148–53
Gibbons, Abigail Hopper, 151
Gifford, O. P., 141, 156–58, 159, 161, 266n47
Gill, Gillian, 54, 58, 141
girls, education of, 22–24. *See also* women's rights and equality
Glover, George Washington, II, 28, 29–30, 42, 55
Glover, George Washington "Wash," 26–27, 55
Glover, Mary. *See* Eddy, Mary Baker
Goen, C. C., 100
Gordon, A. J., 140–47, 159, 161
Gottschalk, Stephen: on Conger, 184; on Eddy's revelation, 8, 76; on Gestefeld's theory, 150; on healings, 191–92; on liberal vs. conservative support of Christian Science, 157; scholarship on Christian Science by, 5, 234
Gove, Mary, 193–94
Graham, Sylvester, 32
Great Litigation (1919–20), 223
Gutjahr, Paul, 9, 235

Hacker, Jeremiah, 45, 90
Hahnemann, Samuel, 33
Hale, Susan, 188–89
Hamlin, Kimberly A., 85
Harmon, Joseph, 220
harm vs. healing, 72–73
Harper, Frances Ellen Watkins, 45
Hatch, Nathan, 80
healing beliefs and practices: Christian Science testimonies on, 2–3, 92, 174–86; criticisms of, 37, 211–12; divine healing, 73–74, 140–47, 161, 191–92, 264n13; Eddy on early understandings of, 51–55, 59–60, 264n11; Eddy on metaphysics and, 78–80; Eddy on personal recovery experience, 71–73, 77, 132–34, 137; food reforms, 32; homeopathy, 31, 32–33, 43, 57; hydropathy, 32, 34, 248n25; hypnotism, 108, 254n11; of Jarvis, 50–52, 55, 75, 134, 135, 251n31; mesmerism and, 38, 46, 71–76, 108; mind curists, 10, 34–36, 46–47, 59, 146, 156; of Mormonism, 35; of Pentecostals, 142, 145, 264n15; performed by Eddy, 50–51;

healing beliefs and practices (*continued*)
  physical manipulation in, 75, 255n13; of Protestantism, 10; of Quimby, 46–48, 50; water cure, 34, 35, 46–47, 59, 248n25. *See also* neuralgia; salvation
"The Heart's Unrest" (Eddy), 41, 90
Hedge, Frederic Henry, 34, 47, 59
Hegel, G. W. F., 79
Hersey, Heloise Edwina, 196
Hicks, Rosemary, 116
Hill, Samuel S., 142–43
Hindu philosophies, 147, 154, 231
Historical Sketch of Metaphysical Healing (Eddy), 138
A History of the Work of Redemption (Edwards), 105
History of Women Suffrage (Stanton and Anthony), 115–16
Hitchcock, Edward, 36–37, 39, 72, 102
Hodgkiss, Andrew, 25, 246n38
holidays, 169–70, 249n47
Holland, David, 107, 209, 212–13
Homeopathic Advocate and Guide to Health, 33
homeopathy, 31, 32–33, 43, 57. *See also* healing beliefs and practices
Hopkins, Emma Curtis, 150, 154, 156, 267n79
H. S. C. (critic), 96–97, 98, 99, 130
Hughes, Richard T., 80
Huling, Caroline A., 189
Human Life (publication), 212
Hunt, Lucian, 23
Hunter, Tera, 58
hydropathy, 32, 34, 35, 248n25. *See also* healing beliefs and practices
hymns, 168
hypnotism, 108, 254n11. *See also* healing beliefs and practices
hypochondria, 7, 25, 247n38
hysteria, 7, 25, 247n42, 247n44

If Christ Came to Chicago (Stead), 158
indexes, annotated by Eddy, 113, 126, 127, 171, 172, 198, 201, 218, 228
Indian rights, 179
India paper, 172–73, 177
insanity case against Eddy, 209–13

insignia, 170, 172
intellectual property rights. *See* copyright; plagiarism
International Sunday Bible Lessons, 171
Ivey, Paul Eli, 185, 224

Jacksonianism, 20–21
James, Amanda, 179–80, 181
James, William, 190, 197, 211, 231–32, 234, 244n9
Jane Eyre (Brontë), 29
Jarvis, Ann Mary, 50–52, 55, 75, 134, 135, 251n31
Jefferson, Anderson, 181
Jehovah's Witness, 4, 142
Jesus by the Sea (engraving by Bida), 83
Jesus Christ: Eddy on divinity of, 171, 175; engravings of, 83, 84; New Thought on, 121; resurrection of, 39–40, 83, 85, 102, 124, 128, 158. *See also* biblical interpretation, overview; Christian Science
Jewish Christian Scientists, 180
John M. Tearle Company, 172
Johnson-Reed Act (1924), 185
John Wilson and Sons of University Press (company), 94
Jones, Ellen C., 201
Jones, Georgina, 1
Jones, Randall, 1, 277n23

Kansas City Sun (publication), 224
Kearney Daily Hub (publication), 195
Keene, John Henry, 204
Kellogg, Merritt Gardner, 100
Kennedy, Richard, 72
Kilde, Jeanne Halgren, 220, 261n8
Kimball, Edward, 118
Kimball, Florence, 179
Klassen, Pamela, 143, 183, 184, 215
Knapp, Krister Dylan, 38, 231
Knox, Anna H., 205
Kuyper, Abraham, 87

Ladd, Clara E., 92
language and expression of thought, 95–96
Lathrop, Laura, 116, 205
Le Bosquet, John, 33
Lee, Ann, 8, 101, 106–7, 127

legal controversies: on alcohol consumption, 20; on authorship of *Science and Health*, 132, 196–97; of child custody, 29–30; Great Litigation of 1919–20, 223; libel suit by Woodbury, 196; Next Friends suit, 209–13, 214; over medical licensing and efficacy of Christian Science, 194–96; on voting rights, 125
Letts, Colonel, 97, 259n26
liberalism. *See* Christian liberalism
Lichtenstein, Morris and Tehilla, 180
Life (publication), 215
Liliuokalani, Queen of Hawaii, 187
linotype printing, 93–94
Linscott, Ellen Brown and John, 120, 121, 148
literacy, 1, 17, 42
literal, as term, 67, 83
literalism, 83
Livermore, Harriet, 27
Long, Charles, 185
Lord, Nathan, 101
Loughran, Trish, 91
Lowell, Spence, 213
Lucifer (publication), 150, 266n53
Lynn Transcript (Eddy), 71–72, 134

magnetism, 36–38
Maine, 44–45
Mann, Joseph G., 204
Manual of the Congregational Church, 170
Manual of The Mother Church (Eddy), 169, 170, 223, 277n26
Marble, Oliver W., 196
Marsden, George, 100–101
Mason, Frank E., 171
Massachusetts Metaphysical College, 168
matter, 78–79, 144
Maxwell, James Clerk, 36
McClure's (publication), 211–12
McCrackan, William, 213
McCullough, J. D., 87
McGill, Meredith, 150
McKenzie, Daisy Stocking, 199, 225
McKenzie, Guilford Stuart, 199
McKenzie, William, 198–201, 202, 208, 213, 220, 221, 225
McLaren, George, 92, 96, 98

McNeil, Keith, 54, 69
McPherson, Aimee Semple, 8, 210, 224
medical theory on education of girls, 23, 24
Mendez, Francisco, 183
Mendez, Susana, 182
mental malpractice, as term, 73–74
mental science, as term, 88
Mental Science Magazine (journal), 154
mesmerism, 37, 38, 46, 71–76, 108, 234. *See also* healing beliefs and practices
The Messages of Paul, 82
Messenger, Frank M., 102, 103
metaphysical science, as term, 88–89, 232
metaphysics, Eddy on, 6, 9, 13, 78–80, 91–92, 109, 132, 157, 227, 231, 233
Methodists: Christian Science and, 102, 145, 146, 163, 179, 183, 197; on restorationism, 80; at Sanbornton Church, 19, 39
M. E. W., 178
Mexican Christian Scientists, 182–83
millennialism, 99–106, 129–30, 247n52, 259n46
Miller, William, 27, 100, 250n6
Millerism, 27, 28, 100
Milmine, Georgine, 212
Mims, Sue, 204
mind curists, 10, 34–36, 46–47, 59, 146, 156. *See also* healing beliefs and practices
Ministry of Healing, or, Miracles of Cure in All Ages (Gordon), 142, 144
Minor, Virginia, 125
miracles, 85, 89, 142. *See also* divine healing; healing beliefs and practices; salvation
Miscellaneous Writings (Eddy), 120
Moody, Dwight L., 142
Moorhead, James, 100
"moral science," as concept, 24, 34, 77, 87–89, 109, 257n33. *See also* Christian Science
Mormonism, 4; Buckley on, 146; Christian Science and, 155, 232; death of Smith and, 27; founding of, 8; Hatch on, 80; healing practices of, 35; on temperance, 20. *See also* Smith, Joseph
Morrill, Alpheus, 33
Moses, Alfred G., 180
Mother Ann. *See* Lee, Ann

The Mother Church, 2, 169–71, 182, 208, 220, 223–24, 227, 261n8. *See also* Christian Science
Mott, John R., 197
Mullin, Robert Bruce, 143
Munger, Theodore, 157

Napheys, George H., 25
Nartonis, David, 32, 33
National American Woman Suffrage Association, 184, 271n70
National Christian Scientist Association (NCSA), 168
National Medical Association, 1
natural science, 80, 86–87, 91, 109, 234. *See also* Darwinism
Nature and the Supernatural (Bushnell), 38
Neal, James, 195, 275n6
networks and nodes of religiosity, 5–6, 12, 107, 140, 231, 233–34
neuralgia, 7, 24–26, 30–31, 43, 59, 247n42, 248n9
New Departure, 125–26
New England farming sensibilities, 17–18
New Hampshire Journal of Education, 94
New Hampshire Medical Association, 23, 32
New Hampshire Patriot and State Gazette (publication), 18
New Thought: Christian Science and, 231, 232, 234; emergence of, 11, 141, 153–54; on gender ideals, 124; on Jesus, 121; Quimby on, 75–76; religious objects in, 175
New York Sun (publication), 97–99
New York Times, 132
New York World (publication), 209–12
Next Friends lawsuit, 209–13, 214
nodes. *See* networks and nodes of religiosity
Norton, Carol, 128–29, 174, 263n57
Noyes, John Humphrey, 28

Ogden, Emily, 38
oil anointing, 143, 184
On the Origin of Species (Darwin), 27, 38. *See also* Darwinism
Opp, James, 191

Orcutt, William Dana, 208, 218
orthodoxy. *See* Christian orthodoxy
Osgood, Jacob, 27
Osgoodites, 19, 27
Ostrander, Rick, 70
Our Saviour from the Only Authentic Likeness of Our Saviour Cut on an Emerald by Command of Tiberius Caesar (Sartain), 83, 84
Oxford University Press, 172, 177

pacifism, 19, 45, 211, 275n19
paganism, 147, 149, 266n65
page clips, 172, 173
Paine, John C., 92
Palmer, D. D., 196
pantheism, 78–79, 81, 140, 144, 147
paper, 172–73, 177. *See also* printing and publishing technologies
Paradise Lost (Milton), 23
Paretsky, Sara, 36
Parham, Charles, 73
Parker, Theodore, 122, 128
Parsons, Charles M., 25, 26
pastoral books, 173–76, 201–6. *See also Science and Health with Key to the Scriptures* (Eddy)
Patterson, Daniel, 30–31, 41–42, 49, 55, 58, 76, 250n10
Payne, Eva, 11
Peabody, Andrew P., 159
Peabody, Frederick, 209, 210–12
Peel, Robert: on Eddy's interpretations, 31, 68, 91, 234, 254n10; on Eddy's writing process, 8; on healings, 192, 261n8; on ministers, 159; on use of Eddy's work, 151, 272n25
Pentecostalism: American influence of, 4, 232; beliefs on healing of, 145, 264n15; racial developments within, 224; religious objects of, 175; as restoration of Christianity, 80; Robins on, 244n11
Perry, Seth, 170–71
Phipps, Joseph, 81
physical manipulation in healing practices, 75, 255n13. *See also* healing beliefs and practices
Pickens, Israel, 180

Picton, J. Allanson, 78
Pierce, Franklin, 22, 23, 44
Pietsch, B. M., 5, 244n11
Pitchford, John H., 180–81
plagiarism: accusations against Eddy, 127, 132–34; by Gestefeld, 150; by Hopkins, 150. *See also* copyright
Plath, Sylvia, 218–19
poetry, 136; by Eddy, 24, 30, 41, 70, 90; on printing errors, 93
Porterfield, Amanda, 124
Portland, Maine, 44–45
postmillennialism, 100, 101. *See also* millennialism
poverty, 55–56, 58
predestination, 19. *See also* salvation
premillennialism, 99–100, 101. *See also* millennialism
Presbyterianism, 142
"Printer's Mistakes," 93
printing and publishing technologies, 9, 17, 81, 91, 93–95, 207–8. *See also* paper; *Science and Health with Key to the Scriptures* (Eddy)
prisoners of war, 41–43, 45, 49, 250nn10–12. *See also* wartime experiences
Puck (publication), 188, 189, 193
Purrington, William Archer, 194

Quakers, 81, 92, 211, 275n19
"Questions and Answers" (Eddy), 69
Quimby, George, 53–54
Quimby, Phineas P. "Park": attempts to cure Eddy by, 43, 45, 46–47, 48, 49, 60; death of, 53, 57; on Deity and Wisdom, 90, 255n12; Dresser on Eddy's work and, 132–34; Eddy's understanding of, 51, 52–54, 60, 68, 74, 76, 108; on George as heir of practice, 53; healing methods of, 47–48, 50; writings and publications of, 251n16
Quimby, Susannah, 53–54

racial identity, 183–84, 221
racism, 125–26, 180, 184–85, 222–24. *See also* slavery
Rand, Avery & Co., 94

Rathvon, Ella, 204
Rathvon, William R., 171
Reading Room, 169
recitation, 174
reformation, Eddy on, 119–21
"Reformers" (Eddy), 120
R. E. K., 179
religiosity, networks and nodes of American, 5–6, 12, 107, 140, 231, 233–34
religious portraiture, 84, 176, 214, 217, 222
restorationism, 6, 13, 27, 80–82, 92, 100, 109, 227, 231, 236. *See also* apostolic Christianity
resurrection, 39–40, 83, 85, 102, 124, 128, 158
Retrospection and Introspection (Eddy), 138
retrospective ethnography, 12
revelation: *vs.* academic explanation, 83; as concept, 66; Eddy and Christian Science on, 76, 134–38; Theosophy on, 149–50
Revelatory Events (Taves), 8–9
Rice, Miranda, 77
Roberts, Jon, 85
Robins, R. G., 5, 244n11
Robinson, Harriet H., 115
Roget, Peter Mark, 96
Ropes, James Hardy, 213
Rudimental Divine Science (Eddy), 149

sacrament, 82–83, 184
sacred text, defined, 9. *See also* pastoral books
salvation, 3–4, 129–30, 161. *See also* healing beliefs and practices; millennialism; predestination
Sanborn, Dyer, 23
Sanborn, Mahala, 29
Sanbornton (later Tilton) Congregational Church, New Hampshire, 18–20, 22, 77, 82, 90, 170, 269n13
Sartain, John, 83, 84
satirical cartoon, 188
Satter, Beryl, 144, 162
Scenes and Incidents in the Life of the Apostle Paul, 71
Schoepflin, Rennie, 192, 193, 194, 195, 272n25

science, as term, 86–87
Science and Health with Key to the Scriptures (Eddy): overview of, 3–9, 84, 89, 109, 233; concordance of, 198; critical reception of, 96–99, 109–10, 140, 163, 210; disputed authorship of, 196–97; Eddy's markings in, 104, 127, 172, 235; editions and revisions of, 94–95, 168, 169, 198, 218, 237, *238–41*, 276n2; examples of reader notations in, 201–6; final "authorized" edition of, 216–17; final notations by Eddy in 1908 edition of, 207, 213–15, 228; first printing and description of, 78–80, 167, 227, 257n5, 259n52; foreign language translations of, 183, 218; Genesis manuscript, 65–70, 74, 108, 117, 136, 253n2; indexed annotations by Eddy in, 113, 126, 127, 171, 172, 198, 201, 218, 228; Jarvis account in, 50; Next Friends suit and, 209–10; page clips and bookmarks for, 172, *173*; publication of, 2; readings in *Christian Science Bible Lessons*, 171–74, 269n15; on reformation, 119–21; significance of, 9, 12, 168–69, 235–36; style elements of, 91; testimonies on, 131; title and subtitle of, 77, 80, 89, 136; typographical and production errors of, 94, 207–8, 213, 217–18, 257n5; Webb's testimony on, 2–3. *See also* Christian Science; Eddy, Mary Baker
"Science of Health," as term, 89, 132
"Science of Life," as title, 77, 89, 136. *See also Science and Health with Key to the Scriptures* (Eddy)
Science of Man (Eddy), 69
"science of the soul," as term, 34, 89. *See also* Christian Science
scientific *vs.* religious inquiry, 85–87, 98
Scott Abbott Manufacturing Company, 173
scrapbooking, 31–32
scriptural metaphor, Eddy's use of, 83–85
Sears, Dr., 189
Seaver, W. F., 179
Second Coming of Christ, 59, 101–2, *103*, 107. *See also* end-time rhetoric; millennialism
Second Congregational Church, Lynn, New Hampshire, 77

segregated churches, 223–25. *See also* racism
Seventh-Day Adventists, 74, 76, 232. *See also* Adventism
sex and sexuality, 46, 107, 246n28
S.&H. *See Science and Health with Key to the Scriptures* (Eddy)
Shakers, 4, 106–7, 232
Silver, Mr., 97, 98
sin, 144. *See also* evil
Singleton, Andrew, 190
S. J. H., 176–77
slavery, 20–21, 119, 220, 245n16. *See also* abolitionism; antislavery; racism
Smith, Alice Weston, 188
Smith, E. J., 136
Smith, Joseph: as come-outer, 77; criticisms of, 210; death of, 27; divine messages of, 8, 80; on temperance, 20. *See also* Mormonism
Smith's Bible Dictionary, 83
social reform, 157–58, 179, *188*, 263nn57–58
sola scriptura, 170–71
"Song of the Printer" (poem), 93
soteriology. *See* salvation
"The Soul's Inquiries of Man" (Eddy), 69
Southern Presbyterian Church, 21
Spanish translations, 182–83
spinal neuralgia. *See* neuralgia
spiritual healing. *See* healing beliefs and practices
Spiritualism, 28, 37–38, 75–76, 91, 146
spiritual journaling, 24
Squires, Ashley, 7–8
"Standards for All Time" (publication set), 216
Stanton, Elizabeth Cady, 39, 127; on gender roles, 124–25; racism and, 126; on social reformer, as label, 121; *Woman's Bible*, 114, 115, 121–22; on women's role in child custody, 29
Statement of Christian Science (Gestefeld), 151
Stead, W. T., 158
Stein, Stephen, 9, 106
Stepping-Stones in Truth for Christian Scientists calendar, 172, *173*
stereotyping (printing technology), 17

Stewart, Allison V., 214, 276n2
Still Life with Science and Health and Roses (Hunting), 177
Stone, Barton, 27, 80. *See also* Disciples of Christ
Stowe, Harriet Beecher, 34
Strachan, William, 24
Strang, Lewis C., 205
Streeter, Frank A., 209, 212, 248n27
suffrage, 114, 115, 125–26. *See also* women's rights and equality
"A Suggestion to the Buffalo Exposition" (Dalrymple), *188*
Sumner, Charles, 221
Sunshine and Love (Spear), 197
"Superstition Has Always Ruled the World" (*Puck*), 189
Sutton, Matthew Avery, 210
Swedenborgians, 97, 163
Swensen, Rolf, 182
symbols, 170, 172

Taves, Ann, 8–9, 74, 75, 92, 232
technological innovations, 67, 81. *See also* printing and publishing technologies
temperance movement, 19–20
Thanksgiving, 169–70
Theology at the Dawn of the Twentieth Century (Gifford), 158
The Theosophical Society, 147–48
Theosophy: Anthony on, 261n11; boundaries and definition of, 149–50; Christian Science vs., 10–11, 139–41, 147, 149–56, 159, 161–62, 234; Gestefeld and, 148–49, 265n41; origins of, 133, 147–48; Stanton on, 124
thesaurus, 96
Thesaurus of English Words and Phrases (Roget), 96
Thomas, Laura, 195
Thomas, Robert David, 65
Thomas, Tracy A., 29
Tilton Congregational Church. *See* Sanbornton (later Tilton) Congregational Church, New Hampshire
Time of the End (Messenger), 102, *103*
Tolstoy, Leo, 187
Tomkins, George, 204

Tomlinson, Irving C., 193, 204
Tower of Babel, 9, 93, 95
Transcendentalism, 34
transmillennial, as term, 10, 100, 107, 109. *See also* millennialism
Trinitarianism, 33, 39, 77
Trinity, 81, 109
Trudel, Dorothea, 27
Truth, Sojourner, 39
Twain, Mark, 99, 189, 196, 212
Tyndall, John, 70
typesetting technologies, 93–94. *See also* printing and publishing technologies
typographical errors, 93–95

Unitarian Congregationalism, 70
Unitarianism, 24, 34, 44, 59, 77, 81, 83, 92, 204
Unitarian Universalism, 33
universal salvation, 39, 125–27, 155–56, 255n8, 259n43
Up from Slavery (Washington), 220
Upham, Thomas Cogswell, 257n32
Ute, 179

van den Hemel, Ernst, 82
van der Leeuw, J. J., 150
The Varieties of Religious Experience (James), 197, 234
Vaughan, Henry, 149
Vedanta, 154
Ventimiglia, Andrew, 7, 150–51, 170
"Veritas Odium Parit" (Eddy), 146
voting rights, 114, 115, 125–26. *See also* women's rights and equality

Wacker, Grant, 5, 7, 244n11
Waldram, James B., 190, 191
Wallner, Peter A., 209
Warfield, Benjamin, 142
wartime experiences, 55–56, 58. *See also* Civil War; prisoners of war
Washington, Booker T., 185, 187, 220
water cure, 32, 34, 35, 46–47, 59, 248n25. *See also* healing beliefs and practices
Webb, Hiram, 1, 222
Webb, Hiram "Orlando," 1–2, 220, 222, 226

Webb, Marietta T., 1–3, 184, 198, 219–26, 277n15
Weddle, David, 68, 99, 234
Weekly Reporter (publication), 57
Wells-Barnett, Ida B., 121, 260n63
Whidden, Parsons, 29
White, Armenia, 33
White, Ellen Harmon, 7, 8, 28, 39, 77, 83
Whitley, Dorothy, 218
Whittier, John Greenleaf, 92, 257n47
Whittle, J. F., 33
Wiggin, John Henry, 196
Wilbur, Sibyl, 212
Wilcox, Martha, 204
Willard, Frances, 33, 120, 121, 262n27, 271n70
Willis Baines-Miller, Minnie, 145
Wilson, John F., 100, 101, 214
Winslow, Abigail, 81
Winslow, Charles, 81
Wisdom, as term, 90
"Womans Bible" (Eddy), 114–15
Woman's Bible (Stanton), 114, 115, 121–22

Woman's Cause (Norton), 128–29
women's rights and equality: athleticism and, 246n28; Chapman on, 246n27; child custody, 29–30; copyright and, 255n16; Eddy on, 10, 114–19, 122, 129, 171; education of girls, 22–24; feminism and Eddy, 113–14; gendered attacks against Eddy, 99, 196–97, 210; Stanton on, 124–25; suffrage, 114, 115, 125–26. *See also* gendered theology
Woodbury, Josephine, 196, 209–10
Woodbury, O. A., 33, 35
Woodhull, Victoria, 126, 137
Woodworth-Etter, Maria, 73
Worcester, Elwood, 184
World's Parliament of Religions (Chicago, 1893), 155
Wright, Livingston, 196

Yankee Farmer (publication), 17
Youmans, Edward L., 78
Young's Night Thoughts, 23

www.ingramcontent.com/pod-product-compliance
Lightning Source LLC
Chambersburg PA
CBHW032056230426
43662CB00035B/436